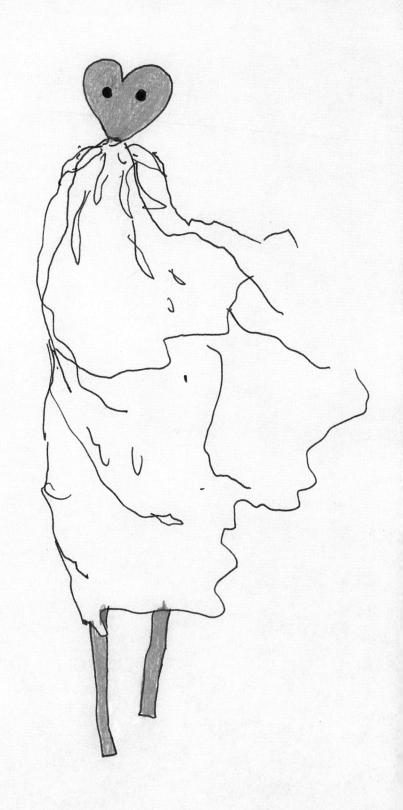

EROTIC ISLANDS

Art and Activism in the Queer Caribbean

LYNDON K. GILL

Duke University Press   Durham and London   2018

Printed in the United States of America on acid-free paper ∞
Designed by Heather Hensley
Typeset in Whitman by Westchester Publishing Services

Library of Congress Cataloging-in-Publication Data
Names: Gill, Lyndon Kamaal, author.
Title: Erotic islands : art and activism in the queer Caribbean /
Lyndon K. Gill.
Description: Durham : Duke University Press, 2018. | Includes
bibliographical references and index.
Identifiers: LCCN 2017051307 (print) | LCCN 2017056661 (ebook)
ISBN 9780822372622 (ebook)
ISBN 9780822368588 (hardcover : alk. paper)
ISBN 9780822368700 (pbk. : alk. paper)
Subjects: LCSH: Gays—Trinidad and Tobago. | Gays in popular
culture—Trinidad and Tobago. | Blacks—Trinidad and Tobago. |
Carnival—Social aspects—Trinidad and Tobago. | Calypso
(Music)—Social aspects—Trinidad and Tobago. | AIDS
activists—Trinidad and Tobago. | Trinidad and Tobago—Social
life and customs.
Classification: LCC HQ76.3.T7 (ebook) | LCC HQ76.3.T7 G54 2018
(print) | DDC 306.76/60972983—dc23
LC record available at https://lccn.loc.gov/2017051307

Duke University Press gratefully acknowledges the support of
the Office of the President at the University of Texas at Austin,
which provided funds toward the publication of this book.

Cover art: A dancing Dame Lorraine, Trinidad Carnival, 2006.
Photograph by Cyrus Sylvester.

Frontis. 1 "Love Jumbie" sketch by Peter Minshall, 2006. Courtesy
of the Callaloo Company Archive.

FOR MY ANCESTORS,
GIVEN AND CHOSEN

AND WITH PLENTY LOVE
AND RESPECT FOR
Merlyn, Donna, and Mary

CONTENTS

ACKNOWLEDGMENTS

Everything has its beginning.

But to be the first is a blessing and a curse.

Making something out of the tiresome swim back and forth between two island departments in Harvard University's brackish sea never meant that I had to brave the frigid waters alone. At every moment when my breath and strength nearly gave way, there were arms outstretched to pull me ashore or brave lifesavers willing to meet me halfway. Words alone will always be an insufficient measure of my gratitude to each and every person who gave— many unbeknownst to me—so generously of their minds, bodies, and spirits so that I might survive graduate school relatively whole. If I learned nothing else from my mentors and friends at that "small school in Cambridge," I have learned that my "thank you" must be offered in deed. My chest heaving, my back and brow awash with perspiration, we are building bridges together still. This is the work of gratitude. These words are the beginning of a promise I must honor.

I thank the chair of my dissertation committee, Mary Margaret Steedly (may you rest in peace), for believing all of this possible long before I truly believed it myself. Her steady support and respect for creativity even in the face of all sorts of serious-sounding rules and regulations has long been an inspiration to me. If what follows is at all interesting to read, it is in no small part because Mary encouraged it. Ingrid Monson and Steve Caton also deserve my sincerest thanks for being willing to sign on to this experiment in its earliest stages and for regularly placing a guiding word on the page or in my ear over tea to ensure that this would not explode in my face. And I owe Steve an intellectual debt I could never hope to repay for introducing a cohort of us to Kath Weston—but only after pressing us to read her entire oeuvre. Kath walked into that anthropology proseminar and something shifted into its proper place in my mind.

As exceedingly generous with her precise intellect as she is with her endearing sense of humor, Kath surpassed all I wished for in a mentor. From our first conversations to our latest, she has listened with the same keen interest to my fearful concerns and half-formed theories long enough to encourage my heart, challenge my mind, and point me toward more sustenance for both—often in a single breath. From introducing me to the work of M. Jacqui Alexander almost upon hearing my vague idea for a dissertation topic to checking in with me right when I had begun to feel lost in "the field," Kath has not only made much of this work better, but she has also made me better—a better intellectual and a better person—by crystal-clear example. No matter where you are, Kath, I hope to always keep you close. I am also grateful to Geeta Patel for her concern and support, whether across a telephone line or a small back-porch table.

Very little is possible in Harvard's Department of African and African American Studies without the support of Evelyn Brooks Higginbotham. I am very grateful for that support in matters I knew about and those I did not. I also thank "the other Evelyn," Evelynn Hammonds, for being willing to walk with me through black feminisms despite the ever-increasing demands on her time and attention. Vince Brown, Ajantha Subramanian, and especially the fabulous Glenda Carpio managed to make Harvard an exciting place to think, dress, and laugh. The same should certainly be said for the brief—but no less lasting for it—sojourns of Richard Drayton (who has far and away delivered the most beautifully comprehensive lectures I've ever heard—I suppose the accent and the poetry pushed him over the top), and especially Susan Stryker. Susan's serene brilliance and open mind are an inspiration.

Patricia Powell, Faith Smith, and Tommy DeFrantz made Cambridge bearable while genteelly pushing the limits of my ideas and pointing me still from far off corners toward the minds and texts that they find most exciting in any given moment. I especially appreciate Uncle Tommy for adopting wayward me into the black performance theory family—arguments and all, it truly feels like home.

Desiree Opal Allen was gracious enough to lend me her parents, and now I fear she may never get them back. Desiree, we probably could never have imagined years ago that our trips to hunt "dead people's clothes" would end up in this wonder of a friendship. Mr. Leslie Beckford and Mrs. Joyce Allen-Beckford, thank you for opening your beautiful home and your gorgeous hearts to me. You certainly made Dorchester an oasis from the incivility of Cambridge. Your convincing me to cross that river was my salvation; I just hope I did not disturb your serenity too much by making a life and birthing a beast just above your heads. Thank you for making your home my own and allowing me to witness the heights (literally and figuratively) of Caribbean love.

Ms. Joyce, I must thank you especially for every evening without fail checking to make sure I had survived another day spent battling the dissertation; your voice alone was always enough reward for watching the sun rise and set behind a computer screen. Thank you for the "classes" in floral arranging and managing all types of diversity; I fear I will never be able to pay that tuition bill off completely. If you do decide to subject yourself to the torture of a PhD program, I will be there at your graduation—freshly cut flowers in hand.

I will always owe Weslee Sinclair Glenn sincere gratitude for engineering my salvation from dissertation writing purgatory with love, song, food, laughter, and an infallible spiritual compass.

Staceyann Chin—in her poetry and her person—first set me on this path toward a fascination with queer Caribbean artistry, and her spoken word has been my gospel ever since. If the queer Caribbean is a vast (largely uncharted) landscape, then Thomas Glave is its highest peak—a seemingly omnipresent and certainly reassuring point by which to orient oneself. I will be forever grateful to Thomas for first putting me in touch with the leadership of Friend For Life just before one of my earliest research trips to Trinidad in 2003. With his particular elegance of phrase and gesture, I have been fortunate to have and keep him close. I would want it no other way. Arnold Rampersad has put up with me since I was a headstrong undergraduate with a little too much lip but the good sense to respect an intellectual giant when I meet one. I am grateful for his determined support and encouragement despite the fact that I am determined to make all the wrong choices.

Henry Louis Gates Jr., Vera Grant (who followed me across the country), Abby Wolf, Dell Hamilton, and the staff at the W. E. B. Du Bois Research Institute provided me with another home in Harvard Square, and for that I am most thankful. The vibrant intellectual community you re-create every semester is honestly remarkable. However, by far the most rewarding resource provided by the Institute was Iman James, my tireless and seriously stylish research assistant. Iman's help with seemingly endless transcriptions—defying the illegibility of my handwriting and the rapid or swallowed bits of Caribbean Creole English—has quite literally given this work its voice. For braving the rain (twice) in search of medicinal plant names, for bringing my Hi-8 tapes into this century, and for your reassuring hugs, I reach down deep inside for your "thank you."

No matter the distance, Jafari Allen always holds me close and shows me again and again the type of professor, mentor, and friend I aspire to be when I grow up. I thank him and Phillip Alexander for making their home my own and for showing me with honesty and kindness exactly what black queer love can become. It is an embarrassment of riches to have as examples both Jafari and Rinaldo Walcott, but I refuse to let either go. Tantie Rinaldo and Abdi Osman love me, challenge me, and feed me like only black relatives can, and for that Toronto will always feel like home. For reading so much of my writing out of the kindness of their hearts, and for always helping me to put the pieces (back) together, my humble gratitude to Jafari and Rinaldo is boundless.

As generous with his vast friendship networks as he is with his effortlessly gourmet cooking, Rinaldo introduced me to Dionne Brand, and for that alone, I have incurred another forever debt. Inspired by the pointed beauty of Dionne's writing for almost a decade at that point, I could not ever have imagined spending a morning having coffee at her favorite Toronto café. Thank you both for the coincidence of cordiality that made this moment and many others since possible for a writer and a devoted reader of her work.

For helping me through so many impossible transitions and always making me think as hard as they make me laugh, I thank my dear friends Uri McMillan, Marques Redd, Rachel Bolden-Kramer, Akin Hubbard, Jen Nash, Mia Bagneris, Dalila Scruggs, Choti Komaradat, Laura Murphy, Cameron Van-Patterson, Deidre DeGraffenreid, Vanessa Agard-Jones, Riley Snorton, Lizzy Cooper Davis, Phanuel Antwi, Cassandra Lord, Savannah Shange, Kenshata Watkins, and Angelique Nixon. I have been able to make it this far because you got me off to a running start, kept pace with me on the steepest uphill jogs, and patiently cheer me on even when I stumble or drift out of sight. I hold you close to my heart. You tell the hard truths but make sure I am alright afterward. I hope to one day become experts like you.

Naima Penniman, Alixa García, Sparlha Swa, and especially Kahdeidra Monet Martin-Thelusca (my spiritual "sistah") knew me back before—way back before—and for that alone I honor you. The most beautiful spirits, women, artists, intellectuals, freedom fighters, dream catchers, Spirit seekers, organic sustenance givers, and sweet sweet sound sharers I know beyond the shadow of all doubt. All the best parts of my being have been shaped by knowing and loving you. Even our silences have profound wisdom in them. You make me so very proud of all my ancestral inheritances. With these powerful ladies, all impossible things are possible.

Patricia Mohammed, Rhoda Reddock, and the staff of the Institute for Gender and Development Studies at the University of the West Indies–Saint Augustine campus still have my gratitude for being cordial institutional hosts so many moons ago during the tenure of my Fulbright fellowship. I am so thankful for the opportunity the Fulbright afforded me to spend more time in Trinidad and Tobago than my own graduate student purse would have allowed.

No proper study of Peter Minshall is possible without a conversation with Todd Gulick and a moment in archives of the Callaloo Company workshop. It was a tremendous pleasure and still a humbling experience to have had so many lengthy conversations with you and spent countless hours in the Callaloo archives over the last decade. I have tried my best to honor your remarkable generosity—with your time and your mind. Todd, the absolutely systematic and thorough attention you gave to an earlier draft of this work still overwhelms me with gratitude; this book is better because of you. And I am eager to read your masterpiece on Minshall in print soon. I hope this will be our Jouvay and not our Las' Lap. I thank Austin Fido for reading segments of the work and offering his own feedback as well as helping to translate between myself and Minsh to resolve some of our perennial frustrations into actionable revisions. I also thank the entire Callaloo Company staff for making me feel welcome at the workshop and thereby encouraging me to sit awhile in the delicate debris of Minshall's past on an island where archives are an endangered species.

Anyone even remotely interested in any thing at all queer and Caribbean owes a nod to Colin Robinson. Colin has taught me much even in the examples he did not intend. I thank him for the challenge of him. Cyrus Sylvester has a heart of gold, so it's a good thing he is a fortress of a man. I thank you for opening Bohemia to me—literally and figuratively—and allowing me to interrupt the calm of your hilltop oasis again and again. You made it possible to live on two islands at once. I most humbly thank Godfrey Sealy (may you rest in peace) for loving gay community to death. You may no longer be with us in the flesh, but your spirit is so strong. Talk of strong spirits brings to mind Warren Morgan (may you rest in peace), a kind soul who is surely making a bacchanal up in Heaven. Warren, thank you for helping me to plan my first real "house lime" in Trinidad and turning it into a dinner party.

Jacquelyn Fields, I owe you grand gratitude. Without you, not only would I have been without a conclusion, but I would have had to suffer only the company of gay men for all these years. Dennis James (may you rest in peace) was a force to be reckoned with, and for that, the Caribbean region as a whole is a much better place for queer people. Deni, we all miss you and that runaway tongue terribly. My fellow Friends For Life volunteer and clay magician, Adam Williams, thank you for sharing a friendship with me across continents over all these years. Although I have strayed a bit from my early obsession with drag performance in Trinidad and Tobago, I kept spectacular performers and friends like Andel Simon (may you rest in peace) and Andel McIntosh close. If there are drag shows in heaven (and Lord, I pray there are) Miss Jakuntele Kwelagobe must be center stage every night, making Whitney Houston herself do a double take. The Queen is dead; long live the Queen! And long may you reign, Miss Lotta Ting. If this past decade and more has been a sometimes-tumultuous sea, Rochelle Augustus has been my ROC. I love you, my dear, for teaching me to lime properly and sing fearlessly.

Nadia Buckmire, Rahi High, Najla, and Thorne keep me questioning everything I think I know. They share their dreams as freely and generously as they share their *ital* and have become the salt of my earth. Your family redeems every city you call home. I must also thank Dave Williams for coming to find me find me out in California long before he even knew me. I owe Mother Tim'm West thanks for that link and so so many others. Dave, the grace and freedom of your body in motion—like the grace and freedom of Tim'm's poetry—is like finally catching my breath.

Queer Tobago posse (though many of you have jumped ship to Trinidad or Canada), you made/make a small island home. My days and nights were shaped by your whims and me well happy to call oonu friends: Dirk, Doncil, Nikita (Madam, Madam, Madam, Madam, Madam!), Tyron, Ricardo,

Hayden, Charles, Delano (may you rest in peace), and especially Delia (may you rest in peace). There is a special place in my heart reserved for two of the biggest and gayest troublemakers Tobago had ever seen: Terrence Kenrick Cabrales and Naobi Abiola. You were my salvation—never mind that you probably got me in the mess in the first place. You are dramatic beauties both and an inspiration to live every moment with gusto and a glass.

Jason Guy will always be dear to me for coming back, knocking, stepping into my life, and staying. To come across a beautiful man who has devoted his life to the craft of making beautiful things is a divine find. Kevin Ayoung-Julien is such a find. Your affection for perfection and your passion for pheasant plumes is only part of why I will continue to love you. Charleston "Xxaalahh" Thomas—my intellectual bredren and (okay, I admit it) the biggest Nina Simone fan I have ever known—no matter what I thought I was going to do, I really went to T&T to meet you (again and again). I had long dreamed of the conversations you and I continue to have. There are not words for our spiritual kinship, but do know that I feel you, my BLACK queer brother. Me, you, and Ms. Simone have plenty plenty road to walk together still. Kern Ardillo Alleyne, we nearly drove off a cliff together, but a hand more powerful than mine guided us otherwise. We have always been guided otherwise. Since we almost died together, it is only fair that I hold you in my heart for the rest of my life.

Not only would the present study not have been possible, but I have no doubt that the world would be a much worse place without the work of Linda McCartha Sandy-Lewis (our Calypso Rose), Peter Minshall (our Minsh), Luke Sinnette, Eswick Padmore, and Kerwyn L. Jordan. Auntie Rose, you knew me before I knew myself, and it has been an honor to get to know you well enough to attempt to capture your life in words. Thank you for your melodious love; I'm blessed to be your "son." Minsh, you have not always made it easy, but you have always made it remarkably beautiful. It must have been pure naïveté that made me believe I could write a book about Minshall and anything else; Peter Minshall is a library unto himself, and his life's work deserves an entire shelf of texts—at the very least—devoted to it exclusively. I would be honored, Minsh, if you would allow me to return to expand this story into a full epic worthy of a mas man. A gracious man with an infectious charisma and one of the most beautiful minds of this century and the last, Minshall is a treasure to behold. Luke Sinnette, thank you for watching me as closely and reading me as carefully as I was watching and reading everyone else. I am still impressed by that and by you. Eswick Padmore, my unending gratitude for always opening your "palace" to me, cooking anything I beg you to cook (yuh han' sweet bad), whipping out Dame Gaynor deGay Foster to do a Bassey number on a whim, riding the CAT back and forth with me (". . . like the CAT ridin' hozes' chest!"), keeping granny company while I'm gone, and teaching me the art of listening and listening and listening more closely. Without you, there would have been no Friends For Life, so I thank you most of all for caring. I am your friend for life.

Kerwyn L. Jordan is all the daddy any organization could ever hope for. If FFL gets funding at all ever, it is usually because Kerwyn has spent what may seem like lifetimes preparing, submitting, revising, submitting, revising, submitting, revising, and resubmitting grant applications. I hate to blow his cover, but Kerwyn is an angel in disguise. All the work Kerwyn continues to do for FFL aside, Kerwyn has been my principal informant and well-informed friend from that fateful day in 2003 when I first met him. It is Kerwyn who pulled me into FFL and gave me a queer community from day one. Kerwyn has housed me at his homes in Trinidad without the slightest hesitation or discomfort. For that—he knows—he always has a place to rest his head no matter where I am. He has answered my countless e-mails, texts, and WhatsApp messages, fielding my never-ending questions with a patient and considerate attention that is truly not of this world. I thank him for reading and rereading and offering important corrections on earlier drafts of this work. And I thank him for getting Eswick and Luke to do the same. For all of this and more, I am forever in his debt. Kerwyn, if I could bring you Usher, I would; but for now, I offer you my heart.

For the graduate students reading this (yes, analyzing acknowledgments is a guilty pleasure we all share), rest assured that there is life after the dissertation and life after finally receiving those elusive three letters. But that afterlife can be as frightening and uncertain as any other. I am still humbled and thankful to Princeton University's Center for African American Studies (now a department!) for taking a leap of faith and offering me a postdoctoral fellowship that was like a hand to hold in figuring out what life, what thinking, what teaching, what learning, what knowing looks and feels like after the doctorate. I am especially grateful for the remarkable kindness, open-minded wisdom, and generosity of spirit that is just the modus operandi of Tera Hunter, Eddie S. Glaude Jr., Imani Perry, Wallace Best, Joshua Guild, my fellow postdoc sojourner and old friend Sarah Haley, and the inimitable Cornel West.

Recognizing with their usual precision and compassion that while my head was committed to Princeton, my heart had found a home in Philadelphia, Deborah Thomas and John Jackson worked a kind of alchemy to help me transform that first illustrious postdoc into another equally as brilliant at University of Pennsylvania. Shared between Penn's Center for Africana Studies and the Department of Anthropology and between Deb and John, I had reached scholarly nirvana. A Caribbeanist anthropologist aspiring to write beautifully and engagingly about big ideas in the African diaspora could not dream up better intellectual parents than Deb and John. I am still in awe of your unwavering support and guidance, your magnificent minds, and that way you have of making this profession look so cool. Beyond Penn's purview though is the city that speaks to my spirit even more (I dare say) than the city at the center of the universe where I was born and raised. Certainly it is in part the palpable black freedom in the air and the truths danced into the ground at Congo Square that make Philly so loveable, but it is also the people. Black queer kindred spirits Aishah Shahidah Simmons and James Claiborne in particular keep Philly on the map for me as my heart's true north.

From true north to south by southwest, I would never have dared to mess with Texas if it were not for the unmatched diaspora-conscious, queer-affirming, anthropologist-infused anomaly that is the Department of African and African Diaspora Studies at the University of Texas at Austin. I took a chance on Texas, and UT certainly took a chance on me, but when those big bright stars align and the beating heart of black queer diaspora studies is suddenly at UT Austin, all roads lead to central Texas. Bless the hearts, minds, and backs of those who struggled before I arrived and those who struggle still by my side to make the forty acres ours too. Thank you, Vincent Woodard (may you rest in peace), Ted Gordon, Omi Jones, Juliet Hooker, Simone Browne, Matt Richardson, Cherise Smith, Christen Smith, Eric Tang, Tiffany Gill, Omise'eke Tinsley, Kali Gross, Lisa Thompson, Charles Anderson, Xavier Livermon (my salvation!), Ayana Omilade Flewellen, Stephanie Lang, Tony Araguz, Moyo Okediji, Ann Cvetkovich, Lisa Moore, Neville Hoad, Charles Hale, Alix Chapman, and Celeste Henery (brilliant enchantress) for welcoming me into the clearing and inviting me to shout. Beyond UT, in the wilds of ATX, it is a sturdy shelter to have the state's queer people of color organization all go camped close by and under the magnanimous leadership of Priscilla "Big Bill" Hale and Rose Pullium, the black lesbian aunties we always wanted. My black queer Austin kin (no matter how far we roam) are a powerful village of artists, healers, intellectuals, activists, lovers, warriors, dreamers, and strategists. Odaymara y Olivia (Las Krudas!), Katrina Simpson, Wura Ogunji, Tameika Hannah, Toi Scott, Tonya Gbeda Lyles, Daryl Harris Jr., Jeremy Teel, Raymond Rashad Jones, Antwon McNeece, and Carre Real, thank y'all for making ATX into our black queer Mecca.

Thanks to Ken Wissoker, Sara Leone, Jade Brooks, and Olivia Polk at Duke University Press, as well as Laurie Prendergast at Moonmarked Indexing, for your Jonah-like patience, keen eye for detail, and capacious ease with big ideas. I am also most grateful to the anonymous reviewers of the manuscript for their encouragement and suggestions on how to make this book more lucid and less crowded. Carol Boyce Davies, Roderick Ferguson, Tom Boellstorff, and Don Kulick have all very generously read earlier drafts of the book and offered extensive comments that have improved the text by leaps and bounds. But of course, I claim full responsibility for any of the sure shortcomings of the text. I am indeed only human after all.

And finally (I know, I know, but it takes a village to write a first book!), I have saved my most intimate appreciation for last. From the first push that brought me here to the final push that has delivered the work to you, these extraordinary spirits have been absolutely, positively crucial. And it is precisely at this important point that words begin to fail. I have a lifetime of deeds ahead of me to show my gratitude to the following people.

My granduncle Horace Gill has dutifully left his comfortable corner in Port-of-Spain and his bread and pastries half-made in the bakery to drive all the way to Piarco International Airport to retrieve me or send me off time and time and time again. For never once forgetting me, I thank you deeply Uncle Horace. I must also thank my brother, Lyithbrandon Kwei Gill, for trying to be a decent younger brother despite my impoverished efforts at meeting him halfway.

Merlyn Veronica Gill danced her way from Port-of-Spain to New York City (after seeing much of the world in between), and just like that my grandmother assured my deep devotion and ecstatic fascination with Trinbagonian artistry. It is in large part because of the grace, timeless beauty, larger-than-life charisma, and bravery of one spectacular limbo dancer that I am the man I am. I thank you, grams, for much too much to be expressed here, but do know that I am most grateful for the house in Tobago that you toiled through New York winters to build for us all. Thank you for allowing me to interrupt your retirement with requests for wheat bread or corn soup or fried plantain or pone or black cake or mauby or sorrel or a trip to Swallows to take "a dip in the salt." I'll hold the memory of us picking peas and watering your Julie mango tree with me forever. Your sparkling laugh, the way you make the best tales out of such mundane things, your sweet sweet sweet hand, and your tendency to break into dance without missing a beat have inspired me for as long as I have known myself. I love you, grandmother.

Donna Veronica Gill, you share with your mother a middle name and all of her very best qualities. You know, mother, that I love you with all of my heart. Thank you for always standing in my corner, by my side, and behind me all at once; I am powerful because of you. Any true wisdom I have, you have helped me to gather. We do not get to choose our mothers, so it is divine intervention indeed that you were chosen for me and I for you. Everyday, I realize that I am becoming more and more like you. And I could not be happier about it. I hope I have made you even a quarter as proud of me as I have long been of you. I love you very much, mother dearest.

Last in this accounting, but always first at the dawn of each new day, I honor my ancestors—those whose names I know and those whose names I will never know—for your guidance, your protection, and your faith in my capacity to claim my destiny. Thank you for making this work and all the work I am here to do possible. I am grateful for the opportunities and the challenges, for the obstacles and the rewards. I am humbled by your presence and present for your purpose.

Thank you, Audre Lorde, James Baldwin, Langston Hughes, Zora Neale Hurston, Bayard Rustin, Essex Hemphill, Marlon Riggs, Joseph Beam, June Jordan, Sylvester James Jr., Assotto Saint, Marsha P. Johnson, Melvin Dixon, Venus Xtravaganza, Stacey Blahnik, Islan Nettles, Ty Underwood, Veronica Banks Cano, Shante Thompson, Keisha Jenkins, Lindon Barrett, Don Belton, Curt Blackman, Devon Wade, Prince Rogers Nelson and the countless unnamed. Thank you. May your blessings rain down upon us all.

Ashé

A PORT OF ENTRY

Fetish and Folklore in a Yearning Region

Writing is an act of desire, as is reading. Why does
someone enclose a set of apprehensions within a book?
Why does someone else open that book if not because
of the act of wanting to be wanted, to be understood,
to be seen, to be loved? And desire is also an act of
translation. . . . To write is to be involved in this act
of translation, of succumbing or leaning into another
body's idiom. . . . To desire then, to read and translate,
may also be to envy, to want to become. To desire may
also be to complicate.

DIONNE BRAND, *A Map to the Door of No Return*

The Antilles are a lucid dream. Their imagination predates the mid-fifteenth-
century birth of the Genoese explorer credited with introducing them to
Europe.

A phantom island that appears on Italian portolan charts of the Atlantic
as early as 1424 and disappears after 1587, "Antilia" is a specter haunting
the archipelago that arcs between the Atlantic Ocean and the Caribbean
Sea. Medieval maps chart the fluctuating presence of Antilia as it moved
throughout the Atlantic in the imagination of European cartographers,

expanding and contracting in size over time—a moving, breathing geological phenomenon. The Antilles then, from their first appearance, are invested with a fantasy that precedes them, a longing that quite literally names them.

A fetish of misplaced and mistaken desires across various geographies and intimacies, the Caribbean region itself—these affected Antilles—are a hundreds-of-years-old allegory for the frighteningly tangible effects of a complicated desire that both circumscribes the region and compels this book. The lauded Trinidadian-Canadian lesbian poet, novelist, and activist Dionne Brand—whose epigraph sets the tone for this opening—considers the literacy of desires that bring us to texts (be they manuscripts or perhaps cartographies).[1] Brand's imaginative curiosity about the terrain of desire in the act of reading/translating/writing provides a capacious entrepôt for the present engagement with the profound work of various desires on as well as within the fertile Caribbean imaginary. We begin here with a brief interrogation of the desires mapped onto the Caribbean as a necessary prelude to a deeper investigation of the cartography of desire within Caribbean cultural production and community building.

European efforts to map materially that which once lived wild in their imaginations was in no small part inspired by an anxious postlapsarian desire to return to paradise. Here the meaning of "paradise" is instructive especially because it remains one of the most persistent tropes used to define the Caribbean region. The word "paradise" is derived from the Avestan word *pairidaêza*; the literal meaning of this Eastern Old Iranian language compound word is "walled (enclosure)" from *pairi* (meaning "around") and *diz* (meaning "to create or make"). Eventually used to describe primarily royal parks and menageries, which were often walled, the term first appears in Greek as a description of a park for animals and is most notably used in the Greek translation of the Hebrew Bible from the third to first century BCE (the Septuagint) to approximate the Hebrew word for "garden."[2]

The Judeo-Christian Garden of Eden (literally a garden of "pleasure and delight"), the primary symbolic referent for the conceptualization of paradise in the Euro-American West, is described as a paradise as a result of this etymological ancestry. An idyllic enclosure for exotic flora and fauna, paradise quite literally contains a fantasy; it encloses a perverse fertility in the walled domain of private ownership. Thus, to call the Antilles paradise over and over again summons a zoological and botanical surrealism that is planted in the region long before the first Europeans set eyes upon the land itself.[3] And so the Antilles remain, a *there* that is not ever there completely, but shifting perpetually like an uneasy spirit between the material world and a fetishistic longing. Quite literally, these islands are called upon to stand in for that which is desired and immaterial (a disappeared Antilia, the elusive Indies), essentially that which they are not and yet still forced to become.

Trinidad and Tobago: A Caribbean Contact Zone

The unfulfilled fantasy (or wet dream?) of the Antilles exists always in precarious relation to the actual materiality of the region. Approaching this forced relationship from a different vantage point, the present analysis uses the firm grounding of site-specific artistry and activism as the principal coordinates by which to launch an ideological and semantic remapping of the very notion of erotic desire itself. The actual ground of this text is in fact an archipelago: the Republic of Trinidad and Tobago (T&T). The southernmost island nation of the Caribbean, T&T is only about seven miles northeast of Venezuela and just outside of the chain of islands known as the Lesser Antilles, though it is informally considered to be part of that chain. And yet, turning toward T&T does not necessarily mean turning away from the Caribbean as a whole.

Not only one of the most culturally complex nations of the Caribbean region, but also one of the primary sites of intra-Caribbean migration because of the strength of its economy—largely the result of being an economically and politically stable oil-producing nation in a sea of fickle tourism-dependent economies—T&T is here metaphorically representative of and quite literally composed of a pan-Caribbean cosmopolitanism. This old cosmopolitanism— created by pre-Columbian settlement routes, the layering of colonial histories, and contemporary migratory circuits—makes T&T a quintessential example of a very Caribbean cultural paradox in which unique singularity results from all manner of cultural contact, comingling, and creolization. Here too is a kind of desire and intimacy. The region, as the stalwart Caribbeanist anthropologist Michel-Rolph Trouillot reminds us, is nothing but contact perpetually drawing the past into the present: "Caribbean societies are inescapably heterogeneous . . . this heterogeneity is known to be, at least in part, the result of history. Caribbean societies are inescapably historical, in the sense that some of their distant past is not only known, but known to be different from their present, and yet relevant to both observers' and natives' understanding of that present" (Trouillot 1992, 21–22).

Caribbean history defies the West/non-West dichotomy that at one time was the guiding premise of anthropology; Caribbean "natives" were some of the earliest postmodern subjects. In fact, it was, in large part, colonial exploration and exploitation in the Caribbean and Latin America that provided an "Other" against which modern European nationalism defined itself and provided the raw material for the industrial revolution, the harbinger of modern global capitalism (Anderson 1983).

In essence, what makes T&T particular is the persistence of regional cultural complexity within its borders. So, although the specificity of T&T as a geopolitical and cultural site is significant, that specificity does not allow one to dismiss the nation as a regional anomaly in large part because so many parts of the region—figuratively and quite literally—rub up against each other there. In this relatively young republic, a thickly layered cultural flesh is matched by an intimately layered temporality; in this geoconceptual site, approaching the contemporary requires traversing the past.[4] So, the study that follows must be as interested in the historical genealogy of contemporary phenomenas as it is in the complexity of the modern moment. More precisely, if Trinidad and Tobago is the result of an intimate temporal quilting—characterized by a creative patchwork of past and present, legacy and innovation—then we must attend to the unfolding of time in the narratives about Trinbagonian artistry and activism that follow. Part of the reason, then, for attending so closely to the historical throughout this book is to make an explicit ideological and methodological statement against so frequently beginning and ending conversations about Caribbean life and work in the vanishing present.

Part of the work necessary for telling new kinds of Caribbean stories from the vantage point of T&T and other elaborate historical crossroads in the region involves creatively revisiting the past and perhaps even our relationship to time itself. Trinidadian lesbian transnational feminist theorist M. Jacqui Alexander's meditation on the palimpsestic nature of time is instructive here for this remembering as remapping:[5] "The idea of the 'new' structured through the 'old' scrambled, palimpsestic character of time, both jettisons the truncated distance of linear time and dislodges the impulse for incommensurability, which the ideology of distance creates. It thus rescrambles the 'here and now' and the 'then and there' to a 'here and there' and a 'then and now' and makes visible . . . the ideological traffic between and among formations that are otherwise positioned as dissimilar" (Alexander 2005, 190).

Alexander's "here and there" and "then and now" provide points of entry for speaking about sites sedimented with layers upon layers of disparate cultural and historical narratives. These distinct time-and-place stories are intricately intertwined in the Caribbean. Attending to the sensual flesh and the spiritual debts of postcoloniality as a political (im)materiality, this book's approach toward Trinbagonian history and culture makes an epistemological proposition. This proposed interpretive frame attends persistently and simultaneously to the political, sensual, and spiritual in the past/present of Trinbagonian artistry and activism. I introduce this political-sensual-spiritual—the combined master trope of this text—later in this preface briefly as the principal interpretive posture the book adopts for reading contemporary T&T through a historical lens. On these islands, as in the rest of the Caribbean region, the past and the present greedily consume each other.

Fantastic Anthropophagism: On Ravenous Metaphors

This mutual consumption across time brings to mind the ravenous trope of the Caribbean cannibal. If a fictive Antilia as paradise describes one tropic extreme—and here "tropic" signifies multiply as referent to the tropics, to the trope, and to a pivot point from which the word is derived—then the savage cannibal represents the other (as well as the Other) in the Caribbean region (Trouillot 2003). These two tropes are not mutually exclusive; in fact, the savage cannibal is thought to inhabit the Edenic paradise, wrapping purity and danger together in a perverse embrace (M. Douglas 1966). This ideological coupling, though contradictory, nevertheless persists into—both imported and homegrown—contemporary popular perceptions of the region. The Caribbean as "dangerous paradise" is most likely the result of overlaying the fantastical Antilia of the European imagination with nightmarishly exaggerated tales that returned with European explorers from the not so New World. The principal character in these grossly fictive tales of encounter and consumption was (and in a much more metaphorical sense continues to be) the cannibal.

It may have been the case that the peoples referred to as the "Caribs" actually did consume portions of human flesh as part of their war rituals in a symbolic gesture used to signify the ultimate defeat of the enemy and the incorporation of his strength into the body of the victor (Knight [1978] 1990, 22). However, there is little to no evidence to substantiate a claim that the entirety (or even the majority) of the Carib diet relied upon human flesh. The anthropophagist fantasies of the European explorers seem to have been allowed to run wild in the presentation of aboriginal peoples as bloodthirsty, flesh-eating monsters. It may even have been the case that Arawakan descriptions of the Caribs' pursuit of them in order to "eat" them may have been a metaphorical reference to the well-documented forced incorporation of Arawakan women into Carib society, thus referencing the symbolic consumption of one cultural group by another (inevitably undermining presumed distinctions between these groups) (Knight [1978] 1990, 21). So, it is highly probable that this combination of symbolic methods of consumption, as ritual and as metaphor, may have lead to the misperception that the Caribs were indeed an anthropophagistic people.

Yet this perverse misinterpretation and its contingent exotic eroticism haunt the European in the Caribbean islands from the very moment of first contact. Transnational sociologist Mimi Sheller's thoroughly piquant *Consuming the Caribbean: From Arawaks to Zombies* exhumes the legacy of the spectral cannibal, which haunts the Caribbean region, as the guiding framework within which to read the figurative and literal exploitation of the region. Sheller proposes that as much historically as contemporarily, "Caribbean islands and Caribbean bodies have been made to work as sites for seeking pleasure, in the form of 'consumer cannibalism' of Caribbean 'difference'" (Sheller 2003, 145). Sheller transfigures the tropic (again in all three senses) cannibal by foregrounding it as metaphor for an exploitative political economy. She does not contest the symbolic presence of the cannibal in the region but rather responds to the ideological persistence of the figure with the disruptive inquiry, "Who was eating whom?" (Sheller 2003, 143). This question serves as a point of entry into a reconceptualization of the ways in which plantation economies and colonial capitalism in fact consumed the bodies, health, and lives of the indigenous peoples of the region as well as generations of enslaved and indentured laborers (Sheller 2003). This opportunistic capitalist consumption of Caribbean bodies provides the material and ideological legacy for the contemporary Caribbean tourist industry, which is the primary means through which the Euro-American West engages the Caribbean (Nixon 2015, 3–32, 89–125). The exotic fetishization of the Caribbean calls attention to the use to which Caribbean "difference" is put; here the familiar Other—as body and as location—is in essence consumed as an attractive commodity.[6]

Sheller identifies the ways in which this attraction is explicitly sexual, returning us to the previously mentioned paradisian fantasy of the Caribbean, but with one flagrant difference: "The new Eden is a perpetual garden in which sexuality can run rampant; rather than being expelled from the garden, humanity can indulge all the temptations of fertile nature and fertile sex, without guilt" (Sheller 2003, 69). The Caribbean as a postlapsian sexual paradise is one of the primary global locations for both heterosexual and homosexual sex tourism (Brennan 2004; Kempadoo 2004; Alexander 2005; Padilla 2007; Nixon 2015). Sheller identifies the way in which this lush auto-poietic paradise serves metonymically for the wild, abundant, and available sexuality of Caribbean "natives." Caribbean governments appeal directly to these tourist desires and vie competitively with each other to placate these fantasies of the region in order to maintain the substantial contribution that tourism makes to their gross national products. Returning to its etymological roots, "paradise" in the Caribbean has been summarily enclosed in all-inclusive resorts whose walled-in, well-manicured greenery, pristine private beaches (overflowing with imported white sand and eager dark sex workers), starched grinning servants, and round-the-clock security details have come to look more and more like elaborate menageries where the exotic animals are indeed the sun-hungry tourists themselves. While beyond the walls, the gates, and the barbed wire, the rest of the island most often remains off-limits precisely because it refuses to be "tamed."

Skin Deep: The Soucouyant as Queer Mythos

Sheller reframes Caribbean cannibalism. She redeems the mistaken legacy of anthropophagy in the region by situating the Caribbean deep in the aching belly of (neo)colonial capitalism. Reframing is one way to tame this feral myth and its attendant fantasy of an innately bloodthirsty Caribbean savagery—a centuries-old expectation of the deadliest incivility, still flourishing today in the crime-anxious popular imagination within and beyond the region. Another approach is to reposition the cannibal within a specifically Caribbean mythic universe. For this repositioning then, I return to Trinidad and Tobago for a metaphysical presence: the soucouyant. A contested figure of Trinbagonian mythography, the soucouyant is a syncretic phenomenon that relocalizes the cannibal at the same time that it reveals the gendered and sexual implications of Caribbean mythography.[7]

Usually figured as an elderly sorceress living in solitude on the margins of a community, the soucouyant seems a mere feeble old woman during the day. But when night falls, she sheds her skin and takes to the sky. Placing her leathery husk in the spiced mouth of her kitchen mortar or in the womb of a silk-cotton tree, the soucouyant—now a ravenous burning flame—bursts into the balmy night. She leaves her berry-stain kiss on the tender neck or inner thigh of her victims as they sleep, her calling card a collage of broken blood vessels below the skin surface. These nocturnal visits are commonplace for most Trinbagonians. "A soucouyant suck you, or what?" might be the playful retort to a fresh blood-bite blossom. This is a rhetorical question to be answered with a blush or a proudly mustered smile. When it comes to soucouyants, knowing glances and seductive grins are language enough. Man, woman, child—all can fall prey to this love *jumbie*, who slips through key-holes, floorboards, and seductively parted windows eager for the slightest Cereus breeze.[8] She is the most fantastic of jumbies perhaps because she is known only in dreams. Her blood appetite sated, the sorceress returns to her skin before the coming dawn and spends her daylight hours dreaming of sweet bloods.

It is believed that to catch a soucouyant—if you had a mind to do such a frightful thing—there are at least two effective methods. The first is to find her skin and season its inside with coarse salt; the second requires fistfuls of rice scattered at a crossroads. According to folk wisdom, the salt prevents the soucouyant from returning to her skin, leaving her exposed to the withering daylight and vulnerable to the aggressions of her prey. Similarly, unable to pass the rice-strewn crossroads without stopping to pick up every individual grain, the soucouyant is left vulnerable to the merciless dawn. But there are always other solitary old women at the edges of unassuming villages; and among these, there will be one spirited enough to rub herself down with liver oil from a freshly interred corpse so she can slip her skin and explode aflame into the craving night. The soucouyant is reborn.[9]

Captured within the corpus of her myth is a long tradition of vampire folklore throughout Europe (usually with an anxious eye toward Eastern Europe), which is matched by similarly lengthy and fleshy traditions of blood-sucking apparitions traced back to Western Africa, the pre-Columbian Americas, and South (as well as island Southeast) Asia. One of the avatars of a characteristically Caribbean mythology, the soucouyant pierces the layers of the Trinbagonian cultural body, revealing cross-bleeding even in the mythic imaginary. Though the term "soucouyant" is believed to be derived from the terms *sukunyadyo* (male) and *sukunya* (female), both describing a cannibalistic witch, in a hybrid Fula/Soninke tongue, the spirit—like the islands that birthed her—contains much more than this naming can manage (Warner-Lewis 1991; Anatol 2000; F. Smith 2006).[10]

Rubbing the soucouyant up against the cannibal reveals not only how these figures ghost each other—if blood is a synecdoche for the body, consuming the blood is in essence consuming the body—but also reveals gender as the point at which the flesh gives way in this comparison. Much like the always presumedly male figure of the cannibal haunts the region, the always presumedly female figure of the soucouyant haunts Trinbagonian mythography; both of these jumbies—including the defiantly imagined female cannibal and male sukunyadyo—attest inadvertently to a sensuous homoeroticism imbedded in their narratives yet largely ignored. If the gendering of the soucouyant is imagined to persist even beneath her skin, then she cannot fly from a kind of queer intimacy as she places her ghostly lips upon her bisexed dreamers. This bisexual intimacy is often overshadowed by an understandably critical feminist reading of the soucouyant as a sexist mythos used to socially chastise—especially postmenopausal and thus postreproductive—Caribbean female sexual autonomy (Anatol 2000; F. Smith 2008).

Although I am in solidarity with the project of exposing how the soucouyant myth has been (and continues to be) used to constrain Caribbean female sexual agency, I am less concerned here with readings of the figure as metaphor for nonproductive Caribbean women than I am with expanding the allegorical potential of the narrative. A figurative body through which to approach the sensual (bisexual intimacy), the spiritual (ritualized anthropophagy, as in Holy Communion), and the political (gender-based social discipline), the soucouyant recalls the tropic trinity I introduced earlier. By foregrounding this trinity, I am able to propose for the soucouyant a different kind of metaphorical significance for the region. If the Antilles are indeed an *oneiro-ecstasy* first dreamt up in Western Europe but now sustained by the shared slumbering consciousness of the Euro-American West and the postcolonial Caribbean, then I propose conceiving of the soucouyant as a queer symbol of that which persists outside of the manufactured dream sequence of Caribbean fantasy. The soucouyant flies outside of the fleshy margins of the lucid dreamer's surreality, a testament to the incompleteness of the dream. This flaming symbol shifts our attention from fetishistic dreams to the reality of a region.[11]

The soucouyant is an instructive queer metaphor precisely because it resists the flights of fancy threatening to seduce us away from the intimate relationship between the dreamer and this fleshless spirit. The two are so sensuously intertwined that it is impossible to see one without a glance at the other. In fact, their separation is contested by ingestion, the blood-as-body of the dreamer clotting in the soucouyant's thirsty belly. Capturing the full picture requires a perspective broad enough to see the lucid dream (the fantasy Caribbean), the enraptured dreamer (tourism's dream seekers), and the feasting queer (quotidian life in the region) simultaneously.

Concluding Notes on a New Beginning

This opening engagement introduces two central themes of the book: historical consciousness and erotic desire. We have laid a firm foundation for a careful attentiveness to how thoroughly the past haunts the present in the Caribbean. And we have begun to explore the expansiveness of a tropic trinity I use to redefine our relationship to the erotic. The political, the sensual, and the spiritual as abstract principles and as precise (meta)physical social systems are at once conceptual and experiential isles that this study reveals to be an interconnected archipelago; an archipelago whose "unity is submarine" (Brathwaite 1974, 64). Across this underwater mountain range, vast peaks break the surface and give the impression of distinction despite profound continuity just below the waves.

This archipelago as metaphor holds the islands of Trinidad and Tobago together as closely as it holds these island elements—the political-sensual-spiritual—that I propose give new geography to erotic desire. As my argument progresses, I will elaborate more on this new topography of the erotic; however, for now, it is sufficient to mark these constituent elements as traceable cues that will reappear often. The political-sensual-spiritual represents precisely the pivot points around which this study can be turned—a tropical analysis in the broadest etymological sense. And yet we must not lose sight of Trinbagonian particularity, the accrual of grounded experiences that exist in an intimate relationship with the Caribbean as lucid dream but are not wholly present in the fantasy. This is an entry point into those experiences and the vital lessons they hold for our thinking and our living. Open your eyes. Come see.

A Queer Cartography of Desire

Erotic Islands: Art and Activism in the Queer Caribbean is about the long history of sophisticated strategies same-sex-desiring Caribbean artists and activists have used to make social and cultural interventions. Homophobic exclusions are certainly as unavoidable in the Caribbean region as they are globally, but the present study is far more concerned with the means by which same-sex-desiring people *survive* by literally and figuratively clearing space for themselves in the public domain through artistic expression and community-building techniques.

How do queer Caribbeans claim fertile spaces for themselves in places that have long had a queer relationship to formal legal and moral dictates, in places where authority—colonial, postcolonial, neocolonial—has historically been and continues to be precarious and imperfect at best?[1] To what extent do overemphasizing exclusions prematurely blind us to various kinds of queer *embeddedness* seldom remarked upon in a scholarly literature racing to demonstrate and document systemic homophobia in the region?[2]

Informed by seventeen months of uninterrupted field research and nearly a decade of itinerant research trips around Trinidad's capital city, Port-of-Spain, and all along the Western tip of Tobago, this study contends that the survival strategies of lesbian and gay Caribbeans are at least as dynamic as the systems of structural and ideological oppression that have attempted to marginalize nonnormative bodies and desires. Through foregrounding a queer presence in Carnival masquerade design, calypso musicianship, and HIV/AIDS prevention and care services—the artistic genres and the activist cause that hold pride of place in T&T's national imaginary—*Erotic Islands* documents a grassroots lesbian and gay artistry and activism that has long been culturally rooted.

This book positions specific works created by two of T&T's most renowned and revered living artists as focal points for a historically attentive engagement with the genres over which they reign—calypso and Carnival. Wedded to this analysis of artistry is a local, regional, and internationally informed investigation of HIV/AIDS prevention and support services provided by and for same-sex-desiring communities in T&T. A reconceptualization of the erotic serves as the organizing hermeneutic that holds these various constitutive elements together and provides the conceptual backbone of this analysis. This redefinition of eros is profoundly inspired by the thought of Afro-Caribbean American lesbian feminist warrior poet Audre Lorde. In fact, following Lorde, I attend so closely to reworking the erotic because the book is to a significant extent also an ethnography of a new praxis of eros—of the thought-action possibilities the renewed concept opens.

And yet this new approach to the study of (same-sex) desire in a Caribbean context cannot ignore the fact that it inherits a nearly seventy-year academic history of investigating Trinbagonian gender and sexuality. The most widely circulated early academic studies of quotidian life in the anglophone Caribbean that integrated discussions of gender and sexuality date back to the 1930s and 1940s. These early ethnographic studies were the ambitious work of famed anthropologists Frances and Melville Herskovits (Herskovits and Herskovits 1934, 1936, 1937, and 1947). The Herskovitses' Caribbean ethnographies actively contest the systematic pathologization of kinship structures and sexual behavior patterns in the region that American sociologists (most notably E. Franklin Frazier [Frazier 1932 and 1939]) had deemed the ontological inheritance in particular of Afro-Caribbean working-class communities as part of the legacy of slavery and the plantation system. Melville Herskovits made his best effort to valorize Caribbean—and African American—patterns of sexual interaction and familial organization through exploring their West African cultural heritage. A heritage that while distinct from a Euro-American behavior model was not ontologically rooted at all but rather taught, learned, contextual, and far from pathological.

In their monograph *Trinidad Village* (1947), one of the earliest ethnographies of the island, the Herskovitses briefly mention homosexuality among working-class men and women in the northeastern Trinidadian village of Toco: "Homosexuality is considered a disgrace. The homosexual is an object of ridicule and abuse . . . among women, it is termed 'making zanmi' and there is much talk and 'plenty song' about such persons" (Herskovits and Herskovits 1947, 128). Perhaps the earliest ethnographic mention of homosexuality on the island, the Herskovitses' frustratingly brief reference nevertheless marks a homosexual presence on the island as part of its early entrance into the ethnographic record. Though the homosexual—"object of ridicule and abuse"—remains commented upon but voiceless, the Herskovitses' merely mentioning the persistent presence of male and female homosexuals in Trinidadian discourse performs a parallel task of introducing homosexuality into the scholarly discourse.

Importantly, the Herskovitses make explicit reference to female homosexuals. Indeed, they go so far as to introduce a very important linguistic particularity that deserves closer attention. A classic term with waning contemporary resonance, $za(n)mi$ is believed to be a creolized form of the French *les amies* ([female] friends). This term marks a close friendship between women *or* men. While researching over the last fifteen years in T&T, I have heard primarily gay men in their mid to late thirties and older use the term to refer to their close gay male—perhaps somewhat effeminate—friends. I seldom hear younger gay men or lesbians use the term *zami* in casual conversation. However, upon asking about its usage explicitly during a lesbian group interview, the women insisted—as the Herskovitses note—that one "makes zami" (literally a descriptor of intimacy between women) so that the term describes "what you do, not who you are"; it defines here a behavior, not an identity. However, one woman admitted that the word had fallen out of usage, poetically explaining, "Words are like fruits. There are lots of fruits that are no longer with us. And there are lots of words that are no longer with us" (Las Cuevas 2008). Ironically, even the words used to describe fruits may in time ripen and rot. And yet, though present here in some region-specific semantic detail, same-sex desire amongst women or men is still abandoned by the Herskovitses to the margins of their study. Trinidadian homosexuality is one sexual behavior pattern that the Herskovitses make no attempt to contest with their West African cultural inheritance hypothesis.

And yet this early kinship and sexual behavior study is a critical beginning for a discussion of same-sex desirous communities in T&T in large part because of the role of social scientists—especially anthropologists—throughout the Caribbean region in defining the Caribbean sociocultural norm for family structure and sexual behavior against the imposition of Euro-American moralizing models of sex-kin normality.[3] Although in many other respects quite thorough, the Herskovitses' hasty treatment of homosexuality nevertheless maps queer presence as part of their topography of the conjoined territory of Trinidadian sex-gender-sexuality. As feminist sociologist Kamala Kempadoo has highlighted, studies such as *Trinidad Village* confirm the presence of same-sex relations in preindependence anglophone Caribbean territories such as Trinidad (Kempadoo 2004, 45). Thus, the present study inherits the Herskovitses' legacy as both a significant precedent that must be acknowledged and a pernicious haunt that must be exorcised. In the more than seven decades since the Herskovitses published *Trinidad Village*, a book-length scholarly study of same-sex-desiring communities in Trinidad and Tobago has yet to flesh out and contest the blanket dismissal that has for too long stood in as the final published word on Trinbagonian homosexuality—the final word until now.[4]

However, much more than a mere recuperative text, *Erotic Islands* marks a significant shift away from the emphasis on cultural disavowal, juridical exclusion, and unmediated violence in the scant more recent treatments of queer English-speaking Caribbeans. Certainly, it has been (and continues to be) necessary to mark exclusionary practices—at the local, national, and international levels—in the region, but the conversation about queerness in the Caribbean has become stuck in demonstrating ideological, structural, and individual (often violent) erasures and exclusions. Insisting on moving beyond this impasse in the analysis of Caribbean queerness is not intended as a subtle side step of homophobia as a vector of oppression, but rather as a refusal of homophobia as a stopping point in the conversation.[5] In fact, it is by centering Audre Lorde and her attempt at expanding the erotic that we are able to shift the discourse on queer Caribbean experience toward a new conceptual horizon.

Precious Lorde: The Book of Eros

In what are perhaps the most conspicuous—and certainly the most concise—articulations of an emergent black queer diaspora studies and its correlative budding black queer diaspora theory, cultural studies scholar Rinaldo Walcott lends lead voice to a now distinctly resonant chorus of interest in Lorde's oeuvre among a generation of scholars determined to hold together black studies, queer studies, and diaspora studies (R. Walcott 2005,

2007).[6] For Walcott, this return to Lorde is primarily about recognizing that conversations between black diasporic feminism and postcolonial feminism form the nexus at which black queer diaspora studies and its new register of black queer theorizing take shape (R. Walcott 2007, 36). Putting an even finer point on Walcott's assertion, the queer Caribbeanist literary theorist and feminist Omise'eke Tinsley continuously encourages my attention to the fact that one of the distinguishing features of an emergent queer Caribbean studies is its grounding in black (lesbian) feminist scholarship. This lineage is certainly one the present work proudly inherits while working hard to earn its place at the (kitchen) table.

A (black) queer theory unwilling to relinquish its engagement with feminist of color critique cannot avoid recognizing Lorde—though the recognition comes belatedly—as a queer theorist. Lorde is a theorist so queer in fact that two decades after her passing, academics have finally begun to brave the broadest and deepest implications of her thinking; Walcott ushers us in her direction: "I want to read Lorde as a queer theorist, a queer theorist for whom queer theory's disavowal of feminism and its white gay masculinity means that she is too difficult to digest in terms of its institutional claims and positioning" (R. Walcott 2007, 36). What might it mean to add "theorist" to the mantric litany of descriptors used to summon the warrior poet? In part, it may mean that the existing scholarship on queerness in the African diaspora comes one breath closer to recognizing some of the fruitful theoretical interventions cultivated from the soil of black queer diasporic experience and artistry. But what if this recognition of Lorde as a theorist—a black queer theorist of diasporic scope—just barely misses placing a fine enough point on the value of thinking deeply through the legacy Lorde has left us?

Inspired by philosopher Lewis Gordon's insistence that the abstract thought of critical reflection (the principal domain of the theorist) reaches toward philosophical inquiry in part on the shoulders of perennial questions (*What does it mean to exist? How is life meaningful? How do we know what we know?*) that echo through Lorde's oeuvre, I consider what it might mean to read Audre Lorde as a philosopher continuing in the tradition of august Caribbean thinkers such as Sylvia Wynter (L. Gordon 2008, 8). And even more precise still, I propose that we include Lorde's work—poetry, prose, fact, fiction, and all the supple spaces she delighted in between them—in a long pedigreed lineage of what Gordon calls "existential philosophies" and places apart from, but by no means subordinate to, the distinct ideological movement christened "existentialism" (L. Gordon 2000, 10). A prolific thinker who may not have defined herself as an existentialist, but whose positions nonetheless have an existential dimension (among others, of course) premised on philosophical questions about embodied agency and situated experience, Lorde has bequeathed us a vast intellectual inheritance that I would not pretend to properly parse here in toto (L. Gordon 2000, 10–11, 16). However, as a means by which to frame the current inquiry, it is vital to foreground one theme in Lorde's work that has garnered very eager attention in recent scholarship about African diasporic communities, queer sexualities, and composite subjectivities: the erotic.

Nowhere in Lorde's oeuvre is her conceptualization of the erotic more explicit—though perhaps not the most transparent—than in the conference paper she first delivered in 1978, which would by 1984 be enshrined as "Uses of the Erotic: The Erotic as Power" in her now near-canonical collection of essays and speeches *Sister Outsider* (Lorde [1978] 1984, 53–59).[7] These seductive and yet troublesome seven pages have been the most heavily cited and strategically deployed by the cadre of scholars deeply interested in using a Lorde-inspired erotics to think through quotidian experience and imaginative possibility in the African diaspora (Weir-Soley 2009; Tinsley 2010; Allen 2011; Sheller 2012; King 2014).[8]

Come Again: Rereading Lordean Erotics

Although the details of the context within which Lorde delivered her paper "Uses of the Erotic: The Erotic as Power" seldom find their way into even the most otherwise attentive discussions of the text, these details are crucial if we are to adequately meet any of the challenges the paper seems to pose to its broadest theoretical applicability. Delivered on August 25, 1978, as part of the Fourth Berkshire Conference on the History of Women hosted by Mount Holyoke College in western Massachusetts, Lorde's "Uses of the Erotic" was intended for an audience primarily of women historians (exceedingly white and heterosexual), who had organized their own conferences in response to the isolation they had experienced within the exceedingly male American Historical Association (De Veaux 2004, 220).[9] Amid significant protest and rallying about the exclusion of lesbian history from the Berkshire Conference's main agenda, Lorde delivered what has since become her classic treatise on the importance of women scholars—lesbians like herself among them—resisting a dangerous urge to embrace a pseudoscientific objectivity sanitized of feeling, emotion and intuition (stereotypically "female afflictions" then, perhaps, as now, in the academy and beyond it) in an attempt to contest sexist presumptions about the inadequacy of female scholars and the significant work they produce.[10] And while these details of context and audience cannot explain all of what Lorde said that day—nor do they give us any clue as to why the irreverent poet uses the language she does for an audience of women historians—I propose that these bits of information do tell us something about why Lorde articulates the erotic as she does in the paper.

Lorde's black lesbian feminist underpinnings are undeniable in her oeuvre, and one cannot (certainly should not) avoid the centrality of women's struggles and especially the challenges faced by women of color in general and black women in particular to the vast majority of Lorde's writings. So, I do not mean to undermine the ideological and political importance of Lorde foregrounding women in "Uses of the Erotic," but I do want to better situate the seemingly singular emphasis on women and the erotic in the text. Remembering that Lorde is delivering a paper to a conference of women historians, honoring Simone de Beauvoir at a women's liberal arts college perhaps begins to help us explain what might be misread as Lorde confining the erotic to the exclusive domain of women—or at least of the female within each of us—as seems evident (without contextual considerations) in the troublesome second sentence of the essay: "The erotic is a resource within each of us that lies in a deeply female and spiritual plane, firmly rooted in the power of our unexpressed and unrecognized feeling" (Lorde [1978] 1984, 53). This sentence is merely the beginning of Lorde's return again and again to articulating the importance of the erotic for women exclusively. Even if one is willing to accept that Lorde's "deeply female plane" may exist within men as well, scholars would be more comfortable perhaps with the notion that the erotic exists in a deeply *feminine* plane that men can also access within themselves. And this feminine erotic may have been Lorde's implicit intention, but of course the text predates more recent gender theory on sex-gender distinctions, and there really is no way around Lorde addressing women directly about women exclusively with regard to relationships (sexual or otherwise) between women. So, most scholars who take up this essay either embrace what appears to be Lorde's theorizing of the erotic as exclusively female or chalk that emphasis up to an essentialist failing on Lorde's part and make use of her erotic while ignoring her gynocentrism.

While it may be the case that Lorde conceived of the erotic as the exclusive domain of women, I contend instead that we must read Lorde for the audience gathered and not presume that she would reject the proposition that eros as a principle be allowed to retain the widest possible applicability—without losing its necessary attention to the ground of lived experience (of women, of men, of trans people, of heterosexuals, of queers, of people of color, etc.). Perhaps Lorde would disagree with my reading and insist on a politically and ideologically vital essentialist perspective on the erotic, but for the task at hand I require a broader eros that places Lorde among a long lineage of philosophers who have wrestled with the concept from early in the history of human thought throughout ancient Egypt and Greece. Most conspicuously, this lesbian poet philosopher's engagement with eros brings another to mind: Sappho—the classic lesbian poet-turned-philosopher by classicist and creative writer Anne Carson in her luxurious essay *Eros: The Bittersweet* (Carson 1986).[11] Carson's reading of Sappho (among others, most notably of Socrates' revelrous reasoning on Eros in *The Symposium* (Plato [385–370 BC] 2008) and our reimagining of the erotic through Lorde position us to recognize eros's sweet bitterness as a philosophical metaphor.

As an important orienting mechanism, Carson defines the Greek word "eros" as "want/lack/desire for what is missing" and then proceeds to unfold the concept's inherent pleasure-pain paradox primarily through Sappho's poetics (Carson 1986, 4, 10, 11). With individual romantic relationships as her primary referent, Carson describes eros as an ultimately unfulfillable desire; for her, it is the simultaneous delight (sweet) of reaching toward a love ideal and the pain (bitterness) of always falling short because one cannot have a thing and still want it in the same way (Carson 1986, 30, 62, 70, 171). Other fissures of desire open to replace the sated wish, and we rush to fulfill those new wants, whose satisfaction will surely birth others. In line with Carson's reading, I want to expand Sappho's bittersweet eros beyond solely romantic relationships toward a larger affective metaphor for other social dynamics within which the sweet bitterness of desire describes a relationship between lived reality and hoped-for ideals in various spheres of existence. I will discuss what it may mean to merge Carson and Lorde—mindful of the defining tensions that merging reveals—for our redefinition of eros shortly, but it suffices to recognize here that eros reveals realms of experience (like love/pleasure and hatred/pain) that seem disparate but are in fact linked. Those of us familiar with Lorde's oeuvre will recognize this bridging work as indicative of the warrior poet's philosophical impulse to connect (experiences, ideas, identity categories, people, places, and feelings, often through poetry's metaphors and similes) across difference through the rallying of artistry and the poetry of activism. Approaching Lorde's erotic as a philosophical principle about which she is offering a theory positions us to more accurately read Lorde's definition of the erotic and focus our attention here on what Lorde might be trying to say about the principle of eros itself and how it may indeed save our lives.

Much scholarship on "Uses of the Erotic" has been hesitant to admit what appears quite clearly from even the most cursory reading of the essay. True to its etymological roots and to its historical usage, Lorde's assay of the erotic is far from an easy definitive statement. In fact, in it one recognizes Lorde herself trying to write through a still uncertain investigation of what it might be while struggling with the inadequacies of how it is popularly defined. In this struggle with the erotic we are able to witness in a single finished piece—perhaps more readily than in much of Lorde's other prose work—Lorde as existential philosopher *and* poet pushing her theorizing to uncertain extremes in an attempt to redefine an ancient principle. Nearly in the perfect center of the paper—at its heart, if you will—Lorde offers her clearest (though still not absolutely transparent) definition of what she means by the erotic:

> It has become fashionable to separate the spiritual (psychic and emotional) from the political, to see them as contradictory or antithetical. . . . In the same way, we have attempted to separate the spiritual and the erotic, thereby reducing the spiritual to a world of flattened affect, a world of the ascetic who aspires to feel nothing. But nothing is farther from the truth. . . . The dichotomy between the spiritual and the political is also false, resulting from an incomplete attention to our erotic knowledge. For the bridge which connects them is formed by the erotic—the sensual—those physical, emotional, and psychic expressions of what is deepest and strongest and richest within each of us, being shared: the passion of love in its deepest meanings. (Lorde [1978] 1984, 56)

Even in her attempt to define erotic knowledge as that which defies false dichotomies between the political and the spiritual as well as between the spiritual and what Lorde eventually calls the sensual, one recognizes a slippage (a seeming redundancy) in which she struggles to decouple the sensual from the erotic.[12] This decoupling must not be misunderstood as Lorde's attempt to deny the sensuality of her new erotic, but rather to accommodate the political and the spiritual alongside sensuality in her new theoretical architecture. If "our erotic knowledge" requires that we attend to the political and spiritual alongside sensuality, intimacy, feeling, affection, empathy and love, then the erotic as mere euphemism for sex or even sensuality cannot persist. It is in the moment when Lorde is forced to replace "the erotic" with "the sensual" that her reconceptualization of the erotic itself achieves its most potent coherence. If the sensual ("those physical, emotional, and psychic expressions of what is deepest and strongest and richest within each of us, being shared: the passion of love in its deepest meanings") provides a bridge between the political and the spiritual, then "the erotic" constitutes the entire structure and ought not to be reduced to an easy symmetry with any of its composite elements.

Extending Lorde, I propose that the erotic must be reconceptualized as a perspectival trinity that holds together the political-sensual-spiritual at their most abstract; in other words, "the erotic" describes various formal and informal power hierarchies (the political), sexual as well as nonsexual intimacy (the sensual), and sacred metaphysics (the spiritual) simultaneously. And here, if we merge this logical expansion of Lorde's erotic with Carson's interpretive framing of eros as paradoxical desire, we can recognize the defining tensions governing this new tripartite conception of the erotic. The three constitutive elements of the erotic each represent a negotiation of the tension between an ideal vision and our lived reality. What if politics at its grassroots is a desire for more just power dynamics despite the seductive imbalance that present power dynamics foster? What if sensuality at its heart is a desire for the dissolution of the seemingly bounded self despite the epidemic of selfish individualism? What if spirituality at its core is a desire for a metasystem of accountability and a larger continuity of existence despite the persistence of tangible immediacy and the seeming finality of mortality?[13]

Then, political desire, sensual desire, and spiritual desire might provide the interconnected infrastructure that gives substance to a new erotic. Again, areas of experience that may seem disparate lend themselves—across a bridging desire—to the linking work that Lorde reveres in eros. These conceptual linkages provide a mirror for the personal connections (seldom easy, effortless, or safe) that are a vital resource in Lorde's work. If connection in general proves an important governing principle for Lorde, then connection specifically between human beings—a deep sharing of pursuits (physical, emotional, intellectual)—"forms a bridge between the sharers which can be the basis for understanding much of what is not shared between them, and lessens the threat of their difference" (Lorde [1978] 1984, 56).[14] Lorde reassures us that once in touch with the erotic—which can be achieved only through fostering deep connections with others across a range of political, sensual, and spiritual desires—one is not only less willing to accept feelings of powerlessness, despair, and depression, but also more inclined to pursue structural changes in society (Lorde [1978] 1984, 58, 59).

I will return to the erotic as a community-building tool and as a motivation for social change (or at least arts-initiated ideological shifts) in the chapters that follow, but for now it is sufficient to recognize eros as a radiant prism through which to interpret the lesbian/gay artistry and grassroots activism presented in the chapters that follow. This use of eros as a lens, vital for surveying the elaborate topography of connections we share as political, sensual, and spiritual beings, is the principal theoretical and methodological proposition of this book. Through this erotic looking glass, an intertwined political-sensual-spiritual provides a strategic wellspring that lesbian and gay Trinbagonians use not simply to persist despite attempted marginalization but, more profoundly, to summon the courage to push back against homophobia with creativity and determination.

At the heart of eros as a renovated concept is the confidence that political, social, and cultural exclusions can (and must) be confronted through community building, through touch, and through faith. Politicized power hierarchies, sensual intimacy, and spiritual metaphysics present interrelated obstacles *and* opportunities that the lesbian and gay artists and activists at the center of this study must negotiate not only to survive cultural disavowals, juridical exclusions, and various forms of institutional and individual violence but also to clear a space for queer imagining and queer fellowship in their midst. And perhaps this strategy for how to remain undeterred in the face of oppression might prove instructive for other similar (or very different) communities in other contexts, communities of interlinked beings desperately searching for a path out of depression, despair, and self-effacement. The erotic may just be our way out.

A Matter of Method, or How to Write an Ethnography That Is Not One

As much a methodological proposition as it is an interpretive intervention, the erotic also provides a way in. What might it mean for scholars to work inspired by this broadened conceptualization of the erotic? How might this new eros shape our expanding cartography of the queer Caribbean? It is important methodologically to emphasize here again that this book has not been written in isolation. Conceptualized, researched, written, and revised in the intellectual and actual company of a cadre of queer Caribbeanists, this text is touched by over a decade of countless interactions, conversations, upsets, revelations, distractions, coincidences, visions, hugs, and debates. Recognizing the presence of the political, the sensual, and the spiritual in the community of minds who continue to inspire, intrigue, frustrate, and preserve me is part of recognizing the methodological implications of the erotic.

However, even beyond the kinds of erotic interlinkages that one might be able to mark in acknowledgments or follow through citation practices, the erotic has been central to the methods by which I have gathered all of the data central to this book. My ideas, my perspective, my questions, and my very sense of self have been influenced not only by a community of black queer scholars but also by a community of diasporic black queer intellectuals, artists, and activists within and beyond the academy. Although the various ways in which my academic kin—the queer family that we are—show up in the work are archived in this text as in any other, I marry this archive of citations with another that explicitly documents the dynamic relationships I developed as part of same-sex desirous communities in Trinidad and Tobago. This sister archive is as vital a constitutive element of the book as the chapters surrounding it.

Based on excerpts from my field notebooks, *From Far Afield: A Queer Travelogue (Parts I–IV)* is a reflection segmented into four interludes placed between the chapters of this book. These interludes document my quotidian experiences in T&T over a period of a year and five months, from February 5, 2007, to July 22, 2008, and create a collage of this finite period of time, my relationship to that moment, and the various relationships in which I became entangled during that time. Beginning with prefield research trips during the summers of 2003, 2004, and 2005 ranging in length from two weeks to two months, my journeys to T&T culminated in a ten-month research trip from October 2007 to August 2008 under the auspices of a Fulbright fellowship, which extended a previous seven-month research trip undertaken in February 2007. My field notes over the course of this period map my time in T&T but also provide a partial cartography of my inner thought landscape. The erotic is unavoidable here again not only in explicit reflections hyperconscious of the interworkings of power hierarchies, sensual intimacy, and sacred metaphysics, but also as a frame within which to read the kinds of interactions and revelations—saturated with the political, sensual, and spiritual—that this travelogue documents across my own body of experiences.

As a queer Afro-Trinidadian, born in New York City and raised on the nostalgia of my immigrant mother and grandmother—who returned me to Nelson Street, Port-of-Spain enough to settle a little Trini English Creole under my tongue—I am also a subject of this inquiry. "Subject" here in two senses: the authoring subject and an implicit subject (for better or worse) of this study. *From Far Afield* is my negotiation of this subjectivity alongside the other same-sex-desiring Trinbagonians who populate this analysis. These are subjects with whom I share "an equally affect-saturated subjecthood" to this day (J. L. Jackson 2013, 243). From the vantage point of this shared affective landscape, this travelogue narrates two stories simultaneously: a trip into the field that is at once a journey "home," and a return home that is at once an immersion in the unfamiliar familiarity of T&T.

Although these patches of narrative are stitched together chronologically, they still—for the most part—challenge any simple telling of the overarching tale they suggest. But they do tell a story just the same. Principally, I offer these interludes as—at least in part—an acceptance of anthropologist Deborah Thomas's elegant and welcomed invitation to experiment with narrative voices as a means by which to methodologically dilate the boundaries of ethnographic work (D. Thomas 2011, 17). Together, these reflexive breaks expose my coming upon and coming to terms with the integration of the political-sensual-spiritual in the lives of lesbian and gay Trinbagonians while also demonstrating the not-always-flattering unfolding of erotic complexity in my quotidian negotiation of my own presence in the field. While not necessarily foregrounding the day to day in my chapters, I nonetheless summon elements of the quotidian on terms closely tied to my own imposing body in order to symbolically and quite literally frame the analysis.

It is by design that my chapters refuse the kinds of anecdotal displays perhaps most traditionally characteristic of ethnography. Deborah Thomas has noted that my ambivalence toward a more "traditional" ethnographic style is reassuringly far from singular:

> [A disinclination toward ethnography is] part of a growing reconfiguration of anthropological research that is thinking through how one does ethnography in the present, and who one does it for. In other words, many scholars are moving beyond an earlier sense of ethnography as translation, indeed refusing the impulse completely, in order to instead demonstrate how particular sites and relations at multiple levels of scale can help us to clarify complex [and indeed proximate] theoretical and real-world

problems (without the voyeurism and presumed break between writer and audience that characterized much early anthropology, and that is still probably dominant today). (D. Thomas 2012)

I am accompanied then in offering here an ethnography that is not one in any traditional sense. Perhaps I offer here an ethnography that refuses— if you will. This study resists the tempting compulsion toward ethnographic totality encouraged in part by the etymological imperative of the term "ethnography" itself literally describing the "writing of (a) race/culture." And instead, I experiment here with what it might mean to decouple classic ethnography from participant observation.

In large part, this would mean following anthropologist John L. Jackson Jr.'s definitional guidance to recognize ethnography as the "descriptive social science writings that attempt to capture groups' cultural beliefs and practices" and set that genre of writing apart from the methodological practice of participant observation, which is the data collection process dependent on "methodological observations and face-to-face interactions over an extended period of time" (J. L. Jackson 2013, 207). If we can resist the presumptuous consumption of the latter by the former, then we are better positioned to respond to Jackson's elegantly disciplining call in his *Thin Description: Ethnography and the Hebrew Israelites of Jerusalem* (2013) to embrace the fact that anthropologists' most baroque ethnographic accounts reveal the complex workings of little beyond our own thick delusions of omniscience: "Ethnographic spaces become dense with the swelling, inflation, of resident anthropologists, and all the thicker, ironically, when they choose to shrink from view, omnisciently offstage, puppeteering things from far above the storyline. It is a thinness invested in an occulted version of anthropology, one that would pretend to see *everything* and, therefore, sometimes sees less than it could" (J. L. Jackson 2013, 14; emphasis in original). This particular telling resists ethnography as totalizing translation and embraces participant observation as a central method, requiring my presence in the field as vitally as its documentation requires my presence on the page, in the text—my body figuratively and literally on the line. What other kinds of scholarly writing might an anthropologist use to share research findings (including the various kinds of relationships "found" in the field)?[15] This text is an experiment in answering that question, an attempt to "write up" on the experimental borderlands where ethnography begins to look like something else entirely. Out here, there are no curtains; there is no offstage per se; we are at once puppet and puppeteer—but the show must go on.

The Cartography of This Body: A Chapter Outline

Three chapter pairs follow this one. Each pair is composed of an introductory historical chapter that provides a bit of context for the more specific engagement with artistry or activism that follows it. In each of the three pairs, I approach the idea of the erotic through a distinct sociocultural institution (Carnival, calypso and HIV/AIDS activism) and a particular aesthetic principle. Here the definition of the aesthetic returns to its etymological root to describe roughly "the art/science of sensory perception" in line with German philosopher Immanuel Kant's insistence on the proper usage of the term.[16] So, the aesthetic experiences brought to the fore in what follows are principally sensory experiences.

While it is nearly impossible to isolate our senses—and more often than not a kind of synesthesia confounds even our own presumably clear sense of our senses—I foreground certain sensorial points on the path toward recognizing a new expansive eroticism. Sight and the visual provide the sensory reference points for the first Carnival masquerade chapter pair, sound and vibration for the second calypso chapter pair, and touch and sensation for the final HIV/AIDS activism chapter pair. Taken together, this linked "sensoryscape" grounds the book as an aesthetic treatment in the truest sense of the term. This treatment in each of the chapter pairs returns us repeatedly to the concept of the erotic from various vantage points in an effort to map three related paths through queer sociocultural embeddedness to an identical goal: eros reimagined. Between these chapters, I have placed the reflective interludes I discussed previously. The first interlude follows this chapter.

Chapter 1, "Inheriting the Mask: A History of Parody in Trinidad's Carnival," provides a brief history of traditions of race and gender parody—as primarily sight-bound erotic endeavors—in Trinidad's Carnival in order to set the stage for introducing Peter Minshall. The island's over-two-hundred-year-old Carnival provides the primary palette for the over seventy-year-old white, gay, Caribbean Carnival masquerade designer. This chapter marks the place where Minshall enters Trinidad's Carnival history, the erotic traditions of masking and performance that he inherits, and the legacy his oeuvre of designs has left as part of the cultural heritage of the nation. Chapter 2, "Peter Minshall's Sacred Heart and the Erotic Art of Play," focuses in on the artist's 2006 HIV/AIDS awareness masquerade band *The Sacred Heart* not only as an HIV/AIDS intervention but also as an eros-driven critique of the nation. As an interpretive frame, the erotic encourages a fuller recognition of the elements that have sustained both the artist and the nation's admiration of him. A second interlude follows this chapter.

Chapter 3, "Echoes of an Utterance: A History of Gender Play in Calypso," tells the brief history of gendered crossings and appropriations that have birthed a singularly Caribbean music genre. This history provides the melodic background for the introduction of Linda McCartha "Calypso Rose" Sandy-Lewis, a well over seventy-year-old black lesbian musical virtuoso and the very first female performer to rise to highest prominence in calypso music. Lewis clears a definitive space (again) for female calypsonians while guaranteeing her unique position as godmother of the genre. Chapter 4, "Calypso Rose's 'Palet' and the Sweet Treat of Erotic Aurality," gives the artist's calypso "Palet" (1968) a close listen. A playfully bawdy tune laced with homoerotic double entendre in which Calypso Rose transforms herself into an ice lolly vendor, "Palet" documents female same-sex desire in calypso through the sung symbolism of the Caribbean lesbian phallus. This phallus functions simultaneously as a political, sensual, and spiritual fetish. A third interlude follows this chapter.

Chapter 5, "A Generation with AIDS: A History, A Critique," offers a brief historical assessment of the HIV/AIDS pandemic—up through the end of the first decade of the twenty-first century—in order to address a few of the statistical and terminological inexactitudes plaguing international HIV/AIDS work. The chapter begins by mapping the state of HIV/AIDS globally, in the Caribbean region, and specifically in Trinidad and Tobago up to the end of my fieldwork period. This survey of the disease then shifts into a critique of the terms, discourses, and presumptions circulating around HIV/AIDS in order to provide an even more precise historical and ideological cartography of the pandemic locally, regionally, and internationally. Chapter 6, "Between Tongue and Teeth: The Friends For Life Chatroom as Erotic Intervention," introduces the Trinidad-based nongovernmental organization (NGO) Friends For Life (FFL)—one of the only HIV/AIDS service provision organizations run principally by and for working-class gay men in the Caribbean region. This final chapter demonstrates the grassroots usefulness of various kinds of contiguous intimacies in FFL's most resilient program, the

Community Chatroom Experience. This chapter broadens our perspective on the importance of touch for subtle successes in HIV/AIDS prevention and support work. The fourth and final interlude follows this chapter.

The concluding chapter, "Black Queer Diaspora and Erotic Potentiality," reviews the cross-workings of the erotic in the work of Calypso Rose, Peter Minshall, and Friends For Life while proposing a methodological intervention that advocates for holding situated, speaking subjects at the center of an emergent black queer (diaspora) studies. This chapter provides not only a way to integrate the ones that come before it but also voices a hope for the relationship between anthropology and black queer studies that the project has instantiated all along. Ultimately, this study offers this proposition as well as the potential uses of the erotic—as a theoretical intervention that may extend even beyond this particular contextualization—to both the reader and the various disciplines across which it lies. Thus, this conclusion serves as a surveying tool indicating how far we have come, the ground beneath our feet, and the path ahead.

By insisting on a promiscuous multidisciplinary topography, *Erotic Islands* offers an intervention that is not simply relevant for anthropology, African diaspora studies, and queer studies, but rather indispensable for these increasingly interconnected fields. What follows is informed by and promises a contribution to the avant-garde work currently reshaping these scholarly fields.[17] Most important, though, this book claims space as a key text within the nascent field of black queer diaspora studies. Informed by the scholarly and artistic work at the forefront of this new thought project, the present study further articulates and outlines the expanding terrain of the field. A future-looking intellectual enterprise that is nevertheless attentive to the long history of black (lesbian) feminist scholarship that cleared a path for its existence, black queer diaspora studies is the newest direction toward which fresh approaches to anthropology, African diaspora studies, and queer studies are pointing. *Erotic Islands* journeys across these proximate domains—its course set on their convergent horizon.

From Far Afield / A QUEER TRAVELOGUE (PART I)

FEBRUARY

2/5/07

I feel this journey in my hands—a rough ache, unfamiliarity with the most familiar—and so I take this as metaphor. Small incisions—from packing, storing, cleaning, moving—have pressed into the backs of my hands. These hands are not mine for this beginning. Finally, I am in flight—exhausted, a week delayed. Leaving is a gift. I wonder—the muscles strained in my fingers and across palms—if I will ever be the same, ever so soft and untouched, so delicate and well cared for again. What will become of these hurt hands? Will I come to know myself again—even in pain, even when made into an odd new thing? I have learned that whoever walks with me is most powerful, most forgiving, and most kind. My existence is miraculous, and I am thankful. I raise and clasp these hands—ritual.

2/6/07

"Where in Trinidad you from?" a nice enough woman asks me on the plane. I smile a quick mischievous child's smile. But knowing the unyielding truth of passports, I say, "I was born in New York," and my accent confounds her. I am awake when we land in Trinidad. First off the plane, I am caught in the advertisements for this place. A foolish thing, I think to myself, to advertise a place once you have already arrived. If I am here, I must be convinced. But I read anyway for the best face this nation would put forward. I meet Uncle Poule, my grandmother's youngest brother.[1] He is frozen in time and wearing that smell—a familiar body, brought forward by the heat. He is a patient man—quiet, calm, dutiful mostly—like most of the surviving men of that generation in my family except for Uncle Mauby. But he was once Mr. Universe—exceptional, I suppose. Nelson Street: the anecdotes of cruelty precede it—not crime per se, but that does have its place here. This time it is petty jealousy. Uncle Poule tells me that his old determined white pickup truck—held together by his goodness and that smell—freshly painted had been keyed. Now though, it has been restored, its insides a thick skin of grime and affection. He tells me the car battery is bolted down so as not to be stolen again. I watch the sky in the side view mirror, titled toward less mundane things. People are haunting the corners and front yards, like they do in Harlem summers. The roaches are as familiar in this home of a youth that is not my own as anything on this island—small and fast or the largest I have ever seen. My mother calls them "mahogany birds." That way with words is my mother's forte. This place—perhaps a shadow of itself, perhaps a ghost—is where my family as I know it began. This three-flight walk-up—barely distinguishable from the other neatly decrepit government housing projects surrounding it on all sides—in one of the worst neighborhoods in the bustling heart of Port-of-Spain is home. Return.

2/7/07

The ceiling leaks. The water running down from the washhouse on the roof is a waterfall in the dead of night. The drops upon the mattress soothe in a torturous kind of way. I sleep still and deeply. Zooti has stories he tells easily between cigarettes. His home and his love are beautiful, quiet, and unimposing. The view—the edge of downtown falling into the sea—is tremendous, and I cannot think of anyone who deserves it more. I see everyone my mind passed over fondly before leaving. I run into Mazay near Green Corner while mourning the disappearance of a bookstore. He crosses the street toward me—fresh faced and smiling—and the world disappears. We hug and settled in for *tea*—slow, steady sips on the hot, sweet gossip of the moment. Roukou is holding court on the Promenade—his "downtown office." Since last I saw him, he has sold his childhood home and planned a permanent move to England only to suffer British Immigration's refusal and detention in London. A diabetic, denied his insulin, he nearly died before being allowed to return home. After that, living in Trinidad again might have been unbearable. So now he lives in Tobago. Britain, beware a long-memoried Caribbean femme. Zooti tells me he had a nervous breakdown and checked himself into an insane asylum—the infamous St. Ann's Psychiatric Hospital. And he was almost kept there permanently. How does one leave a Caribbean madhouse? He might have been there still but for his persistence, his family, and his friends. A tormented beauty, Zooti—he is as powerful as he is troubled. How easy it is to be pulled back into the fold with stories of the time in between this visit and my last. My coming and going at whim is a luxury I take for granted. Just before sleep takes me, I consider the awe of this place. Beside me, the water still falls.

2/8/07

Tref is not well. Finally, Mazay admits mid-tears that his *daughter* is in danger of losing *her* life. Tref has been taken to the hospital. Earlier, he sounded himself on the phone. I've missed him—tall elegant, untouched, a laughing mystery with a sugary singing voice. Stories keep Mazay distracted, a history of drag queens long passed on: Betty Wright stepping out down Frederick Street with poodles in tow . . . Ericka . . . Mackie (the first to die of that mysterious disease before it had a name). His stories fill the empty corners of the day. Mazay calls down longtime *hozes* (maybe short for "homosexual" and "whore" at once—a telling convergence). He remembers being pelted with glass bottles. He returns to family—gay family—with talk of his *mati*. "That's my *mati*," he says, "that means my good good girlfriend. That means me and she does *go down*." The sharing of deep secrets, confiding—man or woman: my mati. Or my *macomeh*: (1) a godmother (creolized form of *macomère*, or "co-mother" in French) who noisily watches out ("to *maco*," an abbreviated verb in its own right) for her good good girlfriend who would do the same for her in turn; (2) so, a *macomehman* is a man who is inclined to maco just like a good good godmother. And thus, he must be gay. Tref is my Tobago mati, my small-island macomeh—I want to see him today.

2/9/07

The boat to Tobago takes two and a half hours; high-speed catamarans have replaced the big cargo vessels with the underdeck cabins that still take six hours but mostly transport only goods now. I remember that overnight journey; it is still a recent memory for most Trinbagonians. Roukou and I chat until the rocking takes over. I have never felt seasickness before, but, as Roukou quips, "The CAT is riding hozes' chest." He tells me about wanting to go, needing to leave, emigration on a feeling. He sold all he had, put faith in the soon-to-come, and went . . . only to be detained in London. The plainclothes officers have their suspicions. He is fingerprinted and sleeping in a detention center, nearly without his insulin—his sugar soaring. But he finds a nurse to make it right and *rip* (or tongue lash) the immigration officers in the process. Family. Roukou tells me about his family, the difficulty of brothers abroad (older in Canada and Los Angeles) and sisters "not here" he says to mean "not with us" (alive) or not all there (distant in mind). He starts fresh in Tobago. But not a moment before mourning the lost plane ticket money. This is a long low period, but he is still resilient, still optimistic about his plan. Roukou teaches me lessons about new beginnings that seldom come as you planned them. But they come, and we must find a way to embrace them even when unsure about what we have learned and where it leads. His plan does not refuse change but is not merely change either. I can only hush and watch the approaching horizon.

2/13/07

Here there is much to tell, an archive of life stories rots in the tropics. Some seem mere fiction—likely stories—but most are the truest accounts of unbelievably surreal lives. Here fact is fiction and fiction fact. We live according to what we are willing to believe in any given moment. Betelmi—that *Grenadian woman*—is a contrast in sharp elegant features and beautifully thick hair. He is a master at brandishing *tone* (attitude) with the best of them. The red light is soft on his cheek, on his bed. The curtains blow softly into this glowing room. He tells me about Grenada, the hurricane, his head nearly busted open, saving his mother's windows he had imported from Trinidad, and saving his sister's life. This is 2003 and nearly all he has the hurricane has blown away. Grenada is devastated. Betelmi worked for the relief service, searching for dead bodies, bearing gruesome witness, and keeping vigil in the morgue. He tells me about *clipping* (stealing) from Radical Designs, explains the politics of gay Grenadians making community in T&T. He has a British mother, he says, and a British passport. He has broken stories too—a German boyfriend, the promise of emigration, stolen by his closest friend; his revenge is tricky, hard-edged spite. A set of hozes is living in Betelmi's apartment. Their kitchen counter gossip wraps around a murdered gay boy, caught in a vicious drama, mutilated and disposed of in Black Rock by an old lover. The dead boy's new lover survives his stab wounds.

2/22/07

Early on a morning, Vervine comes to wake me and whisper that I am the only one who pronounces her name correctly. Sometimes, I do not trust her. She is too phenomenal a storyteller. The day is wrapped in her for the most part, carried by her borrowed car with the bottomless trunk. She tells stories of the gentlemen she is raising and then collects her two sons to prove it. This is as close to a day at the beach as I have so far been allowed. She was raped—she says that casually—in a cab going toward San Fernando on a Carnival Tuesday. With this, she soils and weights the playfulness of the "Carnival baby." And just as soon as she plants the seed, she harvests the thought with a quick distraction: nobody knows I'm a lesbian. A banner in precise white letters on her favorite black T-shirt, this bit of irony insists that she is perhaps the island's most visible and certainly most vocal lesbian. This everyone now knows for sure.

2/25/07

He left me—I suppose the others had no choice but to go or be left themselves, but *he* left me. I can understand the logic of wanting to go home once the party has come to an end. But I refuse it still. I am drunk and enthralled in the beauty of a dreadlocked prince adorned with seed jewels. He is a déjà vu infatuation. I had made note of him in the airport, followed him with my eyes even after the staring became obvious: Mowan. But Seme—a monstrous mix of nonchalance, remove, and judgment—sours the longed-for encounter by deciding it is fine to be on his way without me. He is unconcerned. My ride has gone. I am near the sea and far from home. One dollar, one red note in my wallet folded and lonesome stares me down. I have spent an evening buying drinks for others, hardly noticing that nothing has been bought for me in return until now. But I am proud even if stranded. The *jumbie* (spirit) that comes when I drink was more or less kept under control, occupied. I am mindful of this shift and pleased. The flaming bottles are still rooted in the sand—a flambeaux romance. The low light is a revelation. The ocean beckons but stays distant and black except for the moon watching itself. The warm glow of these lights is impeccable. Between us—Mowan and myself— words are exchanged, gifted to one another. Some are more precious than others, but they are treasures. We share the gentlest of kisses, tender like the light. We are just barely here. He has a tenderness that I have forgotten exists, that I never knew could exist here. I sit down in the dusty graveled road. If I was to be left to receive him, I am gladly left behind. This single sobering thought eases me away from anger.

MARCH

3/2/07

We kiss for hours. We have crossed boundaries, Betelmi and I. The breeze is an invasion. Pants slack, flesh taking starlight, we have only darkness between us, just beyond the reach of a nearly full moon. I am back and forth between us in my mind. The road is not paved. This bold-faced moon is witness to a secret revelry. Then, more gasping kisses.

3/4/07

The day is his to have, but just because I anticipate that Mowan takes the evening instead. He comes chauffeured by a friend—a young woman, who recognizes the double tone of my accent right away. She asks me where I am from, hears the Yankee in my vowels perhaps. It is then I know this will be an evening for exposure, for laying bare. We begin with coffee— this woman and I. I'm trying to read him without looking at him. He has peppermint tea, and I want him and the tea just the same I think. We say our goodbyes to her and we are alone atop this cliff. The view we share. All of Scarborough tumbling into Rockly Bay before us as close as fingertips. I am nervous and stripping walls nearest my heart. I ask enough questions to learn the beauty of pheasant plumes—shade, length, miraculous hybrids.

One must treat natural jewelry with linseed oil, he says, to preserve it. I wonder what oil might keep time still. Mowan's expressions are to be savored. His visions are a mix of fabric and passion. He is a young artist. Even jittery for a cigarette, there is an elegance and a grace about him. This is strangely, subtly overbearing. He is "distant" from gay communities here, he says. Alone with his work here, he explains, but still dating and *doing up* (fucking) on occasion. He is honest. He is alone. Gorgeous. Mowan is a mix of the simple and the extravagant. I am dancing ambivalence until his hands are around me. He is behind me. We are in front of a gunpowder dungeon—the spirits of this hill are quiet tonight, but probably not at rest. A stone cave is our witness. He has been here before—less clothed, feistier. We stand for hours holding, then kissing, then approaching with the slightest touches. Soon we are descending home.

3/12/07

We pepper the morning with swift kisses, lips searching tender alcoves across fleshy expanses. But we do not make love. We have fallen into the deepest part of a relationship without ever touching its shores. I am longing, but resolved that even perfection is not without its heartbreaking flaws. Mowan cooks for me. This man pulls a fish he has never seen before from the deep freeze, stir-fries ginger into rice he has never cooked before. He makes a potato salad with a flick of his wrist, and the sparkling ring of his silver bangles is mesmerizing. His legs are endless, shaved. These breathless hugs are salvation. Our breathing together is ritual. He strips down to his boxers but leaves his black ankle socks. He lays claim to a kitchen and my bed. I follow. We still do not kiss too deeply, perhaps like lovers growing weary of each other. I devour him. We kiss only lightly still. An overripe emotion rests between us.

3/19/07

"They're not together. They have no kind of cohesion. Up in Laventille there is a church every few feet and everyone wants to do things their own way," Mayoc says. "I'm a Spiritual Baptist, you know," he reminds me. I have not forgotten. He's a *stargazer* he tells me. He reads stars. A few years ago, I saw him initiating this *daughter* of his who is neither his daughter nor woman by birth—gay kin. A strict fish diet, ankle weights, and a house perched on the hill in Belmont are all I remember. That house held all of Port-of-Spain below it. The "Shouters" all believe the same things—in the saints principally, he emphasizes the saints most—they used to preach loudly at the side of the road, to shout (some still do), and hence the name. He shows me stills from Ochro Cass's *Paradise Garage* that he's mixed to music. This is a tender mourning.

3/25/07

A haphazard pool *lime* (hangout) jumps up and happens despite the weather and precedent having set their mouths against. This lime is unlikely for a whole host of reasons. It must be the work of Vervine, yes Vervine, with her smile and that hot pepper mouth that could cuss you and love you up same time. She is a performer, and a good one. No shame is permitted around this woman, no hiding. And that must be part of her draw. Roukou cooks that sweet pot way he does—sweet and sour sauces, flaky roast bake. That would have been all—would have been enough—then Mowan calls to say he's on his way. And the prospect of his arrival is so unbelievable that for a moment I cannot recall his face. In shock, my memory outright refuses. We seize legs in the family-sized pool. A child looks on, not having perfected the adult art of seeing without looking. Then, a shower together. The private cleanse we had been waiting for—a release. We relish the tenderest bites. This is a begging in water.

3/27/07

I return to the mangrove. Its boardwalk is sleek and mossy, wooden and unimposing, winding its way through this exclusive swampland. The sea at the end of this one simple path lies just beyond a motley crew of wooden chairs, constructed with careless affection. I return, freed to wander about, catching the bloody scarlet of a mud-caked crab's pincer. The long fingered roots extend across these paths that have a logic if they are not watched too closely. Two days ago was the two hundredth anniversary of Britain's abolition of the slave trade—not the holding, the working, the beating and killing of slaves as property, but an end to a certain capitalism of flesh. No more buying and selling of slaves according to the law, but the world is still in no rush to comply. Sunday, March 25, 2007. Tobago seems to have missed this event altogether, or perhaps it took no interest in reminding me. I visit Mowan's workshop today. The hours creep round the edges of us and through. He sorts the fabric. The heat is nearly unbearable just before I begin to relax. Questions hang uneasily, backless, not quite stitched in place, like prototypes on mannequins. We are a work in progress. And then that evening, unexpectedly, Betelmi says I have let him go. And he is almost right.

APRIL
4/12/07

A familiar place was made foreign last night. This is a metaphor for the darkness now come upon Mowan and me. Close your eyes, allow them to adjust. Walk unsure, fearful, but not swallowed by either. I return to the Mangrove, a sacred place cast into darkness—no moon, no path lights, a playground for the wickedest imaginings. But then, the sea—agitated, black, beautiful. Here, the most stars I have ever seen undisturbed. Shooting stars showering us with wishes, but still we strain. We pull at the edges of each other. I decide to decide against us a million times only to rethink things again. We talk in the car, pulling away impossibilities. We are vulnerable and afraid in the pitch dark. The rains threaten to fall. Will we begin again—text messages, awkward phone calls? Why are we so afraid? The familiar made sublime.

4/13/07

Nearly two months we waited, dancing around each other. Nearly two months before last night—a feverish intercourse, a coming together muffled for decency's sake in the half-light. This is the patience that poetry must endure. Mowan has made a remarkable entrance, a second coming of sorts. I pray he stays.

4/14/07

There is always more going on than meets the eye with Tref, Mazay, Pursley, and Gimauve, who is flinging his waist swift enough to shame the baddest dancehall queen. Herb and a taste of scotch in his head, Gimauve is gyrating *bumsie*, winding head, splitting down and coming back up. But this is just a taste. He flings down stories about life in London—the clubs, the parties, the cold—and I know there is more there, the not-told that makes the telling so sweet. Seasoning is coming out of our pores. Chicken, pork, fish, cleaned and seasoned until the apartment's floor is washed in blood and scales. Preparing for a big cook-up, we are taking music any way it comes—cell phone, stereo, hum. I am trying to keep up with Tref. Mowan is slyly mentioned in conversation with eyes and smiles upon me—this is the way information comes to light, pushed by nosy queens with secret-intentioned eyes. We are preparing for today's barbecue on the beach—a benefit and a fashion show. I have stumbled back into this world where a loose tongue can be your downfall. Knowing how to hold and release things as simple as smiles can be your salvation.

4/25/07

I meet Agouma *again*: he comes toward me as graceful as one can be while walking too many dogs—small things, more fur than anything else. He is a sleigh being pulled. These are his babies, he says. Agouma's accent is DC metro area—maybe more Maryland—but with a rough-tongued Trini finish. He sounds like a Yankee trying too hard but catching it every now and again. But he was born here. It is just that he grew up in the States. He went to Howard University, he says. There is something about the way he throws that accent around that comforts and frightens me at the same time. "We're neighbors, you know?" He points out the web of dirt roads between us. I ask him about Kuze. That topic is a tender one we share. I watch him walk in his strappy neon orange-and-pink pumps, teaching the young ladies a bit of graceful sexiness in their carriage. The gays are attempting a modeling agency. Agouma is the photographer. Lozei has been invited from Trinidad to do the makeup. I'm the chauffeur. Bruka styles the shoot using his own clothing. Gimauve is the hair stylist. Pursley is a snake, a cunning *woman* with a swiftness of tongue that pushes out insults like razor blades, but this is his idea. Though his enthusiasm for the agency is genuine, Tref is slow to follow fashion. We are a clique of gay men—living in Tobago—building a new agency or an elaborate joke.

4/30/07

Mowan says that was the last straw. He says he cannot take this up and down any more. He says I should call him when I get it together. There is a tense aggression in his voice like the reserved anger of a disappointed father. And what did I do? I could not—would not—accept him putting money on my mobile. It is not that it was weird for him to call me, ask me to write down a series of numbers, and then tell me to put the money from that card on my phone. Well, perhaps that *is* it—the disrespect of his tone in the giving. I tell him I do not think we should link tonight because there is no precise plan or destination and because spending time with him has become work for me. For him, it is effortless—answer, answer, answer. There is nothing between us now but questions about him and his work—questions that I must always pose, questions that have begun to tire me. He is seldom curious about my work or about me. He never asks. This imbalance aside, I have grown less generous with him; his presence is costly. When do I get cared for, I wonder? I plan and prepare, and Mowan offers nothing in return. It is an insult to accept anything thrown down so haughtily. I am not your child. Neither am I your whore. I can afford to put money on my own mobile, thank you very much. Give me something more. Give me something that requires a little of your immense creativity, some of that hot spirit passion that draws me to you. I do not think I will be ready to call you anytime soon. Or maybe we can talk, but on very different terms: What do I do, Mowan? Why am I here? What do I study? What are my favorites? What are the dreams on my horizon? Who do I turn to when I feel lost? How might you brighten my dreariest days? He does not know. He does not even care to ask. He is self-centered, and I have allowed it. He needs a personal assistant with whom he can have sex, not a partner, not a lover, not a boyfriend. I break down in tears while driving much too fast on the main road. I have to pull over and let them come—tears for this boy I have fallen in love with, tears for this boy who hardly knows me at all.

CHAPTER 1

Inheriting the Mask

A History of Parody in Trinidad's Carnival

Attention to same-sex desire in the Caribbean region—but especially in Trinidad—is haunted by a titillating fascination with Carnival.[1] By no means unique to the Caribbean region, this fetishization of Carnival as *the* principal site of sexual possibility tends to foreclose—even in polite conversation— any other possibilities for an engagement with same-sex-desiring communities in T&T. Surely there is ethnographic research to be done about the various kinds of sexual fantasies enlivened by Trinidad's Carnival, but this is not that study. Instead, this particular engagement with Carnival foregrounds the artistry of design and performance in order to catch a glimpse of the epistemic possibilities imaginable in Carnival fantasy. By focusing briefly upon the history of racial play within the centuries-long tradition of the Trinidad Carnival, this chapter first sets the stage for an introduction to lauded mas man Peter Minshall.[2] A retrospective of the life and work of this white gay Caribbean artist provides the context for the following chapter, which focuses in on Minshall's 2006 Carnival band, *The Sacred Heart*, which many prematurely presumed might be his last.[3] This first chapter pair explores the lens the erotic provides for seeing the layered flesh of the political-sensual-spiritual in the performance history of Carnival spectacle as well as within the particular performance through which Minshall hopes to offer the nation symbolic salvation. By bringing this new erotic into view, Minshall's mas also gives first flesh to my epistemological intervention, challenging it to accommodate a specifically situated stage. Carnival provides this stage—at once literal and symbolic. So, although I may be approaching from an unanticipated angle, I admit that the following analysis is indeed—in its way—about desire in the Trinidad Carnival. Please allow me to *reset* the scene for you.

In Trinidad, Carnival is a season. Annually, the festivities begin with elaborate band launches as early as June and come to an end by Ash Wednesday (the Roman Catholic day of repentance). The word "carnival" likely originated in the Latin *carnem levare*, which became the Italian *carne levare* or *carnevale* and the French *carnaval* (Francophone Catholics are believed to have introduced the celebration to Trinidad). Literally meaning the raising, removal, or putting away of the flesh (as food), "carnival" most often refers to the season of revelry immediately preceding the Lenten fast, during which the consumption of meat is traditionally prohibited for Catholics.[4] Gluttonous indulgence in the flesh (as food and as a synecdoche for corporeal excess) serves to prepare the devout to do without in preparation for Easter, the celebration of Jesus Christ's resurrection. Trinidad's Carnival reaches its climax on the day just before the symbolic mourning of Ash Wednesday; however, during the long sultry dance up to Carnival Tuesday's Parade of the Bands, the sheer quantity of fêtes, concerts, and other Carnival-related events is easily overwhelming, even for the born-and-bred Trinidadian. Still, Trinidad's adaptation of this Catholicized "pagan" rite—in various different incarnations, most certainly—has been celebrated on the island for at least the past two hundred years.

A Brief History of the Trinidad Carnival

Although the earliest Spanish settlers most likely introduced pre-Lenten festivities to the island, there is scant documentation of an annual Carnival celebration in Trinidad before the influx of French-speaking Creoles in 1783 (E. Hill 1972, 6; Cowley 1996, 11).[5] Already a syncretic European ritual—the result of Roman Catholicism having been forced to assimilate pre-Christian rites that were too deeply rooted to be excised—preemancipation Carnival in Trinidad was reserved for the Creole upper class, who combined British and French celebratory traditions in their revelry (Campbell 1988, 8). Traditionally, this season of events would have included indoor masked balls, *fêtes champêtres* (pastoral or outdoor festivals), house-to-house visiting, hunting parties, street promenading, small musical bands, and practical jokes (Riggio 1998, 12–13; Brereton [1975] 2004, 53; Franco 2007, 28, 44). Although the influential minority white and mixed-raced participants summarily excluded the sizeable population of free black people from participating in these activities, these freed Africans were at least allowed to don masques in public during this period—a privilege altogether denied the enslaved people of the island (Campbell 1988, 8).

However, this prohibition did not prevent the enslaved from forming their own social societies from as early as the beginnings of the nineteenth century in Trinidad. Common throughout the island and ostensibly for the purpose of dancing and "innocent amusement," these organizations were generally known as *convois* (convoys) and later adopted the name *regiments* (Cowley 1996, 13)—both terms whispering rather loudly and audaciously about the other purpose some of these bands served. Frequently, these societies proved to be organizing nodes not only for revelry but also for revolt of various kinds and degrees of severity, especially during celebratory seasons such as Christmas and Carnival, when the social authorities would be engrossed in merriment (Campbell 1988, 3).

Hiding rebellious organizing in plain sight, these societies adapted the hierarchical structure of the European aristocracy and its attendant military for social structures also informed by familiar West African models of royal hierarchy; black kings and queens reigned over a family of fictive royal kin that extended as far as lesser nobility, all ostensibly presiding over an equally elaborate military hierarchy often appointed with flags and uniforms that the European colonial military had cast off (Campbell 1988, 3; Cowley 1996, 13–14). It is important to emphasize that this satirical play was not simply a mask for rebellion but also a symbolic enactment of the very challenge to authority that might ultimately culminate in a revolt of the enslaved. Here the mask and that which it attempts to hide share a single purpose, though it is approached on the surface with the ideological weaponry of mockery; beneath the mask, these enslaved people were preparing other, more tangible weapons. Postemancipation, this tradition of playful parody perfected in symbolic warfare would continue through to its performative formalization with the artillery band of 1834; this legacy dances right into the present century, followed by a long march of military and naval masquerades, which have become characteristic of Trinidad-style Carnival (E. Hill 1972, 14).[6]

If Trinidad's white elite—whose prized militia was often the subject of farce grandly orchestrated by the enslaved (Cowley 1996, 27)—could not always appreciate the subject matter that the enslaved chose for pointed jest, they did share with them a penchant for parody.[7] Perhaps it was this taste for mockery, most piquantly evidenced in their elaborate *cannes brûlées*–inspired enactments, that permitted the ruling elite to entertain humor at their own expense. From the French for "burnt canes," *cannes brûlées* in its earliest usage referred to both a phase in the sugarcane crop cycle and a narrowly averted plantation catastrophe. After the sugarcane harvest, the remaining stubs of this tropical grass would be burned in order to fertilize the soil for the next planting season and to guard against infestation by rodents or other crop pests; in the instance that crop infestation did occur prior to the harvest, fire would have been used to purge the vermin, resulting in an emergency harvest (Cowley 1996, 20). A spontaneous wildfire (a common enough occurrence during the parched-earth dry season) or a strategically planned conflagration—a form of surreptitious rebellion ignited by the enslaved—would also have required an emergency harvest.

Faced with an extremely time-sensitive challenge—a race against gluttonous flames to save the sweet cane before it began to ferment and sour in the heat—plantation owners would welcome bands of enslaved field hands (*nègres jardins* in French Creole, from the French *nègre de jardin*, "field slave") sent from neighboring estates; each band worked under the whip of its own slave driver, carried torches (*flambeaux*) for nighttime illumination, and moved in time with the pulsing rhythms of its drums and waves of chants used to maintain the pace of work (Cowley 1996, 20). Forced to cut and grind sugarcane night and day, these bands of enslaved laborers not only salvaged the season's crop but also provided a form of perverse entertainment for the unnerved planters, stimulated by the event despite haunting suspicions about machete-wielding, torch-bearing, chant-singing bands of the enslaved surrounded by their burning livelihood. For centuries, Carnival parody has been one of the principal means by which such social anxieties are performatively addressed; just as the enslaved used satire to strip naked the social hierarchy, the plantocracy used their position at the top of that hierarchy to ape those at the very bottom. In Trinidad's preemancipation Carnival, the island's French Creole elites enacted elaborate parodies of cannes brûlées; these planter aristocrats costumed themselves as tattered approximations of nègres jardins, toted lit flambeaux, and danced farcical versions of dances performed by the enslaved—the *belair, bamboula, ghouba,* and *kalinda*—in public street processions to the rhythms of "African" drumming and under the orders of whip-wielding, jestful slave drivers (E. Hill 1972, 11; Cowley 1996, 21; Riggio 1998, 13).

After emancipation and in commemoration of the end of apprenticeship on August 1, 1838, formerly enslaved peoples would annually perform their own reenactments of the cannes brûlées on the first day of August in symbolic defiance of the plantocratic parody, reappropriating this plantation event as part of a celebratory ritual. Symbolizing the burning spirit of resistance that could not be extinguished across generations of enslavement, the ceremonial Canboulay (a creolized rebaptism of the original French) extended over three days and nights, beginning with a spiritual ritual by torchlight during the predawn hours of August 1 (E. Hill 1972, 31; Elder 1998, 38; Cowley 1996, 33). At once a ceremony, a celebration, and a performative means by which to undermine the plantocracy's pointed parody—symbolically stoking their suspicion that the enslaved had intentionally lit cane fires as an act of revolt and were thus thoroughly enjoying the long last laugh—the Canboulay would be significantly shortened to a predawn rite and adopted as the opening ritual of Carnival before the close of the nineteenth century. Carnival scholars have not been able to determine the precise means by which Canboulay became Carnival's initiating rite. However, attention to the tradition of symbolic inversion and racial role reversal during the pre- and postemancipation Carnival season in Trinidad provides insight into the function of this repeatedly overwritten reenactment of forced plantation labor, an aristocratic mockery of it, rebellious resistance to that labor, and a commemoration of freedom from it. Canboulay is perhaps an appropriate beginning for Carnival because it is pregnant with the racial plays that have always characterized the season in Trinidad.

By the 1860s the character of Carnival would change significantly. The emergence of Jamette or Jamet Carnival during this period would lead to increasing efforts to suppress certain masques deemed obscene according to the imported Victorian moral structures of the middle class and colonial government (Brereton 1979, 152–75; Franco 2007, 29). A creolized form of the French diamètre ("diameter"), the term jamette or jamet referred to someone who existed below the diameter of "decent" society; petty criminals, commercial sex workers, pimps, the chronically unemployed, and various other members of the "social underworld"—including members of Port-of-Spain's nascent working class and newly arrived immigrants from the neighboring islands—were thought to reside on the wrong side of the social divide between respectability and ill repute in part because they all shared the city's crowded slums (Pearse [1956] 1988, 259–61; D. Wood 1968, 245–46; Campbell 1988, 10; Scher 2003, 39; Brereton [1975] 2004, 54).[8] If the middle class—across the color spectrum and including francophone and anglophone alike—found what they perceived to be the unabashed impropriety of Jamette Carnival generally objectionable, they were particularly unnerved and appalled by the sexually explicit play and the transvestitism that were quite common in the final decades of the nineteenth century (Cowley 1996, 73, 128–31; Brereton [1975] 2004, 55–56).

Encouraged by the middle class, the colonial government would take increasingly bolder steps toward suppressing "indecency" in the Carnival, beginning with the Canboulay; however, at each turn bands of masqueraders met the challenge to their festival with aggressive resistance and creative indignation. This pas de deux would eventually culminate in the Canboulay Riots of 1881 and various succeeding conflicts between colonial authorities and Canboulay celebrants, resulting ultimately in the passage of punitive legislation in 1883 and 1884 that effectively banned the Canboulay completely by criminalizing drum playing, stickfighting, and torch bearing—especially in urban areas (E. Hill 1972, 25; Batson and Riggio 2004, 32–33; Brereton [1975] 2004, 60, 63).[9] Between 1896 and 1919, the Carnival itself was effectively purged of its most undesirable elements through bans against what were presumed to be the jamette elements of the festival, including transvestitism and other disparaged masquerades as well as obscenity in speech or action. Determined to tidy up Trinidad's Carnival, but refusing to relinquish this quintessentially Creole fête, the island's elite began to return to the celebrations they had largely stepped away from in the mid-to-late nineteenth century. The Victory Carnival of 1919 marked another character change in the long history of Trinidad's Carnival—the island's well-to-do had returned to the ball. Appropriating the festival for burgeoning nationalist purposes, the Creole middle class created "a new public culture that preserved elements of the working-class Carnival dressed in middle-class costume" (Cowley 1996, 132–33; Scher 2003, 50, 52–53).

This middle class tolerance of the Carnival as a celebration of protonational identity would be combined with the very early commercialization of the festival in Trinidad's post–World War II years (E. Hill 1972, 85, 87). If Carnival represented the nation's cultural uniqueness and vibrancy as the colony marched toward Independence in the late 1950s, after Trinidad gained Independence in 1962, Carnival also increasingly represented a source of revenue. By the 1970s, it was this revenue in turn—provided by a new middle and upper class enjoying the wealth of the nation's increasing oil revenues—

that ushered in a gilded age of masquerade over which reigned the royalty of masquerade design: George Bailey (who died prematurely on August 14, 1970), Harold Saldenah, Carlisle Chang, and Wayne Berkeley—each artist leaving his imprint on the modern history of Carnival aesthetics.[10] During these boom years, masquerade designers expanded on the increasingly elaborate presentations—enlivened by growing numbers of masqueraders—that many had begun experimenting with as early as the 1950s (Gulick 2016d). Many of these well-educated, middle-class artists used more modern materials and their knowledge of design to set different aesthetic standards for the Carnival genre (Green and Scher 2007, 15). But by the time Peter Minshall entered this lineage of mas designers, the era of epic (historical) pageantry had given way to decorative extravagance, middlebrow fantasy, and escapist bourgeois revelry (Gulick 2016d).[11]

Minshall: The Life and Work of a Mas Man

Peter Minshall himself most succinctly explains how one of the most iconic Trinidadian artists of at least the last five decades comes to be born in Guyana: "I was born on July 16, 1945. The world was at war. So apparently were my parents. On account of their impending divorce, I was ferried to [then] British Guyana in my mother's womb, to be delivered into the world at the Georgetown General Hospital, surrounded by her loving family, soon thereafter to be brought back to Trinidad in her arms. I was the last of four children. The others were all born in Trinidad" (Minshall 2015).

Conceived on the island if not born there, Minshall's easy reassurance that Trinidad has always been his true home makes the matter of his birthplace moot for the people of T&T, who wholeheartedly embrace him as a son of the soil. And yet the ground of his conception ironically does not provide as firm a native claim as the fact of his foreign birth. Having been born somewhere else and yet still identifying keenly with a society long characterized by the foreignness of its "natives," Minshall is the consummate Trinidadian.[12] His mother Jean's father left England for Guyana in the 1920s as an engineer tasked with helping to build the nation's railway; and his father, Wilson, had come to the colony in his twenties from a struggling West Yorkshire family from the wrong side of the tracks in Bradford, England (Minshall 2015). Jean would eventually raise young Peter—the youngest of four children—on her own in a rented house in Cascade, a prominent suburb of Port-of-Spain.

FIGURE 1.1 Peter Minshall with The Pierrots characters he designed for the band *Carnival Is Colour*, Trinidad Carnival, 1987. Photograph by Rick Simon. Courtesy of the Callaloo Company Archive.

White immigrants from Guyana like the Minshalls would likely have reaped the benefits of white-skin privilege in a British colony even as they suffered the slights of exclusion from Trinidad's white Creole elite.

Consistent with many other colonial holdings in the Caribbean region, Guyana's preemancipation white population was significantly more homogenous than Trinidad's, and yet—even among these mainly British whites—tensions persisted, fragmenting the English, Scottish, Irish and their descendants. However, emancipation in Guyana brought with it a new incentive for white solidarity and a preoccupation with guaranteeing the sympathy of the colonial government should an intervention become necessary. Aggressively aligning themselves with British culture in order to prove that living in the tropics had not sullied their whiteness nor degenerated their Britishness, these white communities would even go so far as to stretch whiteness to include Portuguese laborers and traders—largely from Madeira—by the later twentieth century (B. Moore 1998, 97, 112). However, with a significantly more diverse white population and a system of intraracial stratification dominated by French Creoles, Trinidad's white community would not begin to move toward a similar solidarity until the 1920s, and still British, Portuguese, and Syrian/Lebanese whites would struggle to be recognized by the French Creole ruling families (Brereton 1979, 33–34, 52). And many of these not-so-subtle distinctions still haunt the contemporary community of "local whites" in Trinidad despite the elasticity of whiteness over time. Leaving a colony where whiteness was initially much more homogenous, or at least came to seem so, from as early as 1834 to enter a significantly different colonial racial terrain in which whiteness had only two or so decades earlier begun to imagine itself a single ruling class out of a single ruling race, the Minshalls would have encountered quite a different social milieu in this new odd British territory overrun with a French Creole elite.

It is perhaps this outsider position even ostensibly within a disproportionately influential racial minority that has in part contoured Minshall's racial sense of self—a self that has come into view against a multiracial and multicultural mise-en-scène in which it is generally understood that even whiteness is far from simple. Minshall's mirror is his island—an island whose face gives a glimpse of an entire region. Minshall's mirror is a region:

They say I am white, but that is not my measure . . .

I am not a European.
I am not an African.
I am not an Indian.
I am not Chinese or Syrian.
I am not Amerindian.
I am not American, North or South.
I am none of these.
I am all of these.

I am a Caribbean.

I am a rare hybrid.
I am a richly textured, multi-layered creature.

I am precious as a pearl.
The world is my oyster.
I see the world clearly from my island vantage.
I do not harbor the vanities of a big city dweller
or someone from a vast continent.
I am at the tip of the spear that leads into the future.

I am a Caribbean.

They say the Caribbean is a sea.
Yes, I am an island in it.
Much blood has spilled in that sea.
All the waters of humanity wash my shores.

I am a Caribbean.

(Minshall 2002, 1, 3; 2005; 2008; 2013b, 5–6)

Minshall refuses to have the coordinates of his racial and cultural identity confined within the geography of a European descendant whiteness. However, this refusal ought not to be read as Minshall's inability to recognize his whiteness as a marked category of racial privilege reliant upon an overvalued European cultural prestige. Instead, this refusal is an insistence on contextualization, contact, and the unavoidable concomitance of cultural influences across any seemingly discrete racial categories. Noted performance studies and Carnival scholars Richard Schechner and Milla Riggio read this insistence as particularly tragic:

> Richard Schechner: [Minshall is] a kind of tragic figure in the sense of being a contradiction. And he has to live through this contradiction. . . . What makes tragedy is not compromise. What makes tragedy is that you live two contradictory things at the same time, so, . . . yes . . . he is black . . . but he's also white. He can't deny the culture of his skin at the same time. And he has to live that tragedy.
>
> Milla Riggio: But that is also . . . part of the source of his power. And that is the fact that he has to live that contradiction all the time and he has to come to terms with it . . . [Schechner interrupts: Or not come to terms with it] . . . or not come to terms with it, but he himself feels that the island has to come to terms with it as well . . .
>
> Richard Schechner: He embodies the fact that . . . that black is a cultural category and not a skin color. (Narine 2009)

Minshall bristles at what he perceives as Schechner and Riggio's presumptuously foreign assessment of his familiar place in T&T's racial landscape (Minshall 2016a). And yet, comic, tragic, or some creole of the two, the mas man's relationship to Afro-Trinbagonian and other African diasporic cultures—within the decidedly *racial* category of "blackness," which is in fact principally about phenotype if not exclusively about skin color—is a complex drama still without its denouement. Undoubtedly, Minshall is a *white* Caribbean, but this adjective has a rich palimpsestuous quality to it; "white" does not simply modify "Caribbean," the former also holds a place—among others—within the latter. Perhaps it was an affinity for this type of incessant cultural cross-pollination—encouraged by a lush orchid house of an island—that inspired Minshall's racial cross-identification and play from an early age.[13]

Encouraged by this father—himself a visual artist with a penchant for painting—Minshall's creative curiosity soon found its way from the easel, oil paints, and steady supply of canvases that his father provided from as early as age twelve to his own bodily frame (Schechner and Riggio [1998] 2004, 110). At the age of thirteen, Minshall constructed upon his own body a mas that would allow him to play a spirited imagined other.[14] He tells the story of this early performance to Richard Schechner and Milla Riggio:

> At the age of 13, with a cardboard box and Christmas tree bells turned inside out as eyes, and some silver and some green paint that I begged from the Chinese man who ran the grocery at the bottom of the hill, and some grass from San-San, which is the name of that very hill behind the house, and bits of wire, and bones the dog had left around the yard dried in the sun and bleached, I prepared all by my precocious little self a costume for the Saturday afternoon children's [Carnival] competition. I called my mother to the balcony:
>
> > [Young Peter:] "Mummy, mummy, mummy! Come see my costume!"
> > [Mummy Jean:] "Oh very nice, darling! Tell me what is it?"
> > [Young Peter:] "But, mummy, I'm an African witch doctor."
> > [Mummy Jean:] "Oh, but darling, you're the wrong color. Here, come."
>
> And she gives me a dollar, sends me down to Ross's drugstore on Frederick Street for eight ounces of "animal's charcoal" [which Minshall recalls cost forty-three cents]. That's all I remember. To this day I don't know what "animal's charcoal" is. So I get this stuff, and I am transformed into

FIGURE 1.2 "The African Witch Doctor," a mas for the Children's Carnival created by thirteen-year-old Peter Minshall, Trinidad Carnival, 1953. From the personal collection of Peter Minshall. Courtesy of the Callaloo Company Archive.

a black that is as deep as velvet. Then I go down to the Savannah [Port of Spain's central park and the primary stage for Carnival mas competitions] and dance my mas and I am awarded the prize in my age group for "the most original." (Schechner and Riggio [1998] 2004, 109–10; Minshall 2015)[15]

Obedient young Peter's first foray into mas—a largely naïve exploration of imagined blackness channeled through a shamanic Africa—dances him innocently into a long history of playfully pointed racial inversions (Minshall 2016a). Although teenaged Minshall did not know it at the time—and certainly had no need to blacken his actual face behind his elaborately adorned cardboard mask—race play performances of this sort had been daubed with the tarbrush of American blackface minstrelsy from as early as the mid-1860s in Trinidad (Cowley 1996, 62).[16] Unaware of the full resonance of this mas and certainly ignorant of his tremendous future in the art form, young Peter finds himself folded into the layers of a Carnival tradition of racial mimicry that had so absorbed the influence of traveling white *and* black American minstrels that both white *and* black Trinidadians have been documented performing in blackface from as early as the 1890s (Cowley 1996, 115).[17]

This performance of American blackface minstrelsy by black Trinidadians is part of a long local tradition of using the repeated gestures of racial play to open a space for improvisational agency (Aching 2002, 17, 32–33). Over four decades later, Minshall would articulate the sophistication of the very minstrelsy his childhood mas only obliquely referenced: "The traditional [Trinidad] minstrel . . . is notable for the high level of wry mockery in the mimicry. The mas is derived from the American travelling minstrels, which were originally performed by blacks, but popularized by whites in blackface. The Trinidad minstrel imitated not the original blacks, but the whites in blackface. He is thus, as [calypso scholar Daniel] Crowley puts it, 'a Negro imitating a white imitating a Negro'" (Minshall 1985, 15–16).

If this play with blackface refuses racial ownership, then young Peter's mas pulls him into a complex theater of contentious racial script sharing and exchange that had been following scripts written and overwritten for over six decades. So that by the time Trinidad was approaching the mid-1950s, Jean Minshall's white boy-child playing an "African witch doctor" inadvertently summons an uncomfortable early mas tradition (mocking racial inversion dating back to late eighteenth-century Trinidad) interpreted through a relatively modern technique (late nineteenth-century Trinidadian blackface). Perhaps not in fact the most original, the witch doctor would indeed prove originary; limbs blackened with animal charcoal, the shaman of Minshall's imagination—an embodied mixture of the traditional and the modern— foreshadowed the art practice that would usher in his reign as Carnival's most beloved *bête blanche*.[18]

Despite the small success of his witch doctor, it would be some time still before Minshall received the call to devote himself creatively to mas design as an art form. Instead, the son of a painter found himself following in the illustrious footsteps of his father; proof of Minshall's early acclaim as a painter—a work titled *Metamorphosis*—still hangs in the National Museum and Art Gallery in Port-of-Spain. But the artist could not be satisfied with only two dimensions. A teenaged Minshall would explore theater arts—as an actor, makeup artist, and most especially set and costume designer—in various creative corners of Trinidadian society, including a stint at Trinidad's Light Operatic Company (Gulick 2016e). Having made the decision to leave Trinidad for art school training, a precocious twenty-one-year-old Peter followed the austere advice of his father and applied for admission in theater design (instead of painting) at London's Central School of Art and Design in 1963.[19] He gained admission due in no small part to the guidance and personal advocacy of the Trinidad-born, London-trained, and internationally renowned textile designer Althea McNish (Gulick 2016e). Minshall often describes in meticulous detail the artistic awakening he experienced while in England—a lucid dream enhanced by the inauguration of London's annual World Theatre Season festival in 1964, during which the city overflowed with invited theater companies from all over the world putting on some of the most spectacular and avant-garde productions imaginable (Schechner and Riggio [1998] 2004, 110–11). Ironically, it is precisely during his immersion in London's cosmopolitan art world that Minshall began to appreciate the artistic sophistication of his small-island Carnival. By 1966, Minshall had earned his diploma in Theater Design; it is no coincidence that he wrote his final thesis on the Trinidad Carnival.[20]

Even after the Scottish Ballet founder Peter Darrell and the well-known British director Colin Graham choose Minshall to design the costumes and set for the Scottish Theatre Ballet's inaugural production of *Beauty and the Beast* at Sadler's Wells Theatre in 1969—convinced by design renderings for a Carnival queen costume from 1967—Minshall still resisted shifting most of his artistic attention and talent away from the theater of the proscenium to the theater of the streets. It would not be until 1974, when Minshall's mother visited him in London and requested that he return to Trinidad to design a hummingbird Carnival costume for his adopted sister, Sherry Ann Guy, that Minshall would have no choice but to answer the call of the mas (see plates 1 and 2).[21] If Wilson Minshall's practical sensibilities made him push his son toward formal training in theater design, then Jean Minshall's heart pulled her son back to the Trinidad Carnival. No easy return, Minshall took up the Herculean task of making a winning mas out of a national cliché for a dark-skinned black girl competing for a title usually reserved for the white and light-skinned daughters of the island's elite (Minshall 2013a, 325).

With his characteristic storytelling flare, Minshall is second to none in his description of this watershed moment; I quote the mas man at some length:

> It was some months before the Carnival of 1974 that Jean Minshall informed me that it was my duty to design for my adopted sister Sherry Ann, then thirteen, a Carnival costume. But this was no ordinary costume. My mother wanted her daughter to be Junior Carnival Queen. Me, professional designer in avant-garde London, design a children's Carnival costume in Trinidad?! Worse again, she wanted it to be a hummingbird! A hummingbird?? But a mother's wish is a son's command—thank God.
>
> As it happens, the son of Wilson and Jean has never known how to do something halfway, to "toss off" a little design and get on about his business. And so I launched myself into this hummingbird project as though it were a world premiere at Covent Garden. I went back to the bat, the simple old Trinidad Carnival bat, the most kinetic and alive of all the traditional [mas] forms. I took him apart and put him back together again, and tried to find out how "to make the cloth dance" [a prized turn of phrase Minshall says he received from his father, who adopted it from an old mas man]. (Minshall 1991a, 11)

> I must've spent off and on about five months just fiddling—in between whatever jobs I was doing—putting into this diminutive little work all my theories about playing the mas and its energy: it's about performance, it's about mobility. It was Christmas Eve night I came [home to Trinidad] with £100 worth of fabric, which was a lot of money back then.
>
> On New Year's Day we start to construct the costume. It took five weeks, twelve people. It was totally meticulous, 104 feathers, each one made of 150 different pieces of fabric, the blue to the purple to the green, stuck with transparent nail varnish over bits of plastic over a pattern. All pinned up, then finally assembled. It has to be finished. We haven't slept for three nights. One person is holding the thing onto Sherry standing there like a little girl crucifix—there's not time for zips [zippers]—while we sew her into it.
>
> We lift her up onto the jitney, drive to the Savannah in a dream, in a daze, mindless. This little 13-year-old girl is going up the path [onto the stage]. I've rehearsed with her with canes and an old sheet and told her, "Forget you're a bird. You're a flag woman [a flag bearer at the head of a Carnival band, usually though not always a woman]. Wave your flag, dance, you're not flying, these are not wings, you're a little girl enjoying

yourself." This little thing exploded like a joyful sapphire on that stage, and ten thousand people exploded with her. On that afternoon, a moment of revelation. "Christ, so this is art too!" I did not choose the mas—it held me by the foot and pulled me in. (Schechner and Riggio [1998] 2004, 111–12)

Minshall's now iconic *From the Land of the Hummingbird* mas is a shimmering turning point in his life not merely because an audience fell in love with it on that fateful day, but more importantly because it held in its very wings Minshall's nascent propositions about the kinetics of mas design (Minshall 1982). This proposition had grown out of the design traditions of the Carnival, but it would not be confined by the anachronistic strictures of those traditional forms; instead, Minshall had distilled the design impulse of the bat mas—the desire to marry structure with the dancing human form—in order to give flight to something new (Minshall 1991a, 10).[22]

The mas pulled Minshall into designing his first band, *Mas in the Ghetto*, in 1973 for London's Notting Hill Carnival. However, not until 1975—as a result of a quarrel with their designer, noted Trinidadian artist Carlisle Chang—did bandleaders Stephen and Elsie Lee Heung invite Minshall to design their band for the 1976 Trinidad Carnival (Schechner and Riggio [1998] 2004, 113).[23] The band Minshall designed—*Paradise Lost*—proved nothing less than a sublime re-imagining not merely of John Milton's mid-seventeenth-century epic poem but, much more importantly, of the aesthetics of Carnival masquerade.[24] For the Carnival of 1978 Minshall finally stepped into the role of bandleader and designed his very first band, *Zodiac*, an austere work mounted on the backs of revelers long-limbed and awash in primary colors. Or, as Minshall describes it,

> Discipline. Not a damn sequin, not a piece of braid! Primary colors—red, blue, yellow, black and white—spinnaker nylon . . . Zodiac was aluminum backpacks, extensions here, spring-steel wires there, and great shapes attached to the ankles. As Balanchine said, "I want you to 'see' the music and 'hear' the dance." So the whole band is coming down, and every step to the music moves the fabric ten feet in the air and you get this kinetic madness. . . . You're challenging people. You're saying, "Come on, let's stop being so quaint." (Schechner and Riggio [1998] 2004, 113)

With *Zodiac*, Minshall had finally stepped audaciously into the artistic genre that was to become his lifelong passion; for decades to come Minshall would rise again and again to the challenge of pushing the limits of his chosen art form without losing the lessons of its rich past. A nation danced in awe.

Since the band *Zodiac*, Minshall has designed twenty-four mas bands for the Trinidad Carnival, including two three-year epic trilogies.[25] The first of these unprecedented three-part Carnival productions began in 1983 with the band *River*, followed in 1984 by *Callaloo*, and concluded in 1985 with *The Golden Calabash*. Undeniably a masterpiece of mas, Minshall's *River Trilogy* was a minimalist leap forward in Minshall's design acumen and an avant-garde innovation in mas theatrics.[26] The design innovations especially in the principal characters of the trilogy were in large part the result of Minshall having been awarded a Guggenheim Foundation fellowship in 1982 for the study of "Carnival design and kinetics." The Guggenheim fellowship provided Minshall with the time and resources to refine the kinetic design breakthrough that he terms the "dancing mobile." A mas construction proposition based on the legacy of traditional bat mas, Minshall's dancing mobiles are sculptures on an architectural scale that are designed to be brought to life by the unencumbered, dancing human form (Minshall 1982, 1984a). The *River Trilogy* would be followed by Minshall's second three-part Carnival epic, which began in 1995 with the band HALLELUJAH, continued in 1996 with *Song of the Earth*, and concluded in 1997 with *Tapestry*. Beyond the Trinidad Carnival, Minshall has also designed four bands for London's Notting Hill Carnival, two bands for New York City's Brooklyn Carnival, and a band for San Francisco's Carnival.

Following from his early work in the theater, Minshall's oeuvre also extends beyond the Carnival genre without losing the aesthetic consistency that is the artist's signature. Beginning in 1965 with a production of Alain-René Lesage's *Turcaret* in the United Kingdom and concluding in 1979 with a production of Federico García Lorca's *La casa de Bernarda Alba* in the United States, Minshall has designed the sets and costumes for twenty theatrical productions in both countries over the course of fourteen years (Minshall 1982).[27] In 1985, Minshall designed and directed a theatrical street protest— *The Adoration of Hiroshima*—as part of a Washington, DC, Peace March against nuclear proliferation and in remembrance of the fortieth anniversary of the bombing of Hiroshima (Minshall 1982). His work has been a part of group exhibitions at the IFA Gallery in Bonn, Germany (1990), the National Museum of Scotland in Edinburgh (1993), the Museo Extremeño e Iberoamericano de Arte Contemporáneo in Badajoz, Spain (1998), and the 7th Biennial of Havana in Cuba (2000). Discussions of his artistry have also appeared in the catalogues of the preeminent art exhibitions *Caribbean Festival Arts: Each and Every Bit of Difference* (Nunley and Bettelheim 1988) and *Caribbean Visions: Contemporary Painting and Sculpture* (Lewis 1995).

Minshall's dancing mobiles have been included in two of noted French composer Jean-Michel Jarre's large-scale outdoor music spectacles: *Paris la défense: Une ville en concert* (1990) and *Concert pour la tolérance* (1995), both in Paris. Minshall has been the subject of at least seven solo exhibitions: *Callaloo by Minshall* at Riverside Studios in London and Arnolfini Gallery in Bristol (1986); *Peter Minshall: Callaloo, an Exhibition of Works from the Carnival of Trinidad* at the 19th International Biennial in São Paulo, Brazil (1987); *The Coloured Man* at Gallery 1 2 3 4 in Port-of-Spain, Trinidad (1989); *The Dancing Mobile* at the Leicestershire Museum and Art Gallery in Leicester, England (1990); *Minshall: The Early Years* at On Location Art Gallery in Port-of-Spain, Trinidad (1990); *Looking at the Spirits: Peter Minshall's Carnival Drawings* at the Drawing Center in New York City (2005); and *Minshall Miscellany: Paintings, Sculpture, Drawings, and Design Renderings, 1967–2012* at Y Gallery in Port-of-Spain (2012) (Riggio 2004, 126–28; Gulick 2016e). Minshall has also been a leader on the design and direction teams for the opening ceremonies of the 10th Pan American Games (1987); the opening ceremony of the Summer Olympic Games in Barcelona, Spain (1992); the opening and closing ceremonies of the Summer Olympic Games in Atlanta, Georgia (1996); the opening segment and other performance segments of the Miss Universe Pageant in Port-of-Spain, Trinidad (1999); and the opening and closing ceremonies of the Winter Olympic Games in Salt Lake City, Utah (2002). In 2001, Minshall was chosen as a Principal Prince Claus Award laureate for his work in the mas and the contribution it made to "culture and development." And in 2002, Minshall received an Emmy Award in the category of "Outstanding Costumes for a Variety or Music Program" for his presentations at the Salt Lake City Olympics (Schechner and Riggio [1998] 2004, 126–28).

Despite Minshall's accomplishments beyond Carnival, the beating heart of his artistic corpus has been and continues to be the mas. A ceremonious theater of the streets—a living, breathing, dancing contemporary art that happens only by permission of and in collaboration with his masqueraders— the mas is undeniably Minshall's creative core (Minshall 2015). Wherever else Minshall's mind roamed over the course of nearly three decades, he religiously returned to design mas for Trinidad's Carnival. By 2003, Minshall had only thrice missed consecutive years in his twenty-seven-year history of designing mas for the streets of Port-of-Spain.[28] In this time, the interval between bands had never stretched beyond three years. This unofficial timetable being well marked among Carnival revelers devoted to Minshall's artistry (sometimes colloquially referred to as "Minshallites"), the uproarious opening and somber closing of the 2005 Carnival season sans a Minshall band would likely have given many devotees cause for alarm. Was it possible that Minshall's 2003 band *Ship of Fools* had indeed been his last? Would the Ash Wednesday rumors of having experienced the last band of a mas legend prove sobering truth?

In 2006, as January stumbled to a close and the nation set its sights longingly on Carnival's climax, it seemed as though Minshall's reign over the mas had come to an unceremonious end. The three to eight months prior to the frenetic whirl of Carnival Tuesday has become the loosely-agreed-upon season for Carnival band launches—that long-awaited unveiling of themes and costumes for the year's Carnival. However, the planning for a band is the planting of a seed just after the sun has set on the previous year's Ash Wednesday. Carnival bands are often a year in the making, their launch long preceded by months upon months of preparations. Once a certain unofficial threshold has been passed and the few remaining weeks crowd toward Carnival's two-day dénouement, it seems unimaginable that any band leader would dare risk conceiving a band without time enough to advertise, make and sell the costumes even in this contemporary age of sparse bead, sequin, and feather assemblages. But Peter Minshall is a master of imagination.

CHAPTER 2

Peter Minshall's Sacred Heart
and the Erotic Art of Play

On Sunday, January 29, 2006—four weeks to the day before the height of Trinidad's Carnival festivities—Peter Minshall assembles a congregation of artists and craftspeople at the workshop of the Callaloo Company in order to deliver a call to arms; the artist is planning an urgent return to the mas (see plate 7) (Ward et al. 2006; Bowman 2006; Laughlin et al. 2006).[1] The T&T government's partial financial sponsorship of the band—through its National AIDS Coordinating Committee (NACC)—certainly incentivized the return of a Minshall mas to the streets of Port-of-Spain.[2] In fact, it is because the NACC approached Minshall to request a partnership just before Christmas—excruciatingly late in the Carnival season—that he so belatedly assembles his faithful that Sunday morning in Chaguaramas. Nevertheless, Minshall is decidedly not the type of artist who surrenders his creativity to the whims of a sponsoring body. Although fundamentally he may share the NACC's concern with fostering a sexually conscientious citizenry, Minshall is also deeply concerned about the state of the Carnival and the conscience of the nation; for Minshall, these concerns share a single corpus. And his 2006 Carnival band provides a metaphor through which to envision a political project that not only attends to the intimate enfolding of HIV/AIDS, Carnival, calypso, and the nation but also wages a symbolic battle against diseases— literal and figurative—that threaten the body *and* the mind.

FIGURE 2.1 *The Sacred Heart* stage presentation, 2006. Photograph by Jim Stephens.

FIGURE 2.2 The Callaloo Company building, Chaguaramus, Trinidad, 2007. Photograph by the author.

The Sacred Heart and a Politics of Play

The Sacred Heart is an army of urban, samurai cowboys and cowgirls in undulating white or bleeding blue robes, wrapped in red slashes of fabric snaking down standards, foreheads, and flanks, strapped firmly into wide two-dimensional black chaps fastened with red ribbon pressed against the rough second skin of blue denim, and crowned in intricate galvanized metal headpieces and masks (see plates 6 and 15).[3] A classic heroic spirit pierces and pulls together the seemingly disparate elements of this eclectic band. Part of a society seduced across genre by this cinema-worthy heroism, Minshall offers a filmic lens through which to reconcile the Wild West and the Ancient East: "The greatest movie ever to come out of Japan was 'The Seven Samurai' [Akira Kurosawa's film of 1954] and the cowboy reply to that was 'The Magnificent Seven' [John Sturges's film of 1960], which produced the greatest of all movie themes [jumping up from the chair, conducting], 'Pam Pam-pa-pa-dam!' Right! We Caribbeans are the most hybrid people on the planet. Nobody is better placed than us to marry cowboy with samurai" (Pires 2006b). If a cultural and temporal distance defies the relative geographical proximity of these distant worlds, there remains, nonetheless, an imaginative overlap that Minshall uses film to highlight. He suggests that a Caribbean sensitivity to the fertility of a "samurai-cowboy" hybrid is the affective inheritance of a highly creolized people who understand all too well the seemingly impossible possibilities for coherence across the collapsing of time and space. The figurative cinematic crossroads at which Minshall positions his band may have a literal location at the actual crossroads where the now shuttered Globe Cinema (formerly Metro Cinema) stood open for over eighty years in the heart of downtown Port-of-Spain (Bagoo 2013). Overlooking Green Corner—where St. Vincent Street, Park Street, and Tragarete Road converge—this balconied cinema's single silver screen long provided a frame for seemingly unlikely juxtapositions that saw Hollywood and Bollywood sitting comfortably beside classic Samurai and Kung Fu films in legendary double features.

And yet beyond its mixed aesthetic lineage, *The Sacred Heart* holds a deeper ambivalence that the work of art does not hope to definitively resolve. A layered text—true to the complex flesh of the Carnival tradition that has for centuries placed performances one upon another—*The Sacred Heart* exposes an internal struggle that Minshall uses his creative

RAINBOW

FIGURE 2.3 Peter Minshall's developmental sketch for "The Rainbow Heart" section of *The Sacred Heart*, 2006. Courtesy of the Callaloo Company Archive.

resources to see more clearly. An aggressive despair contends against a luminous hope in the division of the band's sections. Minshall sets five sections of "dark hearts"—the Broken Heart, the Heart of Darkness, the Heart of Fear, the Bruised Heart and the Heart of Greed and Power—against five "hearts of light"—the Heart that Sings, the Shining Heart, the Rainbow Heart, the Heart of Hearts and the Heart of Hope (see plates 3, 4, and 5) (Pires 2006b).[4] This single band of nearly four hundred masqueraders is a struggle between two opposing forces—like Minshall's band *The Golden Calabash* (1985)—a political battle for the body (or citizenry) and soul (or

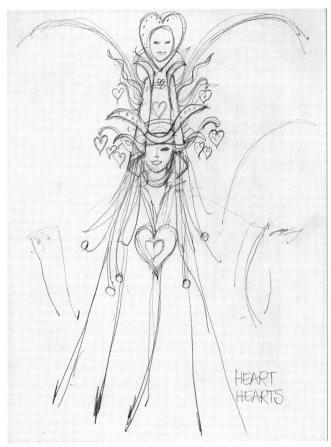

FIGURE 2.4 Peter Minshall's developmental sketch for "The Heart of Hearts" section of *The Sacred Heart*, 2006. Courtesy of the Callaloo Company Archive.

spiritual/ethical core) of the nation (Laughlin et al. 2006). An ancient allegory, the dialectic between good and evil has been a favorite frame within which Minshall himself consistently positions his oeuvre. For Minshall, *The Sacred Heart* is part of a long lineage of bands—including his *Callaloo* (1984), HALLELUJAH (1995), *Song of the Earth* (1996), *Tapestry* (1997), and *The Lost Tribe* (1999)—that have attempted a politics of reconciliation and unity through the visual metaphors of mas (*T&T Express* 2006; Gulick 2016a).

A governing trope for Minshall's band, the heart serves well as the pumping metaphorical core of this hoped-for reconciliatory unity. This heart is expansive enough to hold a critique of the current state of the Trinidad Carnival as well as an HIV prevention and antidiscrimination salvo. If the heart of the nation (its vibrant aesthetic center) is the Carnival, then for Minshall, *The Sacred Heart* reclaims an artistic integrity lost to a feverish pursuit of profit in the streamlining business of Carnival costuming. Trinidadian visual artist and critic Christopher Cozier gives precise language to a sentiment he shares with Minshall about the overbearing economic interests and bankrupt creative economy of Trinidad's contemporary Carnival: "There is something very dark about the overt industrialization of mas and something very sardonic about the thousands of bikinis moving through Port-of-Spain—some with three or four beads per flank—and the way in which it has suddenly been imposed upon us as our culture. When one small element of the Carnival dominates because of financial expediency and people start struggling to find words to give it meaning, to give it value in a kind of promotional frenzy, I can't imagine anything darker than that" (Narine 2009). In response, Minshall offers his *Sacred Heart*—a light vessel launched into the darkness: "In the sea of feathers and sequins, it will be a little ship of hope and bravery . . . we can communicate just an oomph of hope against the sea of despair those feathers and beads represent, the sea of mindlessness" (Minshall quoted in Pires 2006b). For the mas man, this recuperation of Carnival is the symbolic heart of his call for the redemption of the nation. If the ancient allegorical battle between good and evil has remained Minshall's focus for several decades, then Trinidad and Tobago has been his battlefield and the mas his most formidable weapon. But by harnessing these tropes to an HIV prevention and destigmatization initiative—as part of a larger AIDS awareness effort—*The Sacred Heart* charts new terrain.

Functioning simultaneously as an aesthetic, biologic, and metaphoric reference point, the heart provides an interpretive axis that is at once a bridge. Archived references materials at the Callaloo Company workshop indicate that Minshall's use of the symbolic heart is informed by the neo-Dadaist paintings, sculptures, and "Happenings" of American pop artist Jim Dine (J. Gordon 1970; Livingstone 1998; Joubert 2007; Noel 2008). However, Minshall's hearts are equally kin to an aesthetic lineage that passes through a family of traditional Trinidadian Carnival characters—the Nègre Jardin, Pierrot and Jab Jab—each adorned with an elaborate heart-shaped *fol* (Riggio 2004, 96–97).[5] And yet Minshall's use of the heart as an associative

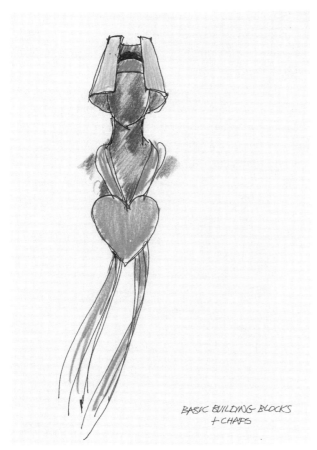

BASIC BUILDING BLOCKS
+ CHAINS

FIGURE 2.5 Peter Minshall's developmental sketch for the design of mas costumes for *The Sacred Heart*, 2006. Courtesy of the Callaloo Company Archive.

biological metaphor steeped in blood and compassion—the bleeding heart, if you will—thrusts his aesthetically hybrid *Sacred Heart* into the highly politicized body of HIV/AIDS activism. For Minshall, mas has always been part of a political corpus; he resists the false dichotomy between culture (as manifested in the arts) and politics, between "real" life and performance. Minshall contends that people make the mistake of trying to put a wedge or a division between what is called culture and what is called politics or life. But on a little island, these many parts—like the many parts of a body—are indivisible. The mas of politics is no less a playing than the mas we play on the streets (Minshall quoted in Dass 2008).

However, if a persistent political project has always animated Minshall's mas, his little-island artistry has never so wholeheartedly lent its global voice to a government-sponsored initiative. By sponsoring the construction of several of the band's principal characters—including its King and Queen—the NACC attempts to make of Minshall's band yet another of its hypervisible HIV/AIDS awareness campaigns. Unavoidable though they may be for having employed various entertainment media, saturated various entertainment venues, and rallied various local and regional entertainers as spokespersons from about the early 2000s, the NACC's oblique HIV awareness and antidiscrimination campaigns appear to lack the proper policy and programmatic focus ultimately to be widely effective. In marked contrast, Minshall's *Sacred Heart* not only focuses in on condom usage as a particularly effective HIV prevention strategy but also models in microcosm the type of compassionate social inclusion of HIV-positive persons that the NACC had previously only gestured toward abstractly in the public domain.

Arguably the principal ideological meeting ground of the samurai and the cowhand, heartfelt heroism provides the moral center of *The Sacred Heart*. This heroism requires a hero around whom the narrative of the band can be told. It is only upon discovering such a figure and deciding to make him the central axis of the band that Minshall is able to confront one of the most challenging questions plaguing HIV destigmatization: the mas man asks earnestly,

> How do you take "HIV positive" and make people think and feel positively about it? It was one of those times when an answer comes literally in the dead of night. . . . He is the *Son of Saga Boy* and he is HIV-positive. It could be your son, her son, the neighbor's son, and the only way to deal with that affliction is to shower it with affection! The only way to deal with pain in the community is to heal it with love.
>
> [The interviewer asks,] The young man portraying the king is actually HIV-positive?
>
> Yes, and he is the hero in our midst. . . . [He] was a name on the Internet. This is how strange this journey has been so far: his Internet handle was, "The Crystal Heart." I couldn't believe it. And I wrote a little note to this HIV-positive stranger, who is 22, and said, "I'm looking for a person such as you. You will have to be brave." And then we spoke. And then we

shared a meal. And he's never played a king before, far less a character. But, my God, he has spirit and character and true grit! . . . First, there was a king, the *Son of Saga Boy*, and I needed a hero to play it; and the hero presented himself: a brave, a good man. His name is Kerwin Paul. (Minshall quoted in Pires 2006b)[6]

A cybernetic, futuristic rainbow child, the *Son of Saga Boy* (see plate 8) inherits an innovative kinetic legacy and deploys it toward a visionary political intervention. Minshall's King character is at once an impressionistic crouching figure of bristling black coque feathers below an animated blue visage crowned in a rainbow of ostrich plume dreadlocks *and* a spirited, HIV-positive, Afro-Trinidadian young man brave enough to shoulder the weight—actual and ideological—of this mas (Gulick 2016a). The heroism involved in Paul's decision to become the public face of HIV infection for Trinidad Carnival 2006 following a chance encounter with Minshall in an anonymous, sexually charged alley of cyberspace ought not to be overlooked. Through Paul's bravery, Minshall is able to model the inclusion he symbolically proposes as one of the principal affective strategies used to combat the social and emotional isolation of stigmatization.

And yet Paul's willingness alone proves insufficient for the challenging technical task of truly playing a Minshall King character:

He [Kerwin Paul] put on the costume. He was able to carry the costume. But he couldn't play the mas. And that was the bottom line. He couldn't play the mas. . . . He was not used to carrying such weight. Because it is quite heavy. Knowing how to move to carry it, dealing with the wind, you need to be a seasoned performer to do something like that. And this was baptism by fire. . . . We were asking too much of him. We knew this. We were just hoping against hope that yes he could pull it off, which would have been the biggest statement. . . . The reason why he was unable to do it had nothing to do with his status . . . it was the lack of experience with dealing with such kind of a costume. And that was the bottom line. (Guy James 2008)

Longtime designer, prototypist, aesthetic confidant for Minshall, and seasoned Dame Loraine performer, Ronald Guy James here gives voice to the general sentiment that would eventually lead to Brian Pantin replacing Paul as the handler of the *Son of Saga Boy* by Carnival Tuesday. However, Pantin barely did a better job than Paul. Minshall readily admits that he quite inadvertently designed his King character for a veteran large mas character handler like the inimitable Peter Samuel—who had over a decade and a half earlier brought Saga Boy to life for Minshall's band *Tantana* in 1990. Samuel was even invited to the Callaloo workshop to demonstrate the mastery necessary to "play" the mas adequately, but he decided against stepping into the character himself and perhaps also into forbidding rumors about his HIV status (Minshall 2008). Although they are only barely able to carry the weight of the masquerade, Paul and Pantin valiantly shoulder the very stigma against HIV that the *Son of Saga Boy* intends to contest; through the embodiment of Minshall's King, these two men share the burden of representing an "HIV positivity" (taking "HIV-positive" and asking people to think and feel positively about it) that is still extremely difficult to grasp for many who believe contracting HIV to be a death sentence.

Nevertheless, it is ironic that the very symbolic politic that compels Minshall to choose HIV-positive Paul to play the King of his *Sacred Heart* in part forces the artist to replace the young novice for fear of the representative repercussions of his individual shortcomings. Minshall is quite frank about being haunted by a nightmarish vision of Paul falling during his debut as the *Son of Saga Boy*. The mas man vividly recalls a single moment when it seemed as though Paul's entire being would break under the weight of the character, but Paul pushes on just long enough to reach the Callaloo Company tech crew, who grab him just in time. As a result, Minshall reluctantly replaced Paul; the artist could not bear the dread of collapse and the unforeseeable damage it might do to Paul's psyche and public image, never mind the larger project of destigmatizing HIV-positive people in T&T by demonstrating their health and strength (Minshall 2008). The argument might be made that by choosing compassion for Paul and succumbing to his fears about the potential symbolic tragedy of his fall, Minshall backs away too quickly from his early commitment to challenging debilitating presumptions about HIV and capacity; however, one recognizes how difficult it must have proven for the mas man to compromise one particular politic of representation for a modified politic of presence. For although Paul does not ultimately shoulder the King character, he remains king of Minshall's band.

The Sacred Heart is unique among Minshall's Carnival bands for being a performative kingdom grand enough to accommodate four monarchs and among them two kings. Although Brian Pantin handles the band's dancing mobile King, Kerwin Paul still appears in a shimmering silver gown and

FIGURE 2.6 Peter Minshall pulling the "Body Politic" character he designed across the stage, Trinidad Carnival, 2006. Photograph by Jim Stephens.

white fabric crown as King of Carnival to accompany the Savior of the Sacred Heart, a queen mas portrayed by Wendy Fitzwilliam—T&T's beloved winner of the 1998 Miss Universe pageant and a widely recognized HIV/AIDS awareness advocate, especially on behalf of AIDS orphans (see plate 9).[7] A queer monarchy to be sure, *The Sacred Heart* is a symbolic intervention into an HIV/AIDS politics of representation that crowns two sovereign couples in order to resist compromising the integrity of either the mas or the message.

For Trinidad Carnival 2006, Minshall comes to the stage—in part—on behalf of the body politic by virtue of having accepted the sponsorship of the state for his HIV awareness band. And yet, as part of the stage performance that precedes the arrival of the band at the final judging point, Minshall literally steps into the body of the spectacle to soberly pull a bruised effigy of the ailing state; this gesture serves as a critique of the very body financing many of the band's principal characters. Minshall's The Body Politic character is a prostrate, gigantesque Gulliverean state mounted on wheels that is at once a requiem for a post colony and a symbolic call to resuscitate the nation and its legislative representation. In one crucial sense, then, *The Sacred Heart* is a political project that attempts to pump new lifeblood into the nation by battling corporeal and cultural affliction with dignified island affection. However, the centrality of affect, corporality, and sexuality to this project makes the band also a highly sensual intervention.

On the Uses of Desire: The Sensuous Core of *The Sacred Heart*

On its fleshy surface, *The Sacred Heart* mobilizes sensuality in order to contest a "beads-and-feathers" aesthetic that threatens to overrun Trinidad Carnival. If this aesthetic contestation is one of the principal battles that Minshall wages with the band, then desire is the wide voluptuous terrain upon which this battle is fought—a battle waged for figurative and literal space in the Carnival. With an army of what he calls "urban samurai cowboys and cowgirls," Minshall refuses the lewd equation of sexiness with exposed flesh and instead calls for sensuality in mas enhanced by costuming and not by nudity: "You see this little band? It is going to be the sexiest band on the streets of Port-of-Spain. In my mind, denim against the human skin, especially against sapodilla-coloured human skin, is so much more sexy [*sic*] than feathers and beads. Boy or girl, that denim that is like an extra skin . . . low down on the hips . . ." (Minshall quoted in Pires 2006b).

By summoning an earthy comparison that reaches for the sugary fruit of the sapodilla tree while likening the firm tightness of denim to a second flesh, Minshall emphasizes the sensuous strain of the bulging seam where the corpus and the costume converge.[8] The literal frame for this display of behinds in the close cut of denim—black two-dimensional chaps—add another layer to Minshall's play with the eroticism of exposure and concealment, the dialectic between the flesh and the imagination (Minshall 2008). The leathery flesh of this centuries-old equestrian garment—brought to the Americas by the Spanish and worn in the American West as early as the nineteenth century—offers the subtle temptation of the flesh beneath by exposing the derrière outlined in denim. In gay camp and in bondage/dominance-submission/sadomasochism (BDSM) this denim is stripped away, revealing the framed bit of bare behind that has for decades provided a common visual trope for the overlay of camp's flamboyant parody and BDSM's fetishistic seriousness. Although Minshall refuses any conscious referent to camp or BDSM culture in his band's aesthetic, his sensual use of the cowhand nevertheless rides the friction of representations that layers leather (upon denim) upon flesh (Minshall 2016b). And by proposing a sexiness to this layering of referents, Minshall's band also encourages doubts about the presumed sexual expressiveness of fetishized beads-and-feather costuming, an ornamented nudity designed principally to maximize profits and not to tantalize the imagination.

A representational politic of desire in part determines the look of *The Sacred Heart*, but there exists beneath this initial reading of the band a much deeper relationship between desire and Minshall's artistry. The mas man has long been unabashedly nonchalant—or if he finds himself boxed in, particularly prickly—about his same-sex desire:

> I neither advocate, advertise nor conceal my homosexuality. I have determined to live it with the same ease that my next-door neighbor lives his heterosexuality. I'm not going to let it get in the way. Anybody who's anybody in this town knows I'm gay. Most of them don't give a damn. They care far more for my work as an artist, as a mas man. They care for my understanding and contribution to island life, all of it, everybody, men, women, children, of whatever race or tribe, rich, poor, hetero, homo, the whole lot, the whole world. I do not belong to a gay ghetto. I belong to humanity.
>
> . . . I am exactly as I am supposed to be, with all the joy and all the suffering of love and life in me. I love me. I want to be no other person but me. I want to be exactly as I am. I want to be who I am for you to be who you are. (Minshall 2015)

Minshall reaps the gracious privileges reserved for homegrown icons—perhaps momentarily turning a blind eye to the merciless scrutiny that is the bane of the public figure—in a society not unfamiliar with homophobic recriminations of various sorts. The mas man's complex decades-long relationship with white American-born Todd Gulick—who now maintains a purely professional relationship with Minshall as managing director of the Callaloo Company—was certainly no secret even if it is not particularly overemphasized by either man.[9] Indeed, their romantic relationship was acknowledged—even if subtly so—and respected by nearly everyone with whom the two interact regularly (Gulick 2008). It may be the case that this level of silent acquiescence is the sole result of Minshall's artistic genius, but it is more likely the social reward for a tremendously talented artist willing to keep the matter of his homosexuality unspoken, at least in the public domain. But Minshall—at nearly sixty years old—would trouble this arrangement of permissibility by broaching that very subject for the first time in a public address in 2002.

As part of an invited lecture that he delivered to coincide with Christopher Cozier's *1981* art exhibition, Minshall uses a description of his art practice and his homosexuality to defend the necessity of art and the procreative potential of same-sexuality. I cite the mas man at some length here because of how vital his position proves:

> I want to deal with the word "draw" as it applies to human beings. Human beings—us, you and me—we go to the well to "draw" water. Without water we would soon die. You and me, we "draw" a breath of fresh air. Without air we would soon die. We make a mark; we "draw" a line on a piece of paper or on the wall of a cave.
>
> I suggest that the language is not accidentally arranged, this one word for these three activities. I suggest that if we couldn't make that mark—if we couldn't draw that line, that line that says "I am, I exist"—we would surely die. We have a consciousness. Just as we breathe air to live, just as we drink the water to live, we need to feel a sense of being to live. That line, that which we "draw," that which many centuries later we call art, defines us. It describes us. It says "I am" or, in some cases, "We are."
>
> . . . It is my observation of the art that I've experienced in my lifetime that the best of it has come from three groupings. I'm speaking mainly of the art of the 20th Century, and the three that I speak of are the blacks the Jews and the homosexuals; and I wondered to myself, why? They share in common: suffering, persecution, discrimination. And going back to where we started tonight, I wonder if that's the reason why they had more need than others to make a mark, to draw a line that said "I am." My own sexuality has been the cause of great suffering in my life. It has also been the gift of great insight. I've experienced great love. I've experienced ecstasy. My homosexuality has provided me with an understanding of life I would not have otherwise had. (Minshall 2002, 1, 10)

Minshall begins his lecture with a proposition: like water or breath, art is a vital necessity—an existential necessity that sates our thirst for an affirmation of presence in the now *and* calms our gasping for legacy. And he ends his lecture by extending his initial proposition: the best art comes from a crucial need to affirm a presence under threat or a legacy facing the possibility of erasure. Proving Minshall's claims about the twentieth-century artistry of blacks, Jews, and homosexuals is decidedly beyond the scope and interest of this analysis; however, Minshall's interpretation of the vantage point his homosexuality offers on life is especially germane to the present discussion.

Although Minshall quite fervently refuses to be considered a "gay artist" if it means that his artistry will not be interpreted broadly or taken seriously— here a concern (not altogether unfounded) about the frivolity associated with earlier, once widely held interpretations of the adjective "gay" haunts the mas man, whose art form is already not taken seriously enough—he nevertheless lays claim to his homosexuality as an interpretive frame. And it is from this epistemological position that Minshall creates his work, drawing insight from his well of suffering, drawing love from the thin air of persecution, and drawing ecstatically across the blank space of discrimination.

If Minshall creates from a perspective informed—but not narrowly confined—by his homosexuality, then a consciousness about the consequences and potentialities of desire has always framed his artistry. *The Sacred Heart* calls attention to that frame by centering an epidemic spread, in part, through sexual contact and once widely presumed to be the sole concern of homosexual men. The immediate stigmatization *and* mobilization of gay male communities in response to the alarmingly indiscriminate spread of HIV/AIDS have for over two decades encouraged among gay men a hyperawareness of and direct identification with those infected and affected by HIV and AIDS. Although the mas man came of age in cosmopolitan London two decades before the discovery of HIV in 1981, there can be little doubt that an engagement with the issue of HIV/AIDS proved unavoidable once Minshall had reached middle age and settled comfortably into his unique place in Carnival history. The fact that Minshall's first mas trilogy (*River* in 1983, *Callaloo* in 1984, and *The Golden Calabash* in 1985)—and in the mas man's estimation perhaps his most exquisite work to date—coincides with health officials' realizations about increasing rates of HIV prevalence in the anglophone Caribbean, has largely gone unmentioned in the existing literature on Minshall's artistry.

Disparaged early on in some corners of society as an "AIDS band" for being overrun by—if not for being under the direct leadership of—well-known, same-sex-desiring artists from various creative enclaves in T&T, Minshall's mas would be gravely influenced by much more than the prejudicial, peppertongue rumors that seldom dissuaded even the most casual Minshallite. In the final decades of the twentieth century, as Minshall learned of the death of a former lover in London and experienced the loss of various members of the Callaloo Company to AIDS-related illnesses, his empathetic imperative strengthened steadily (Gulick 2008). As early as his band *Tapestry* (1997), Minshall had weaved HIV/AIDS into the fabric of his Carnival presentation—a fitting symbolic nod in living, dancing fabric toward the quilted memorial began a decade earlier by San Francisco–based AIDS activist Cleve Jones. And in 1998—as the keynote speaker at an international Caribbean consultation on HIV/AIDS hosted in Port-of-Spain—Minshall delivered his first public speech on the global epidemic (Gulick 2016a). In this poetic call to conscience, the artist provides a wide view portrait of our personal responsibility to combat the virus with connection and compassion: "Consider AIDS. A threat to all of humankind. To have any hope of surviving against it, we must all see, and share, the logic and inevitability of the fundamental human connection. We must connect. We must communicate. We must love" (Minshall 1998, 2). Minshall's *The Sacred Heart* would prove to be the culmination of the mas man's nearly decade-long public concern about the ravages of and resources for an incurable dilemma—a virus that has fundamentally changed the way the world thinks about sex and intimacy.

Admittedly, any particular Minshall Carnival band might easily serve as the single subject of this entire analysis—to this rule *The Sacred Heart* is no exception; however, as I have decided to devote only the present chapter to Minshall's latest band, I must also focus the scope of my attention. To this end, I look to a particularly compelling segment of the staged presentation of *The Sacred Heart* in what follows. For at least two centuries, Trinidad's Carnival has belonged to the streets of big cities and small towns all over the island. However, Port-of-Spain—where publically judged, staged presentations of bands en plein air date back to the late 1940s—boasts the biggest and most elaborate parade of bands and remains the indisputable center of attention (E. Hill 1972, 101–2; Scher 2003, 50). And the beating heart of the capital city's Carnival revelry is the Queen's Park Savannah—the city's central park and purportedly the world's largest roundabout.

For over seven decades, bands of street revelers have annually queued up to dance across a massive stage erected in front of a grandstand (once used for the appraisal of racehorses) on the edge of the Savannah for the final judging of each band. *The Sacred Heart* is in part momentous for being possibly the last full-sized Minshall band to cross that Savannah stage, marking an end of sorts to exactly three decades (if we begin with *Paradise Lost* in 1976) of designing, developing, and directing mas productions for Trinidad's Carnival. An emotional experience for many of the masqueraders and spectators, who participated in or witnessed that crossing with the legendary mas man, *The Sacred Heart*'s stage show may have been subject to an even higher level of scrutiny than customary for a Minshall band precisely because of the beginning ache of nostalgia. If this increased scrutiny has resulted in a particularly memorable performance overall, then I hope here to spotlight a particular moment that stands out even more prominently in the collective memory.

Deploying the Dames: Minshall's Prophylactic Stage Show

Between "The Heart of Hearts" and "The Heart of Hope"—the final two sections of the band—the opening strains of soca artist Alison Hinds's hit single "Roll It Gal" (2005) clear a space on the stage.[10] Twelve characters sway into that open space in ankle-length, Valentino-red, A-line skirts lifted by exaggeratedly generous posteriors. Each dame wears ample metallic-silver breast cups strapped to the chest and a red plastic colander with a heart-shaped base as a mask attached to a band of red foam surrounding their crown (see plate 10).[11] Across broad bare shoulders or draped across their napes, these soft-bellied performers hold swaths of rainbow fabric (see plate 14). Each padded derrière finds its own rhythm as ten of the characters carry a silver polystyrene phallus onto the stage, five dames holding each side of this eighteen-foot-long and three-foot-wide dancing missile (see plate 11) (Gulick 2016a). These ten undulating figures jerkingly center the phallic object on the stage and then turn it around to face the remaining two characters. These two remaining dames have entered the scene behind the phallus holding a large sheath of what appears to be red fabric, rolled into a circular ring that resembles an unused condom. The audience hums in anticipation of the scene's coming resolution. As Hinds approaches her third chorus, the characters begin rolling what is now revealed to be a rainbow sleeve onto the phallic object (see plate 12). There is a contortion of bodies—skin-to-skin and bulbous posterior-to-bulbous posterior—as the pair of dames pull the fabric taut, trading places and shifting grips with their ten sisters. And once the object is fully sheathed, the ten characters release it to the stage, assemble on a single side of it, and roll it offstage, followed by the remaining dancing pair (see plate 13).[12]

It is principally through his redeployment of the Dame Lorraine character that Minshall is able to preserve a necessary balance between morbid seriousness and ribald humor across the penetrative possibilities of his spectacle. This balance alone makes the project of an HIV/AIDS awareness Carnival band conceivable, and its effective negotiation is perhaps what determines the success or failure of Minshall's *Sacred Heart*. For such a delicate pas de deux between discipline and indulgence, Minshall looks to the Trinidad

Carnival tradition for a masquerade not simply adept at the dance between sobriety and satire but born of that ambivalence. A folk play believed to have been performed in Trinidad as early as 1884—replacing the banned Sunday night Canboulay procession—the Dame Lorraine performance formalized a long tradition of performative mockery that enslaved peoples had used to entertain themselves at the expense of their enslavers; this annual Carnival tent theatre production—which would traditionally end at the break of dawn just as Jouvay began—continued until the beginning of World War II (E. Hill 1972, 40, 41). Originally performed in two acts, the first part of the masque mimics the fanfare, dress, and mannerisms of the eighteenth-century French aristocracy in the re-creation of an elegant ball complete with servants peeking in from the peripheries. In the second act—a parody of the first—a presumably well-meaning elite attempts to teach his servants to dance in the style of the European gentry. His rambunctious pupils are dressed in ragged imitations of aristocratic finery and a grotesquely exaggerated physical feature—from which the character's French Creole name is derived—marks each servant; these characters were usually all masked, and farcical transvestitism was quite commonly employed (E. Hill 1972, 40; Crowley cited in Seidman 2008).

This multilayered farce enabled Trinidad's servant class to embed a bold-faced mockery of the colonial elite within what appeared to be an elaborate mockery of themselves. This particular open mockery of the bodies, manners, and pretensions of the elite class had to have been sophisticated enough by its later years to be performed for a paying audience of the mocked (E. Hill 1972, 41). Perhaps it is the involved sophistication of this layered parody that led to the eventual abandonment of the practice, beginning with the disappearance of the first act and leading to the demise of the entire tradition save one oddly decontextualized character. No longer used to refer to the Carnival folk play, the term "Dame Lorraine" in modern Carnival parlance refers to a farcical cross-dressing masquerade (usually) for men. Although the excessively padded posterior and breasts of this character indicate that the mas is a survival from the second act of the folk play, it has taken on the name of the entire performance. It may be the case that the Dame Lorraine folk play was originally named for a character—a caricatured well-to-do lady from France's Lorraine region—who traditionally formed part of the performance but has since been forgotten; how appropriate then that this performance named for a character would in time become the name of a character again.

Born of this heritage, and with its grotesquely sensual masquerade, the Dame Lorraine is arguably the most appropriate character to midwife the clearest HIV prevention message that Minshall delivers through his *Sacred Heart*. Minshall is able to use an exaggerated ribaldry to approach the most serious of matters in an artistic genre—Carnival—that the mas man has always insisted need not sacrifice conscientious critique to heedless frivolity. And yet the Dame Lorraine has long held this dichotomy between serious threat and playful entertainment within its masque even if it would take the mind of a contemporary mas man to recuperate the cutting edge of what threatened to become merely a misogynistic clown masquerade fading in Jouvay's predawn light. Minshall is able to put this traditional character to effective contemporary use, demonstrating in practice his philosophy on the uses of Carnival's history in its present:

> A responsible approach to the making of mas . . . requires knowledge of the traditional figures. However, if one is to do art, and not merely art history—that is, if one is to do mas, and not merely mas history—one must delve deeper than the forms themselves to determine the themes, the disciplines, the unspoken principles behind those traditional figures. The important thing, then, is not merely the traditional figures, but the tradition of those figures. That tradition is mimicry, and the adaptation and transformation of outside cultural influences, and, above all, relevance to the contemporary society. (Minshall 1985, 12)

Minshall's attention to the performative tradition of the Dame Lorraine and his application of its aesthetic make his twelve red dames such a forceful presence. They resonate as loudly as they do in the visual symphony of the band because they are familiar, and yet their familiarity comes with a difference. As part of a symbolic HIV prevention message set to Alison Hinds's soca homily, these Dame Lorraines prove impressive in large part because they are centuries old and yet utterly contemporary.

The Dame Lorraine character is also particularly interesting in part because of Minshall's early intimate relationship to this masquerade. In fact, it is by stepping into the body of the Dame Lorraine at the age of fourteen that Minshall corporeally experienced the intimate transformative potential of that mas in Jouvay (Minshall 1991a, 9; Minshall 1993; Schechner and Riggio [1998] 2004, 110). In the predawn half-light, this masquerade offered young Peter a brief moment of corporeal displacement, a passionate rapture that pulled him outside of himself and in one sense drew him closer to the undifferentiated divine.[13] This is the potential for transfigurative ecstasy that lives within the Dame Lorraine, a seductive character who provides a bridge—across the archipelago of meanings "ecstasy" spans—between the sensual and the spiritual. Thus, the dame serves as an apt point of departure from which to consider the spiritual lifeblood of Minshall's *Sacred Heart*.

When the Artist Is a Priest: Compassion and Transcendence in *The Sacred Heart*

No consideration of Peter Minshall's 2006 work could hope to avoid the band's titular reference to the Sacred Heart of Jesus Christ, a pervasive symbol in Roman Catholic iconography. This surreal representation of a divine heart—engulfed in flames, wrapped in thorny vines, bleeding before the cross and yet luminous—is often centered over the chest in depictions of Jesus that recall his violent crucifixion. A corporeal synecdoche for Jesus himself—crowned in thorns, crucified, but luminous—the Sacred Heart also serves as a sublime metaphor for "Christlike" compassion. It is this other-worldly compassion that Minshall exhumes from the Christ narrative to serve as the principal affective reference point of his band. For a culture deeply influenced by Roman Catholicism—Trinidad and Tobago's pre-Lenten Carnival testifies to these roots—Minshall's turn to Jesus Christ for an exemplar of unconditional affection (despite HIV/AIDS stigma) resonates resolutely. And yet this gesturing toward the sacred in the space of Carnival performance did not resonate with all groups harmoniously. A Roman Catholic prayer group at a secondary school in one of Port-of-Spain's early suburbs took absolute offense to any association between Minshall's band and the Sacred Heart of Jesus—deeming the presumably implied marriage of Christ with bacchanalian revelry "sinful, to the extent of blasphemy" in a letter to the editor of a local newspaper (Shears-Neptune 2006). However, his long history in the mas over the previous decade had already prepared Minshall for just such an outcry against his work.

Considering the fierce chorus of dissent that greeted his 1995 band HALLELUJAH on similar grounds, it is to be expected that Minshall and the Callaloo Company would masterfully hold their footing when fighting the same ideological battle a decade later. The letter of protest from one seven-member Catholic prayer group in 2006 could not even begin to compare to the fiery objections that spurred the controversy in 1995 when fifty-two evangelical pastors threatened legal action if Minshall refused to change the name of his band (Riggio 1998, 20; Shears-Neptune 2006).[14] The mas man did refuse, and no legal action was ever taken, but the tumultuous clash with religious leaders (and many others) has had a lasting impact on Minshall in part because it demonstrates the unwillingness of some congregations of Trinidad's religious community to believe in the spiritual objectives of the Carnival. This disbelief wounds Minshall deeply; for the mas man, this too is tantamount to blasphemy. Perhaps Minshall was well positioned to respond to the accusations levied at his concept in 2006 because he has not stopped responding since 1995. The mas man confesses,

> It's not easy. I suppose that not-easiness came to a mighty crescendo with the experience of HALLELUJAH, where nothing I had done in my life had prepared me for two and a half months of daily diatribe in the newspapers, every single day, the most extreme Pentecostals saying it is sacrilege to use the word "hallelujah" in Carnival—"the mother of all rot," they called it—and columnists, editorials, politicians, bandleaders, priests debating the pros and cons . . .
>
> I went through my own spiritual transformation. I am sitting right here [in his garden] one day, I hear a rustle over there in the heliconias, and I look: there is the cat, Missy, having just missed the hummingbird that was about to touch the heliconia flower. In a flash, I understand that the cat, the hummingbird, the heliconia, and myself are one. I can explain it no other way. And I was paralyzed. This is my life's work, I want to bring celebration into the mas. This is the only way I know. Hallelujah!
>
> Curses were heaped on people. [Rumors spread that] "If you play in this band, the island will be cursed." . . . Then Carnival came. The people had a joyful, transcendent experience. The people who played in the band and the people who watched it. HALLELUJAH was Band of the Year. It is a week after HALLELUJAH, and I am on the north coast, by the sea, alone. The rocks, the crashing waves, the horizon. Mr. God says to me, "It was a beautiful hallelujah. But whatever made you think it would be easy?" (Schechner and Riggio [1998] 2004, 116)

In this interview—conducted in 1997, a full two years after the controversy—Minshall is not only still exasperated by the backlash against the title of his band, but the mas man is also quite lucid about the transcendental revelation that resistance encourages in him. Able to see a divine interconnectedness in the mundane sanctuary of his yard, Minshall resolves to insist upon his sacred celebration despite the difficulty; ultimately, the mas man believes—as he stands alone in nature's temple—that he received divine sanction for his work, but he could perhaps never have anticipated the challenge it would pose.

As with the "baroque praise-song" of Minshall's HALLELUJAH trilogy, the gospel of *The Sacred Heart* is in part a challenge to recuperate the spiritual imperative of Trinidad's Carnival (Laughlin et al. 2006). However, unlike those who dismiss Carnival as blasphemous, the mas man honors the necessary duality between the sacred and the profane in Carnival by resurrecting a spiritual consciousness in the mas (Minshall 2002, 6). In recognizing that there is nothing inherently sacrilegious about Carnival—a tradition adapted from pre-Christian sacred rituals, after all—Minshall simultaneously contests the presumed insurmountable dichotomy between the human and the divine, the carnal realm and the spiritual realm. Instead, the artist's work might be imagined as offering a vision of the intimate relationship between revelry and prayer by turning a mirror upon divine (and yet fleshy) creatures capable of both: human beings. Minshall's *Sacred Heart* demands recognition of human sacredness, a delicate originary balance that begets Minshall's oeuvre: "I do believe. I know not in Whom or What or Which, but there is a tremendous unknowable force that has brought all of this into being . . . and it is my duty as part of that sacred force—each of us is sacred— . . . to do my best. From somewhere it came to me: *The Sacred Heart*" (Pires 2006b). Consciously or not, Minshall's approach to his artistry offers an indirect retort to his grandmother's supposition that her young grandson would be either an artist or a priest.[15] The mas man chooses to become both.

If Minshall's mas is a tool for "looking at the spirits," then it provides a conduit between the mundane and the magnificent (Camnitzer 2005, 6). In one sense, this is precisely the role of religion under the attentive eye of a faithful priest. Minshall insists,

> I go back to that oft-used dictum: a good artist is a priest. He's responsible to his tribe. He's a deeply spiritual man. He has to speak of and for his people. By the same token . . . a good priest is an artist. . . . The rest are charlatans—both artists and priests—they're out there to make money, all of them. I would like to think I'm a good artist. (McCommie 2008; J. Williams 2008)

The artist-priest is driven by the needs of his community and by his own need to communicate. He gives his community its sense of being. (Minshall 2013b, 4)

My work is my prayer, my prayer is my work! . . . I know no other way. (Pires 2005)

Minshall testifies to the shared creative conscientiousness of the artist and the priest while identifying spirituality as the hallowed grounds upon which they meet. It is important to note that although Minshall's *Sacred Heart* repeatedly looks to Roman Catholicism for visual tropes and affective themes, Minshall's conceptualization of spirituality extends beyond any particular organized religion while incorporating many of the world religions into a larger sacred tapestry. If the convergence of artistry and priesthood is a union consecrated by spirituality, then it follows that this bond will be honored across the overlapping territories of various religions. As an aesthetic and spiritual conduit, Minshall attributes his multireligious consciousness about spirituality to his having been raised on an island that holds many of the world's most populous religions—including various sects of Christianity, Islam, Hinduism, and Orisha worship, among others—with an insouciant nonchalance (Gulick 2016c). Growing up in Trinidad prepares Minshall to see spirituality beyond the moors of any particular religion. He admits, "In fact, I have to be grateful for being of this island. The very seed of my existence was planted here. A little Presbyterian having the Roman Catholic experience and the Anglican experience and the fundamentalist Christian experience and the Hindu experience and the Buddhist experience and the experience of Islam—all of these experiences of mine, I am all of these. And being a Caribbean, I will be the first to say too that I am none of these" (J. Williams 2008). It is through the mas that Minshall is able to speak across religious niches to a spiritual complexity that models a philosophical proposition about a broader understanding of sacred consciousness.

Various religious traditions inform Minshall's sense of the transcendental sacred. And it is through attention to this sacred consciousness that we are able to better understand the spiritual work Minshall intends for his mas. The mas man insists:

The artist touches the eternal infinite and relates it to the observer, who sees it, touches it himself, discovers himself in the midst of it. The human moment is evoked, infinitesimal, yet momentous and essential, the inevitable link between all that has been and all that will be. The moment is beyond time and yet contains time. The vanity of us all, as well as our profundity, is plain in that moment, elucidated by art. Mas captures that moment inescapably. (Riverside Studios 1986; Nunley 1993, 306)

The moment of the mas is no less a moment than the moment of the pyramids. (Minshall 2016b)

Perhaps one of the most interesting revelations about the mas comes with the recognition that this artistry-induced transcendence that looks outward and inward at once is achieved not simply by faith in an intangible other-worldly presence but also by the actual carnal presence of the masked worshipers aroused (sexually and spiritually) by a frenzied revelry. *The Sacred Heart* is no exception to the fleshy exploration of the sacred that Minshall's mas has for decades encouraged. And yet blood as a literal and figurative signifier of a sensuous life force—proof at once of a miraculous vitality and a mortal vulnerability—reminds us that the band's HIV/AIDS imperative has heightened an attentiveness to mortality and the metaphysical in this Carnival performance. If an awareness of HIV/AIDS encourages (at the very least) an abstract consideration of mortality and permanent impermanence—much like the pyramids of Giza—then it raises the very questions that spirituality endeavors continuously to address.

The Sacred Heart provides such an appropriate intervention in part because it redeploys a theme (mortality) that has been central throughout the long tradition of Carnival in concert with a contemporary crisis that resonates directly with that theme. In a nation that provides free universal access to antiretroviral therapies—presumed by the Western medical establishment to be the most assured way currently to control the virus adequately enough to ensure a decent quality of life for people living with HIV/AIDS—contracting HIV is by no means an absolute death sentence. However, the virus remains a mortal threat even for those brave enough to get tested, come to terms with their positive status, and submit to indefinite treatment. As with HIV, so too with Carnival; both find a means by which to call the ecstatic embrace of life and death into question. In fact, "ecstasy" provides what is perhaps the most apt means by which to understand this dialectic between the corporeal and the spiritual that Carnival is always attempting to resolve. From the Greek for finding something or someone literally "out of place," the concept of "ecstasy" lends itself to descriptions of a spiritual transcendence (or death) in which the spirit is thought to leave the body, and yet the very same concept describes a sensual rapture that results from focusing in upon a corporeal hyperstimulation. The latter experience is so profoundly rooted in the body that it figuratively pulls one outside of one's self in an experience that mirrors the former. This convergence of meanings is rooted in a divergence of perspectives: looking away from the body versus looking toward it. This is the very divergence that *The Sacred Heart* strains to hold tightly in red ribbon. Minshall's ecstatic band plants the proposition that spiritual transcendence is possible not in spite of the body but rather through it; this seeming contradiction offers a path by which to leave the imperfect body through feeling so deeply within it that one discovers there a sacred potential expansive beyond any individual body. If Carnival spectacle has traditionally brought this ambivalent ecstasy to the fore, Minshall's HIV/AIDS awareness Carnival band revels in that tension in part because the disease demands attention to the materiality of the fragile body and the intangibility of spiritual strength.

Conclusion: Eros and Epistemological Vision

If Peter Minshall has made a mantra of contesting flat suppositions that *The Sacred Heart* is merely an "AIDS band" (Pires 2006b; Minshall 2008), he has done so in order to continuously call forth a conceptual space expansive enough to hold the various figurative and literal battlefronts to which he sends his band of warriors. Minshall is able to deliver a sophisticated HIV awareness and prevention message in large part because he dares to use HIV/AIDS as a metaphorical lens. The band's salve of hopeful affection is intended to heal: (1) the "affliction" of beads and bikinis plaguing the cultural body of the Carnival; (2) the infectious anti-HIV/AIDS prejudice weakening the national body; and (3) the compromised body fighting an intruding virus. As political metaphor, HIV/AIDS remains elastic enough in Minshall's hands to stretch toward each of these wounds while simultaneously connecting them. If sensuality endangers the body (national or individual) caught in a frenzied revelry, this same sensuality has also deeply penetrated the artist's creativity. Minshall invites us to touch HIV/AIDS as a metaphor for perilous pleasure. This threatened death summons a sacred vision that looks to Catholic iconography for a symbol of compassion that stretches beyond any particular religious doctrine toward an expansive spiritual consciousness. It is precisely because this sacred attentiveness cannot ignore the vulnerabilities of the flesh that HIV/AIDS provides such an inspired metaphor for the ecstatic contestation of a body-spirit dichotomy. If an embodied metaphysics focused intently upon mortality provides an interpretive link between HIV/AIDS and Carnival, then Minshall's *Sacred Heart* is a ritualized dance at the crossroads of that overlap. The mas man uses his HIV/AIDS band to do very serious political, sensual, and spiritual work.

An interlinked political-sensual-spiritual spectacle, *The Sacred Heart* offers a glimpse of our newly expansive erotic—a performative means by which to *see* the interrelation that forms the structural core of this epistemological position. Minshall's *Sacred Heart* holds our gaze on an artistic genre that attends at once to power, desire, and metaphysics in order to represent all three as part of an integrated performance work. The mas man's band from 2006 provides such a clear vision of the erotic principally because the band's HIV/AIDS awareness and prevention objective is met primarily through visual cues—within a performance genre in which the visual reigns. Minshall's warrior revelers use their performance to do battle against prejudice, willed ignorance, and forgetfulness. And it is the degree to which the band is able to "find a place and make a stage" for itself in the fickle terrain of memory that determines the success of *The Sacred Heart*.[16] For this aesthetic warfare, Minshall does not simply rely upon the worn visual tropes of HIV/AIDS; he redeploys a select few of these symbols in the process of creating his own local HIV/AIDS awareness and prevention iconography.

The effectiveness of this iconographic innovation depends upon Minshall's creative use of the epistemological imperative he recognizes in all Carnival performance (Laughlin et al. 2006). If the Carnival has long been a means by which the peoples of T&T come to understand themselves and their sociocultural context, then working in the mas is working upon this reflection of a people upon themselves. Like other cultural performances, the mas brings to light that which is lost in plain sight (Turner 1987, 22). Minshall's band from 2006 focuses upon HIV/AIDS in the visual and conceptual landscape of a culture while widening this reflection just enough to draw the collective gaze toward an interweaved political-sensual-spiritual frame. In other words, the mas man's artistry opens a space for precisely the "performative reflexivity" that brings our new erotic to light (Turner 1987, 24). Viewed through the prism of the erotic, Peter Minshall's *Sacred Heart* delivers a challenge. And if we dare to look long and hard at him and at the metaphors he makes of us, we may yet get a transcendent glimpse of ourselves as we are *and* as we might be.

From Far Afield / A QUEER TRAVELOGUE (PART II)

MAY
5/1/07

I awake to a revelation. The cousins who I had always presumed were Rastafarians are in fact sumptuously dreadlocked Spiritual Baptists. This discovery is incidental to a tragedy. Auntie Kaya has been terribly burned. Our family is told that her *ras* went up in flames on the *mourning ground*. I do not yet know what that means, but somehow this mysterious mourning ritual may be foreshadowing another. She was the "nurse" in the ritual we are told; she was to be vigilant against potential danger. Quick and sharp, the ironies fold in upon themselves. My grandmother's eldest sister, Aunty Hibis (though her true true name is not Hibis at all), is a strong Spiritual Baptist just like her daughter, Auntie Kaya, who is technically my mother's cousin. My grandmother's face is drawn long from crying, but for now tear spent. My mother, on the phone, tells me to look after her. I am not sure exactly what that means right now, but I promise I will. Yesterday was uneasy, heavy footed in its rush to end. My head ached from sunset and would not ease with nightfall. Aimlessly, the pain just lingered. I spent an afternoon at the Tobago Oasis—the island's underdog HIV/AIDS NGO run primarily by and for HIV-positive Tobagonians—preparing for the coming candlelight memorial. In the midst of preparations, it is subtly revealed that Coraili and Pursley are both HIV-positive. I knew as much about Tref and Mazay, though they seem to refuse to discuss it. I will see how willing Mazay proves tomorrow if in fact we have our interview. Perhaps Coraili will be next, but I suspect most likely Vervine on camera and then maybe beginning the tape-recorded interviews. Soon, I will start preparing for that month in Trinidad. I hold this overripe sadness in my belly for Mowan still, but I refuse to call him. I still dream about us. We are so strong-minded and fragile. Today, I am a little less upset. I hope he is okay, hope he is almost happy really as he prepares for work. This is emptiness—spiteful and selfish—easing its hold on me.

5/2/07

Today, I finally meet with Zeba Pip—a nearly middle-aged gay white Trini businessman now living in Tobago. With the pointed nonchalance of the wealthy, he mentions being raised by his Grenadian maid and I hold my tongue. He is a source of information. He tells me about "old-time" gay organizations in Trinidad like Lambda Lambda. We sip our shandies, adjust our beach chairs. The sun is hot and insistent; the sea is cool and calling. I ask him about yachting—Tobago's Sail Week and Great Race—and gay male communities in Trinidad. I ask him about his childhood and his family. We spend a few hours together. I get the halfway promise of an actual recorded interview. For now, Zeba Pip talks mostly of love. There was the time he and his lover found their way to Tobago's highest point—the moon so close they nearly reached out to touch it—flooded the car with music, and danced in the headlights. Romance. There is a little restaurant nearly in the sea, he says, the charming magic of the place matched in abundance only by the plates full of food, a kind of belly full ground provision and dumpling food. I must go see for myself, he admits; take a drive to Parlatuvier, Castara, maybe even quite to Charlottesville. You must try bread hot from a clay oven on the beach and fish grilled fresh, salted from the sea. . . . This is a kind of courtship he invites me into with this island, miraculously mundane as his living breathing presence. Before he left Trinidad, he survived being run over by a Maxivan—he says so coolly that I nearly miss its severity—and I might not have believed him except that he sits beside me alive and astonishing.

5/5/07

Red Day. An evening fair skirts a Cubanesque mansion—the paint-chipped grandeur of Havana Vieja. As the day closes, the booths open. This is at once an HIV/AIDS awareness event and an opportunity to support queer business, queer activism, and sex-positive initiatives in Trinidad. There are just a few booths and a scattering of people—older couples, lesbians, gay men. Ribbon-red fabric frames us all. Balloons dance everywhere indiscriminately. I volunteer at the Caribbean Anti-Violence Project booth, following behind my ride—Bois Cano—a ruddy white Australian and his Guyanese partner in crime, Alan Tukai. We wait a few hours behind our table. Lozei's performance in drag dazzles as usual. I pull on a last bit of charisma for our final moment in the booth. Many are heading off to Sky bar—almost a gay club really. I say I may go. Then I do. I run into nearly everyone—planned or otherwise. The music is unnoticed, except perhaps for the soca. I am making a few rounds, buying a few drinks—these are mostly for myself. I leave Sky. I'm not fully present. The alcohol descends like fog and I lose myself in the haze. The next thing I remember, I am in a car full of strangers—one of them fondles me. I recognize a somewhat close acquaintance in the car with us: Sapodi. He is drunk, very drunk. Even through my own haze this much is clear. The car stops every now and then; he vomits at the side of the road. Keet and Papolola take us to their place. They are not a couple as far as I can tell, but even that is uncertain. Sapodi has a dysfunctional polyamorous relationship with Keet and Papolola and Vori (his sometimes boyfriend), but I could not have known that then. I get *bulled down* by Papolola and remember virtually nothing of it. I don't even remember ever saying a single word to him. He is handsome, tall, muscular like a marine, but soft too somewhere I cannot quite put my finger on. The next morning, he is a stranger lying naked next to me in an unfamiliar room. We meet like we're seeing each other for the first time.

5/10/07

"Canap. Afternoon, Canap. This is Lyndon. How are you?" He has grown tired of that question and the "You going good, right?" asked with a speed that makes it rhetorical truth set safely just beyond an actual response. He will tell you how he is. He's always the sincerest—cursed as he is with a bitter clarity—but you can't ask for it, you can't ask to know. And that is the beginning. He has so much to say, but it is peppery. I want to see him for tea and a conversation. He says, "Aren't we talking now?" He says he wants sex, wants me to fuck him because he has had to dig too deeply within himself to do what he does. He has had to find his own muse within without a black cock to worship, without a black male muse. These are almost the exact words he uses—raw desire, longing like a wound. He is hungry, a poetic hunger. In his old age, the creativity comes more wildly now. His imagination has birthed a dreadlocked choir. This is a blazing sun forced into the darkness, he says. They promised light by promising time, but in the Caribbean such promises of time are empty. They are hopeful but unlikely. Against the darkness, this man's great work emerges—his greatest ever he says—and I say flatly that this is metaphor. He ignores me. Or perhaps he hears me only after our conversation ends. The "black tribe" is killing itself, he says, the "black tribe" in its self-loathing is killing itself and this white man's burden has become too much. His overwhelming mission has been to return Africa to the Africans, to represent that Africa by re-presenting that Africa. What a task indeed for a "nonwhite white," a Caribbean white man who has fallen in love with his island but can find no black muse to inspire him. He has a solution presented to him. A friend now in Barbados suggests over the phone an Indian hard-prick to fuck him good. I ask Canap if that's what he wants. He says that's what he has.

5/16/07

"What you doing? We coming for you just now, *get ready.*" Roukou calls, Susi drives, but Vervine Bamboo is most certainly behind the way it is done. This is how a lime happens at her house—impromptu and assertive, a directive to prepare to have a good time. "If nothing else, the characters—old and new—will not fail to entertain," Susi says as I climb into the backseat of her car, its floor is rusted straight through to the road. I snuggle up next to Syrio and take a quick sweet glimpse at her girlfriend, Parvu—hair freshly braided, eyelashes on, made up and polished off. "We going for an orgy," Vervine offers. We meet a woman on the beach—beautiful woman, divinely dark-skinned. She is most certainly a presence; her raw charisma makes this plain. And she has plenty charisma. She is a whore she says with a painful pride. The stories begin to ease out. The rum comforts us. We take turns. We are spending hours finishing this chapter we are now writing together. I fell in love with a woman at nineteen, Parvu admits with a gallant tenderness, and she stays for the regular *cut ass* that woman gave her—hard-hearted abuse. This is her first love.

5/17/07

Parvu at nineteen: she has never been with a man, no never, not once. She lives with her first love for ten years and this is a kind of bliss. These ten years she glosses in a few seconds—retrospect is unforgiving. Then one morning, she says, her lover wakes up and decides some younger woman's pussy is sweeter than hers. These are her words, raw and tearing at the edges. Perhaps this is all said for effect, but it is effective—each syllable a pinprick of spite. And just as nonchalantly as she smiles, this red-skinned big-boned Grenadian explains how she beat that woman she once loved. "I beat her to a pulp," she says, "then I went to run her business," presumably as she always had. The woman gathers enough of herself to call Parvu—obviously not all of herself, because had she gathered all her wits about her she would have dialed otherwise. But she calls and told Parvu she is broken; she can't walk straight. And Parvu—rage purged—tells her she doesn't care. That is the end. She fast-forwards to a party in Trinidad—the rum washes away chronology and fine detail. In walks Syrio and now here she sits beside her. It has been nearly two years now, but their relationship seems perpetual. Now it's Syrio's turn. She comes out late, she explains—late like in her thirties. Realizing only then, she says, what she is, what she likes, realizing only *then*, she says, without disturbing the patience on her face. The caress of time has been nothing harsh for Syrio. Her cap rests upon her graying hairs, but it does not hide them. Hers is a butch elegance—she is a distinguished gentleman this woman. She has just ended a relationship. She finds herself at this party. She falls for this woman. Two years pass in an instant. She is almost forty-nine. Originally from Trinidad, she lives in Tobago now, her Grenadian love by her side. But before Syrio and before Parvu, Susi acts out her attempts with *totie* after we have laid her curiosity about anal sex and hemorrhoids to rest with talk of sitz baths in plum bush and Epsom salt. (A racial aside: everyone says Susi looks German—she is a common enough Trini mixture of Chinese and Portuguese—even though I am convinced she looks like a woman of color somehow. But "Trini white" is not the world's white, even if the world's white turns out to be uneasy territory upon closer inspection. "Trini white" might be better understood then not as the fringe of whiteness but one of its numerous fault lines. Beware Teutonic shifts!). It was nine inches—the prick Susi first attempts to take. Drunk, a big strapping man is sucking her breasts in the car going home—her *sagging* breasts, she mentions more than once. She was in her forties; she has never *taken man* before in she life, she nearly sings, and she start out *braps* with nine-inch *totie*! The walk finishes the story for her. Susi demonstrates an aching-vagina, wide-legged waddle for the laughs it certainly receives. "No more *totie* for me!" Susi delivers her punch line and means it. Vervine has been offering tiny bits of stories all along, but now she explains where her sons came from. This story I have heard. She is transparent at least about lesbian motherhood. Then Rachie—Rachette— this silky black beauty of a woman begins. She made a list, she confesses, of all the men she's had in life—a long list . . . what a number . . . *big* number, she says almost inaudibly to herself. There are nearly three hundred names, she admits, and perhaps this is hyperbole, but the silence it evokes is tangibly precise. And then, at the bottom of that list, she writes with a deep pain that I can only tearfully imagine, "I am a whore and that is why I cannot find anyone to love." You can hear hearts breaking in that silence. She was being beat badly by a man who has fathered her child; so, she runs away. She runs from him. She runs from love. She gives up on love proper that same night and comes to depend only on her purse—her source of income, her vagina. Her "Visa card"—according to Vervine's mother—because everywhere you go, it has the same value. It is something to sell one day and have the next. The lesbian child of a prostitute, Vervine says her mother took enough man, so she would never have to take one. Now Rachie—after burning that list— is living in a shack here in Tobago and renting beach chairs. She's attempting a life. She *zami* once and it was sweet, she says, but she love prick. In fact, she live by it—and her *nani* still tight. There is a light in this woman, but pain too, just around its edges is all.

5/29/07

The boat trip back provides just enough hours in the ocean to wash what was left of Trinidad out of me. On return, I anticipate the relaunch of Tobago's Chatroom.[1] A second launch since the first had managed only to bring together those of us who helped to bring it along—Roukou, Betelmi (they were still friends and roommates then) and myself—in Vervine's apartment. This time though we have a central location—privately public in its way—Kings Well Inn. I negotiated for it and paid twice the price to secure it—more involved than I should have been in any of this if it is to be sustainable. And although Yakit could read that overextension—over the phone all the way from Trinidad—and we could agree together on it not being good for the Chatroom in the long run, here I am still calling and reminding a week before, texting a day before (calling some again to be sure), and on the day arranging who I would pick up. I have even attempted to find a lesbian to cofacilitate with Roukou. All this preparation—games, tricks, gifts to keep people engaged—but I am determined not to be pulled in as a cofacilitator; it is not my place, and it sets a bad precedent. It is challenge enough that Roukou is a Trinidadian—even though he lives here now—and not a born and bred Tobagonian. Foreign as I am, I resolve to participate as minimally as possible, but a creeping anxiety about it going "wrong"—the space and money wasted—does not allow it. Here I am taking notes on everything that is said and the intricate ellipses between, on the way bodies say and silence; and then, nearly by surprise, I am adding my two cents. I am still resisting cofacilitating, but now trying to facilitate *through* Roukou—an unworkable puppet show. I should not have sat on that stage next to Roukou. I should not have convinced Coraili Regosa to come. I should not have tried to guide the conversation back, and back again, to the matters at hand—establishing a Tobago Chatroom and the state of the smaller island's gay community. I should not have expected too much beyond a few bodies in chairs talking. Then the gay Trinidadians arrive. They come "straight from the boat" and antagonistic about having performed heterosexuality for the three hours it takes to cross the sea between. Disgruntled as Trinis can be, these gay men seem determined to prove that Tobago is—they insist indelicately—"backward." I try to ease some of the discursive blows and keep the conversation from becoming a competition—a Trinidad has and has and has and Tobago needs to, desperately needs to, so long overdue. A gay revolution, someone says, but nothing homegrown mind you, nothing local. Instead, all imported from Trinidad, transplanted perhaps but not, absolutely not, Tobagonian. The circle mostly agrees that a Tobagonian gay movement is impossible; I have seen much to disprove this, but I stay silent. If this circle does not see it, I cannot force it. We end. Really, it is a kind of falling apart. People stand without sharing their feelings about the experience. We do not manage to pick a topic for next week. And we do not pass the hat to try to make back some of the money I spent on that space and will spend next week and the week after perhaps. I drive home all who can fit into the car uncomfortably. And then I head home myself. I am upset—although I should not be—that I ended up more involved than I promised. On edge still from the sleeplessness of this day between islands, I comfort myself with a bit of hope. This is only our second Chatroom in Tobago—and this one mostly attended by Trinidadians, who really should have known so much better. There is an ongoing lesson here for me on learning to step back just far enough to see what is going on without trying always to *be* what is going on. This is slow-won wisdom.

JUNE
6/9/07

The Tobago Chatroom is being held right in the middle of Scarborough, tucked away in a hidden pocket of the center of town. The open, greenery-concealed upstairs space gives a kind of bohemia feel when it's ready. This is a feeling of possibility. The chairs we arrange in a half circle around the stage. Nine people attend the first public session and then eleven the next. Vervine and Susi—the resident lesbian couple—pepper the conversation. Vervine facilitates. There are more Tobagonians this time. And the chat walks its own confident path. I get back some cash after we pass the hat to pay the TT$100 for renting the space. This is the beginning of continuity, of a kind of assurance. And now Roukou is considering moving to a free space. I cannot disagree.

7/6/07

There will be a memorial cabaret for Feuille Band, Mayoc tells me the evening my boat arrives in Trinidad. Time has aligned itself such that I must go. I did not know Feuille—either as himself or as Lady F—but many many did. He was a godmother of drag here in Trinidad and he has passed. "AIDS-related death" whispers the rumor once it has made its way to Tobago; the talk comes days before he actually dies. It's just so *hozes* does be fast, *oui*, not just fast but premature—putting *goat mouth* on the man life as he was still living it. But die he does and such is the clairvoyance of gays—many of us often-reluctant spirit mediums. And now those same spirit whisperers offer the crossing soul a drag cabaret as a form of remembrance. It is perhaps the best-organized and -coordinated drag show I have yet seen here in Trinidad—truly a kind of cabaret with individual and group numbers all tied together with recognition of Lady F. His cousin comes up to acknowledge the support, to acknowledge the family, friends, and coworkers present. This is a celebration of life, an informal Pride event in honor of a life well lived. The usual suspects lip-synch to the songs of the moment. Standing out among them, Lozei's remarkable Whitney Houston works through a tough song brilliantly—an eerie mourning song that is not one in anticipation of Houston's death and his own only a few slim years later. To this, add various costume changes and Sage, our saucy drag host—who pulled me up quickly for talking, for not paying sufficient attention, who clawed her way onto my chest till I was too frightened to say anything to anyone. Oh yes, that is the power of the drag queen over her audience; I had nearly forgotten. After intermission I move from my seat, partly out of fear, but really because my brother calls to tell me my mother's cousin—Aunty Kaya—has died. After the bad burns on the Spiritual Baptist mourning ground and the long hospitalization, she dies, and my mother has been trying to reach me to tell me. My brother is still speaking, but all I can hear is my grandmother crying in the background. This phone call seems surreal. I've been pulled into a family tragedy. But we are already mourning, a drag mourning in sober anticipation of Pride.

7/7/07

The evening of the Pride party, I decide to go. I decide this will be it for me. I have prepared an all-black outfit around that elastic skin of a shirt I have been dying to wear. I leave Nelson Street that night in a blur and head to the guesthouse where Ditay is staying over from Tobago. We have become conveniently close it seems. So, I have a place to dress. We coordinate a ride to the party and back. We are set to go. My attempts at flirtation nearly make the boy a liar—but no, nothing happens, just as he tells his boyfriend; he makes sure of that. I respect him for this later. After various outfit modifications, everyone is ready; Yakit comes with us too. Japana is just giving us a drop and she's gone; a lesbian, yes, but she's not going to the party. The large hall has a high school dance feel still at half past twelve. We survey outfits and notice several pockets of young—too young—Indo-Trinidadian boys and their requisite straight female friends swarming them like flies do overripe sapodilla. Early I realize that this evening has the potential to be nightmarish. But Yakit is making the rounds; I make them with him. "Elements— The Evolution of PRIDE": a theme into which nobody is really putting much effort, a grand theme largely ignored even by the decorations. This party is little different from any other I've experienced here in spite of being a Pride party. It is a slapdash of rainbow balloons and streamers, flanked by two impromptu bars, flooded with soca and dancehall music. Many here have just barely refined their look. Many more are quickly unlaced, their free-spirited pretension ripped down now and again by a true true smile and hug from an actual friend. People I had expected, I finally see. Betelmi looks amazingly mundane in heels and a short white cotton skirt (all ripples) and a country club polo, but the wig is perfect and it works. Maho is a walking disco ball, all lamé and cliché shimmering, but still that same frowsy smell that lingers with him—unwashed this woman—but somehow approaching elegance with all of that. Titip is a beauty, absolutely, undeniably gorgeous in wig and dress. He has an effortless sexy appeal that is alluring, deserving a drink at least. Of course, Bouca and his adorable boyfriend are hemmed in a corner. They are not worth much effort. Mayoc's heavenly but cool embrace is comforting. Seme and Senna show up—guru and protégé now—and we talk a little, dance a little. I do see when Zebton arrives, but I only barely recognize him. The alcohol has begun to creep in upon me. Before I realize it fully, I am gone. I do not remember this: I chatted up a few other people. We did probably unmentionable things on the dance floor. And I end up outside sitting, head bowed low, on a low pile of scaffolding materials, fighting sleep. The moment when I leave my body and a familiar sensual force returns to claim it is the precise ecstatic moment that I reconnect with Zebton. His mind is phenomenal; this much I remember well. The irony of our meeting again in that moment proves to me that our link is spirit ordained, encouraged by forces beyond us. It is Tuesday now. I have one more day left in Trinidad. I meet Zebton for tea at the university. We go back to his place for the most sublime nonsexual connection I have yet had with a man.

CHAPTER 3

Echoes of an Utterance

A History of Gender Play in Calypso

A woman can be a bridge, limber and living, breathless,
because she don't know where the bridge might lead,
she don't need no assurance except that it would lead
out with certainty, no assurance except the arch and
disappearance. At the end it might be the uptake of air,
the chasm of what she don't know, the sweep and soar
of sheself unhandled, making sheself a way to cross
over. A woman can be a bridge . . . A way to cross over.

DIONNE BRAND, *In Another Place, Not Here*

Calypso is the original Trinbagonian leitmotiv.[1] In fact, music is altogether
unavoidable throughout Trinidad and Tobago's cultural landscape. Corrobo-
rating anthropologist and ethnomusicologist Alan Merriam's emphasis on
music as a primary tool for sociocultural analysis, generations of scholars interested in Trinbagonian culture have had to not only include music in their
ostensibly non-music-orientated studies but also rely upon that music—at
least in part—as a means by which to understand these islands' uniquely
polyphonic cultures (Herskovits and Herskovits 1947; D. Miller 1994, 1997;
Munasinghe 2001; Yelvington 1995; Birth 1999, 2008, 5). If it has remained
the case for centuries that "in Trinidad [and in Tobago], music is an important

means for making and contesting cultural claims about identities and the nation," and more than this, that "music is also an important means for *thinking* and generating *feelings* about such claims" (Birth 2008, 12; italics in original), then calypso stands always in a spotlight on the Trinbagonian epistemological stage. This responsibility to engage calypso begs us to listen more closely not only to the music and the artists who create it but also to its troublesome beginnings. Calypso is an aural pastiche. A mischievous laugh in the face of questions of origin, this quintessential national music genre is the sonorous chorus for a culture composed of harmonious dissonance. Nevertheless, even if no attempt at calypso's origin narrative can ever be definitive, it is still possible that the search for origins itself may prove instructive. I propose here a brief history of calypso then not only as an introduction to the genre—a standard overture in calypso scholarship—but also as a discursive contribution to the ongoing narration of its history.

Well over three centuries old by most scholarly accounts, modern calypso's earliest form likely combines two vocal traditions—the *lavway* and the *calipso*—both closely associated with the *kalinda* (also *calinda*), or stick fighting, tradition of early eighteenth-century Trinidad (Elder 1967, 91; Cowley 1996).[2] A call-and-response challenge song led most often by *chantuels* (loosely meaning "singer/chanter" and typically referring to the very stickfighters who were soon to engage in physical combat), the lavway was a means by which to lure an opponent while boasting of one's stickfighting prowess. In fact, the term "lavway" may be a creolized version of both the French *la voix* (meaning "the voice") and *le vrai* (literally meaning "the true") (Cowley 1996; Mendes [1986] 2003). The translational double entendre of "lavway" may be indicative less of a linguistic imprecision than of a flexibility in the French Creole unmatched in the standard French. In essence, the lavway is a voiced oath of challenge that immediately declares its own truthfulness. This ambiguity in the term would set a precedent for the clever playfulness with language that would come to be one of the defining elements of modern calypso.

Although stickfighters and chantuels are almost invariably considered to have been male, there is a well-documented history of formidable female *bâtonnieres* and sharp-tongued chantuelles (Pearse 1956; Campbell 1988; Elder 1967, 1998; Maison-Bishop 1994; Dikobe 2003; H. M. Smith 2004):

> Each band [of roving stickfighters] was led by a soloist known as a chan-
> tuel/chantuelle whose role was to boast the accomplishments of his, or

more often her, band in song while pouring vituperation on rival gangs. It is important to note that in this period ca'iso, as calypso was called before 1890, was usually sung by women. A well-known chantuelle of the 1870s was Bodicea, whose life "was devoted to three things: singing, drinking and fighting" [according to an 1875 local newspaper account]. (Campbell 1988, 12)

Notorious stickfighting kalinda women existed. In Trinidad popular canboulay history, noted in the early 19th century are: Sarah Jamaica, Bobull Tiger, Techselia, B-Bar the Devil, called matador women. (Elder 1998, 42)

Although the calypso and Carnival historian Susan Campbell is unequivocal about the predominantly female voice in the chantuelle shout, other calypso scholars, such as the folklorist J. D. Elder, recognize the significant presence of women in the kalinda—as stickfighters, as chantuelles, and even as drummers—but stop short of claiming that the majority of chantuels might have been women. In fact, as a somewhat ironic twist, Elder concludes his ethnographic taxonomy of the postemancipation *cannes brûlées* processions (of which the kalinda formed a part) by noting, "On Carriacou island in the Grenadines there is in the Big Drum Dance, an 'Old People' (ancestors) kalinda played by two women armed with large white towels. They enact a 'battle' of Right and Wrong, the steps corresponding to the bois [from the French for "wood" and used to describe the stickfighter's staff] kalinda of Trinidad. The music and drumming are by females (Elder 1998, 42).

The similarities in the danced contests that Elder notes are not surprising considering the substantial inter-Caribbean movement of enslaved as well as free black populations, especially among black French Creoles. However, this all-female kalinda ritual proved noteworthy to Elder in part because he might not have imagined it to be one of many similar scenes enacted throughout the nineteenth-century Caribbean.[3] Susan Campbell's insistence on the recognition of female presence in the kalinda lends scholarly credence to thinking the Carriacou scene remarkable still, but perhaps not quite a singular anomaly. Attention to the second vocal tradition—the calipso—out of which calypso comes may help to account for Elder and Campbell's difference of scholarly opinion. This clarification serves well as a preface to the briefest engagement with the extended debate about the origin of the term "calypso" and its relationship to the term *kaiso* (*ca'iso* in Campbell above).

The *calipso* (also called *cariso* or *caliso*)—to which the modern calypso most likely owes its name—was both a song and an accompanying dance form that shared the same name, performed predominantly by women during the rest periods of stickfighting matches (Elder 1966, 1998; Rohlehr 1990; Cowley 1996; Dikobe 2003). These derisive banter songs would have had more elaborate compositional structures and addressed a wider breadth of themes than the lavway. Despite attempts at neatly gender-segregated suppositions about calipso and stickfighting, it is especially important for this analysis to emphasize that just as women were often centrally located (both figuratively and quite literally in the center ring of drummers, spectators, and possible combatants) in the stickfight, so too must it have been the case that men often lifted their voices in calypsos, challenging opponents in song as the fighters rested. So, it would probably not have been uncommon to come across a kalinda in which some of the fighting and drumming bodies may have been female and some of the singing bodies male. A somewhat anachronistic insistence on an impermeable gendered division of performance roles in the kalinda tradition may explain why it is that the chantuelle and the calipso singer have been so closely aligned in calypso scholarship, which often makes no mention of calipso song or dance, obscuring the distinctiveness of the largely female vocal tradition about which little thus far has been written. By 1881, however, that distinctiveness would fade as a result of the Canboulay Riots and the British colonial government's subsequent repression of the stickfight and other seemingly threatening elements of the kalinda tradition; this danced tradition would be most aggressively compromised by an 1884 ordinance against the playing of drums.

The Canboulay Riots were a gasp for breath in response to the colonial government's steady constriction of Carnival since its dip below the *diametre* (French for "diameter," which would be creolized as mentioned previously into *jamet/jamette* and lend its name to the scandalous mid- to late nineteenth-century Carnival) of "decent" society after 1860 (Campbell 1988, 10). An expected, though no less striking, result of official legislation against stickfighting was the increasing transfer of aggression from the contest of the *bois* to the tongue-lashing. As male chantuels and stickfighters took refuge in song, they adopted elements of what had been a predominantly female song of playful ridicule for well over a century (Elder 1967, 109; Rohlehr 1990, 213; H. M. Smith 2004, 35). As the aural distinctiveness of the calipso song and the lavway began to fade, female calipso singers were nearly flooded out of the song tradition. The principal elements of a new syncretic vocal art form were in place; the dawn of the twentieth century witnessed the birth of a new genre of music—*calypso*—characterized by a mixture of musical elements inherited from the lavway and the calipso: a driving 2/2 or 4/4 rhythm, leader-and-chorus cooperation, consistent syncopation, and predominance of the minor mode (Elder 1966, 200).

However, this unique new form was largely reserved for men. The final decades of the nineteenth century into the first decades of the new century had seen not only regulations against the stickfight but also the quite severe repression of female public performance simultaneous with the eager institutionalization of calypso into a middle-class sanctioned performance spectacle (a further attempt to distance calypso from the officially maligned stickfight) housed in tents for the enjoyment of a paying audience (Elder 1964; Campbell 1988, 18–19; Rohlehr 1990; Reddock 1994; Maison-Bishop 1994, 102–3; H. M. Smith 2004). Ironically, the emergence of this newly hybrid form coincided with an extremely class-conscious and unduly gender-biased Trinidadian Victorianism, the result of Queen Victoria's new "moral" order (beginning with the British queen's accession to the throne in 1837). As fiercely defended by the colonial government as it was by the local middle class, Victorian morality would discourage female performance while not actively discouraging the calypso genre. In fact, the bawdiness of calypso provided just the appropriate balance of restraint and hedonism so relished by the Victorian era just as long as female performers were confined to the chorus.

The mass popularity of the calypso genre also resulted in part from a language shift in calypso singing that made the genre more accessible to the non-French-Creole-speaking inhabitants of the colony. The lingua franca of black peoples in Trinidad and Tobago and throughout the Caribbean in the nineteenth century, French Creole was the expected language in which the lavway and the calipso were composed and performed (Cowley 1996, 231). It would not be until 1898 that calypso composers would first experiment with lyrics sung—in part—in English, leading verse by verse to the composition of the first full English-language calypso "Jerningham the Governor" in 1899 (E. Hill 1972, 59; Cowley 1996, 126, 138).[4] However, even once English had become the dominant language of calypso, a French Creole call-and-response was often retained in the refrains of songs for centuries still (Campbell 1988, 18–19). Over the course of two centuries the genre had undergone a significant language flip—English and French trading places nearly completely in the mouths of calypsonians; this language change is perhaps indicative of a more fundamental tectonic shift in the topography of Trinbagonian linguistic affinities.

If the new mass popularity (and controversial unpopularity) of calypso was in part the result of calypsonians' new affinity for English, then this language recognition was heard on top of a chorus of other sonic and structural affinities. The various influences on calypso beyond the shores of Trinidad and Tobago were initially addressed in the scholarly literature in the service of hypotheses about the origin of the term "calypso" (Crowley 1959a, 1959b, 1966; Elder 1967; E. Hill 1967; Quevedo 1983). This etymological debate holds within it competing claims about the "true" geocultural origins of the music genre, claims that Trinbagonian culture has taken delight in confounding since its birth and continues to confound centuries later. Nevertheless, the scholarly treatment of etymology-as-origin is instructive—though far from definitive—in that it allows one to mark a few of the various music traditions calypso incorporates or perhaps simply resembles.

The most consistently repeated origin narrative traces the origin of "calypso" through a contemporary synonym—*kaiso*—to a Hausa-language word, *kaito* (or *kaico*), pronounced "kaitso" (or "kaicho"), which is an exclamation either declaring one is owed pity ("What a pity!") or affirming that one shall receive none ("Ba ka da kaito": "You will get no sympathy/pity" or "It serves you right") (Bargery 1934; Elder 1967; E. Hill 1967, 361; Crowley 1959a; Quevedo 1983; Newman 2007). The theatre scholar Errol Hill suggests: "The term *kaico* might have been introduced (or reintroduced) into the argot of Trinidad Carnival songsters and masqueraders by the newly arrived Hausa-speaking immigrants sometime in the first half of the nineteenth century. . . . At an early stage the word was probably changed to the more euphonious *kaiso*, which served as an expression of both approval or disapproval as the context warranted" (E. Hill 1967, 362–63; italic in original).

The contemporary usage of the exclamation "Kaiso!" to mark a particularly adept calypso performance while at the same time attesting to the authenticity of that performance ("true true" kaiso as opposed to the substandard) lends credence to Hill's meticulously argued proposition. Hill further contends:

> I would like to suggest, further, that *kaiso* had a dual development. On the one hand it could have been retained as an expression of approval by the calypso audience and thence have given its name to the song itself.

Passing through a folk etymology of, let us surmise, *cariso* (French: car-rousseaux), *ruso* or *wuso* (Creole), *aliso* (Venezuelan Spanish), it eventually became established, under the growing dominance of the English language in Trinidad, as *calypso*. On the other hand it is possible that the term *kaiso* continued to be used as part of the song lyric where it carried a noncomplimentary meaning. This usage could have been translated into the Creole *sans humanité* and thence became established as a conventional way of ending certain types of calypso, especially in the late nineteenth century when the *calinda* chants of the stick-playing masqueraders were of a notoriously belligerent character. This would account for the retention of the Creole phrase as a calypso refrain out of context in the early years of the present century.[5] (E. Hill 1967, 364–65; italic in original)

I quote Hill here at length not only because he proposes such a seductive etymological kinship map for the term "calypso" but also because the "folk etymology" he charts incorporates (albeit to his own ends) the two other etymology-as-origin narratives that attribute calypso somewhat dubiously to medieval French chansons or quite plausibly to topical songs of the Venezuelan highlands (Crowley 1959a, 59–60). In fact, the influence of Venezuelan string band music instruments (most notably the four-string *cuatro*) can be heard in calypso from as early as the late nineteenth century (Campbell 1988, 12; Cowley 1996, 116, 124–25; Bethell 1998). Considering the layered history of settlement, colonization, immigration, and indentureship in Trinidad and Tobago, it would be nearly impossible to imagine a Trinbagonian aural landscape absent the resounding musical cross-influences of Native American, European, West African, Indian, Chinese, American (North and South), and even Middle Eastern music from the fifteenth century up through the nineteenth and early twentieth centuries.

Linda McCartha Monica Sandy-Lewis: A Rose by Any Other Name

Four decades hence, I focus our attention through this intricately entangled sonic milieu—rich with the music of five continents and now firmly established as a distinct music genre—upon the lifework of a particularly prominent figure in the calypso tradition. The artist to whom this study proposes to give a close critical listen is by many accounts the grand dame of calypso music: Linda Sandy, better known by her delicate (though thorny)

FIGURE 3.1 Calypso Rose, n.d. Photographer unknown.
Photograph courtesy of the personal collection of Merlyn V. Gill.

sobriquet "Calypso Rose." Born on April 27, 1940, in the hilltop village of Bethel on the island of Tobago, Lewis is the fourth of eleven children.[6] A farmer, a fisherman, and a Spiritual Baptist minister, her father, Altino Sandy, had to have had a hand for cultivation and the steady patience that abundance rewards. An Afro-Caribbean syncretic faith, Spiritual Baptism developed in part out of a US Southern Baptist tradition brought to Trinidad and Tobago by African Americans recruited into Britain's West India Regiment and Core of Colonial Marines during the War of 1812. Promised freedom from slavery and land (but only in British territories) for their service to the Crown, many of these soldiers remained in the region once their units were disbanded, combining their ecstatic spiritual practice with West African spiritual traditions by then firmly rooted on the island.[7] This Creole faith of her father's would profoundly influence Lewis's spiritual mooring in adulthood. And yet Altino Sandy's great patience with land, sea, and spirit would not have amounted to the patience of Dorchea Sandy (née Ford)—a mother of thirteen, who had lost one child young and another right at birth (L. M. Lewis 2010). Naming her daughter in part after highly decorated United States Army general Douglas MacArthur, Lewis's mother may have had an intuitive sense that her fourth child was going to be a fighter. However, neither Lewis's mother nor Lewis herself could possibly have anticipated the figurative war she would wage—as an Afro-Tobagonian woman—on an entire genre of music held firmly by men, planted deep in Trinidad, and already centuries old. Having spent nearly a decade of her life in rocky Bethel village—named for an anointed stone that would become a biblical city—Lewis was busy with the serious play of nine-year-olds when an opportunity walked right into her home, rubbed her head, and changed her life forever.

A mother longing for another child to raise—after her own son had found his way to England—the common-law wife of Lewis's uncle eagerly set sail for Tobago on her husband's suggestion that they take in one of his brother's eleven children. Lewis remembers the moment her destiny chose her:

> She [Lewis's aunt] came the Saturday and spoke to my mother. We were outside; I didn't know what the conversation was about at the time. But then, my mother called all of us in the house. So, we went into the house. They put us in a line; we were in a line standing up. And the lady—her name was Ms. Edith Robinson—she came to me and she touched my head. And in those days—when I was small—I used to suck my finger, so I had my finger in my mouth. She started rubbing my head. She says, "You want to come to Trinidad with me?" So, I shake my head [Lewis nods] meaning yes. She says, "You sure?" And I [Lewis nods again] yes. She says, "Okay, well tomorrow I will come for you and take you to Trinidad" . . . my aunt came and took me the Sunday and brought me to Trinidad. (M. L. Lewis 2007)

What a thing to be chosen for a new life—perhaps better, perhaps worse—from among your ten siblings standing at either of your shoulders. Each sister, each brother would be hoping to be chosen or perhaps wishing away the most troublesome with all the nearsighted will of a child or perhaps simply waiting patiently to return to the elaborate world of their imagination in the yard just outside. What a precocious nine-year-old, bold enough to leave all she had ever known behind and nod toward a life in a place she had never been with a woman she hardly knew. Lewis had grasped at an opportunity. And yet opportunity too comes with its petty prejudices. Lewis describes her welcoming committee at school: "The kids in my class used to taunt me. They used to say, 'Small islander, why you don't go back where you came from!' And I used to cry. Because I figured Trinidad and Tobago—despite the fact that you have to cross the ocean to get to Trinidad—well, I figured we were one. But they used to taunt me and call me 'small islander.' But after a while, I adjusted" (L. M. Lewis 2007).

Although the cruelty of adolescents is disappointingly common in T&T as elsewhere in the world, this childish mockery highlights a centuries-old tension that has made the metaphorical waters between these two islands at times quite rough. These children beg us to recall that Trinidad and Tobago—two relatively small islands when compared to Cuba or even Jamaica perhaps—were in fact coerced into a sisterhood by the British colonial government; there is no reason to believe that sharing independence and subsequently sharing a republic would allay the angst of these rivalrous siblings. Any sustained ethnographic engagement with Tobago as well as Trinidad almost immediately reveals the complex life of this tension that is at once antagonistic and quite familiar.

I dwell here briefly in this house of difference in order to emphasize the importance of Lewis's Tobagonian heritage. The scant scholarly literature that has thus far directly addressed Lewis's life and artistry has made only cursory mention of her place of birth—if Tobago is mentioned at all—some texts summarily baptizing her a "Trinidadian" (Maison-Bishop 1994; Mahabir 2001; Dikobe 2003; H. M. Smith 2004). Undoubtedly, Lewis's time in Trinidad from the age of nine well into adulthood must have had a lasting impact on her character and the character of her art; however, one cannot turn a blind eye to Lewis's first nine years in Tobago and over seven decades returning *home* regularly for kin and kind. The consummate "Trinbagonian" for having lived significant portions of her life on both islands, Lewis is quick nevertheless to sing the praises of her Tobagonian roots as a figurative battle cry against the too frequent elision of Tobago and Tobagonian cultural specificities in the popular and official discourses about Trinbagonian culture. In fact, it is precisely the shock she receives at the age of fifteen to her Tobagonian sensibilities one market Sunday in Trinidad that propels Lewis into calypso.

It 1955, Lewis's adoptive "aunt" Edith Robinson sent her to the market with six years' experience on this new island and money enough to buy the week's provisions:

> Coming through the gate—after I finished shopping—I heard a commotion. And when I turned around there was this lady running, bawling, "Thief! Thief! Thief!" . . . [at the same time] a guy was scampering through the gate. "Thief! Thief! Hold him! Hold him! He thief my glasses! He thief my glasses!" The guy snatched a pair of glasses off the lady's eyes and started running. That's the first time I ever see anybody steal because Tobagonians were not accustomed to that kind of life . . . it was new and shocking to me. So, I went home and I told my aunt what I saw and she says, "Well, this is Trinidad and anything could happen in Trinidad." So . . . I start writing and that's the first Calypso I wrote.
>
> And the lyrics are [Lewis sings]:

> Well Tobagonian boys, Tobagonian boys,
> stay on your island and rear your fowls.
> Jane went into the market to buy piece of ice
> and a fellow snatch she glasses from off she eyes.

> (*Laird 1989; Obolo 2005; L. M. Lewis 2007*)

"Glasses Thief" marked the birth of a calypsonian who was soon to steal the entire music genre. A laughing Tobagonian critique of the more metropolitan "big sister" isle, Lewis's first calypso quickly gained audience— no doubt as a measure of playful yet prideful mockery in the tradition of calypso—with Trinidad's first prime minister, Dr. Eric Williams, during a visit to Tobago in 1956.[8] Lewis herself was on holiday from school, visiting her family in Tobago. A good-natured despot, Williams encouraged Lewis to pursue the art form in a moment that remains vivid in Lewis's memory: "He [Dr. Williams] said, 'You are very good. You should be in Trinidad in the Calypso tent singing'" (Obolo 2005; L. M. Lewis 2007). Williams's enthusiasm would become prophecy a few years later when Lewis began performing in the Original Young Brigade tent, under the venerable tutelage of a calypso giant—Theophilus "The Mighty Spoiler" Philip—on Nelson Street in Trinidad's capital, Port-of-Spain. Although Lewis had originally chosen for herself the sobriquet "Crusoe Kid" (an oblique reference to her Tobagonian heritage via Daniel Defoe's 1719 fictional novel *Robinson Crusoe*, believed to have been based, in part, on Tobago), the managers of the Original Young Brigade tent rechristened her "Calypso Rose"—hoping to justify this change with the perfumed proposition that "the rose is the mother of all flowers" (Mahabir 2001, 416; L. M. Lewis 2007). And like a keen thorn, the name stuck. From 1963 to 1965 Lewis would perform in the tent of the internationally legendary calypsonian Aldwyn "Lord Kitchener" Roberts. And by 1966, Lewis would be performing alongside another renowned calypso master and friend, with whom she frequently shares the spotlight—Slinger "The Mighty Sparrow" Francisco.

Although Lewis herself acknowledges that she was not the first woman to sing calypso in the tents, she is the first female calypsonian to garner significant recognition and reap the rewards for the mastery of her craft.[9] In 1963, following the local success of her calypso "Co-operation," Lewis made her first trip beyond the shores of T&T as part of a region-wide tour of the nation's calypsonians; while on that tour, Lewis outperformed eleven other male contestants (some rather well known) to win her first crown in Saint Thomas, US Virgin Islands (Ottley 1992, 6). Lewis was the new Virgin Islands Calypso *King*; she also collected the UVI Road March title for that Carnival season.[10] However, back at home, Lewis would have to wait until 1977 to become the first female calypsonian to win the national Road March title (with her hit song "Tempo").[11]

That same year, anticipating that Lewis (or perhaps another female calypsonian) could potentially win the highly coveted national "Calypso King" competition during the upcoming Carnival season, the Carnival Development Committee introduced the newly renamed national "Calypso Monarch" competition. The name change marked a new possibility in the predominantly male calypso arena, returning women—almost a century after their near exclusion from the genre—to center stage in the art form that chantuelles, female calipso singers, female drummers, female stickfighters, and female calipso dancers had helped to midwife. During the Carnival season in 1978, Lewis reclaimed this legacy, becoming the very first female national Calypso Monarch (singing "Her Majesty" and "I Thank Thee") while again winning the national Road March title (with her song "Come Leh We Jam"). The first calypsonian—female *or* male—to simultaneously win both titles in a single year, Lewis had successfully executed a calypso coup.[12] A little black girl—

the daughter of a preacher no less—with a halting speech impediment from a small hilltop village in Tobago had become the new reigning monarch in a Caribbean kingdom of song.[13] Her Majesty had made a way—her own: "I am like a river overflowing its bank. You try to stop me, I'm going to find room to pass" (Dunn and Horne 2008).

Coming to "Palet": Calypso Masculinity and the Scholar Who Refuses

A river can be a bridge—a rippling way between two shores. A swollen river, ravenous and bankless, does not cease to be a bridge, but the rushing water has another way in mind. This crossing into uncertainty is precisely the path Dionne Brand brings to life breathlessly in this chapter's epigraph: "No assurance except the arch and disappearance. At the end it might be the uptake of air, the chasm . . ."[14] Lewis is a flooded path that I entreat you here to follow, toward an expanded horizon of possibilities suddenly visible because we seek it with a newly crafted compass (Alexander 2005, 8). I offer a steady introduction to calypso music and Calypso Rose—carefully situating the latter in the former—as a means by which not only to orient us for the analysis that follows but also to prepare the way for a potentially disorienting remapping.

In his article "I Lawa: The Construction of Masculinity in Trinidad and Tobago Calypso," the revered calypso scholar Gordon Rohlehr provides the most prominent scholarly treatment—though brief—of Lewis's calypso "Palet" (1968).[15] And it is Rohlehr's analysis of the song that has prompted, in part, the present close engagement. I do not intend to represent Rohlehr's arguments in full here, but his handling of phallic symbolism in calypso and its correlative import for Trinbagonian masculinity opens an irresistible space for intervention into the gendered politics of calypso masculinity. Although Rohlehr quite accurately identifies the calypso music genre as one of the most elaborately articulated archives of the nation's masculinity, he stops short of being able to recognize that masculinity anywhere but in the male body.[16] If for him masculinity is always already confined to the male body, then it comes to function as little more than a euphemism for maleness. This troublesome conflation of sex (maleness) and gender (masculinity) all too subtly undermines Rohlehr's reading of the "phallus" and its relevance for his interpretive approach to Lewis's "Palet."[17] Unfortunately, Rohlehr anticipates a significant shortcoming in Caribbean masculinity studies, which

FIGURE 3.2 Calypso Rose and Loren Doris, Saint Thomas, US Virgin Islands, 1966. Photographer unknown. Courtesy of the personal collection of Merlyn V. Gill.

has yet to insist upon this sex-gender distinction and instead leaves largely unchallenged the presumption that masculinity is the rightful and "natural" domain of men only.[18] In this particular instance, a sex-gender conflation is matched by an equally troubling correlative conflation between the phallus and the penis that I must first address in order to recuperate one of the principal leitmotivs for masculinity—the phallic symbol—that Rohlehr uses (to tell an origin narrative of calypso masculinity) and refuses (just when it seems that Lewis too might possess it).

A Working Definition of the "Phallus": Risking Unnatural Synecdochism

Without getting lost in psychoanalysis, and mindful that the very act of attempting to define the phallus is invested with its own highly charged philosophical and psychoanalytic implications, I nevertheless attempt here a working definition of the term (Butler 1993, 60). The most effective means by which to explain this rather counterintuitive concept may be to begin by clarifying what the phallus is *not*. Despite its original Greek etymology, the phallus as redeployed by Freud and Lacan is summarily *not* the penis:[19] "In

Freudian doctrine, the phallus is not a phantasy, if by that we mean an imaginary effect. Nor is it as such an object (part-, internal, good, bad, etc.) in the sense that this term tends to accentuate the reality pertaining in a relation. It is even less the organ, penis or clitoris, that it symbolizes. . . . For the phallus is a signifier . . . it is the signifier intended to designate as a whole the effects of the signified, in that the signifier conditions them by its presence as a signifier" (Lacan 1977, 285). I turn reluctantly to Lacan in an attempt to clarify a term whose popularity is largely indebted to his elaboration of Freud in his invited lecture "The Signification of the Phallus" delivered at the Max Planck Institute in Munich, Germany, in 1958 (Lacan 1977). Neither imaginary apparition nor material object, I understand the Lacanian phallus—informed by Lacan's elaborate forays into the baroque science of semiotics—to be a symbolic ideal with no adequate direct object referent; in essence, an idea without a material thing to which it corresponds. Following Freud, Lacan is ostensibly clear about the fact that the phallus is not the penis and yet there remains an inherited slippage in his work that threatens the very conflation that both theorists claim to resist (Silverman 1992, 91–93, 96).

Feminist theorist Kaja Silverman contends, "It is self-evident that as long as the phallus is designated the 'image of the penis,' and the penis as the 'real phallus,' there can never be less than an analogical relation between those two terms, a relation which often gives way to complete identification" (Silverman 1992, 99). Thus, to concede that the phallus symbolizes the penis—as Lacan indicates in the passage above—reinforces a hierarchy of signification that holds the "actual" object (the penis) above its symbolic referent (the phallus). It is significant that Lacan aligns both penis and clitoris as objects symbolizing the phallus, but this inclusion does not trouble the tempting conflation Silverman contests. Instead, to think of the penis (or clitoris) as phallic symbols, but not the phallus itself, attempts to restore this sense of the phallus as an exclusively symbolic object to which a multitude of material objects refer but none can ultimately fully contain. It is perhaps the case then that Rohlehr's phallus-penis slippage is an inherited one, inherent in the term as long as one fails to clarify the distinction.

If for the purposes of this analysis the phallus is to be read as the whole constellation of associations ("the effects of the signified") that any particular society or culture invests in the penis either directly or indirectly, then the closest we can come to defining the phallus is as a web of meaning that includes but is not contained by the penis. In other words, through an elaboration ad infinitum about the penis, one approaches asymptotically a definition of the phallus. Therefore, the penis is better understood as a synecdoche for the phallus, a part representing a larger whole within which it is incorporated; instead of the phallus symbolizing the penis, the penis is understood to be merely one—granted perhaps the most familiar—of a multitude of phallic objects (including the clitoris). Furthermore, I propose that masculinity is perhaps best defined as the whole constellation of associations that any particular society or culture invests in the phallus— either directly or indirectly—constituting a web of meaning that includes the web of meaning that defines the phallus but is not ultimately contained by it. In other words, the phallus is a synecdoche for masculinity. Therefore, the penis-phallus and phallus-masculinity synecdochic relationships come not merely to mirror each other but rather to form an interpretive chain in which the penis is a synecdoche for the phallus, which is in turn a synecdoche for masculinity.

Before this proposition begins to stiffen too comfortably, I turn to feminist theorist Judith Butler, whose critique of the slippage between phallus and penis that haunts Lacan's text is premised in part upon denaturalizing the very synecdochic chain that I propose. I am referring here and in what follows primarily to Butler's seminal essay "The Lesbian Phallus and the Morphological Imaginary," which appears in her *Bodies That Matter: On the Discursive Limits of "Sex"* (Butler 1993). Returning to critique Freud in her critique of Lacan, Butler emphasizes that there is nothing "natural" about this penis-phallus-masculinity linkage through associative webs of meaning; these relationships are of course the result of social construction, but what is important about this social construction for Butler is that it is inevitably unstable and thus requires constant reaffirmation often through the repetition of precisely the slippage that Freud, Lacan, and Rohlehr commit over and over again (Butler 1990; Butler 1993, 89–90). Butler contends that it is an impotence of the imagination that compels us to interpret the phallus always and only through the penis, naturalizing a link between the two that is the result of our association and not of nature. Although Butler concedes that materiality (where the penis resides as a morphological structure) and language (where the phallus resides as a symbolic element of discourse) are coconstitutive, fully embedded and implicated in each other, she uses this mutuality to refuse the presumption that the penis is the "real" phallus; in fact, for Butler, the phallus is fundamentally transferrable property (Butler 1993, 59–69).

Perhaps what is most immediately relevant for this discussion is Butler's proposition (by evoking the possibility of a "lesbian phallus") that the imagination—or imaginative play with this transferrable phallus—can trouble that unstable link between the material and the ideal by disrupting the seemingly natural order precisely at its moment of repetitive reaffirmation:

> The lesbian phallus may be said to intervene as an unexpected consequence of the Lacanian scheme, an apparently contradictory signifier which, through a critical mimesis, calls into question the ostensibly originating and controlling power of the Lacanian phallus [or the thinly veiled penis, in Butler's estimation], indeed, its installation as the privileged signifier of the symbolic order. . . . Consequently, it seeks to open up a discursive site for reconsidering the tacitly political relations that constitute and persist in the divisions between body parts and wholes, anatomy and imaginary, corporeality and the psyche.
>
> . . . Precisely because it [the phallus] is an idealization, one which no body can adequately approximate, the phallus is a transferable phantasm, and its naturalized link to masculine morphology can be called into question through an aggressive reterritorialization. (Butler 1993, 86)
>
> . . . The phallus (re)produces the spectre of the penis only to enact its vanishing, to reiterate and exploit its perpetual vanishing as the very occasion of the phallus. This pens up anatomy—and sexual difference itself—as a site of proliferative resignifications. (Butler 1993, 73–74, 86, 89)

Butler's rhetorical posturing with the "lesbian phallus" is intended to function as a discursive intervention that through insisting upon the coherence of a seeming contradiction actually opens up a site within which to identify implicit gendered presumptions. If the phallus is kept true to its symbolic form, there ought to be no reason why one could not imagine the phallus without men; this discursive reterritorialization vanishes the penis while simultaneously enacting the recuperative potential of "reiteration with a difference" (Muñoz 1999). The phallus seemingly displaced is thrust into such high relief that it, in effect, becomes more clearly identifiable. Queer studies scholar J. Jack Halberstam has made a nearly identical case for masculinity, arguing that the notion and enactment of "female masculinity" actually provides the clearest picture of masculinity as such (Halberstam 1998).

If Butler's proposition is an invitation to see the phallus more clearly, then this engagement with Butler hopes to focus that vision even further by calling into question the universalist pretensions of Butler's purview. In other words, I propose with this analysis a particular cultural location from which to challenge the tacit politics of unsituated gender theory. If Butler is aggressively reterritorializing the phallus by emphasizing its transferability, I am here aggressively territorializing that attempt by calling for an attention to place, a mindfulness of cultural territory. A Trinbagonian cultural geography—like any specific cultural geography—contains its particular landscape of phallic objects, at once contributions to and reflections of a national phallic symbolism. It is by virtue of recuperating one such phallic object—the *palet*—that Calypso Rose's playful gender politic becomes audible.

The Uses of the Phallic *Palet*

Referring to an iced lolly (or popsicle), the word *palet* is most likely a French Creole rendering of the French *palette* from the Latin *paleta* or *paletta* for a flat instrument or flat-bladed tool with a handle used for a variety of purposes. The French *palette* would thus refer primarily to a thin, flat board or tablet; it was these flat boards with holes for thumb grips that were often used by painters to mix their colors. So, the term "palette" would come to refer also to a range or selection of colors or any assortment of items from which one chooses.[20] The word "palet" may have been used to describe the frozen lolly because of the flat wooden stick inserted into them, the assortment of colors or flavors from which to choose, or perhaps a syncretic mix of both. Unable to deny the seductive double entendre Lewis writes into her tune "Palet," Rohlehr is nonetheless unwilling to recognize these palets as potential phallic objects; he insists, despite figurative incongruence, that Lewis's song is suggestive not of fellatio but of cunnilingus (Rohlehr 2004, 368). Perhaps the most plausible explanation for this misalignment of a metaphor is to be found in Lewis's own female morphology; the specter of her vagina appears to prevent Rohlehr from recognizing Rosie's phallic treats. If Rohlehr is unwilling to buy the phallic palet, this is in large part because of his unwillingness to relinquish the phallus-as-penis conflation already dissected. There is a deeper refusal that Rohlehr enacts, perhaps not altogether consciously, which turns a deaf ear to an implicit critique that Lewis nimbly disseminates through the penis-phallus-masculinity synecdochic chain. Relying precisely on an impotence of the phallic imagination, Lewis levies an indirect critique of the penis; this is a critique that simultaneously allows Lewis as Rosie-the-palet-vendor to repossess the phallus (a reminder of the long tradition of female stickfighters and the symbolism of this practice) while allowing Lewis as calypsonian to playfully critique the penis through an understated yet ribald mockery characteristic of the music genre.

If Rohlehr's history of masculinity in calypso foregrounds the stickfighter's *bois* as the symbolic object representing the penis and thus alluding (quite unnaturally) to a particular kind of Trinbagonian masculinity, then the historical presence of the formidable female stickfighter—a specter that even Rohlehr cannot avoid—inadvertently demonstrates the accessibility of the symbolic penis for the Trinbagonian woman willing to grab hold of it (Rohlehr 2004, 328–30, 335). By replacing the bois with the palet (a truncated stick), Lewis is able to hold the penis in song just long enough to critique it by measuring it through a more palatable phallic object. Reading the palet as a phallic object does indirect work on the penis precisely because the penis occupies such a prominent place as the unnatural phallic object par excellence. The penis-phallus slippage that Rohlehr, Lacan, and Freud allow, but which Butler and Silverman critique, is precisely the location in which Lewis inserts her intervention. This sung gender politic must be heard as part of a long oral tradition resounding with *picong*. From the French *piquant*, meaning "pricking" (the pun is instructive here), picong describes the exchange of stinging/biting/pointed humorous insults, usually between friends (Mendez [1986] 2003, 145). Lewis's loving mockery offers up the penis as a sweet treat at the same time that it snickers at its melting.

Lewis's melting phallic object—and in the tropics, the palet is perpetually melting—is a playful dissolution of the unforgiving hardness of even the most formidable erect penis. Lewis reminds us of the inevitable flaccidity of the penis, which metaphors such as "wood" and "iron"—perhaps the most common indirect referents for the penis in Trinbagonian speech and song—would pretend to obscure. In essence, the erect penis is always vanishing, never able to be the mythic, perpetually erect ithyphallus. The song's double entendre, then, is more than a mere mask for the penis; rather, it takes the opportunity of the unimaginative association of all phallic objects to the penis as a means by which to critique the sex organ. This critique is able to trouble the penis-phallus link in the synecdochic chain by demonstrating— through association with the *palet*—the failure of the penis to be the phallus. These phallic objects are returned to their rightful place, both disallowed from materializing the symbolic. The restorative rupture, sung in a Trinbagonian key, alludes to a broader potential for masculinity, unmoored from the penis or the phallus as an always already penis. Hearing "Palet"—reminded of the central female presence (in song, dance, and fight) as part of Rohlehr's aggressively masculine, precalypso, kalinda tradition—only sweetens the gender picong, pointing to a long tradition of assertive female masculinity in Trinidad and Tobago. This tradition is Lewis's rightful inheritance, and she preserves it with a full-throated forcefulness.

CHAPTER 4

Calypso Rose's "Palet" and the Sweet Treat of Erotic Aurality

Released in 1968 on a seven-inch album and shortly after on an LP, Linda McCartha Lewis's song "Palet" provides the sonic focal point of this chapter:

PALET
Composed by Calypso Rose
[Lyrics transcribed by the author]

Is palet I selling
to make a shilling.
Is palet I selling
for meh living.
That is my occupation
to be a palet woman.
Stretch out yuh hand I bound to stop;
I selling meh palet from ten cents up.

If you hear me:
(Chorus:
Palet, palet, mama.
À la petite palet, mama.
Palalalala lala lalet!

FIGURE 4.1 Calypso Rose, n.d. Photograph by John Crow. Courtesy of the personal collection of Merlyn V. Gill.

À la petite palet, mama.
Palalalala lala lalet!
À la petite palet mama.)

I going all about—
East, West, North and South.
All by the college
I have meh privilege.
I have all kind of flavor:
orange, pine, soursop and vanilla.
I pushing meh cart all through the rain.

Coming down I singing the same refrain.

If you hear me:

(Chorus)

From Sunday to Monday
and public holiday,
I selling meh palet;
Me ent have no limit.
Any time that yuh thirsty,
yuh could suck a palet from Rosie.
I don't care if meh business bus';
I selling palet and I giving trust.

If you hear me:

(Chorus)

Through this song—as situated in the echoing history of calypso music—Lewis helps to strengthen the voice of the erotic in this analysis. In her very breath, Calypso Rose affirms the harmony among the political, sensual, and spiritual in her life (and deaths) as well as in her artistry. And it is through an interpretation of "Palet" that this chapter encourages one to *listen* for the erotic as part of a contestation of the primacy of the visual. By imagining herself as Rosie-the-palet-vendor chanting through the streets of Barataria, Trinidad—summoning customers (or perhaps the occasional sweet tryst)—Lewis puts calypso to work in the tradition of the genre, without forcing the pleasure out of her play. This play takes the quotidian "real" and imaginatively recrafts it so effectively that it pointedly calls into question that reality as a means by which to challenge the listener's imagination.

This chapter is curious to consider what it might mean to conceive of the erotic as a hermeneutic with which to listen? As an interpretive frame in the service of calypso critique, the erotic compels us to listen for the political, the sensual, and the spiritual in precisely those places where other kinds of listening, informed by other epistemological moorings, have turned a deaf ear.[1]

Sensual Symbolism: On the Pleasures of Giving Suck

Although Lewis's usage of the *palet* as metaphor is a form of sung critique, we ought not to ignore the fact that its sweetness—its desirability—persists nevertheless. One of the long-enduring gustatory tropes of Trinbagonian sexual discourse, the figurative "sweetness" of the penis is quite literally actualized by its competing phallic object.[2] There is a sensuality to the palet as phallic object that ought not to be subsumed by the previous discussion of the palet as an intervention into a certain parochial gender politics. It is mostly for the pleasure of giving suck, after all, that Rosie sells her palets. The shillings she earns from selling her popsicles are ostensibly the way that Rosie makes her living, but we learn by the last couplet of the song that successful business is not after all her motivation: "I don't care if meh business bus' [if she goes out of business], I selling palet and a giving trust [credit]" (Lewis [1968] 2005).[3] Even if it drives her out of business, the palet vendor is willing to give a bit of sweetness on credit. It is this emphasis on sweetness for sweetness's sake that encourages a discussion of pleasure.

The easiest point of entry for this engagement with pleasure and desire is via the palet's most obvious and seductively apt homonym: *the palate* or the roof of the mouth. The repeated "palalalala lala lalet!" of the chorus requires a repeated delicate tap of the tongue against the palate that not only calls attention to the homonymic pair but also quite intimately pinpoints the exact space the palet is called to fill. This flirtatious coaxing with sung speech emphasizes the highly sensual quality of vocality:

> Not only is the voice felt to be a key marker of identity, representing a person and (usually) carrying the machinery of (always gendered) subject-positions embedded in language, but its site of production— mouth, throat, vocal tract—is associated with a range of sexing tropes. As an apparatus that organizes the passage of energy from inside the body to outside—"desire as articulated air"—this site bears obvious comparison to sexual organs. The mouth, from childhood an important erogenous zone, both sucks in and ejaculates, opens and closes, articulates flows and reproduces them endlessly. In this sense, voice can be figured as standing for, that is, metonymically, our sense of sexuality as such. (Koestenbaum 1991, 205–34; Middleton 2006, 92–93 [Parenthesis in original])

Though not a reproductive organ, the mouth is most certainly an erogenous zone—in *oral* sex (when the mouth comes into direct contact with the genitals) as in *aural* sex when the voice is used to enhance arousal (or even re-place actual physical contact). The voice then as "metonym for sexuality" is saturated with the sensuousness of the space from which it flows and the uses to which it can be put. Even outside of an explicitly sexual encounter, the resonance of sensuality still echoes in the voice. A whole range of subject-positions, gender perhaps being the first cue for which we listen intently, nearly always marks this voice—much like the sensuality it summons.

In "Palet," four lines of its six-line chorus repeatedly call particular at-tention to the fact that both the singing mouth of the palet vendor and the desired mouth of the potential customer are decidedly female. Lewis sings: "*Palet, palet,* mama. *À la petite palet,* mama. *Palalalala lala lalet! À la petite palet,* mama. *Palalalala lala lalet! À la petite palet,* mama" (Lewis [1968] 2005). Echoing the pushcart vendors she grew up hearing seduce their customers with song, Lewis uses song to imagine herself as one such character—but with one substantial difference. Lewis recalls: "There used to be three people passing down 12th Street—well, [really] the whole of Barataria on Saturdays and Sundays. It's the nuts man, the pudding man and the palet redoman. I never saw a female [vendor]. It is only when I came to America that I saw females pushing their cart in the summer to sell snow cones. But in Trinidad, it was men [who] used to be selling, pushing their carts and selling" (L. M. Lewis 2007). Lewis's own female body converts this simple French Creole refrain into a declaration of possibility for Trinbago-nian female same-sex desire.[4] Significantly, Lewis does not imagine herself a male palet vendor—even in spite of never having seen a female vendor when the song was written—nor does she substitute a masculine vocative for the feminine "mama." The sensual pleasure of giving suck is here shared between women over the sticky, melting sweetness of a phallic symbol that critiques the penis's claim to the phallus while offering a pleasurable bridge for a female same-sex encounter. This is precisely the desire shared between Caribbean women across metaphor and symbol to which Omise'eke Tins-ley insists on lovingly returning our attention over and over again in her groundbreaking treatise *Thiefing Sugar:* "In this project, I focus on . . . how same-sex eroticism enters into the history of sexual labor in the Caribbean as a practice by which women take control of sexuality as a resource they share with each other" (Tinsley 2010, 20). The palet as melting phallic symbol subtly vanishes the penis, which is precisely the tool (pun intended) that is presumed to render female same-sex coitus at best unfulfilling (quite liter-ally) and at worst simply impossible. At the throbbing center of a potential female same-sex encounter, Lewis is able to brandish phallic symbolism without the penis getting in the way.

Rumor and the Dilemma of Vanishing Desire

By playfully encouraging the conflation of Calypso Rose and Rosie, Lewis indirectly centers her own same-sex desire. And yet despite this and other quite explicit references to her same-sex desire in song or in conversation, Lewis's highly visible presence as a calypso icon has ironically rendered her largely invisible as a same-sex-desiring Caribbean woman. The rumors of Lewis's lesbianism have been perhaps most notably addressed—if only briefly—by noted Caribbean feminist and literary scholar Carole Boyce Davies: "Calypso Rose had to survive through rumors of lesbianism and for years had a distinctly androgynous appearance; her stage performance was similar to some male calypsonians like the Mighty Sparrow, including dancing and projecting the microphone as phallus. Singing songs of men, sex and satisfaction . . . Rose ably competed with her male peers" (Davies 1990, 183).

Although Davies hesitates to make a definitive statement about Lewis's sexual orientation, she leaves undisturbed the perhaps unintended implication that Lewis's (strategic) masculine stage performance has burdened the artist with seemingly unfounded accusations of lesbianism; Calypso Rose must "survive" a veritable assault upon her popularly presumed heterosexuality. Undoubtedly, Lewis's distinctly boyish appeal offstage, her alluringly handsome charm, and her comfort with an understated—though certainly still stage-worthy—feminine elegance while performing inform Davies's reading of Lewis as androgynous in the true etymological sense of the term.

And yet this unique calypso female masculinity has contributed only to the wide (hushed) recognition of Lewis's same-sex desire. This recognition has often to do with Lewis's refusal of the trappings of "appropriate" Trinbagonian femininity—a femininity that is often assertive, forceful, gregarious, and quite vocal but still adheres to a very particular aesthetic that Lewis largely avoids. The artist's shortly cropped natural hair, her affinity for pants (flamboyant though they may be), and her discomfort with high heels are by now hardly surprising for her audiences in T&T. In fact, over the course of her career, Lewis has become well known for quite literally kicking off her heels rather early—often right after her first or second song—in her stage performance to the noticeable delight of her expectant loyal fans. Although

Lewis frequently sings and dances through most of her sets barefoot, she always steps out on stage first in heels. Decades on, perhaps these now not-so-high heels are worn in anticipation of her entertaining ritual or perhaps Lewis has found a way to compromise her own comfort onstage and certain sociocultural expectations about respectable femininity for the always seemingly disreputable female calypsonian. Nevertheless, even if her fans have come to normalize Lewis's "odd" gender expression as largely idiosyncratic, this signature style would have early on set Lewis apart from femininity in T&T. This position adjacent to appropriate femininity is made even more troublesome by Lewis's obvious corporeal comfort with an ostensibly effortless culturally coded masculinity that is often suave, colorful, and rum-shop sociable.

Davies does attend to the false premise that sexual orientation can be read through one's ability or inability to perform her gender "correctly." As it is most often the case that sex (as reproductive morphology or chromosomal makeup) and sexuality (as sexual practice) are hardly seen in public spaces, gender becomes the cue for these other categories that in actuality have very little to do with gender at all; here Davies is in alliance with feminist theorist Judith Butler's contestation of a *heterosexual matrix* that compulsorily aligns sex, gender, and desire based primarily on gender's legibility (Butler [1990] 1999, 3–44). A person's masculinity (gender) does not make it inconceivable that she may be female (sex), nor should it carry the presumption that she will be attracted to femininity (sexuality)—though she may be attracted to feminine men perhaps just as easily as she may be attracted to masculine (wo)men or androgynes of either sex or perhaps all of the above. And yet, if we are unwilling to explicitly consider the possibility that Lewis may in fact be a same-sex-desiring woman, we indirectly perpetuate a discomforting compulsory heterosexuality (Rich [1980] 1986, 23). This silence disallows Lewis's same-sex desire, which is not directly correlated to her masculinity, but present nonetheless even in spite of her courting (or more often tenderly chastising) men in song.

In an ironic turn that exposes one of the principal weaknesses of textual citatory practices in academe, Davies's unintentional and perhaps even reluctant reassurance that the rumors of Lewis's lesbianism will prove false has taken on the infectious quality of rumor itself. Cited repeatedly in scholarly texts as *the* definitive (non)statement on Lewis's sexual orientation, Davies's attention to Calypso Rose's sexuality might be read a bit more generously as an attempt to side step the matter altogether by noting that Lewis has had to confront rumors of lesbianism regardless of her actual, unstated sexual orientation. However, as is the case with the most resilient rumors, the least generous or subtle readings have proven to be the most infectious (Dikobe 2003, 112; Guilbault 2007, 109).[5] In the limited existing scholarly literature as in the abundant popular media accounts of Lewis's life and oeuvre, the assumption of Lewis's heterosexuality has only been further justified by her marriage in 1966 to Aubrey Lewis in Puerto Rico. Adrienne Rich—lesbian feminist writer and dear comrade in thought to Audre Lorde (who also married and bore children with a man)—reminds us that opposite-sex marriage does not a heterosexual woman make. Rich emphasizes that same-sex-desiring women who do choose to marry men may do so for strategic purposes and not in an effort to divorce themselves from their same-sex attractions (Rich [1980] 1986, 23–75).

Lewis—who in 1966 had been working illegally as a performer in the El Calypso club in Puerto Rico—explains the circumstances of her nuptials:

> One night, immigration came and took me because I was working there illegally. . . . So, they told me I could not perform there anymore and they confiscated my passport. They gave me until September the 29th to come in for an interview [and make a case for] why I should not be deported.
>
> I was in my room one day and there was a knock . . .
>
> (And I was the asset to the club; everybody came there asking for the lady of calypso.)
>
> So, he [Aubrey Lewis, a US citizen and the piano player in the band] comes. He says, "You want to [get] married?" I say, "Ma—who?!" He says, "[Get] Married?" I say, "Ma—who?!" again. He says "I could marry you and they cannot put you out" . . . I say yes and . . . we [were] married the next day.
>
> . . . So, when the date for the hearing arrives now . . . [an immigration lawyer began] "Ms. Sandy (because I am "Sandy" by maiden [name]), we are here today because we want to know the reason why you should not be deported." My husband stood up; he says, "She is not 'Ms. Sandy,' she is 'Mistress Lewis.'" So, they ask, "Who are you?" And he puts [forward] his credentials with the marriage license. He says, "I am her husband." . . . So, they say, "Okay, well, Mr. Lewis, you know what to do. This is her passport. You know what to do. Thank you."

And we got up from there, he held my hand and escorted me down the road . . . we were not living together, but he was a very nice guy.[6] (L. M. Lewis 2007)

True to established historical precedent, Lewis's marriage of convenience proves inconvenient for an accurate reading of her same-sex desire. And yet recognizing the strategic importance of Lewis's marriage ought not to amount to discrediting it as a complete sham. Beyond her married name, Lewis maintains ties of affection and responsibility to the family into which she married; her de facto adoption of her husband's young daughter (from a previous relationship) as her own has kept Lewis to this day in close contact with the woman—now residing in the Bronx—and her five children, who Lewis showers with all the affection grandmothers reserve for their grandchildren.

It is precisely this complexity of familial and romantic relationships that makes same-sex desire among Caribbean women so seemingly difficult to recognize except perhaps when lives and love depend on it (Silvera 1996; King [2005] 2008, 194). More often than not, though, the surreal seeming invisibility of Caribbean female same-sex desire persists despite the materiality of flesh, palms pressed, thighs touched, chests breathing in unison or the flutter of kisses on her body's tender seams (Tinsley 2010). Nearly drowned in swirling silences that swallow like the sea, desire still speaks its name with tongues on fire (Elwin 1997).[7] Speaks still this tongue even when the words vanish:

I am a . . . how you call the word? How you call the word? I have a friend or a lover and she always says, "Your work—because this is what you love—your work comes first." But I still divide [my time between] my work [and] my lover and we are domestic partners. This year will make it eleven years I've been married. . . . September will make it eleven years. We were married in a church in California—a Catholic Church.

I say, look, this is my life. I was raped when I was eighteen, so I have never had a man in my life. I was raped by three men when I was eighteen years of age. So, I never had any man in my life and because of that all the Calypsonians [would taunt me by] saying, "She's a lesbian" because I never slept with any of them. Thank the Lord for that!

So, I made it final [by deciding to "marry" my long-term partner] because this is my life. My family accepts me—my whole family knew . . .

my aunt had known—the lady who raised me; she accepted me. Everybody accepts me. And who can't accept me, chew them!

[People in T&T] do talk about me, but I don't care. They may talk, but
not in a negative way. Not in a negative way at all. If they saying negative,
it's probably in their mind. But they still hug me, they still kiss me, they
still bow to me. Oh yes! Every time I arrive home [to T&T] they bow to
me, man! (M. L. Lewis 2007)

Lewis finds a way around using any particular language to describe her sexual
identity; she offers instead the language of ellipses that Trinbagonians use
as effectively as the spoken word. There is an entire vocabulary for silences,
ways to indicate with different kinds of noiselessness what it is exactly that is
unspoken, ways to mention the unmentionable outside of language.

During the course of the interview, I dared not offer "lesbian" or "homosexual" or "queer" to fill the space that Lewis perhaps intentionally left un-
filled. Instead of attempting a word to describe what she *is*, Lewis shifted
quickly instead to describe whom she *has*. Her long-term, long-distance "domestic" partnership with her female partner (who still lives in California),
consecrated by a particularly welcoming Californian Catholic Church, is a
testament to Lewis's comfort with her same-sex desire, so her hesitance to
name that desire comes from somewhere other than self-denial; perhaps the
available terms are not as effective as the silence. A rape and breast cancer
survivor, Lewis holds as tightly to the love of her partner as she does to her
love of life, a life lived her way to the tune of her own happiness, uncluttered
by any voiced referent for her affections.[8] The fact that her family acknowledges and accepts her bold resolve to live and love in a manner that brings
her joy can only be a boon to Lewis. Later in the interview, upon asking her
explicitly if she would describe herself as a "lesbian," Lewis quickly smiled at
me and with all the ease of a breath said, "I am happy" (M. L. Lewis 2007).
And as best as I can tell, she *is* happy. She is calypso royalty. She must have
a sense of the rumors circulating always just out of earshot—the pests of all
royals it seems—but she is comforted by knowing that her subjects still bow
lovingly before her. She must be comforted too by the fact that rumor feeds
upon secrecy and shame; this over-seventy-year-old woman, who has found
love with another woman, suffers neither. What happens to a rumor once it
proves true?

Spirit Visions: Healing, Mourning, and Ascension

Spectral rumor—and the rituals of ellipsis that surround it—calls attention to the vanished in Lewis's "Palet." This attentiveness to the ghostly in turn summons a force that goes unmentioned explicitly in Lewis's "Palet" but which remains a haunting presence in her consciousness and thus also in her artistry: the spiritual. In the same text in which he discusses Lewis's calypso, Gordon Rohlehr provides a very material bridge between our conversation about sensuality and this engagement with spirit when he points us toward a spiritual object imbued with potential phallic symbolism. When Rohlehr likens the penis to a *poteau mitan* (the "center post" of Haitian Vodou), he inadvertently encourages the alignment of a sensual and spiritual object (Rohlehr 2004, 334, 365–66). At the literal and figurative center of Vodou ritual and ceremony, this axis mundi—usually a wooden pillar or platform permanently lodged in the ground in the center of a worship site and intended to provide a bridge between the spirit world and the mortal world—also appears in the Spiritual Baptist religion as the sacred center pole (Lum 2000). This bridge provides a figurative way between the flesh and the spirit at the same time that it defies the presumed distance between them—a defiance corroborated by a belief in spirit-made-flesh (or the soul "housed" within the body). The shift here from sensuality to spirituality is always temptation to shift back. This crossing is perhaps best represented by the connotative journey of the "fetish" from a spiritual object invested with supernatural force as described by early ethnographers to an object saturated with displaced sexual energy as adopted by psychoanalysis. The intimacy between sensuality and spirituality is familiar—even if avoided— conceptual territory, but for Lewis, this marriage of passion and spirit was also *familial* territory.

The curious daughter of a minister, Lewis recalls asking her father about the source of his religious fervor, which appeared to reach beyond the written word: "My father couldn't read. One day I asked my father, I said, 'Dad, you cannot read, but when you get up on the pulpit you preach [Lewis holds onto this word and pushes into it for emphasis] so much like you ate the Bible.' You know what he told me? 'They does come and teach me in the night.' So, my father was a real spiritual man. I came with the spiritual seed in me" (L. M. Lewis 2007).

A reverence for the unseen sown deeply in Lewis's consciousness from an early age, it perhaps seemed more likely that she might become a church leader than a calypso singer. Presumed diametrical opposites in the Trinidad and Tobago of the 1940s and '50s, the lewd song of the calypsonian and the righteous song of the Spiritual Baptist were thought to serve opposing spiritual allegiances; one could not serve God and the devil at the same time (Lewis quoted in Obolo 2005).[9] And it seemed from her earliest days in the Tobagonian villages named for biblical cities that Lewis had been touched to serve God:

> Before I could have comprehended, my father [used to] tell me that I born with a gift. Because when I was small—before I went to Trinidad—many times they miss [did not know where to find] me; and when they miss me, they have to go hunting the whole of Bethel and Bethlehem looking for me. . . . Some spirit used to come into me and lead me away.
>
> . . . One time when they found me, they found me in a house in Bethlehem—the whole yard was full of people. I was healing people . . . I know that I have a sort of a spiritual gift within me. (M. L. Lewis 2007)

Whether a true child prophet laying hands on the people of a village aptly named or a precociously young girl anxious to minister like her father in a village destined to hope for the birth of a Caribbean Christ, Lewis had indeed been lead by a compulsion beyond her reckoning to the faith of her father.

Although she was baptized into the Spiritual Baptist faith as a child, it would not be until adulthood that Lewis would formally begin her spiritual trials on a quest to deepen her faith:

> We—the Spiritual Baptists—when we go into the inner chamber to gain higher wisdom, we go into a room and are locked away for a certain number of days—it depends—five days, seven days, two weeks or whatever. . . . I did it five times. I was mourned five times. We call it "mourning," when you seclude yourself from the carnal world and you go to the spiritual world. And all you do is pray—all you do is drink water and pray. You are fasting. There is light, but your eyes are banned. And the reason why your eyes are banned is as a symbol that you are banning yourself from the sight of the world.
>
> So, I mourned five times. The first time I mourned, I was a healer. The second time I mourned I was a Diver and Searching Warrior [spiritual roles in the faith]. The third time I mourned, I'm a Mother. The fourth, I'm a Mother; the fifth time, I'm a Mother. A "Mother" is at the head . . . which means to say that I can put bands on my children [offer sacred

protection and guidance to followers]. I can baptize children, put seals and signs on them, and mourn them [initiate newcomers in the faith]. I am very high up there. (M. L. Lewis 2007)

Having mourned the death of her carnal self five times and each time experiencing a transfiguration of spirit, Mother McCartha cherishes her role as the religious leader she was perhaps called to become through various phases of enlightenment.[10] These phases are revealed to the fasting suppliant during the mourning ritual; devotees come to see themselves—their spiritual selves—more clearly as they journey toward higher planes in the religious tradition. First seeing herself as a healer, Lewis believes she has been given the ability to soothe pain with her touch; as a diver and searching warrior in her second journey into her sacred self, Lewis believes she was chosen to be a spiritual warrior tasked with scouring the seafloor in search of lost spirits in order to guide them home. One cannot help but imagine these diving warriors of this syncretic religion having been given the task of walking the watery underbelly of the Middle Passage looking for those unsettled souls, presumed to be roaming the fathoms of the Atlantic yearning for a way home. In her final three crosses into the realm of the otherworldly, Lewis is thrice called spiritual *mother* though she has had no child of her own flesh. She has indeed reached a rarified height in the Spiritual Baptist tradition.

And yet her ascension in the faith has not distanced her from calypso; quite to the contrary, she attributes her talent for reading music, writing music, and playing the piano and the guitar to divine intervention. A musical autodidact, Lewis has never taken a single lesson to augment her craft and yet her musical virtuosity amounts to little less than the miraculous outcome of finding a passion, hearing a message, and claiming a medium. In fact, her spirituality is in many respects the nerve center of her musical sensibilities; Lewis is forthright about her devotion to the Spiritual Baptist faith *and* to calypso music (Guilbault 2007, 110). It is impossible then—in her estimation—to imagine her or her artistry disconnected from a firm religious foundation:

[A strong Spiritual Baptist rhythm is] in me, I born with it [laughter]. As I told you, I born a Baptist . . . I am a Baptist from birth. I grew up with it and don't matter what I do, it's within me. And there is something that one has to know, you cannot hide from that fact—you may try to take me out of the religion—[but] . . . the spiritual aspect, they can't take that out of me because no matter what, it is here in my singing, in my speaking . . . my

spiritual background and who I am spiritually also help me to create. . . .
I believe my music does something for people. That's why I feel that I am
a messenger. (Lewis quoted in Ottley 1992, 11–12)

Suspicious of essentialist presumptions about an ontological spiritual self,
one might best hear Lewis's statement as a testament to the centrality of
her spirituality even in the very sites that seem so far removed from conventional religious terrain. Lewis is quick to affirm the devoutly spiritual nature
of even her "sex songs," among which "Palet" might be coyly considered.[11]
This potential alignment of the sensual as spiritual and the spiritual as sensual is precisely the recalibration that our new erotic in part encourages. If
the messenger offers her testament in song, then she conveys it via what is
perhaps the most miraculous and sensuous ancient instrument yet known:
"The singing voice as a musical instrument is inexactly understood because
its mechanism of production is invisible. Voice is vibration: an exhaled
stream of air passes from lungs to larynx, where it opens muscles like valves
that regulate it, resist its escape and, vibrating, produce sound: to resonating
cavities of the upper body and head; and to the pharynx where sound and
tone quality is shaped, pitched, projected—'placed' by mouth, tongue, palate, lips" (Randel 1986, 926–27, 749–50; E. Wood 1994, 27).

The voice acquires a mysterious sensuality here not merely because of its
relationship to the mouth—as Middleton earlier attested—but also because
its very production is here defined as an intimate and yet transcendent vibration. Flesh and breath—the mortal body and this divine life-giving breeze—
resist or give way as muscles tighten and relax in the soft folds of the vocal
tract. Lewis's voice carries within it—in speech or in song—the echoes of a
harmonized sensual-spiritual that resonates beyond a false dichotomy between the sexual and the religious.

Heeding the Call: Erotic Aurality and the Afterlives of Faith

A "sex song" that deeply engages sensuality alongside a gendered politic and
a spiritual consciousness, "Palet" offers us a conceptual three-part harmony;
this political-sensual-spiritual (our erotic) functions as a hermeneutic
measure, an interpretive frame that encourages a particular listening technique. Influencing the way that Lewis listens to the world and thus the way
that she interprets the world through her artistry, the erotic also expands our
range, permanently broadening our listening capacity. Calypso Rose's exten-

sive musical oeuvre—since the age of fifteen, when she first began composing, Lewis has written well over eight hundred songs—provides a myriad of opportunities to listen closely for our erotic trinity. And yet if one were inclined to dissociate the political, sensual, and spiritual in an interpretive approach to these songs, a tempting tripartite taxonomy might be the result: *political* songs, *sex* songs, and *religious* songs neatly separated just so. However, this severing represents not only a less challenging—and perhaps less interesting—interpretive frame but also reinforces the troubling distinctions that have made the erotic (not simply as a euphemism for the sexual) so difficult to recognize. The challenge undertaken here is precisely to hear the political in the sensual in the spiritual as part of a single sonic landscape.

This critical challenge broadens our interpretation of the erotic in an artistic work that seems confined to the sexual. More than simply another aesthetic language in which to read the erotic, song provides a different interpretive mechanism that loudly contests any attempted primacy of the visual in the present elaboration of the concept. This analysis of "Palet" listens for the erotic as keenly as the Carnival chapters looked for it. Having emphasized attention to the unseen as fundamental for an engagement with the spiritual, I would be remiss to rely solely on the visual for an explication of our newly redefined erotic. A conceptual and interpretive frame—dependent on an interconnection among the senses no less vital than the interconnection among the political, sensual, and spiritual—the erotic demands a sensory matrix for it to exist at all. In fact, although "Palet" is a decidedly aural text, it nevertheless alludes to various mechanisms and methods of perception—from the sweet fruity delight of the melting phallus to the otherworldly voice of a Spiritual Baptist mother—extending beyond even the expansive gaze of the mind's eye. Lewis's life and artistry are not merely testaments to a new gospel of eros; her creativity challenges the concept to listen more keenly even as she puts it to work.

And Lewis has a lot of work to do still as an artist and as a spiritual mother. With an at times quite surreal faith feeding her passion for life, Mother McCartha does not fear death as long as she is certain that the purpose of her living has yet to be fulfilled. In fact—as she recounts at some length with the steady confidence of the faithful—she has died many times:

I am a person with strong faith and strong beliefs. I believe in God—the Father, the Creator—who made heaven and earth. . . . I am here for a purpose and my purpose will be fulfilled before I leave this earth. And

I know I'm not leaving this earth right now because I've died so many times and I've come back . . .

I died in this house [Lewis's home in New York City] on Saturday. . . . I normally go to sleep on my side, but for some reason I was on my back. And I wanted to breathe, but I couldn't breathe. I'm willing myself to breathe. I'm willing myself to start moving my toes. And I'm praying. I am falling deeper deeper like I'm going through a tunnel. And like somebody comes and shakes me and I go [Lewis exhales forcefully] and a big breath comes out of my mouth. And for the whole day on Saturday, I was weak and I had pains in my chest. And it's not the first time it happened to me . . .

I died years ago in my house in Trinidad. I went through the tunnels so many times going down, going down. And when I came out, I came out in a green pasture. I saw a grave. And . . . the grave it had three flowers [on it]—roses—all white. I stood up and I watched the grave; I asked myself, "I wonder who is buried here?" And a voice says, "Jesus." [Then] I was going to the hall—there was a long building on the right and I was walking going to that hall—and my grandmother tells me, "Go back! Go back! Go back! Don't come here! Your time isn't ready yet." And when I woke up, I couldn't move from the bed because I was so weak . . .

[In] 1978, when I left New York and went to reside in California, I died there again. I was in my bed and I could see myself on the bed. I wanted to move and get up, but I couldn't. And when I looked up, I saw the Sacred Heart of Jesus. I wanted to breathe and I couldn't breathe. I saw the heart and the heart was still. I could see the veins. The heart . . . was not pumping at all. And then I start trying to raise my hand to hold the heart, to pump the heart so I could start to breathe and I couldn't.

Then I start going through a hall again and I start smelling tobacco in the hall. And when I look, I see my father's mother now smoking a pipe and she says, "Don't come here. Go back." And when I caught myself [awoke], my right foot and my right hand were stretched off the bed— stiff like a buckram. This left hand was stretched up and I had to wait a long while for this hand to come down for me to take this hand to lift my right hand and put it on my body.

So, I'm not afraid of death. Death is only a door that you pass through. I know I have something to do on earth and I'm doing it. And anytime you see . . . I gone, I finished doing what the Lord wants me to do. (L. M. Lewis 2007)

Lewis, who suffers from chronic heart problems, has survived three heart attacks that she believes each correspond to one of her three deaths (L. M. Lewis 2009). But how can it be possible to die more than once?

In an illuminating prospective study on cardiac arrest and patient awareness during resuscitation, Dr. Sam Parnia—a specialist in pulmonary disease and critical care in the School of Medicine at Stony Brook University—helps us to understand the scientific possibility of multiple deaths:

> Contrary to perception, death is not a specific moment but a potentially reversible process that occurs after any severe illness or accident causes the heart, lungs and brain to cease functioning. If attempts are made to reverse this process, it is referred to as "cardiac arrest"; however, if these attempts do not succeed it is called "death." In this study we wanted to go beyond the emotionally charged yet poorly defined term of NDEs [near-death experiences] to explore objectively what happens when we die.[12]

A transnational study of over two thousand cardiac arrest victims—from which Dr. Parnia's team culled one hundred and forty survivor interviews—in the United States, the United Kingdom, and Australia, the Awareness During Resuscitation (AWARE) Study scientifically defines the death process while also identifying verifiable instances in which cardiac arrest patients remained sentient even once they were technically dead momentarily. Survivors' accounts of this death have previously been presumed to be hallucinations or illusions corresponding to the moments either before or after heartbeat cessation, but the AWARE Study provides leading evidence that consciousness can persist despite the formal death of the body. Parnia continues, "Furthermore as hallucinations refer to experiences that do not correspond with objective reality, our findings do not suggest that VA [visual awareness] in CA [cardiac arrest] is likely to be hallucinatory or illusory since the recollections corresponded with actual verified events" (Parnia et al. 2014, 6).

Calling for further investigation of the experiences surrounding death, the study uses visual cognizance as an indicator by which to assess mental alertness during death; but what if their study could also open our eyes to another kind of now scientifically verifiable vision? A significant step in the direction of medically proving awareness beyond the carnal body, the AWARE Study may also hesitantly point us toward what might be thought of as "spirit perception" or "soul awareness," a consciousness that can step or be pushed beyond the boundary of the body. Dr. Parnia and his colleagues

FIGURE 4.2 Calypso Rose and the author, Roatan, Honduras, 2006.
Photographer unknown. Courtesy of the author.

might disagree with this interpretation of his findings as vehemently as his detractors disagree with the findings themselves, but the question remains: in an out-of-body experience, who or what exactly are we without flesh, without blood, without breath? One potential answer: perhaps we are spirit.

Might it be conceivable that Lewis's detailed recollections of her deaths indicate an awareness parallel to that of the patients in the AWARE Study—who could accurately recount visual and experiential details about their surroundings even while they were technically dead. What if Lewis's experiential purview while dead simply extended beyond the reality of the room she was in toward another realm of the real that science finds it more difficult to verify? I cannot hope here to absolutely disprove the secular presumption that Lewis's experience during cardiac arrest was little more than hallucination, but Dr. Parnia's study does encourage just pause; it challenges a dismissive presumption that death and extracorporeal awareness are mutually exclusive. How do we come to terms with that which lies just beyond the reach of secular logic, especially if few patients or researchers find the courage to document these experiences with any consistency or accuracy? Despite presumptions that this disembodied consciousness must be fictive delusion, Lewis is devout enough to believe and insist otherwise. Nevertheless, her spiritual encounters—actual or allegorical—are unavoidable moments of transcendence as inspired as a marvelous dream, as persuasive as a chilling prophecy. Whether or not one believes that Lewis dies thrice or embarks on spirit journeys to return from those nearly definitive deaths is perhaps not as vital as hearing in her parable a profound belief. A faith that manages to draw together Catholic symbolism (the white rose Trinity, the Sacred Heart) and a decidedly female ancestral presence (her grandmothers) guides Calypso Rose at the crossroads where the life of dreams and the afterlife meet. This faith compels Lewis to live on toward the fulfillment of her divine purpose. And Linda McCartha Monica Sandy-Lewis knows that this purpose is in her music, in the open sound circle it represents. The erotic—a harmony of the political-sensual-spiritual—welcomes us into that ring and clears a space for us to shout.

From Far Afield / A QUEER TRAVELOGUE (PART III)

JULY

7/23/07

She asks me to suck on her breasts. She is a handsome woman. I keep her right nipple firmly in my mouth. But that was all near the end of the night, easing into early morning. First, Japana's arrival—black lesbian salvation. She crosses the "sea bridge" to Tobago, a fathomless bridge between two islands that know each other not nearly as well as one might suspect for being one nation. This is only her fourth time in Tobago, but she has been to Suriname and Canada and so often to Barbados that she code switches playfully from time to time between beers. Every move she makes draws more and more attention to that masculine beauty turned soft around her mouth. Her chipped-tooth smile is passionate and ravenous. I see her first at the port, lording over introductions between the two friends she's brought with her and Senna—the black American I was also expecting. I know immediately that the next three days will be Japana's, uncontrollably hers. She has brought with her a *dougla* man whose nerdy masculinity is confounded by his sexy confidence—Loma. I will see him much later in the nude. With Loma, Japana also brings his best friend—Olive. She is a barrier, but a pretty one; she is sweet and sometimes scandalous. Olive would probably fuck Loma if he gave her the chance (but she might just as easily fall in love with Japana if our bisexual suspicions are correct). Of course, Olive can admit none of this aloud despite having once had a bisexual best friend. And she simply refuses to see that her current best friend—Loma—is a gay man in relentless pursuit of sex with men. This refusal is encouraged by Loma's unwillingness to admit his homosexuality to Olive alone. He's hunting "tops" I gather from his questions. Perhaps he is this direct only on holiday. Masterfully, he is as shameless as he can be behind his best friend's back. I am driving them around. I take Japana and hers to their guesthouse. It is not a guesthouse at all really in any formal way, but it is cheap, private, and does not look altogether uncomfortable. I take Senna to my grandmother's house and her guest bedroom. He is paying to stay by the night and that exchange stands tall and forbidding between us. His is a coy sexiness. And it seems he's not yet discovered his naked beauty because he insists on wearing clothes even though his relationship to them is awkward at best. Awkward not for his movement—though that too sometimes—but because of the fall of the fabric over his ample behind and his concave six pack that could be a paunch if you're not seeing it in the flesh . . . but not that just yet. First, a night spontaneous. We end up at The Deep, an underground club that is nearly in the sea. Dancing, we lay claim to the space, and the alcohol keeps the few other unsuspecting patrons dancing in our periphery. In our raucous circle, men are dancing together. The sparse dancers beyond us barely seem to notice; certainly, no bottles take flight. Splitting, shaking, challenges, we hard wine, bend backs, jump up close-crotch and pull away laughing. We laugh wide-mouthed, holding our collarbones in ecstatic mockery of the affront we must be. We are orbiting Agouma, and he is anything, everything but ashamed. His mischievous bald head, his flaming charisma, he is drinking too much and making magic with this evening. Everyone has had more than enough. But Japana has a plan. As we pile back into the car, she parcels us off—pure sex in mind. Ditay has stopped talking about himself just long enough to notice Senna again and again and again, to dutty wine for him without us realizing, to split for him same way. I drop Senna at Ditay's place with a promise to return. He is horny enough to trust me, horny enough to stay. We drop Olive at Agouma's for protection and make more promises. That leaves Loma and Japana in my bed. She strips us, gives us orders, fondles our penises, and watches close to see what will happen. We are naked, stark naked, and drunk—but not nearly as drunk as Japana. We kiss and kiss and kiss—his tongue is the most insistent I have ever experienced. We are two men on exhibition. Japana—our eager voyeur—is a dominatrix of sorts, a bald-faced puppet master. Neither of us cum. Eventually, she settles into a chair near the bed and falls asleep. But just before that, Japana asks me to suck her breasts. I attach my lips momentarily to her right breast, tasting the nipple with my tongue. That is all. Just before the sun catches us, we return for Olive. She is sitting in Agouma's living room, feverishly willing the minutes by. Agouma is passed out in his bed. I return Japana and hers to their guesthouse that is not one. Then I pass for Senna. He is fresh from Ditay's arms and as uncomfortable in his clothes as I remember. But his body seems to ignore this—if only briefly—when he stands still and does not laugh. Day clean and we return home. I cannot imagine two more days with these people. Tobago was never so eventful. I'm sure I won't survive this.

OCTOBER

10/17/07

I dreamt of violence. Pointed, sharp-edged, unfolded. Wounds and tight grasps. A swift push. Punctuated physicality. Perhaps this is a premonition. Or maybe this violence is a reworking of the vivid stories Susi has told me of suffering Vervine's abuse. A Vervine of multiple personalities, she's convinced, a Vervine who needs psychiatric help. Her "wife" Vervine is a compulsive liar, and that I can nearly believe. I have heard her weave light lies. I have known her to get caught talking small things into being. But that is how the dramatist deals with this life that is mostly lies we tell and believe. The violence: a shattered car windscreen, a cuff or two on a hardback lesbian, and insults that are perverted truths not completely unrecognizable. Susi tells me all this on the phone, all about this woman I have known longer than I've known her. And I've known Vervine just long enough to nurture a certain caution with her, a certain distance. I do not love her less, but I recognize her passion. I know that her creative mind is boundless, her ambition thirsty. Still, I have not heard Vervine's side. I ask. This is what she tells me: Susi tries to replace her with a twenty-one-year-old woman. Vervine refuses. Instead, she uses her best weapons—a bit of truth and an audience—to put on a show. Talking sex in the road—who suck cunt last night, who taking white man prick. I hear her mouth curled deviously around these words even now through the phone. Vervine is a fierce performer, a fierce lesbian, a fierce black woman, a fierce black lesbian performer, and she is dangerous with words. I wonder about the lies unfolding. What is lie, what is truth anyway? Perhaps she doesn't have leukemia, hasn't had a bone marrow transplant, wasn't raped as a young girl? And yet, what to make of a lie that's believed long enough? A con artist, a performative presence, silver-tongued woman struggling to be an artist—an openly lesbian artist—in a world that seems to have no place for that, no place comfortable enough for Vervine. She is a complexity. The on-again/off-again between Susi and Vervine is a saga, a fully-grown lesbian soap opera, and I wonder if it will ever end. Will one have to kill the other? Is that killing close? Susi is off of her antidepressants. Vervine is desperate for money and affection. Will they go to the grave together? Naively, I do not want to believe lesbians capable of such brutality. Still, I ask more questions, stepping into conversations with both women bracing myself for the worse.

10/24/07

I catch my first glimpse of him majestic at the kitchen island—royalty marooned in a no man's land. His locks alone are too much to see at once. The rest: a sensuous abstraction—all angles and cheekbones, the sweet promise of a too-even smile. He is chiseled, stunning: Kojo Piray. His name is a misfit, discomfortingly plain. Whoever named this man had not intended for him to be so remarkable; that name was for disappearing. And anyway, the first name already had an owner—here in queer T&T at least—a vicious queen, a brutal thing of beauty *Ms.* Kojo Papai. "Kojo" seemed wrong, but perhaps it is the name that summons the violence, whispers for blood. At first meeting, though, he is divine—a strong Spiritual Baptist, feet grounded, head uplifted. He sings for me and I am primed to believe anything after that. His is one of those powerful voices trained through pain. Agonizing pain and a blinding devotion to music make voices like his. His voice fills the living room effortlessly as he sings down his repertoire. Time stops to listen. Song after song after song in quick playful succession, I am enthralled and he is slowly circling for the kill. Over six feet of man, he is lean and steady in his late thirties—thirty-seven he would reveal later, and I blush for him, thereafter avoiding the topic. Do not misunderstand me. He is a beauty at this age, but to imagine him in his twenties is to go breathless—the kind of man whose attractiveness swoons both sexes indiscriminately. All this enchantment on the very first night we meet—Wednesday, October 17. I remember because Wednesdays is karaoke at the Tobago Hilton. And I promised Vervine the day before that he could stay the night with me if he came for karaoke, if he came to escape Trinidad for an evening. But really, with Vervine, there is no way to say "no" and mean it for long. Still, I am skeptical about this voice coming to stay at my grandmother's house—decidedly *hers* now that I am considering allowing this man I do not know to come stay the night. I remember deciding midair on a flight to God knows where that I could not allow people over, would not allow the encroachment, the inevitable loss of control this intimacy has fostered before. Summer past, I managed it with bellyfuls of liquor and a sopping resentment, but I promised myself that had to end. Uncontrolled is how I first met the likes of Betelmi, Barbadine, Maho, Ditay . . . not again. But I had made that decision too far from solid ground to give it any weight; these midair resolutions are a fickle breeze. Quickly forgotten, these decisions do not make it through customs. So, aimlessly walking the aisles of Penny Savers—underwhelmed but reacquainting—with the mobile pressed to my temple, I decide against better judgment, past experience, respect for my grandmother, and my flighty resolve to tell Vervine that Kojo is most welcome. A fleeting friend of Vervine's, Kojo comes and that first evening exposes his overturning voice and a stab wound near his left shoulder blade. He asks me if I am gay that first night too, as if it could not be more obvious, and I—in high camp style—feign surprise and delay before smiling and confirming what he surely already knows. But he is setting me up to ask him that same question, perhaps convinced that I might not otherwise because his gayness seems so blatantly obvious even if I am old enough now to know that sexuality is never as obvious as it appears. Still, hardly one to upset a good performance, I do ask him if he is gay and try to make so direct an asking as indirect as possible with the warmest smile I can muster. He says "somewhat" or something equally vague, which means, "Yes, but not how you think" or "Yes, but not really tonight" or "Yes, but I don't want anyone to know that" or "Yes, but . . ." Such is the language of this place—a double speak, a way of saying two seemingly contradictory things at once effortlessly without either one mocking the other. It is at these very moments, in situations just like these, that smart faggots take a step back in their minds. And I consider myself a learned faggot, but my step back wasn't far enough. Really, the step back ought to have been a turn and run. But I didn't. This "somewhat" comes before the song as prelude to the story of the stabbing (I remind you that chronology is a trickster in this telling, and some might argue in this region): He had been involved with a woman. He loved her. In his telling, that love is honest; he has nothing to hide. But previous to her, he had a twelve-year relationship with a man—his ex; whenever he says his "ex" he means this man, not the woman he loved. Ironically, these two men—Kojo Piray and his ex, Canca Piray—share a surname though they could never legally marry here. But Kojo had intended to marry the woman he refuses to call his ex. That wedding day would never come. In an argument in a living room somewhere in Arima, she passes her hand over his shoulder and leaves. She has stabbed him. He realizes this only when he starts to bleed profusely. A doctor whispering about a major artery severed in his neck and the cold cold gurney warmed by pools of his own blood—that is all he recalls of the X-rays. He spends twenty-two days unconscious. Twenty-two days and still his mother refuses to see him die. He is resurrected, weak but thankful for a second life. It is at that moment of rebirth that he decides he cannot ignore the feelings anymore—and that is just how he describes them, "the feelings," and I know he means feelings for men and not *feeling* in general, but both might have been true, to think on it now in retrospect. So, newly enlivened after twenty-two days near death—a prelude to a crossing—he looks to men. This is another warning, much more subtle, but a signpost nonetheless, where smart queens turn on their heels and begin to walk away. But by this point, I am too far gone in awe of this man. Days have passed. I spend more nights than the single night promised wrapped in his arms. We climax together night and day. His penis does not match his imposing frame, but he handles it like a weapon, blunted, uncircumcised, pushed past its curve up inside. . . . I remember—just before he orgasms and I follow—my long-lost decision to be celibate for a time. Come and gone. This island changes everything. Barbadine, Tref, Ditay, Banda, the school girls Banda is supposed to be shuttling back and forth, a boy I do not know but whom Kojo knows well—they all come and go over the course of those days with Kojo. Roukou comes for the weekend. Friends coming to spend time, they all pass through, but only Agouma is a constant—a welcome constant. They all bring something: rum, vodka, wine, hungry bellies. They come. Kojo cooks. They eat. Roukou cooks. They eat. I buy the groceries, buy bread from the baker's hand, but I am careful not to buy too much or they will devour me too. A morning when I am ready for them to leave, ready to reclaim the living room television from the crowded desires of *blues*—a suggestive term for pornography that I have heard only here on these islands—I refuse to buy any more food. And I refuse to leave the bed. But Kojo is determined to feed. I ask him not to, but still he takes sixty dollars from my wallet. He spends his last few dollars too, he says, conveniently omitting how much that might have been. And I am almost certain this is a lie. This is another warning sign. I cringe when I check my wallet, knowing full well that I should not ignore this. But I do. Roukou cooks. They eat. Gay men come and go. Someone is always awake and the front door is always open. I am with Kojo in the other guest bedroom; I have even given over my bed. We are wrapped in each other. Occasionally, when the house is briefly empty, we have this rough hard-edged sex. He is a boy, he says; I say boys can be gentle. He is not a girl, he says; I say girls can be rough. I refuse to accept any of this as is. Seven days have passed and seven nights, 4 a.m. meets us midargument. Once a day he asks me like clockwork if I love him, and each time I smile and say "in time" or nothing at all. Each day he demands that I want him—that I have him "for keeps"—and each day I want him just a touch more, yes, but hardly for keeps. There is something about the finality of "for keeps" when he says it that frightens me. This is the last subtle warning any smart faggot would need, but by now I am not thinking clearly. But, I am not foolish enough to fall in love with him and that alone is my saving grace. Each day, without fail, he also asks for money—four thousand at first, then fifteen hundred, then five hundred. These requests are all weaved effortlessly into a story about a performing arts Olympics in Hollywood, California, where he was singled out to sing gospel for Sony Music, contracted to sing two songs for thousands of dollars. But he has to pay the lawyer and the studio here in Trinidad before he buys his ticket to go. *Trickeydadians*. The money will come right back to me once he gets to California, he assures me. And as his supposed departure deadline draws closer and closer, he becomes more and more distraught. I can maybe give him two hundred dollars; that is the most I can do. This conservative offer comes without story or explanation—a very American refusal. For his trouble, I offer something small to keep company with the blank, cold-eyed look I offer freely—these alone for him and nothing more. I can feel the tension heavy between us. The smart faggot is long gone. Kojo asks me where I am going persistently now any time I leave his side. He must be in the room I am in, touching me, caressing me. He is holding fast to me now. I attempt to leave his side mostly because the television program he is watching has begun to annoy me, but this he disallows. We have been together for seven days without pause and he complains that I am neglecting him for my friends, avoiding him for my chores. He is still playful, but becoming rougher and more imposing in that play. So, I refuse him—money, body, both mine to deny him. I admit my frustration with him and he flies into a tantrum. He is leaving, he says—he says this twice—because I am acting like he is making me uncomfortable (he is) and I do not believe anything he says (I don't). He packs to go—he has pretended at this packing before. The first time, he packed to leave the "characters" and activities I allowed around me—the hungry-eyed strangers and errant school girls, the weed and wine, the blues and vodka—but this time the blame is ours. This time, I do not ask him to stay. We are not speaking, and the house is big enough for that not to be impossible, which makes it so much more frustrating. He goes outside. I find him on the phone, seated at the end of the driveway, surrounded by bush. He says he has called for a ride. The ride never comes. I doubt he ever called one. I ask him back inside. I make up his bed. I invite him to have tea with me; we also have toast. He comes inside, sits at the isle where first I discovered him, then migrates to the couch. I open windows and put on fans so he will not overheat, but in my mind, I am through. Kind, but through. He takes to my bed in his underwear and I leave him there. I blow out the candles in my bedroom, turn down the music, turn off the AC, and turn out the light. I leave him there and prepare the guest bedroom for myself; the expectation of a good night's sleep away from him hums in me like this second bedroom's AC unit. He awakens and comes looking for me. He is upset and resolves once more to leave. It is early Wednesday morning long before sunrise. Kojo is wearing my T-shirt: I [heart] Black People. He thinks it a bit "racial"—Trinbagonian for racist—but agrees generally with the sentiment. For the third time, he says he is leaving, and now I am convinced he is not. I watch television—"In Living Color"—awaiting something. He says again that he is making me uncomfortable, and his seething anger right now is doing just that. He begins to curse and just then there is a change. I begin to feel frightened, but I am fascinated too. In an instant, he is a gorgeous wild animal. He comes closer. I do not move. He comes closer. I do not respond to his questions or respond only when it is unavoidable. He grabs me by my belt and refuses to let me go. I keep calling his name, calling his name calmly, hoping somehow to reassure myself and stop him from doing something drastic. I can feel something drastic coming. Now fear settles in my skin. He has worked for ten years at Trinidad's infamous St. Ann's Mental Hospital and because of this I suspect that he is capable of anything. He knows madness well. In his eyes, I can see that he is barely present anymore as I knew him. He asks me if I love him. I do not respond. He asks me why I don't love him. I do not respond. He asks me to say I hate him, to say I want him to go. I say nothing. He jerks me closer, pulls off my belt and pushes me onto the chaise longue. His sudden weight on my chest forces the air from me. Breathless, I think, "This is surreal." I tickle my way up out of his grasp. All of a sudden I am more tired than afraid. He starts to cry. He bemoans how his life is falling apart right now at this very moment and it is *me* refusing him, he says, that has scattered what remains. He asks himself why he came and why he can't leave again and again and again and cries. I hug him tightly, but I am afraid again and not sure what else to do. I see him clearly in this moment; he is a horrific beauty. His eyes change again. And he begins to poke me, to jab me in my ribs with his fingers first. Then he picks up and positions the metal paper towel dispenser. He is unscrewing the stainless steel rod into its sharpest parts and I know for certain then that he is preparing to stab me, I am thinking, and I want to cry. He gives me his phone to call the police. I cannot remember if 9-1-1 works here too (it doesn't; the number for police assistance is 9-9-9). Then I consider that this is still Tobago and we are still two men who have been sleeping together. He knows this already and that is why he hands me the phone; he is mocking me. I get loud. I use force. I rip one of his immaculate locks from his scalp. But I am still afraid, still feeling helpless, vulnerable. Now my mind is racing. And these frantic thoughts are keeping me safe—these thoughts and the chanting. I am chanting to Eleggua in my head, using the one phrase I can remember over and over and over as I watch him good and steady. I am asking for Spirit to guide and protect me. And I'm watching him with another vision, a deeper vision. He steps away for a moment. I breathe. He comes at me again. He threatens me with karma this time just before he asks again and I finally tell him yes I want him to go. It is 4 a.m. He marks the time and I mark his threat. But I am too assured of karmic justice to be shaken by it. I want him to leave. I want this to end. He is incensed that I am "putting him out." I am still afraid. He threatens to break things, to "mash up things inside of here," he says, and goes to start, but doesn't. I am silent. I am trying to be powerful. I push past him to my bedroom, get my phone, force it on and call Agouma. I am so relieved when he answers that I almost forget where I am. He is half-asleep, but willing. He comes over. He is tired and humorless. But after some talk back and forth, he escorts Kojo out. I am so grateful that I give him money to give Kojo for his boat ticket back to Trinidad. I close the door. I lock it. I check the lock once, then again. I cannot sleep. Agouma is coming back. My mind is chanting backward over all that just happened; I am trying unsuccessfully to ease myself out of this fear. Kojo has left, but he is not gone completely. I light a white candle and a stick of incense. I change the sheets. I am thinking softly now, cautiously trying to step around him in my mind. I cannot bear the thought of him and the heavy realization that this abuse is too often preface to comas, prison sentences, and funerals. I bury that thought in my first deep breath of the morning—my gratitude, a litany.

10/28/07

Last night set up she self to accommodate both a lime *and* a party—only a difference of degree and location separating them. This seems overly ambitious for Tobago's gay community, especially on a rain drenched evening, but few are deterred from either. First, Coraili Regosa's birthday lime: he hosts it just after his birthday at his flat in Sherwood Park with that view, that phenomenal view, out toward where the island's hem falls into the sea. The company, mixed—gay and straight. This much is apparent from the entryway. A carload of gay men, we arrive together—Barbadine, Ditay, Agouma, Tref, Mazay, Rito (whom I have just met). Banda is driving, but true to form he's not coming inside. Everybody knows him and Coraili don't go down good with each other, don't take to each other's blood, don't sit well on each other's heads. The heterosexuals mark their territory with talk of politics and their tone of voice. Or they keep to their corners in silence, baiting the camp performance with a smile or chuckle here and there, now and again. More and more talk, more corners claimed, a few jokes laid out flat, old animosities unearthed by rum and reburied with a shift in attention. Coraili is reveling in his spotlight. Nobody drinks too much. There is a half-hearted birthday song, a mediocre cheesecake cutting, and then we leave. We walk down the grand hill and wait for our ride. A gang of gay men, we are strutting, laughing, parading down the middle of the road in the middle of the night in this very residential corner of Tobago. No curtains flutter, no lights go on, but at this hour, at this volume, everyone is watching and listening so closely that each sound could be a symphony. But *we* are disharmonious. We reach the main road. Banda—our driver for the evening—is returning, but in the meantime we entertain ourselves with the passing cars and our hidden audience. "Bullermen Take Over Tobago," someone declares the headline and we all laugh loud and wide in agreement. Some dance to songs on their mobile phones—Lady Saw is our featured artist tonight, but other rambunctious dancehall tunes occasionally challenge her reign. This is a kind of rude boy music for an impromptu batty bwoy gathering. Banda is on his way. The rain holds up. Banda is back. We are off again, pressed into his car that flings itself around on the road carelessly. Some of us sit on laps—laughing and complaining—but finally we are all singing Cher at the top of our lungs and this feels surreal, a caricature of itself. We stop for cigarettes, then continue. Do you believe in life after love? Whitney's response: it's not right, but it's okay. We arrive at the house rented for the party. Brand new, it is nearly a minimansion, a playhouse without furniture, an immaculate space. The new pool is still very rough around the edges, but it is being filled out back. One of my cousins is here; he is the only one I know of in Tobago at least. There is hardly a place in T&T far removed from family—blood, chosen, or imposed. My cousin is huge—all height and belly, dark complected, and quite the slut if gossip is to be trusted. Gay family. This party is his. There is food I will not touch and drinks not meant to impress. The lights are too low and then off completely. Men who, of course, know each other dance close or grind up on one another. Other small groups of men chat near the windows or outside over a cigarette. Couples, friends, or curious bodies go upstairs where there is more light. I do not. There are rooms and beds up there I am told. Those of us below mark these ascents, keeping mental tabs on who is climbing the stairs to *do up* whom. One never knows what sorts of information will serve one's interests later. More music, more drinking, more dancing in the darkness. Dawn begins to threaten the sky. The party is all men until two women arrive; I have seen one of them before, and the other I have not. Then the party is ending and the drivers are returning. We make our way into cars—this time less confined—and home as the sun gets comfortable in the sky and prepares to hot up a new day.

10/30/07

Yesterday afternoon, I was leaving Kadd's Supermarket. It used to be one of the only markets in Tobago. Now it has succumb to a half-rotten nostalgia. Still, it occasionally surprises me with choice finds like Stolichnaya vodka or Scotch-Brite heavy-duty kitchen sponges or the elusive *Guardian* newspaper or the puppy food the dogs actually eat. As usual, the smaller of my grandmother's dogs, Celine—whom everyone calls "Blackie" because she is, but I never do because I find such lack of imagination slightly irritating—follows me. This she does only when she knows I will be coming right back; how she knows, I don't know. She is often a conversation starter, so on leaving the market, I expect that the man trying to get my attention wants to tell me something about her or ask me if I am breeding. I always want to say, "No, not dogs, not humans. I am most certainly *not* a breeder!"—or maybe that has only now occurred to me as something I might say with a swift smile. The man sits on a beer crate blending right into the front façade of the shop. His face is awash in liquor and sunshine. He extends his coarse swollen hand and introduces himself—Dais. He would not be handsome even if he were sober. I can see that much plainly. Standing opposite Dais, his buddy— an Indo-Trini, maybe a dougla—is handsome though even with the liquor distorting the simplest of his movements. Yes, he is indeed handsome— "Robocop." I could never bring myself to call him that, but this is the name he gives. I quip that surely his mother did not give him that name and he in passing tells me his true true name is Paye. Dais is far far gone in drink and I think it's the vantage point of broad daylight drunkenness that prompts him to finally voice the question his eyes have been asking all along: "Tell me something—are you gay?" It is probably obvious to him though he pretends it isn't, but I check with him anyway. I ask with as little aggression as I can manage if I *look* gay. Paye then—with the help of Dais—explains almost defensively that "fucking guys" is no big deal. And that is just how he says it. Paye is most vocal, regulating his stage whisper depending on who is leaving the shop. "I'd fuck a guy," he says, and I wonder under what circumstances he would. There's nothing wrong with homosexuality, they assure me. They invite me for a drink. I refuse genteelly. I am as suspicious as I am curious. Perhaps they just want a little company now that the Hardwine they've been nursing is coming to an end. I will not stay long enough to figure out their true intentions. They tell me to take their numbers and I do with no intention of calling either. Paye wants to know if I am going out on Friday and I have not thought so far in advance. If I do go out, of course, I do not intend to inform them. I walk away. The dog follows. But the conversation stays with me. I spend a good while considering their eyes, those bloodshot eyes, tearing from the sun and the overproof rum. What to make of two men— presumably straight—watching me so intently, curious enough to approach me with a kind of indirection? If I had said yes to that drink, there is no telling where the afternoon might have gone. But I am cautious. They are drunk. But they do set me to wondering if their finding no fault with fucking men is a common sentiment within the larger population of men here in Tobago or in Trinidad. I have heard this jokingly suggested, but never seriously confirmed. Still, I cannot up to now figure out why these rum buddies choose me to attempt to bull or befriend or bobolee. Their boldness surprises me. Their willingness to strip away embarrassment, extend palms, and make my flaming acquaintance in big daylight outside of a once great market astounds me.

CHAPTER 5

A Generation with AIDS

A History, A Critique

For more than three decades, direct or indirect association with the human immunodeficiency virus (HIV)—and the acquired immune deficiency syndrome (AIDS) toward which this virus can lead—has placed an indelible stigma on gay and bisexual men. And from the very beginning of the pandemic, these men have shared that stigma with Caribbean peoples—especially Haitians—in the region as well as in the Caribbean-American diaspora. These presumably distinct sites—one of sexual orientation, and the other of geographical and cultural orientation—would early on form ground zero for ostensibly preemptive and epidemiologically informed social assaults. This infectious discrimination was supposedly intended to prevent these presumed locations of disease incubation from becoming vectors by which illness might spread to the "general population." Despite presumptions in the US American public health literature of the early 1980s, these locations were not nearly as distinct as might have proved comforting to many concerned with the etiology of this new disease; in fact, self-identified gay Caribbean men provided a largely ignored bridge between them. Contemporary discussions of gay and bisexual male communities in the Americas or nearly all communities in the Caribbean region—recognizing, of course, the unavoidable overlap between the two—are not only haunted by this linked history of stigma but also deeply influenced by a continuing joint struggle against the spread of the epidemic. Therefore, this particular engagement with same-sex-desiring communities in the Caribbean region is doubly compelled to address HIV/AIDS.

The following analysis begins by mapping the state of the HIV/AIDS pandemic in the world, in the Caribbean region as a whole, and specifically in Trinidad and Tobago from its earliest reports up through the first decade of the twenty-first century. Then the survey shifts perspective just a bit in order to focus on outlining the perceived threat that the HIV/AIDS pandemic poses for the troublesome population of "men-who-have-sex-with-men" globally, Caribbean-wide, and specifically in T&T. An opportunity to address various statistical and terminological inexactitudes, this examination of the pandemic lays the necessary groundwork for the introduction of a Trinidad-based HIV/AIDS prevention and support NGO in the chapter that follows. But we must begin at the ostensible beginning; and for the medical establishment, that is the contested moment in sunny Southern California in the early 1980s when HIV/AIDS definitively entered the medical literature.[1]

HIV/AIDS: A Brief History

On June 5, 1981, the first published report in the medical literature on AIDS appeared in the Centers for Disease Control and Prevention's (CDC) *Morbidity and Mortality Weekly Report* (Gottlieb et al. 1981). Although this alarming new syndrome would not receive its official name from the CDC until over a year later, there was little doubt that UCLA immunologist Dr. Michael Gottlieb and his colleagues had discovered a new disease in five Los Angeles–based "active homosexuals," each with symptoms of pneumocystis carinii pneumonia in addition to other rare opportunistic infections usually exclusive to severely immunosuppressed patients (Gottlieb et al. 1981). Still, the world would have to wait until 1983 for the French virologists Françoise Barré-Sinoussi and Luc Montagnier—at the prestigious Paris-based Institut Pasteur—to report in *Science* the discovery of a new retrovirus believed to cause this curious new illness (Barré-Sinoussi et al. 1983).[2] And it was not until 1986 that the International Committee on the Taxonomy of Viruses settled upon a name for this new etiological agent and formally introduced the globe to the "human immunodeficiency virus" (Coffin et al. 1986). Few among that international group of renowned scientists could possibly have anticipated the scale of the transnational health crisis already well underway.

By the end of the first decade of the twenty-first century, the most accurate statistical reports from the Joint United Nations Programme on HIV/AIDS (UNAIDS) confirmed that there were over thirty-four million people across the globe estimated to be living with HIV (UNAIDS 2012, 6, 8). Nevertheless, UNAIDS epidemiological data of the period assured us that the global spread of HIV appears to have peaked between 1996 and 1997, when approximately three and a half million people were newly infected. And as a result of the long interval between seroconversion and symptomatic disease, annual HIV-related mortality appears to have peaked in 2004, when just over two million people died of AIDS-related complications (UNAIDS 2009b, 7–8; UNAIDS 2012, 12). Still, the HIV/AIDS pandemic is far from over.

In 2001, in response to the persistent spread of the disease worldwide and thirteen years after the UN's World Health Organization launched its Global Programme on AIDS, the United Nations convened its first General Assembly Special Session on HIV/AIDS (UNGASS). At this meeting, representatives of the then 189 UN member states reaffirmed the pledge that world leaders had made the previous year—when they named reversing the global HIV epidemic one of the world's eight Millennium Development Goals for 2015—by unanimously endorsing the Declaration of Commitment on HIV/AIDS. The following year, these member states determined the specific core indicators to be used for monitoring the time-bound pledges of this global resolution (UNAIDS 2008b, 12–15).[3] And in 2006, at the five-year review of the 2001 Declaration, the UN member states underscored their commitment by delivering a UN General Assembly Political Declaration on Universal Access to HIV/AIDS Prevention, Treatment, Care and Support, which set 2010 as the global universal access target (UNAIDS 2008b, 12–15). Midway between this strengthened Declaration and the 2010 target, the UNGASS received the highest number of country progress reports since annual reporting began in 2003.[4] These HIV/AIDS progress reports from 2008 submitted by 147 nations—roughly 76 percent of the by then 192 UN member states—included the reports of all thirteen Caribbean countries, marking the region as the first to provide 100 percent compliance with the global monitoring strategy (UNAIDS 2008b, 12, 16, 18).

The Tropical Epidemic

The Caribbean region has considerable incentive to cooperate with UN-
AIDS to systematically monitor the spread of HIV/AIDS. By the end of the
first decade of the century, the Caribbean was more heavily affected by HIV
than any other region outside of sub-Saharan Africa even though the region
only accounted for a minute share of the global pandemic—approximately
0.7 percent of the global total of people living with HIV and 0.8 percent
of new infections worldwide (UNAIDS 2009b, 53). It was the Caribbean's
estimated 1 percent adult HIV prevalence rate—well above the average
prevalence rates for any of the other eight global regions (after sub-Saharan
Africa) for which UNAIDS collects statistical data—that summarily set the
region apart (UNAIDS 2009b, 11; UNAIDS 2012, 15). And yet national adult
HIV prevalence in the region actually extended across a significant range,
from approximately 0.1 percent in Cuba to an estimated 3 percent in the
Bahamas (UNAIDS 2009b, 53). In terms of overall HIV prevalence in that
moment, though, Haiti (and primarily Haitian-occupied sugarcane plantation camps or *bateyes* in the Dominican Republic) still shouldered—then
as now—the largest burden in the region with prevalence rates as high as
5.5 percent to 12 percent early in the decade (UNAIDS 2008a, 3–4). Significantly, since 1986, the principal reported mode of HIV transmission in the
Caribbean region has been unprotected heterosexual intercourse, especially
among migrant populations (Bond et al. 1997, 7; Camara 2000, 2; World
Bank 2001, 15; Kempadoo [2004] 2009, 4; UNAIDS 2008a, 2, 5; UNAIDS
2008b, 53; UNAIDS 2009b, 54).

However, the very first cases of AIDS-related illness and death were
recorded exclusively among gay and bisexual men in the region (Camara
2000, 2; Kempadoo [2004] 2009, 3). There appears to be a consensus in
the scholarly literature that AIDS in the anglophone Caribbean was first reported in Jamaica in 1982 (Narain et al. 1989, 43; Camara 2000, 2; Cobley
2000, xvi; Reddock and Roberts 2009, ix). Nevertheless, there is unavoidable evidence that both directly and indirectly refutes this claim, instead
indicating that AIDS in the anglophone Caribbean was in fact first documented in 1983 in Trinidad. In an article published in 1983 in the *West Indian Medical Journal*, the lauded Trinidadian physician and University of the
West Indies professor emeritus of medicine Dr. Courtenay Bartholomew
and his team reported on two cases of male homosexuals suffering from
AIDS-related opportunistic infections. It is in this report—published in the

region's premier peer-reviewed medical journal housed at the University of the West Indies' campus in Jamaica—that Dr. Bartholomew first makes the claim that his is the very first report of AIDS in the Commonwealth Caribbean (Bartholomew et al. 1983).[5] It stands to reason that if a case of AIDS-related illness had been discovered in Jamaica a year earlier, the editors of this preeminent journal coming directly out of Jamaica would hardly have allowed Dr. Bartholomew such a claim. Nevertheless, there is the distinct though unlikely possibility that a report of AIDS in Jamaica in 1982 might have taken more than a year to reach the medical literature. Even if this were the case, there can be little accounting for the fact that no apparent contestation prevents Dr. Bartholomew from authoritatively echoing his claim in 1984 in *The Lancet* (Bartholomew et al. 1984, 103), in 1985 in the *British Medical Journal* (Bartholomew et al. 1985, 1244, 1245), and in 1987 in the *Journal of the American Medical Association* (Bartholomew et al. 1987, 2604).

It is highly improbable that the editorial teams of three of the most highly regarded, meticulously peer-reviewed, and widely circulated medical journals in the world simply missed the report that predates Dr. Bartholomew's discovery. Is it possible that Jamaica's first case of AIDS could remain a secret from the international medical community for five years? It bears mentioning that much of the scholarly literature that confirms the discovery of AIDS in Jamaica in 1982 rests this claim almost exclusively on an article submitted by the Caribbean Epidemiological Center (CAREC) that appears in the 1989 *Pan American Health Organization Bulletin* (Narain et al. 1989).[6] Although this article does propose that the "first confirmed case of AIDS in the Caribbean occurred in Jamaica in 1982," it provides no official citation for this confirmatory case in the medical literature (Narain et al. 1989, 43). In fact, the article names Trinidad as the first site in the Caribbean to begin HIV antibody testing in 1985 and cites Dr. Bartholomew's study of 1987 as one of the first serological studies conducted in the Caribbean region (Narain et al. 1989, 42, 46, 49). If the first case of AIDS had been discovered in Jamaica in 1982, why would Jamaica not have been the priority for HIV antibody testing and sero-surveillance studies? A closer look at the statistical data in the article reveals a curious trend in Jamaica's figures; the single AIDS case reported in 1982 is followed by no reported cases in 1983, one in 1984, four in 1985, six in 1986, and thirty-three in 1987. In stark contrast, the number of reported AIDS cases in Trinidad totals eight in 1983, nineteen in 1984, forty-five in 1985, seventy-seven in 1986, and eighty-six in 1987 (Narain et al. 1989, 43). Nevertheless, it may be the case that Jamaica suffered early from a plague of underreporting, which helped a seemingly furtive epidemic escape official observation. However, there can be no denying that this new species of epidemic was swiftly recognizable in the official literature in Trinidad. Despite the findings indicating otherwise, it may still have been the case that AIDS was reported in Jamaica in 1982; however, it is undeniable that the AIDS *epidemic* in the anglophone Caribbean came to view first in Trinidad.

HIV/AIDS: A T&T Perspective

In the more than three decades since Dr. Bartholomew reported the first cases of AIDS-related illness in Trinidad, the nation's Ministry of Health has reported on the devastating impact of the disease on this relatively small twin-island republic. In fact, T&T reported its highest number of AIDS-related deaths to date in 1996—when 256 people succumbed to the disease—and its highest number of new AIDS cases to date in 2001 when 440 people acquired the syndrome (NACC 2006, 6). Late in the first decade of the twenty-first century, the nation's estimated adult HIV prevalence rate was approximately 1.5 percent and—consistent with regional surveillance data—was reported to be principally the result of heterosexual exposure on both islands (NACC 2006, 3, 13; NACC 2008, 4; UNAIDS 2008b; T&T 2013, 7).[7] Nevertheless, the overall decline—despite minor fluctuations—in reported HIV infections, AIDS diagnoses, and AIDS-related deaths in T&T since 2003 is in large part the result of increasingly accessible antiretroviral therapy regiments. Beginning in 2002, the government supplied these medications free of charge to just over half of all adults and children in whom the virus had reached its most advanced stages (NACC 2006, 6, 10; NACC 2008, 6; UNAIDS 2008a, 6).

From its launch in 2004 until its dissolution in 2011, the National AIDS Coordinating Committee (NACC)—under the Office of the Prime Minister but funded principally by a World Bank loan exhausted in seven years—directly managed (in the case of Trinidad) or indirectly oversaw (in the case of Tobago) the country's response to the HIV/AIDS epidemic (T&T 2013, 2).[8] This multisectoral policy-advising and program-monitoring body—composed of various interest group representatives—summarily replaced the National AIDS Programme (NAP), which the Ministry of Health had developed in 1986 with assistance from the World Health Organization's Global Programme on AIDS (T&T 2003, i, ii, 7, 10–11; NACC 2006, 15). An

P1 *From the Land of the Hummingbird*, Peter Minshall's individual work of mas portrayed by Sherry Ann Guy, backstage at Trinidad Carnival, 1974. Photograph by Noel P. Norton.

P2 Peter Minshall and performer Sherry Ann Guy posing with trophies for Junior Queen of Carnival awarded to his individual work of mas, *From the Land of the Hummingbird*, Trinidad Carnival, 1974. Photograph by Noel P. Norton.

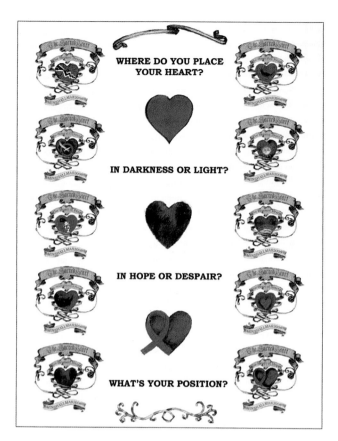

WHERE DO YOU PLACE YOUR HEART?

IN DARKNESS OR LIGHT?

IN HOPE OR DESPAIR?

WHAT'S YOUR POSITION?

P3 Inspirational public message for *The Sacred Heart* featuring logos for the ten sections of the band created by Peter Minshall and Nikolai Noel, 2006. Courtesy of the Callaloo Company Archive.

P4 Graphic logo for "The Rainbow Heart" section of *The Sacred Heart*. Logo created by Peter Minshall and Nikolai Noel in 2006. Courtesy of the Callaloo Company Archive.

P5 Graphic logo for "The Heart of Hope" section of *The Sacred Heart*. Logo created by Peter Minshall and Nikolai Noel in 2006. Courtesy of the Callaloo Company Archive.

P6 (OPPOSITE) *Miss Universe—Tan Tan's Girl Child*, the dancing mobile Queen character Peter Minshall designed for *The Sacred Heart* onstage with a section of the band, Trinidad Carnival, 2006. Photograph by Stefan Falke.

P7 Peter Minshall at the Callaloo Company, 2006. Photograph by Stefan Falke.

P8 The Son of Sagaboy, the dancing mobile King character Peter Minshall designed for *The Sacred Heart*, performing on stage, Trinidad Carnival, 2006. Photograph by Jim Stephens/Cheryl Andrews Marketing.

P9 (OPPOSITE) Wendy Fitzwilliam and Kerwin Paul performing on stage as Queen and King of *The Sacred Heart*, Trinidad Carnival, 2006. Photograph by Jim Stephens/Cheryl Andrews Marketing.

P10 Dame Lorraine characters Peter Minshall designed for *The Sacred Heart*, Trinidad Carnival, 2006. Photograph by Cyrus Sylvester.

P11-13 (Opposite) Dame Lorraine characters performing onstage, Trinidad Carnival, 2006. Photographs by Jim Stephens/ Cheryl Andrews Marketing.

P11 Carrying phallic object on stage.

P12 Rolling sheath onto phallic object on stage.

P13 Rolling phallic object off stage.

P14 A dancing Dame Lorraine, Trinidad Carnival, 2006. Photograph by Cyrus Sylvester.

P15 Masquerader Mark Eastman in *The Sacred Heart*, Trinidad Carnival, 2006. Photograph by Stefan Falke.

P16 Peter Minshall, Port-of-Spain, Trinidad, 2008. Photograph by Curtis Chase. Courtesy of the Callaloo Company Archive.

institutional response to the fragmentation and redundancies that under-mined the NAP for nearly two decades (T&T 2003, 10–11), the NACC was formally convened as part of a *Five-year National HIV/AIDS Strategic Plan: January 2004–December 2008* (NSP) developed by the Office of the Prime Minister with assistance from the Health Economics Unit of the University of the West Indies (T&T 2003, esp. 70–73; NACC 2006, 16). Estimated to cost over ninety million US dollars—with about 40 percent of this amount provided by the substantial loan from the World Bank and a smaller auxil-iary grant from the European Union—over the five-year period, the goals of this first NSP were diseased by inadequate HIV/AIDS surveillance systems and underdeveloped program monitoring and evaluation mechanisms (T&T 2003, iii, 86–97; NACC 2008, 27).

From its very first country progress report, the NACC readily identifies "under-diagnosis, under-reporting, and delayed reporting" in addition to incomplete data sets and the complete "lack of monitoring and evaluation capacity" among the major challenges faced by the nation (NACC 2006, 3, 8, 22, 25). And two years later—in the UNGASS progress report of 2008—the NACC's self-diagnosis had hardly improved. It remained the case that the NACC lacked any adequate, nationwide monitoring or evaluation infra-structure, and the committee still counted among its major challenges the "absence of a comprehensive surveillance system for HIV/AIDS, which cov-ers both the public and private sectors" (NACC 2008, 25, 27). In fact, the national HIV/AIDS statistics provided by the NACC have for decades now not accounted for testing, treatment, morbidity, or mortality data outside of the public sector (NACC 2008, 8). This alarming absence of undoubtedly signifi-cant HIV/AIDS surveillance data from the private sector not only highlights the inaccuracies of the nation's statistics but also points to the limitations of the global data since it is most likely that Trinidad and Tobago is far from exceptional in its reporting oversights. If the United Nations' HIV/AIDS fig-ures are informed nearly exclusively by the country progress reports, then is it quite probable—though extremely disturbing—that over three decades after the start of the HIV/AIDS pandemic, the world still does not have a full sense of the scale of this health crisis.

I devote attention here to calling these statistics into question because it is precisely these figures that are used to determine not only a global strate-gic response to the HIV/AIDS pandemic but also the priority areas to which particularly keen attention and disproportionate resources should be directed.

In the international struggle against the further spread or increased severity of the HIV/AIDS pandemic, action priorities are principally determined not only by rates of HIV prevalence but also by the risk of likely HIV infection. An epidemiological imperative—initiated by the US Centers for Disease Control and Prevention (CDC) in the early 1980s—requires identifying the individuals, groups, communities, nations, and regions of the world most at risk for HIV infection in order to prepare a focused and coordinated global prevention effort. But what exactly is meant by "risk" in the context of HIV infection? UNAIDS—having taken up the epidemiological imperative on behalf of the global community—sets down this succinct definition of HIV risk and its most poignant examples: "Risk is defined as the probability or likelihood that a person may become infected with HIV. Certain behaviors create, increase, and perpetuate risk. Examples include unprotected sex with a partner whose HIV status is unknown, multiple sexual partnerships involving unprotected sex, and injecting drug use with contaminated needles and syringes (UNAIDS 2008b, 65).

In telling contrast to the CDC's initial epidemiological assessments of HIV risk—which focused upon particular categories of people who regardless of behavior remained unavoidably most at risk for HIV infection—the UNAIDS definition pinpoints very specific behaviors and circumstances that increase one's likelihood of contracting HIV.[9] Deeply aware of the damaging stigmatization that resulted from nearly a decade of identifying homosexual men, among others—irrespective of sexual behaviors—as most at risk for HIV infection and most likely to serve as vectors of transmission, epidemiologists have since at least the early 1990s attempted to shift attention away from identity categories and toward behavioral categories. As a result of this shifted focus, the initial risk identity category "(male) homosexual" is effectively subsumed into the new risk behavior category "men-who-have-sex-with-men" by the time the now pervasive acronym MSM was coined in the HIV/AIDS medical literature in 1994 (Glick et al. 1994; Young and Meyer 2005, 1144; Baral et al. 2007, 1902). Over thirty years after the first cases of AIDS-related illness among homosexual men were reported in the medical literature, MSM are still identified across the globe as one of the most-at-risk-populations (MARPs) for HIV infection. But upon what statistical evidence does such a claim rest?

Men-Who-Have-Sex-with-Men and the Trick of Risk

International statistical analyses up through the end of the first decade of this century indicate elevated HIV prevalence rates among men-who-have-sex-with-men when proportionally compared to the rest of the men in the global community. In addition, MSM were estimated to account for anywhere from 5 to 10 percent of all HIV infections worldwide, with MSM in low- and middle-income countries as much as nineteen times more likely to be HIV-positive (Caceres et al. 2006; Baral et al. 2007, 1901, 1902, 1905, 1911; amFAR 2008, 8, 11; UNAIDS 2009a, 2, 6; WHO 2009, 5, 7, 11, 13). These calculations of estimated HIV risk and proportional HIV prevalence among MSM globally were informed by available estimates of the overall size of MSM populations worldwide, which tentatively indicated that MSM make up anywhere from 2 to 20 percent of men worldwide (Caceres 2006; WHO 2009, 11). And yet the overwhelming majority of these very same studies that attested to the disproportionate risk of HIV infection among all MSM—in large part as a result of presumed elevated HIV prevalence rates among MSM globally (surety of this depends of course upon a much more accurate estimation of the global MSM population)—decry the absolute dearth of accurate statistical information on MSM populations (Caceres 2006; amFAR 2008, 6, 9; UNAIDS 2009a, 2, 3; WHO 2009, 5, 7, 11, 19). These studies call for much more systematic MSM surveillance systems in hopes of obtaining the very data one would presumably require before making confident statements about the risks MSM face in the HIV/AIDS pandemic (Baral et al. 2007, 1905; amFAR 2008, 11; UNAIDS 2009a, 8, 10; WHO 2009, 5).

A World Health Organization report from 2009 on the prevention and treatment of HIV among MSM provides an exceptionally dissonant example of this double speak in a single paragraph: "Reports from a diverse range of countries and regions have highlighted that the prevalence of HIV and other STIs [sexually transmitted infections] among MSM and transgender people is high when compared with men in the general population. . . . Existing second-generation HIV surveillance systems, research, and efforts of national HIV/AIDS and STI programmes have not adequately captured biological and behavioral data on these populations, nor implemented prevention interventions on a sufficient scale. Resources to address HIV and STIs among MSM, transgender people and their partners do not match the burden of disease" (WHO 2009, 5).

An absence of adequate surveillance data on global populations of MSM (let alone their partners) perpetually calls into question any accurate estimates of HIV prevalence or any informed assessments of resource distribution. If the UN General Assembly Special Session on HIV/AIDS (UNGASS) country progress reports of 2008 provide the most accurate early twenty-first-century map of the pandemic, then populations of MSM remain for the most part statistically uncharted territory as a result of over half (approximately 54 percent) of the 128 countries reporting from Latin America, the Caribbean, Eastern Europe, Asia and the Pacific, the Middle East, and Africa failing to report on the one UNGASS indicator that explicitly mentions MSM (amFAR 2008, 6, 18; UNAIDS 2008b, 17). If the international community has for some time now been able to collect only an unnervingly scarce amount of statistical data on populations of MSM worldwide, it is perhaps not surprising that the Caribbean intraregional community has fared little better with collecting epidemiological data on the region's populations of MSM.

Replacing "Gay": A Dangerous New Euphemism in the Caribbean Region

Although a secondary route for the spread of HIV far behind heterosexual infection rates, HIV transmission among MSM in the Caribbean region has previously been estimated at around 12 percent (Camara 2000, 5–6; UNAIDS 2008a, 2; UNAIDS 2008b, 54). And yet only seven of the thirteen UNGASS-defined Caribbean nations reported on the UN indicator that explicitly mentions MSM. Importantly, this indicator tracked MSM only with respect to condom use during their last sexual encounter with a male (amFAR 2008, 23).[10] It is likely that much of the statistical information on MSM in the Caribbean region—and perhaps globally as well—has been muddled by an interpretive slippage that presumes the epidemiological category "most-at-risk populations" (MARP) must in all instances refer, if not exclusively then principally, to MSM populations. Of the twenty-five UNGASS Declaration of Commitment indicators, four solicit specific data on most-at-risk populations, including HIV testing frequency and status awareness, participation in HIV prevention programs, knowledge of strategies for preventing the sexual transmission of HIV, and HIV prevalence rates (UNAIDS 2008b, 17). It appears that statistical data on MSM in the region was largely dependent on the excision of figures from the potentially fleshier statistical portrait of the presumably fluctuating epidemiological "MARP" category.

Although the precision of all of the other twenty-one indicators lends credence to the supposition that the UN General Assembly may not have intended "most-at-risk population" to be interpreted as a category in constant flux, it is precisely this possibility for contextual definition that potentially makes the category immune to significant differences in the nature of the epidemic in various locations or to significant changes in the pandemic over time. However, this spatial and temporal elasticity built into the "MARP" category is severely confined when it is interpreted merely as an informal euphemism for MSM. This unofficial standardization of a variable—applicable in some instances but not others—lends itself to statistical and epidemiological confusion at the same time that it fixes MSM as a permanently high-risk group despite sero-surveillance data or specific behavior patterns, encouraging unnecessary stigmatization.

There can be little doubt that in the Caribbean, MSM—like any other sexually active population—put themselves at varying degrees of risk by continuing to have sex despite the pervasiveness of a sexually transmitted pandemic. However, if "male-to-male sexual contact is not inherently dangerous," then determining the degree of risk that Caribbean MSM face requires much more attention to the specific sexual behavior patterns *within* the broader behavioral category "MSM" than has generally been documented in the limited studies that do exist (Baral et al. 2007, 1908). This systematic investigation of the actual sexual practices of Caribbean MSM is often precluded by the implicit presumption that all MSM engage in anal intercourse. In fact, the persistent equation of male-to-male sex with anal intercourse serves to explain in part the correlative presumption that MSM are always the population most at risk for HIV infection. And yet anal intercourse is not exclusive to MSM in the Caribbean nor has there been any substantive effort to statistically document the extent and contexts within which Caribbean MSM partake in it.

Even in the highly unlikely instance that all Caribbean MSM engage in anal intercourse during every sexual encounter, it is important to remember that anal intercourse alone does not put one at risk for HIV infection. The risk lies in *unprotected* anal sex with an *HIV-positive* partner, and even in this instance, the risk undertaken is not shared equally—the receptive partner actually faces a higher risk of exposure (or reexposure if he is already

HIV-positive). The elevated risk faced by the receptive partner engaged in unprotected anal intercourse with a partner of unknown HIV status extends across categories of sex, gender identity, or sexual orientation. And yet this point is too often obscured by the presumption that MSM is merely a euphemism for (unprotected) anal sex and thus inherently high-risk behavior: "Almost universally, even in generalized HIV epidemics, men who have sex with men are more affected by HIV than the general population. Biologically, unprotected receptive anal sex poses a much higher risk than unprotected receptive vaginal sex, whether that anal sex is heterosexual or homosexual" (UNAIDS 2009a, 2).

Although Caribbean MSM are probably more likely to engage in anal intercourse than exclusively heterosexual Caribbean men, it is highly improbable—though not impossible—for all Caribbean MSM to be exclusively receptive partners in all instances. So, even if it is the case that unprotected receptive anal intercourse is the riskiest sexual behavior in terms of HIV transmission, not all Caribbean MSM are exposed to this risk equally; in fact, this "MARP" category also includes Caribbean non-MSM who may participate in anal sex but presume it to be less of a risk simply because they are not having sex with other men. Just as with exclusively heterosexual men, the mere sex of a Caribbean MSM's partner—despite presumptions about the probabilities of sexual behavior unsubstantiated with any data—is insufficient to determine the degree of risk he faces.[11] If identifying specific sexual practices provides a much more accurate glimpse at the HIV risks of men who have sex with other men, then the category "MSM" may indeed obscure much more than it reveals.

A presumably neutral epidemiological category originally intended in part to reduce the stigmatization of particular identity groupings ("gay" and "bisexual" primarily) by shifting the focus of health professionals toward specific behaviors that persist across a broad cross-section of sexually active males despite identity boundaries, the category "men-who-have-sex-with-men"—a full two decades after its introduction into the medical literature—has ironically solidified into what it was supposed to avoid (Young and Meyer 2005, 1144).[12] The most parochial interpretations of MSM imagine it to be merely a more sophisticated—if a bit unwieldy—euphemism for presumably passé identity categories such as "gay" (and perhaps "bisexual"), while those who have been able to grasp the central logic of the new term (namely that all gays/bisexuals are MSM, but all MSM are *not* gay/bisexual) have nonetheless come to use it as if it were merely a newer, broader identity category that says just a whisper more about general sexual practices but remains tight-lipped about the actual specifics most relevant for epidemiological interventions: "Purportedly, one of the greatest advantages of wsw and msm is that unlike *lesbian* and *gay*, they are anchored in concrete behaviors that are more relevant than identity terms to epidemiological investigations. msm and wsw have often been understood as stand-ins for presumed risk behaviors. With this usage, researchers ignore the important task of describing actual sexual behaviors even though this information has greater relevance to public health" (Young and Meyer 2005, 1147; emphasis in original).[13]

Beyond an inability to indicate *what kind of sex* various populations of msm are presently practicing—with especially keen attention to unprotected anal intercourse—the category "men-who-have-sex-with-men" fails to provide a temporal frame. In other words, "msm" may indicate with whom a man has sex, but it leaves one crucial question unanswered: when?

Though largely unattended to in the sparse statistical data on Caribbean msm, there certainly exist epidemiologically relevant distinctions among msm in terms of their sexual practices over time. A man who has at some time in his life experimented with male-to-male sex but who has sex exclusively with women presently is a particular kind of msm distinct from a man who has long had recurring sexual encounters with men and women. Both of these msm are distinct from a self-identified "gay man"—no less an msm—who has long had recurring sexual encounters exclusively with men. These three types represent only the most easily identifiable markers along an extremely complex continuum of Caribbean male sexual practices; this continuum comes fully into view only within a temporal frame: "Where data quality is good and data are readily available, it is possible to distinguish between those men who have ever had sex with men and those men for whom the behavior is more recent and recurring. Where data is limited and no time frame has been applied to reported behaviors, it may be difficult to distinguish between men who have explored or experimented with same-sex behaviors at some point in their lives and those who have recently been or currently are sexually active with men" (WHO 2009, 8).

There are relatively few places in the world where the data on msm is sufficient to highlight the necessary distinctions between msm that just might determine the success or failure of an HIV prevention strategy in that population or a similar intervention with their nonmale partners. Caribbean public health circles have undoubtedly taken interest—for better or worse—in populations of msm in the region principally as a means by which to monitor and stem the presumably rampant transmission of HIV from MSM to their nonmale partners. However, a largely overlooked statistical irony undermines this attempt to focus in upon the MSM who are thought to be primary vectors of disease. The overwhelming majority of the statistical information collected on MSM in the world, as in the Caribbean region, is based upon the data provided by self-identified *gay* men—the very population of MSM probably least likely overall to have recurring sexual encounters with women. Additionally, this statistically overrepresented group of MSM is more often than not composed of men who are frequent visitors to hospitals, STI clinics, or HIV/AIDS organizations and thus easily accessible and trackable for data gathering purposes, but also much more likely to have contracted or be at higher risk of contracting HIV.

Much of the international epidemiological surveillance data on MSM relies so heavily on nonprobability sampling in large part because the full spectrum of MSM is so challenging to access statistically. However, this convenience sampling more often than not focuses in on particular MSM populations without providing an accurate portrait of the general population of MSM in any one location or globally (Baral et al. 2007, 1905). Although these skewed figures on MSM are seldom generalizable, they are too frequently used in the international community to make largely unsubstantiated claims about HIV prevalence rates among *all* MSM—globally, regionally, and nationally. In this regard, the Caribbean region is for the most part unexceptional. From the earliest MSM seroprevalence survey in the region to the most significant one conducted at the beginning of this century—both based on the island of Trinidad—recruitment bias has continually made it nearly impossible to accurately assess the scale of HIV infection outside of the specific subpopulation of Caribbean MSM who are frequent clients of STI clinics or HIV/AIDS organizations.

Tracking Caribbean MSM: Bias and Innovation in a Statistical Blind Spot

Between November 1983 and February 1984 in Port-of-Spain, Trinidad, the aforementioned Dr. Courtenay Bartholomew enrolled one hundred "self-declared homosexual or bisexual men" in the first large-scale MSM HIV prevalence study in the anglophone Caribbean by recruiting subjects from the capital's sole sexually transmitted disease clinic (Bartholomew et al. 1987, 2604). This convenience sample of gay and bisexual men was compared against background seroprevalence rates for a statistically sound random sample of 983 males whose blood Dr. Bartholomew and his team had earlier acquired as part of an island-wide hepatitis B survey conducted in 1982 (Bartholomew et al. 1987, 2605). As might have been expected given the vastly different subject recruitment methods for MSM and presumably non-MSM, HIV prevalence among MSM (40 percent or forty out of the one hundred participants) dwarfed prevalence among non-MSM (0.2 percent or two out of the 983 samples) (Bartholomew et al. 1987, 2606). In fact, Dr. Bartholomew is quite forthright even in this first study about the bias of his sampling methods, noting in his comments on the study that the high rate of seropositivity among MSM is probably the result of having looked to an STI clinic for his population (Bartholomew et al. 1987, 2607).[14]

And yet Dr. Bartholomew's cautionary suggestion for improving the statistical accuracy of seroprevalence surveys among MSM was apparently ignored exactly two decades later when the Caribbean Epidemiological Center's researchers repeated many of Dr. Bartholomew's missteps in a survey of 320 men in 2004 (Lee et al. 2005). Largely due to significant recruitment bias (data collection on MSM primarily through HIV/AIDS organizations), this study found a 20 percent HIV prevalence rate among Trinidadian MSM, 75 percent of whom reported no sexual activity with a female partner within the last year (Martin 2009).[15] This skewed ratio—in which men who have been (at least for a year) having sex exclusively with other men make up the grand majority—was quite irresponsibly reproduced in the NACC's UN country progress report of 2008 (with a one-sentence disclaimer about possible recruitment bias). This sole statistic is the NACC's only response to the UNGASS core indicator "percentage of most-at-risk populations who are HIV infected," which is the only one of the UN's four MARP indicators addressed in the entire report (NACC 2008, 6). And the distorted 20 percent has been re-presented over and over again in the international (and local) literature on MSM HIV prevalence rates minus its minor disclaimer about recruitment bias and certainly without mention of the varying risk differentials involved in the actual sexual practices of this "most-at-risk" population (Caceres 2006; Baral et al. 2007, 1904; amFAR 2008, 5; UNAIDS 2008a, 2; UNAIDS 2008b, 54–55; UNAIDS 2009a, 55; T&T 2013). Although this alarmist statistic on Trinidadian populations of MSM provides a far from reliable glimpse of HIV prevalence in the general population of T&T MSM, it does reveal a frightfully high rate of HIV infection in a particular subgroup of most probably gay-identified MSM, which portends danger for the wider population of

MSM—but especially for gay men—regardless of whether or not the group's overall HIV prevalence rate is likely much lower. It is worth repeating that defining the nature of that danger—in essence, determining which groups of (gay-identified) MSM are most at risk—requires surveillance data on sexual practices. It may be the case that this lack of data is only in part the result of researchers neglecting the very questions to which they wrongfully presume to already have the answers. Two of the earliest transnational qualitative studies of Caribbean MSM (largely gay MSM) populations and HIV prevention—while offering only the most modest engagement with actual sexual practices—inadvertently reveal the challenge of encouraging conversation about sexual behavior patterns among Caribbean MSM (CAREC 1996; CAREC [1998] 2000). Yet the reports themselves are a testament to the fact that—although initiating these conversations about MSM sexual practices can be difficult—it is far from impossible, especially with particular populations of Caribbean MSM.

Focused principally upon self-identified gay men and their overall sexual— as well as psychosocial—health, the Caribbean Epidemiological Center's two-part technical report on populations of MSM in eight Eastern Caribbean nations remains one of the first region-oriented studies of MSM and HIV prevention in the anglophone Caribbean.[16] These complementary studies are quite remarkable for their keen attention not only to the local specificities of MSM experiences in different territories (down to comparisons of colloquial speech) but also to the actual speaking voices of interviewed MSM.[17]

Although these quasiethnographic surveillance studies do not escape the biases of convenience sampling, they are indisputably innovative for including the openly HIV-positive gay Caribbean activist Godfrey Sealy as the field interviewer and coauthor on both reports.[18] Nearly exclusively limited to self-identified gay men as a result in part of the interviewer's accessible social networks—existing and newly formed—these studies perhaps provide a more statistically accurate range of gay-identified Caribbean men; if HIV/ AIDS prevalence statistics had been collected as part of this study, these figures may have proven more comfortably—though not flawlessly—generalizable than the existing data.

Nevertheless, CAREC's Gay Research Initiative has been able to make some of the most substantial contributions to knowledge about HIV prevention strategies for Caribbean MSM through the report's direct and indirect recommendations for action. Both phases of the study speak forcefully though indirectly to the potential uses of focused group conversation—

FIGURE 5.1 Godfrey Sealy holding court on the front porch of his home (christened "Bohemia") in Woodbrook, Trinidad, n.d. Photograph by Cyrus Sylvester.

originally initiated only as a means by which to collect data—not only for HIV/AIDS awareness but also for peer-led sexual behavior change interventions (CAREC 1996, 46; CAREC [1998] 2000, 35, 40). In the late 1990s, facilitated conversations about emotional, social, and sexual health still remained a largely unexplored resource in the fight against HIV/AIDS in Caribbean gay male populations. However, the authors of the CAREC reports point toward the realization that these conversations might be used not only to broaden parochial presumptions about gay men's actual sexual practices but also to encourage collective reflection upon these practices with an eye toward HIV risk reduction. And it is through encouraging this collective assessment by means of conversation that the authors of the CAREC reports appear to unwittingly come upon focus groups as one potentially effective mechanism for addressing the deficiencies they lament in condom negotiation skills among Caribbean MSM (CAREC 1996, 39, 48; CAREC [1998] 2000, 40). By encouraging conversations about patterns of sexual behavior and degrees of potential HIV risk among gay Caribbean men, the focused group chat might discursively prepare these men with the knowledge base and the talk techniques to be able to address condom usage and other risk reduction strategies with their sexual partners.

These indirect suggestions aside, one of the Research Initiative's most re-soundingly direct recommendations is to center Caribbean MSM—especially HIV-positive MSM—in HIV prevention efforts that target MSM populations. The authors propose that community-based interventions led by trained peer educators might be the most effective means by which to reach various MSM populations with HIV prevention strategies as well as with HIV/AIDS treatment, care, and support services (CAREC 1996, 43, 49; CAREC [1998] 2000, 29). Perhaps unintentionally, the study itself models the very involvement of MSM populations (principally self-identified gay men in this instance) that it recommends; not only are Caribbean MSM the principal authoritative subjects from whom qualitative statistics are gathered, but a gay HIV-positive Caribbean researcher is instrumental to the collection and assessment of that data. In essence, the CAREC technical reports on Caribbean MSM might be read—both for what the authors recommend and for the means by which they make those recommendations—as a call to action for Caribbean MSM populations in general and gay male communities in particular. Demonstrating the need for a conscientious, collective, and coordinated HIV/AIDS response orchestrated by MSM populations for MSM populations, the findings of the two-part Gay Research Initiative underlined the very space that a new Trinidadian HIV/AIDS NGO had just been founded to fill. A group of gay Trinidadian men would heed the call—perhaps inadvertently—and form the nation's only HIV/AIDS prevention, support, and service provision organization guided principally by gay men to save and preserve their own lives.

CHAPTER 6

Between Tongue and Teeth

The Friends For Life Chatroom as Erotic Intervention

The following history of Friends For Life (FFL) sets the context in which to consider the organization's longest-running program—the Community Chatroom Experience (or simply "The Chatroom").[1] And this historical accounting is specifically attentive to the importance of the erotic—as an additive political-sensual-spiritual resource—in the formation, leadership, and future of FFL. This expansive notion of the erotic encourages a broadened perspective on the successes of the HIV/AIDS prevention and support work of FFL, while shedding light on the perseverance of its leadership despite formidable challenges. And by demonstrating the uses of the erotic as an organizing practice, FFL stretches the concept beyond representational symbolism and sets it down in the world as practice.

Introducing Friends For Life: A Grassroots Politics of Survival

FFL was founded on October 2, 1997—in the precise interval not only between the Caribbean Epidemiological Center's (CAREC) MSM reports but also between the two years in which Trinidad and Tobago reported the highest numbers of AIDS-related deaths to date (NACC 2006, 6; NACC 2008, 9).[2] The organization holds within its name a double entendre that serves as its

FIGURE 6.1 Group photograph taken by the author at the Friends For Life facilitator training retreat at Mount Saint Benedict Hermitage, Saint Augustine, Trinidad, 2008.

initiating impulse and governing ideal. The simple—though formidable—directive that guided the founders of FFL pivots principally upon the question of mortality. If it is that a *friend for life* devotes himself to supportive companionship until death—his own or that of his friend—then he does so convinced too that this companionship alone may be one of the principal means by which to preserve and extend life—both his own and that of his companion. The perennially troubling dialectic between death and life—made even more ghastly by the ravages of an epidemic at its most ravenous—haunts Friends For Life into existence.

In other words, as FFL's planning and development manager—for over a decade, though this Afro-Trinidadian gay man is just barely in his forties—Kerwyn Jordan explains, the organization's timely birth is the direct result of an unexpected death. Loss of a life gives breath to a collective imperative:

> There was a group of us. I think seven . . . we became a clique, so that anywhere you see one of us, you see all of us. And then we somewhat missed one individual. And I asked, "But you know, it's a long time I haven't seen Reynaldo; has anybody heard from him?" And there wasn't any genuine thought given to it until later on after like four months

FIGURE 6.2 Kerwyn Jordan, Eswick Padmore, and the author, Port-of-Spain, Trinidad, 2004. Photograph by Luke Sinnette. Courtesy of the Friends For Life Archive.

when Eswick [Padmore] and Cleveland [Gervais] and myself sat and we were thinking that something was wrong with him. . . . Because last time I saw him he really wasn't looking that good. But he did not tell me he was ill.

So, Eswick and Cleveland were considering whether to go and see him . . . there was talk about it but everybody had other commitments so it never really came to fruition until the morning after the guy died. When Eswick went to visit him, he was told that he died the night before. We all were very distraught about that because here was a group of friends and we didn't even know our friend was dying. That was March of 1997.

We thought about doing something for these people who are afraid to even tell their own friends that they're sick, who might be discriminated against or ostracized even more by society—other than for being gay—now that they are HIV positive. We wanted to formulate something that we could do for them. We eventually called ourselves "Friends For Life."

The members of that original group were Cleveland, Eswick, me, Kendra [Bernard-Emmanuel], Portia [Guichard], Antonio [Providence], Luke

FIGURE 6.3 Eswick Padmore dressed to attend a wedding ceremony, 2004. Courtesy of the Friends For Life Archive.

[Sinnette] came in a while after, Robbin Thomas who is now deceased, Timothy Nieves who is also deceased, and of course the group is dedicated in the memory of Reynaldo Thomas. (Jordan 2003; 2008b)

Thomas's passing would be the first of many that this group of friends—who became the founding members of FFL seven months later—would have to endure, but the profound regret beneath their grief unearthed a firm resolve to do for each other and for others all that they had not been able to do for Thomas.

Although Reynaldo Thomas's death encouraged increased attention to HIV infection and AIDS-related illness among these original members of FFL, many in this group of friends had long been involved in sexual and reproductive health initiatives. Indeed, Eswick Padmore—the organization's principal founder and, since inception, chairman of its board of trustees—had been involved in this work as a sexual health peer counselor since the late 1980s as part of the youth arm of the Family Planning Association of Trinidad and Tobago (FPATT).[3]

A tall, mixed-race gay man in his early fifties with a demure feminine elegance that lends itself well to drag impersonations of the legendary Dame

Shirley Bassey, Padmore worked for over a decade with FPATT before he began volunteering and finally working for RapPort—the youth arm of T&T's National AIDS Program. While working at RapPort, Padmore unwittingly became one of the most visible sources of sexual health information for gay men, trans women, drag pageant performers, and commercial sex workers across T&T. He had inadvertently become one of the few peer counselors for this increasingly frightened community under siege from HIV/AIDS:

> I realized we needed to do something for the gay people who find out they are HIV positive and don't have anybody to talk to about it. After a while . . . I started meeting with a group of people at RapPort. After a while we couldn't meet at RapPort and we used to meet in the courtyard of the Twin Towers [a public space outside of the Ministry of Finance in down-town Port-of-Spain]. After the courtyard of the Twin Towers, we started meeting at St. Vincent de Paul on Duncan Street. It just evolved; things just happened. . . . And it just grew. (Padmore 2008)

Despite the tense discomfort it caused in the sexual health and HIV/AIDS establishment, Padmore's unavoidable counseling work with gay men at FPATT and RapPort afforded him a glimpse at the landscape of this popula-tion's sexual and social health needs in and around Port-of-Spain. Gradually, gay men would begin to seek out Eswick Padmore from even further away.

Beyond his local network of clients and friends, Padmore was also equipped with a regional information-sharing and support network that had begun to expand virally after a region-wide CAREC training in 1996 based in Trinidad for LGBT activists interested in coordinating HIV/AIDS prevention, treat-ment, and care initiatives for LGBT populations throughout the region (Jordan 2008b, 5; Padmore 2008, 4).[4]

Timing and positioning aligned just long enough to clear space for a new HIV/AIDS NGO to emerge, an organization cohered by compassionate concern primarily for the well-being of gay Caribbean men. Initially uncon-cerned with funding, legislation, infrastructure, or notoriety, Friends For Life—following Padmore's example—held as its core concern the survival of the gay men whose lives in many regards depended on it:

> Friends For Life [he closes his eyes and smiles into a hard sigh]. This was an organization that when you talk about grassroots, it couldn't get any more grassroots than this. We were having meetings on the Promenade [an infamous downtown Port-of-Spain pedestrian thoroughfare] and in

FIGURE 6.4 Delano Ray Thompson, 2004. Photographer unknown. Courtesy of the Friends For Life Archive.

fast food outlets and they were throwing us out and so on because we didn't have a space . . . but we knew what we wanted to do. . . . Finally, we started doing hospital visits, visiting people, giving them that encouragement . . . when you do this you encourage people to go on and then some people actually start recovering because part of recovery is a will to live. . . . We were doing that and people started taking notice. (Thompson 2007)[5]

A decidedly grassroots organization from its very seed, FFL is able to successfully convene and mobilize various networks of gay men in large part because the groundwork for this community building had already been laid by an earlier—though not nearly as well documented—history of gay male organizing across the Caribbean region.[6] In fact, FFL's longest-running program by far—a model for gay community building and assessment that the organization has actively encouraged throughout the region—actually predates FFL itself.

FFL's Community Chatroom Experience began as a series of HIV/AIDS education and community-building workshops for gay men convened at least as early as 1994 and coordinated by the formidable Trinidadian dramatist, dancer, theater designer, and gay activist Geoffrey Stanforde (*T&T Guardian* 2001, 2).[7] Between 1994 and 1998, with the support of CAREC and UNAIDS, Stanforde's education and discussion sessions—provocatively called "Sex Talks"—developed the infrastructure for a MSM HIV/AIDS intervention project.[8] Drafted in 1998 from these talks, the "Project Design Team Address" proposed an action plan for achieving the overarching goals of gay male self-empowerment, sexual behavior change, and community mobilization. As part of this plan, the address established a new collective—called simply TnT M4M—charged with overseeing the implementation of the "TnT M4M 2000 Project," the specific framework for which would be determined and expanded by 1999 into a "Caribbean M4M 2000 Project." This initiative in part formalized the discussion forums that had by now proven to be an effective HIV/AIDS prevention and support strategy among gay men in T&T.

The very first TnT M4M 2000 Chatroom was held on Wednesday, June 30, 1999, in the midst of T&T's 5th annual Pride Week celebrations. The irony of this interactive social space being named for a virtual site—despite their similar appeal for informal "real-time" conversations—is perhaps made less puzzling when one considers that the actual Chatroom (like its virtual shadow) is in fact a space without a place. Instead, this Chatroom is a site that does not simply encourage social interaction but actually comes into being because of it. It is precisely this social interaction—and the informal resource sharing it fosters—that clears the space for another irony early in the history of FFL. Namely, that the very Chatroom that provided FFL with its first opportunity for official funding in May 2001 would ceremoniously become the charge of the organization by July of that same year due in no small part to Geoffrey Stanforde's declining health (TnT M4M 1999; James 2002, 2; James 2003, 2–5; Jordan 2003, 5, 6; Jordan and Padmore 2003, 3; Jordan 2008a, 1, 8; Jordan 2008b, 9, 10; NACC/FFL 2008, 17, 18, 22).[9]

Eswick Padmore vividly recalls the coincidental Chatroom encounter that effectively introduced Friends For Life to the world of international

HIV/AIDS funding—an introduction that though initially warm, would cool significantly in the years to come:

> I had gone to the Chatroom after a while of not going and this gentleman from UNAIDS Ruben del Prado . . . came because he had in his possession a computer and x amount of U.S. [dollars] to set up an organization or to set up a service for the MSM community. . . . He wanted to get x amount of people together "here and now" who would be willing to do something for the Chatroom.
>
> And I was sitting in the Chatroom and I'm looking around because in the Chatroom that night was probably about ten to twelve people. . . . And one of the guys—an Indian guy, I can't remember his name—sitting down next to me pokes me and says, "Ent you have an organization? Why allyuh [you all] don't ting [take the opportunity]?" I say, "Well, I'm looking to see who else is going to say something." I don't know what the hell I was looking for. It had nobody else there to come in front of Friends For Life at the time. So, I said, "OK, I am interested" and . . . we met the next day. And you could say that was the initial start; that was the push forward. Anyhow, it took me a while to get the computer and the x amount of dollars, eh? (Padmore 2008)

Able to provide a social nexus within which Padmore's grassroots organization could come in contact with UNAIDS, the Chatroom directly facilitated FFL receiving—even if protractedly—the computer and just over three thousand US dollars del Prado promised. However, and perhaps much more importantly, this contact—and later one-year contract—with an international NGO would early on highlight the appearance of a new Caribbean MSM-specific HIV/AIDS NGO on the global activist map (Jordan 2005, 6). By July 2003, this visibility would likely make it possible for FFL to receive a nearly eighty-thousand-US-dollar grant from the UK-based International HIV/AIDS Alliance—the most substantial funding agreement FFL has entered to date—promised over a five-year period.[10] The Alliance grant marks what many still believe to have been the organization's zenith. Whether or not this is the case in terms of actual service provision—recall that Padmore and the other early members of FFL had been counseling MSM, referring MSM for health services, and visiting ailing gay men in the hospital for at least six years previous to the Alliance grant—it is undoubtedly the case that FFL as an organization was at its most high-profile during the two years between July 2003 and July 2005.[11]

This increased level of visibility for the NGO and its various programs is in large part attributable to the new office space and drop-in center FFL swiftly opened in the heart of downtown Port-of-Spain:

> Coming to Port-of-Spain was coming out for Friends For Life as *the* gay organization. And it was *good*. It was good because we were providing a service to a particular group of people [for whom] nobody was providing [services] . . . there were organizations that were saying, "Yes, we do provide a service." But when you go to them, they couldn't really come up to scratch. They couldn't answer some of your questions or your concerns about HIV and AIDS and me being gay. They're quick to tell you about changing your life and accepting God and going to church . . .
>
> So, here was Friends For Life now on Abercromby Street, providing a service to the gay individual and people would come. . . . It was about accepting you for who you are and guiding you along the path. It was also a teething time for the straight community because we were in their face now. All kinds of people used to come to Friends For Life—the gay one, the real one, the hen-down one—and then there were those of course who wouldn't be caught dead coming there. But then, I didn't mind.
>
> For the people who didn't come, OK; if you didn't come, you didn't come. . . . And the end result—you know what will happen?—those same people who wouldn't come will call you at home to tell you, "Well, you know x, y, zed and thing, thing, thing, thing, thing [asking for counseling and/or resources]." (Padmore 2008)[12]

Even if FFL has not been able to effectively provide HIV/AIDS prevention, care, and support services to lesbians or nongay/nonbisexual-identified MSM en mass, the organization has from its inception been remarkably successful at highlighting specific populations of MSM inadequately attended to by the vast majority of HIV/AIDS-related initiatives in the nation.[13]

Friends For Life has been consistently successful at reaching populations of working-class, underemployed, or unemployed urban men of African descent who overwhelmingly self-identify as gay—and in many cases are quite vocal about being openly gay. HIV seroconversion or a frightening AIDS diagnosis are likely motivating factors for a significant proportion of these specific MSM, but it is undoubtedly the case that a majority of gay men get involved in FFL because it provides support services—both formal and informal—targeted specifically for and sensitive to the particular needs of gay men. By opening a downtown office space, Friends For Life was able to offer these services in both a highly centralized and highly visible way. This new space would not only house the weekly Chatroom and function during business hours as a sexual health education drop-in center, but would also provide a home base for the organization's new full-time staff.[14] In this new space, FFL staff and volunteers could openly train gay men to serve as sexual health peer educators (particularly attentive to HIV prevention), as home-based caregivers for friends or family with AIDS-related illness, and as outreach workers distributing condoms and other safer sex materials to gay male partygoers and commercial sex workers (Jordan 2003; Jordan and Padmore 2003, 4; Jordan 2005, 7).

At the very beginning of a presumably long tenure of Alliance funding, eagerly setting up a brand new office space in the heart of the nation's capital and overrun with willing volunteers, July through August 2003 proved a nearly surreal moment in the history of the organization. It was in this exuberant moment that I began volunteering for Friends For Life and building many of the intricate friendships that have since survived more than a decade of comings and goings—my own the least remarkable among a host of others. Thirteen years after my last childhood visit with relatives on the island and barely a month after my graduation from university, I decided to return to T&T to begin what I at that time hoped would be a research project on contemporary drag performance in Trinidad.[15] As the present analysis attests, T&T certainly had other plans for me. Gay Jamaican-American author and activist Thomas Glave had put me in contact with Eswick Padmore and Kerwyn Jordan just before leaving the Unites States, but I could never have anticipated that in a few weeks' time I would be moving filing cabinets, desks, couches, and tables and helping a newly endowed organization settle into the important work ahead. It was as a volunteer for FFL that I began to build LGBT social networks in Trinidad and Tobago, and it was through these early relationships that I began to conceive—on the journeys back and forth between my quiet rented room in Point Cumana and FFL's uproarious Port-of-Spain office—the chapter you have before you. During this first of many research trips to T&T, I might never have imagined writing an end to the shining moment I enjoyed—albeit naively—alongside Friends For Life. But just as my most delicate memories of that summer would fade with time, so too would the luster of that moment, giving way to storm clouds gathered to rain down upon FFL.

By July 2005, the Alliance would terminate their five-year funding agreement with Friends For Life after just two years of support due to financial misappropriation.[16] The staff of FFL have hardly contested the Alliance's decision or denied the fact that they made some very poor financial decisions. However, this particular setback—principally the failing of a relatively young grassroots NGO—perhaps ought not to be shouldered by FFL alone. It is undoubtedly the case that the blame for improper spending rests solely upon FFL—as it should—but the financial missteps of the organization may very well indicate much more fundamental flaws in the capacity-building strategies that the Alliance choreographs into its aid distribution. Padmore offers some important concessions:

There's only one person in Friends For Life who [was] at University—well, now there's two. But at the time, there was only one person who was at UWI [University of the West Indies]—Luke [Sinnette]. The other two people: one has been to secondary school, one hasn't. So, we are not a whole bunch of people with degrees and all these set of things who running Friends For Life. We are just normal people who have this grand idea and pushing the idea. And that's as simple as I can make it. So the idea that Friends For Life has this bunch of qualified people that can do accounts and do office management and things—sorry, we can't.

The Alliance now—as far as I'm concerned, how they have fallen short is that—they came and they were willing to support NGOs in this field and they were willing to provide training in the different areas. But then the reality is you cannot take somebody like me, who never did accounts, [have me] spend two days in a workshop—or three days, or even if it's a week—and then send me back out to go and do the accounts. That is spinning top in mud. That is craziness . . . you can't put us in a classroom setting for four days and come out and expect us to do the world of accounts. And I think that's more or less what they expected.

The problem for us in Friends For Life was the accounting practices. I remember we wanted somebody with accounting skills and they weren't willing to pay the salary. And so, that's a problem there. Because if we can't do it and we're willing to bring in somebody who can do it and you're saying no, then that's a problem. [After I press a bit for the reason why the Alliance pulled the funding, he readily admits] The problem was that we had bad spent some money or couldn't account for some expenditures. So, they stopped the funding until we went through the auditor's report. And it just didn't work out in the end in our favor. . . . We have, however, since been able to meet with the Alliance and they have written off the debt. And they're willing to work with us in the future. (Padmore 2008)

FIGURE 6.5 Dennis James, Luke Sinnette, and a participant in the Friends For Life office, Port-of-Spain, Trinidad, 2004. Photographer unknown. Courtesy of the Friends For Life Archive.

It would be naïve to presume that the principal founder of Friends For Life does not have a vested interest in preserving the reputation of the organization—even if only for the most altruistic reasons. I do not cite Padmore at length here in order to deflect blame away from FFL but rather to welcome a wider perspective on the shortcomings of the organization. Perhaps by stumbling along with FFL during its first two years in the Caribbean region, the International HIV/AIDS Alliance was able to learn some crucial lessons about deficiencies in its capacity-building strategies as implemented in T&T. Without falling into agreement with defeatist—and quite often elitist—presumptions about class, educational level, and correlative ability that organizations like FFL contest by their very existence, we might still hear in Padmore's not-altogether-disinterested confession a bit of unblinking reflection on the bare body of the organization. Yet the vulnerabilities of Friends For Life as an organization were demonstrated only in part in its financial misdealings. The eight-year-old NGO had also begun to experience some far more fundamental challenges that easily threatened to destabilize the organization, regardless of funding concerns.

The increased visibility Friends For Life had achieved with the new office space also brought with it an increased vulnerability. Interestingly enough, the most discomforting challenges came not from disapproving heterosexual society but rather from inside the body of the organization itself, as FFL's director—for at least the past decade, though this Afro-Trinidadian gay man is only in his late thirties—Luke Sinnette, explains in elaborate detail:

I think it's inevitable that communities evolve. . . . You probably just don't know when it will happen . . . you can't sustain everything forever . . . . So, you have to go up and down. I think that happened in Friends For Life. We started off doing all of this remarkable—what I would call—activism work and just refusing to have boundaries. And people coming there and having the experience that brought them to their peak.

But then, what happens is you get to that peak and the oppression pulls you back. There are people who have habitual pain in their lives. And then, when they have a really good moment—somewhere in the middle of the good moment—they stop and they [think], "Good things just weren't meant to last and this is going to be over sometime." And so, in the middle of the good moment they're pining about it ending. . . . And I think we went through that in Friends For Life.

And [we in FFL were] also having the experience of ripping away the oppression and so heterosexuals are watching you and [saying], "What is wrong with them? . . . Something is not right. You all not supposed to be gay and be *that* happy or be *that* open about it. You're at least supposed to look sorry that you're gay." Because heterosexuals have that feeling [that] you can be gay, but just feel bad about it. And even gay persons watching it as well and [saying] "No, no, no, no, no"—persons who are oppressed themselves [pleading] "You're not supposed to be like that. Shhh! Quiet down!" And so all those things working against you. The heterosexual community working against you. But the homosexual community working against you [too], wanting to distance themselves. It was that pulling away I think that really wrecked Friends For Life or hemorrhaged it from the inside.

And the only people who would really come to Friends for Life would be the *most* oppressed persons—who were not just oppressed as homosexuals, but were . . . black, poor, living in a depressed area [with] barely a roof over their heads. So, Friends For Life for them was the only place where they had quiet or [could] even be loud because they had to be quiet in the society. So, having that now made Friends For Life even worse for persons looking on. It's a bunch of *unruly* bullermen now. . . . So, all of that "tarnished" the name and persons were not able to see through the thickness of the oppression—to see the beauty of the absolute pureness of this expression of homosexuality. I think that's what really brought us down. Because we made some really horrible decisions about money, but I really don't think that we would have crashed the way we did if we'd had people's support. (Sinnette 2007)[17]

Without getting lost in psychoanalytic suppositions about the circumstances under which anticipated disappointment is most likely to haunt collective accomplishments, it is possible to hear in Sinnette's proposition a particularly uneasy irony of FFL's community-building work. By allowing performative, semipublic contestations of homophobic notions of decency, FFL may have inadvertently distanced itself from portions of the very communities it had hoped to encourage. Sinnette certainly calls attention to the unavoidable challenge that homophobia—especially from within gay communities—poses for the organization; however, he also perhaps unintentionally attests to the possibility for activist work itself to clarify the populations most in need of it. Thus, the "hemorrhaging" of FFL might also be interpreted as a moment of ecstatic clarity in which the leadership of the organization was forced to step outside of what seemed to be an ailing body in order to recognize FFL's vital core. Building the confidence to unabashedly prioritize service provision for the most marginalized populations of gay men has been an important part of the growth of the organization. And this clarity of vision has remained despite having lost the office and the funding that made the space possible.

In fact, the end of the Alliance grant actually began an extended period of collective reevaluation in the organization. And for Sinnette, this critical, wide-perspective reflection is vital for FFL's longevity:

Well, it [FFL] exists but—of course—we're at a low. This is so not anywhere close to where we were when we were at our peak. And strangely enough, it's not anywhere close to how fantabulous I see us being. But I just thought we were going from strength to strength; I didn't realize that you have this ebb and flow. . . . You watch all movements; they spiral. So, they go forward and backward and forward and backward. And so—within the space of probably ten years—it looks like you're going in circles, but if you stretch it out over about fifty years, they're circles that move forward . . . it's inevitable that the evolution will take place.

What has to happen is that other [LGBT] persons have to come to that space in their mind where *they* decide to reject the oppression entirely for Friends For Life to build up. And I suppose we're . . . just waiting for the community to realize that they don't need to accept it. . . . And so, I think right now it's just for us not to die and that's what we're trying not to do . . . just not to fade into oblivion. Because once you keep the embers hot, it's inevitable that some person is going to come stoke that fire.

[But we have] to ride the low part as part of life too. Because there's a way that you could really get depressed and despondent about being in a low space. But [we should try] to figure out what this new space means in the context of the whole movement and how do I work this in the context. Because everything is usable. So, it is possible to use this fact that we are low and we're going through this period of flicker and use that as a tool to start back the fire going. (Sinnette 2007)

It is not Sinnette's background in social work alone that encourages such a wide and forgiving perspective on the lifecycle of FFL. He had for some time been the principal facilitator of the Chatroom and thus charged weekly with overseeing collective reflection and effective crisis resolution among gay men. These are the very skills that Sinnette brings to evaluating the health of FFL. The Community Chatroom Experience offers a model for the long-term reflexivity and quotidian commitment to survival that long kept breath in the body of Friends For Life as a community-organizing entity. The Chatroom served as a mechanism by which FFL could assess the particular needs of gay male communities, the organization's capacity to meet those needs, and the nature of the relationship between those communities most in need and FFL. Thus, in microcosm, the Chatroom encouraged—and thrived upon—the very processes that have sustained Friends For Life. Having emerged as a grassroots organization from a series of conversations that helped to inspire action based on a politics of survival, it is most appropriate that the organization should have been animated by its inherited Chatroom—in essence, a space for discussion devoted to preserving life and enhancing well-being.

A weekly two-hour open discussion forum, FFL's Chatroom is a site for collective reflection and exchange ultimately in the service of community building. And this community building is a vital activist gesture in its own right:

I never anticipated that it [the Chatroom] would last, but the fact that it did last is a beautiful thing because it shows that people refuse to let go of liberation—*refuse* to let go of it. And [we at FFL] use that Chatroom as a place to bring persons in and just to have them yap and quarrel. . . . Because within every movement there's that space where talk happens. And that's all you do for a long time—just talk—even if you're arguing or disagreeing, just talk [and] talk. And somewhere in that talking, the tide starts to turn and it turns and turns until eventually it's pushing in the other direction.

[I ask, "What keeps people coming to the Chatroom?"]

It's the experience. It's the therapeutic value of the Chatroom. You can't deny that talking and venting about things helps. . . . Even persons who don't like to talk, come to Chatrooms to watch other people talk. There's a way that just hearing other people talk about things can [help you] re-evaluate yourself: "Um-hmm, I did that and maybe I should have done this." And that moves you; it's a growth. Human beings have this desire to be better tomorrow than they are today—they really do! The Chatroom itself pushes us forward. . . . The power of the experience is what . . . keeps people coming back.

The most remarkable and most subtle things like just coming to a Chatroom and asking, "So, how does everybody feel tonight?" can [bring about] remarkable life changing experiences for the person who answers, "I really don't feel good, but now that I'm here—phew!"

And to not have this, to not have *this*?! When you think about it, if Chatroom was missing, fifteen years down the line we would still be struggling to find out how do we get spaces to talk. But if we talk now, fifteen years down the line we could be struggling to find how do we open a hospice for battered gay persons? (Sinnette 2007)

A therapeutic space for exchange, assessment, and collective intervention, the Chatroom facilitates individual and joint action while also providing a means by which to evaluate those actions. If this dialectic between conversation and action does not immediately seem to lend itself to a teleology of progress, it begins to come into view as part of movement building once we—as Sinnette suggests—stretch our perspectival time-frame by at least a decade and a half. The relatively simple act of "checking in" with a fluctuating population of gay men on a weekly basis has the potential not only to transform individual lives but also to foster a collective consciousness. This shared sense of community is not only a crucial political project in and of itself, but it also makes most other political activism possible.[18]

The Intimacy of Activism: The FFL Chatroom and the Uses of Desire

One can hardly deny that one of the primary interests of participants in the Chatroom is intimacy and the compelling desires surrounding it. The corporeal proximity that distinguishes the FFL Chatroom from its virtual specter also holds out the tender promise of various kinds of relationships. Most often it is these relationships that provide the connective tissue for the organization's community-building initiatives. It would be naïve to presume that sexual encounters and ongoing sexual relationships would not be included as part of the interpersonal contact facilitated by the Chatroom. In fact, Friends For Life officially recognizes that one of the motivating factors behind the continued attendance of Chatroom participants has long been an interest in meeting potential partners (Jordan 2008a, 2). Still, it would be a mistake to believe that the Chatroom—or any of FFL's programs for that matter—has ever actively encouraged sexual intimacy between participants. The organization's forthright handling of sexuality ought not to be confused with promoting sex per se:

> People might say, "[They're] a bunch of bullermen and they're only encouraging people to bull." I don't encourage anybody to bull—let me don't use the word "bull"—[with a tongue-in-cheek refinement] to have sex. . . . People choose to have sex. . . . Because if I tell you not to have sex and you want to have sex, ain't no way you going to take what I say. What I would like to know is that people in the process of going to have sex . . . they will protect themselves. That's all I would like people to do. In fact, like I was telling somebody, I want to be there to say [he performs this with a comic charm], "Look, [here is] the condom. You want me put it on for you?!" [He is quickly and sobering serious again] I love my people. (Padmore 2003)

Padmore's touching devotion to gay communities remains very honest about the inevitability of sex without ever allowing for complacency about (gay/ bisexual male) safer sex practices. Friends For Life may not have to promote sex, but Padmore's playful—yet urgent—plea indirectly affirms the centrality of sex to the HIV prevention work of FFL. If in Trinidad and Tobago—

as in the entirety of the Caribbean region—sexual intercourse remains the primary route of HIV transmission, then HIV/AIDS activism in the region must attend to individual sexual practices and collective patterns of sexual behavior. Far from avoiding conversations about (safer) sexual practices and (improving) relationships, FFL has institutionalized these discussions and held them at the center of the organization's work for the entire life of the NGO. The longevity of this intervention strategy is in part the result of the Chatroom's ability to hold open a sexually charged space devoted to conversations about sexual and social health concerns.

Although many of these conversations about sexual practices and intimate relationships are far from unrestrained, it is important to consider them in a context where most people still remain relatively tight-lipped about most forms of sexuality:

> You have the experience—and it's very close to my experience as well, so in that way, I'm indicative of a Trinidadian—where you like somebody, eventually you get close to them, and you might get intimate, but you don't really have a conversation about sex. But somewhere in this exploration you do things and figure it out. You get a touch that's not too nice and you don't want that one; you get a touch that's really good and you're *ecstatic* about it. But all of that in body language . . . I think that's how Trinidadian sexuality is represented.
>
> I think in very many respects we're jarred by the nature of sex and how powerful it is. And so it's kind of scary. And so we try to bridle it in many instances, but bridle it without talk. So, like how you have that concept of being politically correct in the [United] States, you have in Trinidad more of a bridling of sexual words and descriptions by using words that are not so close to the sexual words like "butterfly" instead of "vagina."
>
> But at the same time [that you're] not speaking it . . . [you are nonetheless]—in quiet intimate spaces—doing that kind of exploring and touching . . . not being sure about how far we should go and how deep. . . . But through it all, not that talking but that *doing* . . . doing it is allowable, but . . . speaking it is too tough. (Sinnette 2007)

Even though Sinnette eloquently echoes the overwhelming sentiment on the prohibitions and possibilities through which sexuality is negotiated by the various Trinidadians and Tobagonians (gay and not) whom I consulted—

informally and formally—on the matter, articulating some "characteristically Trinbagonian" relationship to sexuality is perhaps less vital than recognizing the ambivalence that Sinnette brings to the fore. This meticulously maintained gap between what is said about sex and what is done—though far from an exclusive T&T phenomenon—is readily recognized as a rather mundane practice among very many in T&T. If it is through touch and not necessarily through talk that many gay and bisexual Trinbagonian men explore their sexual desires, this may be—as Sinnette suggests—because the available language is presumed to outright refuse (or at least restrain) direct engagements with sex and sexuality in discourse.[19] However, a principally nonverbal, corporeal investigation of sexual permissibility poses a very particular kind of challenge for HIV prevention initiatives among gay and bisexual men for two distinct reasons: (1) behavior-change interventions are made exceedingly difficult if men are unwilling to have conversations about their actual sexual behavior patterns; and (2) successful interventions with individual men can be easily undermined if they are unwilling or unable to discuss necessary behavior changes—condom or water-based lubricant usage, for instance—with their sexual partners before or even during a sexual encounter (CAREC 1996; CAREC [1998] 2000). However, it is certainly a mistake to presume that because these types of conversations are perhaps improbable that they are summarily impossible to cultivate. The Chatroom itself articulately contests any such presuppositions.

The FFL Chatroom clears a space for open discussion about a range of different topics—many directly or indirectly related to sexual practices, but just as many not primarily sexual at all—at the same time that it serves as a perhaps undervalued assessment mechanism for (sexual) behavior patterns in gay/bisexual communities. In Trinidad, the Chatroom sessions I recorded addressed nearly every issue from (Internet) dating, commitment in relationships, and the meaning of love to sexual assault, condom usage frequency, and the transmission/symptoms/treatment of sexually transmitted infections—especially HIV. In Tobago, the Chatroom conversations I documented had a similar range in topics, from strategies for finding a partner, dating with HIV, and dealing with fears of loneliness to negotiating sexual roles, heterosexual encounters, and penis size. Although these ranges are far from comprehensive, it is certainly the case that sex, intimacy, and relationships are darling tropes of Chatroom conversations. These particular discussions provide not only a model for the kind of open engagement necessary for condom-use negotiation, but they also provide a discernibly alluring fris-son from engaging in tabooed speech. Thus, desire often determines both the thrust of the Chatroom conversation—despite the facilitator's chosen topic in some instances—and the constitution of the Chatroom itself—a space that exists only as long as the longing for conversation lasts.

Clearing Sacred Space: Mortality and the Chatroom's Spiritual Impulse

Decidedly a favorite topic and an understandable area of heightened concern for individual HIV prevention interventions, sexual practices, and patterns are far from the only recurring theme in the Friends For Life Chatroom. In fact, the organization's commitment to psychosocial holism as a fundamental part of their HIV/AIDS prevention care and support strategy compels a persistent framing of the Chatroom as a space of fellowship—a fellowship ultimately in the service of collective sociosexual and spiritual well-being. Implicitly addressed through group reflection on the sometimes meta-physical nature of that fellowship or explicitly considered in conversations about religious strictures—usually Christian—and agentive belief, spiritu-ality is consistently summoned in the Chatroom in part because it is such a formidable presence in the lives of so many gay men. In the FFL Chat-room—as in the vast majority of the individual interviews I conducted with LGBT people on each of the sister isles—beliefs about the extent to which Christianity condemns or condones homosexuality (even for non-Christians) were perhaps less a matter of concern than individual spiritual communion with God. There can be little doubt that many gay men in T&T struggle to resolve a presumed inconsistency between their sexuality and their religious beliefs; however, the majority of Chatroom participants have at least publicly found some means by which to reconcile their sexual desire and their spiritual foundation. It is often the case that FFL in general and the Chatroom in particular have inspired that reconciliation or at least served as significant support structures for that reconciliatory process.

The commitment of some of FFL's leadership to a by-no-means-uncomplicated spiritual devotion undoubtedly determines the character of the organization and of the Chatroom with regard to faith:

> I don't know if to say, "I *am* religious." I don't know if to say I'm not. Now, of course, you have to understand also that—as far as I'm concerned—you

don't have to go to church to pray. You can lie down in your bed, kneel down in your house, and God will answer your prayer. I believe that. . . . The church is just a place for the community to come together as one. But if you can't [go to church], you can't. Yes, you should; but if you can't, you can't.

We as gay people in growing up try to live to please people. . . . We try to please everybody and in the end we don't please ourselves. . . . And so, I'm going to live my life. I'm going to try in the process to please God because I don't think we can totally please Him. We are going to fall short. . . . We keep trying and we keep praying and we keep asking for forgiveness. But for me . . . I'm going to keep trying.

At the end of the journey, He's the only one who's going to judge me. [I] don't care what my friends say. . . . He is going to judge me according to how I live my life.

And so, I'm going to try to do what I know I have to do and leave it up to Him in the end. . . . Not because you're gay God doesn't love you. He loves all people. . . . And at the end—anyhow you take it—He's going to judge you. (Padmore 2008)

Although he was raised in the Roman Catholic faith and still considers himself a devout Catholic—even if he is a bit errant in his churchgoing— Padmore emphasizes the quotidian intimacy of spirituality over and above any site-specific religious experience. This founding father of Friends For Life does not underestimate the importance of spiritual communion, but he realizes that it is the fellowship primarily that makes a space sacred and not the space that makes the fellowship holy. For Padmore, relationships—*inter*subjectivities— determine the domain of the sacred; one's personal relationship with a metaphysical presence *and* one's relationship with a community determine one's spiritual positioning. As Trinbagonian lesbian feminist theorist Jacqui Alexander reminds us, "We are connected to the Divine through our connections with each other" (Alexander 2005, 283). Padmore's life and work with FFL bear witness to the importance of personal spiritual struggle—a lifelong process—not only within the context of community but also as a means by which to achieve clarity about the particular community within which to seek fellowship. Padmore's personal confidence about his own moral rectitude— the hard-won result of constantly challenging himself to live up to his moral ideals—not only provided part of the push to form FFL but also provides sustenance for his commitment to the organization.

If an intimate spiritual consciousness and a considered spiritual confidence helped found FFL, then the Chatroom—the soul of the organization—is a site for consistent reflection upon and reinforcement of that foundation in communal fellowship. While it is certainly not the case that all participants in the Chatroom consistently share spiritual belief systems or even an interpretation of a shared religion, it is their communion—even if they do not assemble for an explicitly religious purpose—that gives a spiritual quality to the experience. It is in this sense that the Chatroom comes to look like a church, temple, or mosque—not the structural home of a particular religion but rather a metaphorical clearing in which collective relationships (on the physical *and* metaphysical plane) are fostered. Just as conversations in the Chatroom need not always focus on HIV/AIDS in order to be a part of a holistic intervention strategy, so too can a spiritual intervention result from the very act of gathering for fellowship. In fact, the Chatroom's indirect—though no less persistent—emphasis upon HIV/AIDS very likely encourages attention to spirituality as the result of a perhaps unwitting fear of mortality. If HIV/AIDS is central to FFL's organizing mandate and even the most casual reflection upon this ostensibly fatal disease brings our inevitable mortality into especially sharp view, then spirituality—one of the principal means by which most of humanity attends to birth, death, and the "life" after each—effectively haunts considerations of HIV/AIDS and makes it nearly impossible to conceive of the pandemic without confronting death (as actuality or possibility) and turning to spiritual reassurances.

Nevertheless, it would be a mistake to presume that these spiritual considerations—often over and against any particular religious doctrine—are merely incidental for the Chatroom. Indeed, Friends For Life and the Chatroom have both persevered in no small part because of spiritually grounded leadership:

> Luckily, I started to become disenchanted with Catholicism before I really wanted to embrace my sexuality. So, it was easier to make the transition. . . .
> But [this disenchantment] also pushed me to explore who God is a little bit more and to explore spirituality a little bit more, to find it somewhere in the midst of its [Catholicism's] madness.
>
> Growing up Catholic, I really had a relationship with this Creator and—more than that—He started to manifest in certain ways . . . you see Him interacting with you. . . . So even though I was kind of shying away

from Catholicism, [I could] not abandon the fact that there was this God and He was looking out for me in some way.

. . . And then, of course, there are experiences where you feel like if you're touched by the Creator almost. . . . You're wanting something and connecting with Him for it and then receiving it—whether it was something you prayed and asked for or some kind of spiritual awakening or "slaying of the spirit" where you feel the spirit in you. . . . Having all those experiences that really just added up to a whole bunch of ways where I was anchored to this entity that they call "God." (Sinnette 2007)

The organization's resident social worker and longtime principal facilitator of the Chatroom, Sinnette—much like Padmore—remains a devout Catholic, but he makes a transition within his faith that draws him into a more intimate and dynamic relationship with his God. It is not Sinnette's sexuality that prompts a reevaluation of his faith but rather his embrace of a personal spiritual imperative over religious doctrine. By strengthening his spirituality—unrestrained by the seemingly unyielding strictures of Catholicism—Sinnette is able not only to preserve what he believes to be a reciprocal sacred intimacy he shares with his Creator but also to deepen the terms upon which that relationship grows. Sinnette cultivates a more analytic spiritual consciousness not in spite of Christian orthodoxy but rather through it. His transition then is an *intra*religious journey inspired by his desire for a kind of sacred interactionism. The near tangibility of this spiritual exchange serves to ground Sinnette firmly in his faith. And it is this grounding that in part sets the soil for the Chatroom experience by providing an often unremarked upon spiritual base and a metaphysical model for gay male communion. In essence, the fellowship that the FFL Chatroom encourages is based on a willingness to engage in a thoughtful and challenging exchange that proves rather similar in base structure to that which undergirds Sinnette's spiritual infrastructure. Padmore and Sinnette's intimate relationships with the spiritual provide models for (meta)physical encounter and exchange.[20] At the same time, these men's pronounced influence on the organization encourages attention to its principal program—the Chatroom—as a site for underrecognized collective spiritual fellowship.[21]

FIGURE 6.6 Group photograph taken by the author at the Friends For Life facilitator training retreat at Mount Saint Benedict Hermitage, Saint Augustine, Trinidad, 2008.

From Up Above, from Down Below: Eros and the (Meta)Chatroom

It is precisely the various types of relationships—be they political alliances, sexual networks, or spiritual congregations—fostered through the Chatroom experience that have proven to be Friends For Life's salvation. There can be little doubt that the Chatroom has long been the principal program sustaining Friends For Life both in terms of the collective commitment the organization's existence requires and with respect to new funding opportunities directly tied to sustaining and expanding the weekly discussion group. In April 2008, FFL received the very first commitment of funding—to date, this has also been the last—to be granted by the government's National AIDS Coordinating Committee (NACC) for a Chatroom-maintenance and -expansion pilot project, which was first proposed back in 2004 (NACC/FFL 2008).[22] Having been summarily ignored for funding from the NACC for a full four years—and nearly three years since the early termination of the Alliance funding agreement—Friends For Life would finally be able to initiate not only the long-overdue enhancement of the Port-of-Spain Chatroom but also the long-planned expansion of the project to three regional sites

(Chaguanas-San Fernando, Arima-Sangre Grande, and Tobago), each at a considerable distance from the capital city.

In order to prepare the human infrastructure for this new phase of the Chatroom, FFL organized—after troubling bureaucratic delays of the first tranche of funds from the NACC—a residential Chatroom facilitators training workshop held July 18–20, 2008, at the Mount Saint Benedict Hermitage, perched well above Saint Augustine, Trinidad (Sinnette 2008). I had the privilege of being invited to participate in this capacity-building initiative that altogether convened twenty-four gay men—including Padmore, Jordan, and Sinnette, the core organizers—and one lesbian participant at an elaborate monastic encampment on the picturesque edge of a daunting precipice.[23]

One of the most remarkable experiences I have had in more than a decade volunteering with Friends For Life, this training workshop focused the potential and—perhaps unintentionally—the experience of the Chatroom to such an extent that it almost startlingly reveals the fertile intermingling of the political, sensual, and spiritual in the work of FFL in general, but very specifically in the phenomenon of the Chatroom. Understood to be an explicitly named activist organizing environment in which FFL's leadership was not simply fostering individual support-network building—as a facilitator might in a Chatroom—but also training participants to facilitate grassroots LGBT community building using the Chatroom model, the workshop functioned as political work on two levels simultaneously. If the intended task of the workshop was to train potential Chatroom "outreach facilitators" to attract participants to and maintain the stability of satellite Chatroom initiatives, in the process of receiving the training, these outreach facilitators were also building networks of support among themselves—in essence, building a community of activist-minded community builders. While it is unlikely that a single weekend workshop could possibly result in an immediately viable, universally inclusive support structure, there were certainly various interpersonal connections that grew existing support networks and laid the foundation for the formation of new friendship webs. Although hardly the stated purpose of the retreat, the experience alludes to the very relationships that brought Friends For Life into being. The gathering provided a tangible reminder of the individual-cum-collective concern that birthed a political project in the service of survival.

And yet, because this community-building work not only requires collective concern but also demands a consistent corporeal proximity, sensuality figures prominently in the survival project. Enhanced by the retreat's insistence on bodies in sustained contact—for at least three days eating, sleeping, bathing, dancing, joking, listening, talking, and walking together—the Chatroom's sensuality becomes recognizable in the extreme. Seeing, touching, smelling, tasting—figuratively *and* literally—the expressions, the flesh, the presence, and the very air one shares in a Chatroom can be a profoundly intimate experience. The retreat merely provided the opportunity to carry through three days much of the flirtation and innuendo, the furtive glances and swallowed grins, the charged caresses and the breathless embraces that thread their way through the two-hour Chatroom from week to week across a range of various bodies and affinities. This symphony of the senses, accompanying provocative conversations about intimacy, sex, and relationships, serves only to increase the simmering potential for sexual encounter. Without suggesting that sex was the only thing on anyone's mind during the retreat—it most certainly was not—one can still recognize that sex is an unavoidable subject in any HIV prevention intervention in T&T as in much of the world. Far from getting in the way of the important matter at hand, sensuality *is* the way to best attend—fingers outstretched—to an epidemic perpetuated by various kinds of intimate social intercourse.

If contagion inevitably reveals various routes of contact—in essence, the myriad places and means by which we (or any living species) touch—then HIV places a steady finger upon our intersubjectivity, but it also pushes us toward an *intra*subjective confrontation with our own mortality.[24] If considerations of mortality tend to be the center pole in the hallowed ground of spirituality, then the metaphysical haunts any discussion of HIV/AIDS even in its refusal. However, outright spiritual refusal is certainly far from the experience of the majority in the workshop, as in the Chatroom. The absence of formal engagement with spirituality ought not to be misrecognized—in either the fellowship retreat or the Chatroom's weekly communion—as a spiritual lack. In fact, convening the Chatroom facilitators training atop Mount Saint Benedict quite aptly literalizes the figurative sacred space in which Chatroom is cultivated. Not quite a monastic hermitage overlooking a sometimes hostile world, Friends For Life's Chatroom nonetheless provides a weekly space of respite from many of the challenges of living in a world in which self-identified gay and bisexual men are hardly the majority. And like the Chatroom, the retreat also provided a fellowship opportunity that encouraged same-sex-desiring participants to live, love, and perhaps even flourish in this world we nevertheless inhabit.

Friends For Life's founding, its leadership, and especially its Chatroom demonstrate the usefulness of a widened erotic for a grassroots struggle not merely to stay alive but to collectively thrive in the midst of a deadly global pandemic. In the hands of FFL, the political, the sensual, and the spiritual become tools for the building, holding, and transcendentalizing of community. Not always a deliberate frame or an explicitly determined method, the erotic persists nonetheless as one of the organization's most valuable resources, its most fixed capital. If it is that AIDS in the anglophone Caribbean is first discovered among gay men on the largest island of a relatively small archipelagic republic, it might be wise to return to that selfsame isle for one of the oldest HIV prevention and support models those gay men have depended on for decades to preserve their own lives. Welcoming the viral spread of the Friends For Life Chatroom model—throughout Trinidad and Tobago, across the Caribbean, and beyond the region—introduces into a host of sites a vector for not only thinking the political, spiritual, and sensual together but also for *doing* community-based work informed by a hopefully contagious expansion of the erotic.

From Far Afield / A QUEER TRAVELOGUE (PART IV)

NOVEMBER

11/10/07

Zooti has to move, he tells me, because he got a *cut ass*. As casually as that he says it. The boys that have been roughing him up as he goes up and down that hill that leads home in Petit Bourg have gone too far this time. They've been harassing his roommates—they are boyfriends, his two roommates—going up and down. They've made Yakit not want to visit unless he's driving. They've got everyone walking the long way. But things like this don't happen just so. It all started with this *do-up*. Zooti introduced me to him once in town—a cute dreadlocked boy, colored contacts, dark-skinned. They're class-mates, him and Zooti. One night, Yakit and I step in by Zooti only to see that boy's backpack and shoes sitting there obvious as sin in the living room. *She have she fuckin' tings, Ms. Zooti!* Well, that boy was a blessing and curse. He gets into a confrontation with some boys troubling him in the road when he's leaving—probably for "looking gay" though kill *she* dead *she's* the butchest thing alive, color contacts notwithstanding. He's convinced his look is "bad boy" or "prep boy" but certainly not "queen." Queen he is, though. Some boy probably *throw talk* for him and it was the wrong one to fling insult his way because that face this queen recognizes. *She* tells that boy about his house getting burned down, tells that boy how *he-self* was homeless loud enough to shame him back—because really that boy knows all that, but maybe his friends don't or maybe no bullerman *ent* supposed to speak nobody shame so loud. Anyway, is then they start to harass the queen in truth. The language is vague for me. "Cut ass," "harass," "trouble"—they could mean anything, but nobody is in the hospital as far as I know. So, today Zooti gone to get the paper and I'm not sure why he doesn't walk around the way he's accustomed, but on the straight shot down to the main road or back up again, he gets his *ass cut*. The roommates—the boyfriends—see it all and call the police. They are on their way to work. Zooti gets home, changes his clothes and goes to San Juan police station, where the police inform him that they can't do anything for him if he does not have his attackers' names. Everyone knows this is nonsense, but this is often the only protection the openly gay or trans can expect in this country. Zooti makes sure to tell them—with all the sarcasm he can muster—that before he gets stabbed again or killed, he'll make sure to ask his attacker's name. The police hardly ever intend to do anything in cases like these. Zooti will return, he says, for retribution after he has moved. Today or tomorrow, he must move. He will buy a car to speed his search for a new apartment, then sell it once he's found a place. This is much too hasty for Zooti. These are drastic measures, rash decisions. Violence has finally come home and forced a move. And yet this homophobic violence is not necessarily just about gayness, though certainly homosexuality has a lead role to play. This particular round of abuses is also about shame—public shame—and pride. Zooti says he's moving. But until then, he walks the back road. He is forced out of his way. But he believes—well, perhaps he wants to believe—that all this is happening for a reason.

11/23/07

Another phone conversation with Canap: "When I was in my thirties, I was very much in love with Warit and faithful to him for two years—even though there was an entire ocean and the continent of America between us," he says without using all those words exactly. "I ejaculated into a Kleenex tissue and folded that neatly into a tissue and folded that into a clean piece of paper and posted it to him in California," and from that explanation comes some insight into Canap's aesthetic. A "corporeal romantic" I'll call it. And on the heels of that thought, he explains, "I don't mind using the words 'fuck' and 'cock' but to some people, I'm too raw." And I'll end this where we ended our conversation with a reworked Ogden Nash quote Canap offers me, "Heaven is lovely. Orgies are vile. But orgies are nice every once in a while," perhaps without using all those words exactly.

11/25/07

Roukou mentions how well one of the queens "steamed" midway through a performance from DIVA 2002 that we are watching on VHS. These are drag performance—well, technically, they're called *dress-up girl* performances here; "drag queens" *make fares* I'm told. But the border between performance and prostitution is nowhere as thoroughly policed as it is in people's minds. Because Lozei had mentioned "steaming" the night before, I ask for an explanation. One stoops over a basin of hot water, and as the steam shrinks the penis and testicles, you push them back and away to create an illusion. Not everyone who *dresses up* still does this, but the name has stuck. Roukou both understands "tucking" and knows exactly what I mean when I use that as comparison, but here *dress-up girls* "steam." And though I wonder if cold water might not work better for shrinking one's naughty bits, the steam probably makes the goods more pliable. Where might this technique have come from? Or is it an intimate innovation singular to these islands? One can only wonder.

DECEMBER

12/9/07

Vodka is the last thing I remember. A white Styrofoam cup, a succession of shots, and a swirling evening—then *day clean* across my face and I am lying on my back across an unforgiving wooden bench. I've spent the night and much of this day unconscious here outside in this yard, face crumpled and cast to the open sky. With enough clear spirit to baptize a congregation, the dance, the chant, the ritual is the same in the sweet river or a sweating sea of bodies. Either way, someone is reborn. No white robes for last night's high mass, though. Instead, a congregation of gay men nearly nude and pretending not to notice. In fact, many of these men know each other so well that they're forced to feign a big-city indifference, an urban gay-club nonchalance. This impossible aloofness is all part of the art of watching very closely while barely looking. This is my congregation. The bar is our altar. Techno, soca, dancehall—this music is our litany. We are here together. We are very far away. Crowded in on each other, these faces have grown bored and textureless. Spirits in hand—reigning over a kingdom of sweat and smoke— these men entranced the night. But today, in the heavy-lidded afternoon, I can only barely remember them. I nearly drowned last night in the church of open palms and rhythm; I nearly lost my good God-given self to a sea of liquor and long looks. But today—the tide retreated—I am driftwood on dry land.

12/20/07

"I must have left my spirit there." He says this so nonchalantly that I have to ask him to repeat it. "There in the Mangrove," he explains, "I must have left my spirit there." This is no metaphor so far as I can tell. It is not an oblique reference to nostalgic longing. He is not pining for a *soon come* return. Quite literally, he tells me that his spirit still wanders the mossy boardwalk under the leafy canopies, above the clotting black earth, through the ballet of arching tree limbs, pointed seedpods, and aerial roots. Only a few days before, I had introduced him to my most beloved haven on his island; he too had fallen in love. That his spirit is *there* explains his disposition this afternoon— distant, displaced, removed. He is without his spirit. He must return for it; I can hear his conviction subtle as a breath through the phone. And something in the way he is breathing also means that I have to return with him. Or maybe that is what I want it to mean. "Babies leave their spirits often," he is still explaining, "because they don't know to hold them as yet. Ever notice how mothers repeat goodbyes over and over out loud to their infants before going—all to assure that the baby's spirit comes along, to assure that the spirit returns home?" Unsettled, a baby's abandoned spirit disturbs the baby until it can be returned. It does not occur to me then to ask how infant spirits are retrieved and returned. Excitement about any new discovery can loosen our spirit's grasp on us and right there in awe we leave it. There, perched on the edge of the boardwalk, we—a tangle of limbs and lips—watched the Atlantic eased to a frothy calm just beyond the reef and curved into the open mouth of a bay. By the time night catches us, we have gathered what we could of ourselves and left. But his spirit we leave behind. Abandoned, it waits for the moonrise, waits for the stars making mas behind passing clouds. His spirit is not afraid of the darkness or the other wayward jumbies crowding this mangrove. This limbo is home, between land and water, between here and there; the uncertainty is comforting. His spirit waits patiently for flesh to remember, for flesh to return. But sometimes flesh cannot. And so, this place is thick with wandering. "With your spirit there," he admits, "you can describe a place perfectly stone for stone, root for root, tide for tide," and with his next breath he calls this all foolish superstition, convinced I could not possibly believe him. But I do because my spirit is already his.

MAY
5/21/08

Ribbon wrapped around my fondest memories of lovers lost, I place them one beside the next in the battered sandalwood trunk of me. I fasten the warped lid and ease myself—day by day—away from the latest love to grasp at my best portions. I am the sea at low tide, my retreat imperceptible. Taking heart from the spectacular sadness of another sunset, my thoughts— scattered like coconut palms on the coast—are at the mercy of fancy birds and shifting sands. I am also pulling away from the blushing face of Julie mangoes, from their flaming amber flesh, just as mango season dawns. Right as Saint Julie reach the open-air market in town, sweet blessings stacked into pyramids on sooty wooden planks, I am learning to let my lust go. Here too I am falling out of love again. I am preparing to go. Each time, some heartbreak, some distaste attempts to make the pulling away just a little easier. But it cannot be easy. Emotions are the hardest to pack; they are oblong, sticky, uncovered, all smoke or fragile glass. The *soon-come* departure is never fast enough, always much too soon. For now, I am only settling into the ebb and flow, watching moon cycles, practicing my goodbyes. Already, my most tender parts are growing nostalgic for the places I have barely begun to leave.

I forget for a moment not to believe a word Vervine says. This is not the disbelief reserved for pathological liars. Related, but not nearly so suspicious, this disbelief is reserved for actors. And she is an actor of the most dangerously intuitive sort. I have witnessed tightly woven lies unraveling at her feet, picked apart by the gentlest curiosity. Her tongue blunted, this is the actor at her most intriguing. But it never takes her long to recover its edge. Her lies are epic. This I learn from Susi, Vervine's lover, who has no qualms about mentioning how often they fuck. And yet the details of who is fucking whom is never clear even though the talk is so often offhandedly in mouth. Susi dismantles lies; she takes sadistic joy in undoing them. Vervine simply replaces them with more elaborate ones. Their relationship is an elaborate drama, and both women merely players. So when Vervine tells me that she knows Dionne Brand and that the famous Trinidadian-Canadian lesbian writer was here in Tobago on holiday sitting at a popular hotel bar with her statuesque wife, I cannot believe her. When she says she is of course familiar with Dionne's writing, I begin to wonder. I am curious and uncertain. This is the trick of lies, the trick of theater: I know this isn't real, but who's to say it isn't true. Vervine admits all of this with more rum than coke in her glass, in between cigarettes, and I cannot help but think myself twice foolish. A fool for not having known Dionne Brand was on island, and an even bigger fool for possibly believing Vervine Bamboo at all. The principal character in a fiction she is writing with her life—a sort of speculative fiction in which she alone determines reality—Vervine takes artistic license with the truth. Was Dionne Brand actually here or was she imagined, set *just so* on the horizon of the believable? Either way, I have already been warned about pursuing her. Richard Fung tells me one summer in Toronto that Dionne is exhausted with these "dissertation things," which I take to mean—after a coveted conversation with her—that she is weary of budding academics attempting to write about her life and her work as a way to avoid doing our own. But perhaps this too is fiction.

JUNE
6/3/08

Mowan tells me his nonchalance is a "cultural trait." And before his next breath, I'm already running with that notion in my mind, watching where its stride falters and its breath goes shallowest. I am trying to make sense from nonsense; this is a humbling alchemy. "Perhaps you are used to getting what you want quickly," he says "but that is not the way here." I consider the indirection of the enslaved, the indirection of the colonized, the horrors under which the way around is the only effective way through. Maybe this roundabout disposition defies expectation, rests casually in the moment to moment. Perhaps he is trying to teach me something about Tobago that is not readily apparent. This small island sedimented with nepotism and spite, where complaining is futile and arguing for show. A small place where so much seems illogical if taken at face value, where what you see is not half as important as all you don't. Minds here are always already well made up until they are not. After all, one must consider that if a daring mind changes today, where can it go on so small an island to get away from being so utterly wrong yesterday? This is perhaps why apologies, flat straight apologies, are so hard to come by here. And if I expect that I can change anything if I try hard enough, that I can make a life out of my passions, that the world is open to me and full of possibilities, then this is all by virtue of having been born in America, not here. This individualistic idealism is most naïve and most American, but subtle in its seduction of even those of us most skeptical of American exceptionalism. These are the hard revelations that bring the disillusioned among us cheek to cheek with the disturbing imprint of the United States upon us, especially once we've managed to leave it behind. It can never be left behind. A Yankee in denial, my history-blind optimism cannot accommodate small-island cynicism or the hungry depression that consumes so many of the young and talented here. What solace can I possibly offer a young Tobagonian gay man who has lost faith in the world and the importance of his place in it, whose entire world has up till now been this island? Instead, I complain that he is not passionate enough, not driven or ambitious enough, not strategic enough. It is frightening to realize that—and here I paraphrase Essex Hemphill—I love him the same same hurried insensitive way America loves me.

6/24/08

It's mango season—pot turn down. It *ent* make sense trying your hand—sweating away your afternoon, burning up your good pot—because no matter how sweet your cook, it can't compete with what falling ripe ripe from the neighbor tree. Julie mangoes on the ground feeding dog and bird, but you reaching for pot spoon and Golden Ray. Just give the children soft *doux-douxs* to suck for breakfast, slice up a few starch for lunch and for dinner three Julie—six bold faces, three flesh-embedded seeds, all a luscious sunset orange—will do just fine. You ent bound to see the grocery for months if you choose because the best thing ever make coming down by the bucket full from trees nobody can really claim. In the middle of the square, in the middle of town, I make a new friend picking mangoes from trees most people hurry past on the way to work, to lunch, to catch car home, to see about their business, which certainly does not involve being seen picking mangoes in town like some never-see-come-see from country. We eating *mango vert* and all, making chow from the ones that don't end up force ripening in brown paper sacks. Nobody have time to mind callaloo or split peas or *pelau* or curry goat or macaroni to make pie—no, not now, not when mango in season. Not even the market have room enough for all that pick or pelt down from highest branch to ground. Turn down pot! Glory in season.

JULY

7/22/08

Mayoc is an imposition. His height, muscle mass, and blackness are all significant, but incidental. It's his boyish beauty in the midst of all the grand signifiers of manhood that catches one off guard. And if one isn't careful enough, this mismatch can turn everything you thought you knew upside down. When Mayoc is sitting, there is an overwhelming compulsion to kneel or stand in such a way that may as well be prostration. Such is his command of a princeliness he smirks into far too often to be actual royalty. But the bloodline seems to persist, and blood alone is sufficient in these matters. Every now and again, like candy, this born and bred Trini sucks on the most authentic-sounding Bajan accent; his tongue picked it up somehow, but exactly where he cannot recall. And this "authentic accent"—though honestly my assessment is questionable at best; I am a *Yankee-dadian*, after all—sounds the closest to what I recall of Barbados. Mayoc slips into his Bajan tongue: "When Father God was sharing common sense, you went and hide?!" This he says with a devious smile, nearly too big for his face, helping the insult to go down smoother. One cannot but return that grin in the mouth of such biting affection. It does not help that I sometimes rent a room from him; landlords' jokes—even the sharpest-edged ones—are always funny, especially when they aren't. Mayoc deems what is to his mind some foolishness I asked or did worthy of this response, ultimately a long tongue-in-cheek reach back to an originary dotishness. The impossibility of what he says and the water-in-mouth roundness of the Bajan accent make the quick moment deliciously surreal. And yet Mayoc's absolutely pointed jab lands squarely on my jaw without much fanfare or bloodshed. Father God soon come for another round of sense sharing; make sure you not somewhere hiding when he reach.

This white enamel pail is pristine as Chinese porcelain, pouting its cobalt blue lip. Though made for precisely this kind of chore, the pail was in my mind far from utilitarian. I bought it because I found it beautiful, elegant, simple, not because I could appreciate its usefulness for toting water from a standpipe in the yard. But here I am, standing below a six-hundred-gallon rainwater tank, pail on the ground, catching water from a gurgling spigot. I seldom consider exactly where the water I bathe with comes from. Behemoth filtration plants, hundred-year-old pipes nestled below asphalt and concrete, the vagaries of ocean currents and rainfall—these are hardly my daily concern. I could not tell you which rains on which days for how long or which rivers turn waterfalls baptizing which stones before flowing from my faucet. But these past few days, I have bathed in the brisk rainwater— collected in a succession of short showers each day of this rainy season—that fills my pail. Eyes closed, I'm calmed by the determination of water. I hear its first playful pets on the enamel and soon its rolling gurgle. Then the pail is full. Its grooved wooden grip is a blessing against the weight of crystal water that rests on the pail's concave belly. Caught, the rain struggles ever so slightly up over the edge. The metal handle threading the spinning grip bends into long strained smiles from the transparent weight. If not for the promise of cool sweet water anointing, this ritual might be madness. But this wetting down is vital uplift on a morning. So, I tote water, determined to stand briefly between sky and soil—quenched.

Black Queer Diaspora and Erotic Potentiality

To have one's belonging lodged in a metaphor is
voluptuous intrigue; to inhabit a trope; to be a kind of
fiction. To live in the Black Diaspora is I think to live as
a fiction—a creation of empires, and also self-creation.
It is to be a being living inside and outside of herself.
It is to apprehend the sign one makes yet to be unable
to escape it except in radiant moments of ordinariness
made like art. To be a fiction in search of its most
resonant metaphor then is even more intriguing.

DIONNE BRAND, *A Map to the Door of No Return*

By way of conclusion, I offer two interrelated introductions. First, I introduce
Jacquelyn Fields—a formidable Afro-Trinidadian lesbian activist—through
whom I recall the constitutive elements of the new erotic proposed from
various vantage points in the past few chapters. An interpretive frame that
highlights the spectacular and quotidian interworking of the political, the
sensual, and the spiritual, this new eros names a spirited crossroads where
Fields comfortably and adamantly resides. Second, I introduce a methodological proposition that insists on attentive listening to what black queer
people have to say about their lives and work as absolutely vital for a still

emergent black queer diaspora studies. By considering what it might mean to hold situated speaking subjects—primarily though not exclusively—as the focal point of a diaspora-conscious black queer studies, I point toward the larger implications of this study's principal methodology. My elaboration of the erotic is not merely assisted by the voices of same-sex-desiring Afro-Trinbagonian subjects—certainly among others—but actually relies principally on these voices. I propose that this grounding in people and place (which is not the same as hermetic confinement) is crucial for any black queer diasporic engagement. And just as this study could never pretend to exhaust the full range of experiences conceivable under the sign of black queerness—in fact, specificity is one of the healthy results of a situated subjectivity—so too must this analysis merely gesture toward a renewed expansiveness for eros as epistemology.

Jacquelyn Fields and the Mythic Real

Giving new breath and flesh to this concept here is an ever-absented presence: a Caribbean lesbian.[1] If she is invisible, she is the wind. As breeze is the only other way to see her—from breath to gale, knowable first in the rising chest, the rippling sea, the bowing frond. It is hurricane season. An entire region watches the sky for the first sign of wingless things taking flight. A settled presence wise in the meteorology of an island people among whom she has lived for over six decades, Jacquelyn Fields is elemental. She has for over a decade been not only the sole lesbian presence in the leadership of Friends For Life, but also one of the most outspoken HIV/AIDS activists in T&T concerned principally with the health and well-being of same-sex-desiring women.[2] A refined tomboy, self-trained biblical scholar, retired police officer, and absolutely bold-faced Afro-Trinidadian lesbian, Fields swiftly gathers up her face in disbelief when—in an interview—I ask her to describe her race. She tenderly chastises me: "Hello?! African to the bone . . . you'd have to say I'm African . . . that's who I am. I'm of African descent" (Fields 2008). In a postcolony overlaid with centuries of arrivals and cultural transfigurations, holding Africa at the center is a political and ideological gesture that conceives a racial identity category (blackness) in the womb of an identification with the African continent. This type of fervent Africa-centered consciousness is perhaps understandable when one considers that Fields came of age right alongside Trinidad's black power movement in the late 1960s and early 1970s. The "Africa" Fields evokes here is representational.

And yet it is through describing herself as an African that Fields indicates the interpretive frame within which she reads her racial identity; her blackness is contingent upon her Africanness. For Fields, her race and its presumed point of origin roots/routes her back across the Atlantic.[3]

It is this racial imagination—dependent on *and* despite errant essentialisms—that in large part preserves the coherence of diaspora. In fact, our reconceptualization of the erotic sprouts from the soil provided by one of the most fertile minds in the imaginative archipelago that is the African diaspora. Recall that this new approach to eros is deeply indebted to Caribbean-American, lesbian feminist, activist, poet, novelist, and essayist Audre Lorde. It is Lorde's positioning of the sensual as a bridge between the political and the spiritual in her classic essay "Uses of the Erotic: The Erotic as Power" that has made much of the present intervention graspable. For this, it is worth returning to Lorde: "The dichotomy between the spiritual and the political is . . . false, resulting from an incomplete attention to our erotic knowledge. For the bridge which connects them is formed by the erotic—the sensual—those physical, emotional, and psychic expressions of what is deepest and strongest and richest within each of us, being shared: the passion of love in its deepest meanings" (Lorde [1978] 1984, 56). Stretching the erotic so that it might include the sensual alongside the political and the spiritual allows it to approach the deeper resonance—not altogether foreclosed by essentialist slippages—that Lorde brings into view. Both a way of *reading* and a way of *being* in the world, a broadened *Lordean* erotic proposes an interpretive perspective that is at once a mode of consciousness. This epistemological positioning provides a way back through this study that is at once a way forward. Fields leads the way.

The Presence of the Political, the Politics of Presence

In July 2004—as part of Trinidad and Tobago's tenth annual Gay Pride Week celebrations—Jacquelyn Fields took a principal role in organizing the very first lesbian night to be included in the formal roster of events. At the height of the evening's performances, Fields—in her role as mistress of ceremonies—delivered a call to action for same-sex-desiring women in T&T:

> Gay women must wake up. It's time we get [together] as a body. Gay women in Trinidad and Tobago are nobody, you know? . . . We follow the men. We have enough intelligent women in the community and it's time

we do something about it: form ourselves into . . . some group, do something, have some union, have some society, be a voice in the society, let
it be heard. . . . We are intelligent enough to know who we are, what we
want, why we want it. And we are intelligent enough to get together and
form ourselves in [to] some form of organization . . . we could even as-
sist those of us that have HIV/AIDS. Some of us do, you know? Don't fool
yourself because some of us nice and fat and round. . . . As ladies, I think
we should all get together and do something for the community because
it's time. (Fields 2004a)

Having cleared a space for same-sex-desiring women in the usually male-
dominated celebrations of Gay Pride on the island, Fields cannot let slip the
opportunity to provoke community building in the midst of the festivities.
She proposes that it is only in cohering as some form of politicized entity that
same-sex-desiring women will appear as a metaphorical body, a thinking,
acting, speaking, demanding, assisting body—a body that *does* something
and thus exists. In fact, Fields herself is instrumental in convening the first
Lesbian Chatroom—following the Friends For Life model—in the weeks following her plea for collective consciousness.[4] This Lesbian Chatroom—after
having functioned for some time as a rather visible support group and HIV/
AIDS awareness mechanism exclusively tailored to the needs of same-sex-
desiring women—seems to have been disbanded.[5] Yet Fields continues to
be a focal point for collective organizing among same-sex-desiring women
even if they do not explicitly identify as "lesbians"—this despite Field's own
full embrace of the term "lesbian" and her undoubted influence in marking the Chatroom as a "lesbian" space.[6] The fraught politics of semantics
aside, Fields calls forth a community and attempts through discussion to
constitute a collective politicized consciousness. Through Fields, we are reintroduced here to *the political*—an expansive concept that provides the first
means by which Friends For Life, Peter Minshall, and McCartha "Calypso
Rose" Sandy-Lewis have been drawn together in this study.

Whether it is Friends For Life's commitment to the collective well-being
of gay men, Minshall's symbolic battle for the heart of his nation through its
Carnival, or Lewis's sweet critique of the penis despite all stubborn imaginative impotency, the political sets the stage for interpreting each of these
interventions and threads those interpretations together. Juxtaposing these
three efforts within the broader frame of the political brings to light not
only the evident bridge HIV/AIDS provides between FFL's Chatroom and

Minshall's *Sacred Heart* but also the discursive intervention—literal *and* symbolic—central to both Calypso Rose's "Palet" and FFL's Chatroom or the phallic symbolism that makes both Minshall's band and Lewis's calypso such effective interventions. Each in its way a collective, gender-conscious effort to preserve a space for representational or actual existence, the three works operate primarily on distinct political terrains, but thinking them together reveals overlapping boundaries across concerns about a politics of presence. These cross-workings of the political also reveal the extent to which same-sex desire and intimacy determine the connections that draw one outside of the self and into community. This intimacy not only provides the networks upon which activism depends but also encourages the very contact—in an age of HIV/AIDS—that can at once prove so necessary and so deadly.

The Formative Flesh of Intimacy: Approaching the Sensual

Fields's call to action also calls attention to the threat of HIV/AIDS even in the one sexually active population often incorrectly presumed to be beyond the risk of infection. If same-sex-desiring women must also confront the challenges of HIV/AIDS, then Fields is convinced that community mobilization becomes even more urgent. For Fields, this political work relies principally on clarity about female same-sex desire and the relationships it fosters. In an impromptu interview I conducted with her at the conclusion of the Pride lesbian night program in 2004, Fields definitively marks what she believes to be the tender vulnerability and vital strength of female sensuality:

> I am free. And I'm proud to be lesbian. . . . I know I would prefer making love to a woman, rather than man. As a matter of fact, I can't relate to men. I don't know how to start to make love to a man . . .
>
> It's no good pretending to be lesbian because if you're a woman and you're being touched by another woman and she is a lesbian, then you're in trouble. Because there is no way a man will give you that same pleasure or that same feeling. So, your life will be miserable and confused. Don't worry to try it; it's nothing to try. (Fields 2004a)

It is in the touch—the act of making love, the cultivation of pleasure between women—that Fields approaches a same-sex subjectivity. To be a woman knowledgeable of the intimate touch of another, experienced in making love to another, willing to please and be pleasured in return by another is—in Fields's hands—one of the principal characteristics of lesbianism. This touch from a same-sex-desiring woman is presumed to be so charged that it might in fact prove dangerous to ostensibly heterosexual women precisely for being so seductive, so masterful in the art of sexually satisfying a woman. Undoubtedly, there is a moan of sexual bravado in Fields's declaration about female same-sex sensuality. But braggadocio aside, it is Fields's attention to an affective communion shared between women that is most instructive. By emphasizing this "dangerously" pleasurable sensuality, Fields opens a space to contest an overemphasis on penetrative intercourse as the principal means and ultimate goal of sensual intimacy.[7] This broadened perspective on sensuality is precisely what allows room enough in the concept to hold together the distinct parts of this study in a single intricate flesh.

Whether through the sung symbolism of sweetness shared between women, the frisson of expectant flesh and tabooed speech in a weekly struggle against a sexual scourge, or the procreative dialectic between fabric and flesh harnessed in a ritualized display of safer sex practice, the sensual reveals the various tender places where the elements of this analysis rub one another raw. In fact, the body of this engagement is recognizable as such in large part as a result of same-sex desire, the intimacies it provokes, the communities it encourages and the aesthetic possibilities it inspires. Just as the pleasures of the palate—as a site of taste, speech, and song—press Lewis's calypso up against FFL's discussion group, so too does the tantalizing phallus—always melting or just about to explode—maintain the symbolic intercourse between "Palet" and *The Sacred Heart*. And it is precisely the tantalizing threat of sexual encounters that not only provokes both a new HIV/AIDS NGO and an HIV/AIDS awareness Carnival band into existence but also makes their interventions—quotidian or spectacular—so undeniably attractive. If these interventions have been effective, their success comes in large part not from narrow attention to the moment of sexual encounter—even in the midst of an overwhelmingly sexual pandemic—but from incorporating the full body of sensual and affective exchange into their programs. This ecosystem of intimate relations cannot exclude the symbiosis between the mundane and the divine. Thus, spirituality comes to the fore as both a transcendental model for intimacy and a means by which to understand a connection deeper than the flesh.

Mundane Ecstasy/Mysterious Mortality:
Summoning the Spiritual

For Jacquelyn Fields—as for the majority of same-sex-desiring subjects I encountered in T&T—a relationship with spirituality is vital. In fact, she begins her remarks at that lesbian Pride event in 2004 by not only acknowledging the centrality of spirituality for herself but also preaching the divine to her impromptu congregation:

> I am so gay so long that I believe in the Creator. And I believe he made me so. And I believe none of you, none of you has anything to do with it! I love me. God loves me. And I'm walking proud, so I'll always preach God.
>
> Is not no Sodom, it's no Gomorrah thing with me. That has nothing to do with it. Sodom and Gomorrah—He didn't destroy [them] because of no sodomy and all that. Don't study them old people, you know. He destroyed those cities because He couldn't even find three that was righteous. Let me tell allyuh something: it had nothing to do with the bullers and it had nothing to do with the lesbians. And yet, It had to do with all the bullers and all the lesbians still, you know why? We forgot God.
>
> We forgot our creator. And without Him you could do nothing. . . . So, I'm admonishing you all to remember your higher power. *There* is where you get all your substance, all your knowledge and all your power from. And you all would be surprised at how much power you have. Power as lesbians and power as people serving a higher creator. . . . Ladies, the candle that you have inside you . . . it out too long. (Fields 2004a)

Fields was raised Anglican under the watchful eye and swift wrist of a Barbadian mother; her Trinidadian Seventh-day Adventist father was a seaman. Fields began an Anglican; her mother would have it no other way. The iron will of this woman from "little England" also made church and the library unavoidable for even the most tomboyish young lady. However, early the obstinate intellectual, an adolescent Fields would summarily refuse to be confirmed in the church until the rite could be grounded in the Bible. In the wake of this refusal, Fields became a Seventh-day Adventist—following her father and learning a respect for the Saturday Sabbath that she keeps to this day. Much later in Fields's life, a gay male friend introduced her to the Spiritual Baptist faith into which she would be baptized only to return through rebaptism to the Seventh-day Adventist church out of respect for the wishes of her dying mother.[8] These journeys between the different provinces of

Christianity served at every rebaptism only to rejuvenate Fields's faith, to re-affirm a spiritual consciousness that she admits remains unbounded by any particular religious doctrine: "Remember it's not to be 'religious' as much as it is to be spiritual. Spirituality is much more than religion. . . . I don't want to tell people which religion to join because I'm not into religion. But they could read for themselves. Whatever book! Whether it's the Koran or the Bible or whatever book because basically all the books have the same thing in it . . . once you could relate to a God of your understanding—that's it" (Fields 2008). Fields admonishes same-sex-desiring women (and men) to pursue this search for the "God of your understanding" with a passionate intellectual curiosity. She insists this curiosity not be undermined by ho-mophobic religious mythos that distorts the Bible to the point of effectively distancing same-sex-desiring Christians from any kind of spirituality. Sodom and Gomorrah—the Bible's razed twin cities, which are so often deployed to bedevil the faith of same-sex-desiring Christians in the region—are recon-textualized and redeployed in Fields's telling as a warning against rampant secularism.[9] Fields comes to celebrate her lesbianism not in spite of her higher power but rather *through* Him. And with this reassurance, she en-ters confidently into an ideological battle for gay—but especially lesbian—metaphysical consciousness. This necessary recognition of spiritual strength and clarity—unrestrained or obscured by the strictures of any particular re-ligious doctrine—is absolutely fundamental to the communion of subjects gathered for this study.

Whether through the mas—and its transfigurative ecstasy—as a conduit between the mundane and the magnificent, the voluptuous voice that even in singing the secular still carries the undying resonance of the sacred, or the collective fellowship that conversation encourages in a space religiously cleared for concern about communal well-being, the sacred essentially pos-sesses the present project. The epic struggle with mortality—individual or collective, actual or symbolic—inspires Minshall, Lewis, and the leadership of FFL to create as a means by which to reconcile the fragile materiality of the body and the intangibility of spiritual strength. Whether encouraged in part or not at all by the HIV pandemic, this attentiveness to death *and* life is haunted by a perpetual concern with the sacred unseen. Stepping outside of the self through mas, Spiritual Baptist mourning, or a concern for another's well-being, Minshall, Lewis, and the men of FFL each find a way to the other-worldly that is charted across the world we share.

Erotic Redux: An Ancient New Concept

This introduction to Jacquelyn Fields provides an opportunity to reintro-
duce the concept that provides the theoretical infrastructure of this study:
the erotic. Although the preceding chapters are certainly linked through a
host of other concerns, eros is the principal means by which I have brought
together the various subjects that comprise this analysis. Admittedly, an
overarching interest in instantiating a (not-so-new) same-sex-desiring presence in Trinidad and Tobago across three of the most prominent tropes in
Caribbean cultural analysis—calypso (music), Carnival (performance), and
HIV/AIDS (activism)—also fundamentally shapes the study and provides another means by which to hold the body of this text together. Similarly, an investment in a transdisciplinary methodological model that foregrounds the
perspectives, artistry, *and* community-organizing work of same-sex-desiring
T&T in a single study also provides a frame within which to see this engagement as a jointed whole. However, the erotic undergirds this engagement; each of the preceding chapters both instantiates the "new" concept's
interpretive versatility and contributes to its elaboration. Through spectacle, Peter Minshall's *Sacred Heart* offers a fleeting glimpse of the erotic, a
material representation of the interrelation between its constitutive elements. Working in a performance genre in which the visual reigns, Minshall gifts the concept symbolic cues that give it resonance in T&T's cultural
context. Encouraging us to hear the political, the sensual, and the spiritual
as part of a single sonic landscape, Calypso Rose's "Palet" contests the primacy of the visual in our reconceptualization of the erotic. Instead, Lewis
prompts a particular listening technique that attends not only to what is
sung but also to the body singing. Finally, Friends For Life—in its founding,
its leadership, and especially its Chatroom—touches the particular way in
which eros might be used not merely to think across differences but also to
do collective community-building work. Thus, the previous chapters ought
not to be conceived of as having merely provided various illustrations of the
concept but rather as having provided the very coherence of the concept as
it is explored from various perspectives. And in this instance, that coherence
relies principally—though not exclusively—on situated speaking subjects.

Not Quite Silent, Just Not Heard: The Lessons of "Queer Ethnography"

By way of the second introduction that bookends this conclusion, I turn to some of the most prominent scholarly work published on same-sex-desiring communities in Trinidad in order to make a methodological proposition.[10] What might it mean to center situated black queer speaking subjects in an emergent black queer diaspora studies? Queer theorist and transnational cultural studies scholar Jasbir Puar began her career writing about same-sex-desiring (primarily Indo-) Trinidadian communities. Her article "Chutney to Queer and Back: Trinidad, 1995–1998" (2009) polishes quite a few of the arguments she initiated with her doctoral dissertation (Puar 1999, 2009).[11] Puar's engagement with Trinidad in this last article is particularly germane here because of her articulation of what she refers to as "queer ethnography":

> A queer ethnography, along with taking up critical practices of feminist, self-reflexive, and experimental ethnography . . . shatters the disciplinary policing of what constitutes a "proper ethnography." More crucially, queer ethnographies can resist the assignment of discourse to the silenced subject(s), while simultaneously tracing the epistemological conditions of possibility for a/the/any speaking subject to emerge. It might also decenter the fixation on sexual identificatory taxonomies and sexual object choice, focusing instead on reading practices as the basis of its queerness. In other words, at precisely the moment at which one could easily read toward the obviousness of object-choice as a distinction, one must read away from it, and situate queerness elsewhere . . . queer ethnographies also have the potential to disrupt the normative disciplinary production of yet another modernist knowledge formation. (Puar 2009, 7–8)[12]

It is certainly possible to endorse the important challenges and innovations in ethnographic practice—across an interdisciplinary range—that Puar rightfully sets against anthropology's nervous presumptions about ethnographic propriety. At the same time, one might salvage at least one of the methodological tenets of modern ethnography: an extended stay in "the field." This we keep not in the service of defending largely fictive disciplinary boundaries but rather in the service of the subject(s) about which we hope to write. An extended stay (even perhaps in one's own backyard—figuratively or literally) does not necessarily result in an intrinsically better study, but it certainly opens the possibility of a better-informed one. An analysis informed by extensive face-to-face conversations over an extended period of time is well positioned to trace the "epistemological conditions of possibility" under which to identify emergent queer speaking subjects. These subjects are always part of discourse and hardly ever silent even if they are not always properly heard. But what might it mean to include these queer voices in the articulation of various possible epistemological conditions? How might that strategic methodology in turn offer another view of any range of subjects—ourselves included?

Despite the chorus of same-sex-desiring Trinidadian voices heard quite clearly in Puar's dissertation, a decade later she insists that these subjects need not—and probably should not—be determined by sexual-object choice. And this shift aerates the conceptual soil in which Puar plants her notion of queer ethnography. For her, there is fertility in juxtaposing the "non-normative, sexualized racialization of Indo-Trinidadians" (regardless of sexual orientation) alongside same-sex-desiring and sex/gender non-conforming Indo-Trinidadians under an expansive conceptualization of "queer" (Puar 2009, 6). Puar presides here over an ideological marriage not conventionally sanctioned—as she quite rightly notes—by a "traditional gay and lesbian ethnography" that privileges publications about a gay presence, teleologies of "outness," and the "nativized" perspectives of gay and lesbian anthropologists presumed to be studying "their own" even across racial, cultural, or national lines (Puar 2009, 6). This broader perspective on the notion of "queerness" and the sociopolitical potential of the alliances it promises is decades old in queer theory (Rubin 1984; Warner [1999] 2000). However, Puar's intervention extends a much less attended to—though perhaps as old—race and ethnicity-conscious perspective on this expansive queerness beyond the geoconceptual territory of Euro-America (Cohen 1997). There can be little doubt that contesting the parochial fetishization of sexual-object choice (and the "sexual identificatory taxonomies" that rely on it) in queer studies—over and above various other tender sites for potentially non/antinormative subject positioning—is one of the most important challenges undergirding the intellectual project.[13] However, this challenge becomes troubling for lesbian, gay, and bisexual communities at precisely the point that it lends itself to an apparently reactionary avoidance of same-sex desire as a categorical determinant of "queerness."

A complete elision of sexual-object choice in the conceptualization of queerness is certainly very far from Puar's intent; however, if queerness is determined by a reading practice that resists sexual-object choice and seeks to discover the nonnormative in an "elsewhere" not necessarily defined by same-sex desire, then there emerges the threat that queer ethnography could very well lose sight of same-sex-desiring communities altogether. While she has been instrumental in articulating the various ways in which same-sex-desiring communities may very well collude with norm-policing power structures, Puar's insightful engagement with the moments when same-sex desire falls in bed with the norm (and thus outside of queerness) ought not to obscure the presence of LGBT subjects who for reasons of sexual-object choice *in addition to* race, ethnicity, gender, class, and educational level remain—in their particular sociocultural context—undoubtedly queer (Alexander 2005; Puar 2007). Forcing an acknowledgment of precisely this presence is Puar's declared goal; however, in our rush to mark the distended limits of queerness—vital though this stretch may be—we must not allow same-sex-desiring and gender nonconforming subjects to sit silently on the page while theorists court queerness of various other sorts. It is this unfortunate methodological imbalance that threatens to disrupt queer ethnography in its attempt to contest normative disciplinary knowledge production. In an effort to avoid this interruption, I propose not simply allowing for the intervening voices of situated same-sex-desiring queer subjects (myself included among them) but privileging these speaking subjects as fundamental for an emergent disciplinary knowledge formation structured in large part by flux: black queer diaspora studies.

Situated Speaking Subjects: The Center of a Transdiscipline

To say that the black queer diaspora is inconceivable without recognizable black queer subjects is not to say that "queer blackness" appears everywhere always identical. Perhaps by now, social constructivist interventions into cross-disciplinary speculation about race and sexuality have sufficiently transfigured blackness and queerness so as to warrant a healthy suspicion of ontological presumptions about either. However, if it tentatively goes without saying that black queerness is socially constructed—a dynamic fiction of the sort Dionne Brand marks in this chapter's epigraph—and no less material for it, the constitutive influence of sociocultural context begs mentioning. When viewed from the widest possible perspective, blackness and queerness share a fundamentally ambivalent relationship to the interrelated tropes of sameness and difference in that their coherence is contingent on a deep investment in sameness even in spite of a broad range of differences. These differences might be transcontinental, transnational, translocal, trans-communal, or even transitional, but the perpetual challenge they pose to these categories has not yet aborted their conceptualization. This dialectic between sameness and difference is precisely what preserves the fertility of diaspora—the agricultural metaphor within which displaced peoples have planted their narratives of belonging.

If it is that blackness and queerness are articulated differently depending on the meaning systems within which they appear, then might it not follow that each contributes its internal dynamism to the conjunction of black queerness? This is the very tack Omise'eke Tinsley takes when she pushes off from the shore into a black queer crosscurrent: "What would it mean for both queer and African diaspora studies to take seriously the possibility that, as forcefully as the Atlantic and the Caribbean flow together, so too do the turbulent fluidities of blackness and queerness?" (Tinsley 2008, 193). Tinsley's oceanic metaphor floats the proposition that a more profound interpretive frame is in order. And in the wake of this turning tide, one question immediately bubbles to the surface: what kinds of perspectival shifts are encouraged by black queer diasporas if black queerness is an epistemic location in flux? If variously constituted black queer subjects come to understand the world in which they live through some form of black queer subject position, then they collectively arrive at a site that is constantly vanishing, shifting, and reappearing, a breathing locale that perhaps comes to resemble ancient Antilia—the eponymous phantom isle of the fifteenth century with which this study began.

I invoke this perpetually vanishing point of arrival as a departure point from which to query the very sedimentation of black queerness that threatens to truncate the black queer studies project. Resisting the reduction of this multidisciplinary project to an elaboration of the lifeways of any particular group of queer black subjects (most often US American, black, gay, and male) requires a diasporic consciousness attentive to the various specific sociocultural locations black queer subjects inhabit within the geopolitical boundaries of the United States, across the reach of a hemispheric America (extending from Canada to Chile) and beyond the Americas. Again Tinsley takes us to the water: "When black becomes only African American, black queer theory becomes insular; as the crosscurrent between Atlantic and Caribbean, Atlantic and Mediterranean, Atlantic and Indian Ocean are richest in marine life, so they will be richest in the depth of theorizing. Most simply, our challenge is to be like the ocean: spreading outward, running through bays and fingers, while remaining heavy, stinging, a force against our hands" (Tinsley 2008, 212). Attending to this churning challenge is no easy task, but anchoring black queer studies in extensive conversations with black queer subjects, in specific sites, over an extended period of time is a vital means by which to maintain the solvency of that project while also stretching it toward the various corners of the diaspora.[14] In turn, this people-centered black queer studies has the potential to simultaneously push African diaspora studies and queer studies beyond their respective sexual and racial boundaries while convincing anthropology to continue looking for the articulation of local and translocal subjectivities in the most nontraditional places.

The editors of *Black Queer Studies: A Critical Anthology*—a watershed collection of essays on the state of the transdiscipline—anxiously acknowledge the very challenge to contest US American insularity that Tinsley proffers (Johnson and Henderson 2005). In their introduction, E. Patrick Johnson and Mae G. Henderson defend their resistance to thinking black queer studies transnationally:

> In its current configuration, the volume's content is clearly centered within the regional context of the United States. Nonetheless, we are aware of the very important implications of diaspora and postcolonial studies relative to black American sexuality. We are also conscious of the sometimes narcissistic and insular theorizing of U.S.-based academics who do not thoroughly engage the impact of globalization and U.S. imperialism on transnational flows of racialized sexuality . . . our focus here primarily on U.S. racialized sexual politics is not meant to be totalizing or polemic but rather strategic. Black queer studies is a nascent field and we feel compelled to prioritize a concomitant embryonic theoretical discussion within U.S. borders in order to make an intervention "at home," as it were. (Johnson and Henderson 2005, 2–3)

This ambivalent resistance is not simply to a transnational conceptualization of black queerness—though it certainly is that—but also to a sustained interrogation of the various other black sociocultural frames of reference beyond the African American that inform black queer intelligibility even "at home" in the United States.[15] It is at the site of Johnson and Henderson's guilty refusal that anthropology is poised to make its intervention, weaning the nascent field and its twin theoretical discourse off of the bounded comfort of home. In fact, ironically enough, it is "home" as a discomforting trope that noted literary theorist Sharon Holland highlights in her foreword to the anthology, marking the lingering contestation of home as a literal and figurative site over the duration of the black queer studies in the millennium conference from five years earlier that the text is meant to document.[16]

Equally ironic—and yet also keenly instructive—is the fact that the intimate challenge to which the editors are directly responding also appears in the pages of their anthology. The inclusion of Rinaldo Walcott's "Outside in Black Studies: Reading from a Queer Place in the Diaspora" does speak well of the editors' willingness to allow flows and counter-flows in the rippling body of black queer studies (R. Walcott 2005). However, if Walcott's intervention is read not simply for his challenge to black studies but also for its implicit challenge to black queer studies as well, then it becomes possible to read Walcott's essay as a place-specific rupture in the US American discursive fantasy of black queerness. Far from undermining a black queer coherence, this interruption in fact strengthens it by drawing attention to a black queer Canadian context and thus to black queer diasporic potentiality:

> I investigate what might be at stake when the black studies project, diaspora studies, and queer studies collide in our reading practices. I argue for what I call a diaspora reading practice, which can disrupt the centrality of nationalist discourses within the black studies project and thereby also allow for an elaboration of a black queer diaspora project . . . politically the invocation of the diaspora requires us to think in ways that simultaneously recognize the national spaces from which we speak and gesture to more than those spaces. In fact, sometimes it might require a subversion or at least an undermining of the national space. (R. Walcott 2005, 90, 96)

Walcott's black queer diasporic reading practice interprets a script that is always contextual, and even though his contextual referent is primarily the nation-state, he is willing to speculate about the space beyond the nationalist text where other categories overwrite nation to such an extent that it is rendered barely legible. His tentative willingness to read beyond the nation-state represents a definitive step toward a black queer diaspora cohered by sites of elaboration not necessarily confined by geopolitical boundaries. And the argument might be made that Walcott's abiding commitment to a black queer *Canadian* subjectivity is perhaps explained, in part, as a reaction to the pervasive foregrounding of US American black queer life and artistry in black queer studies and black studies more generally.

However, M. Jacqui Alexander, in a panel presentation at the Black Nations/Queer Nations? Lesbian and Gay Sexualities in the African Diaspora conference held in New York City in 1995, voices a resounding warning against taking uncritical comfort in nationalisms:[17] "Admittedly there are different kinds of nationalisms. In fact, it is pretty difficult to imagine anticolonial struggle without nationalism—in Latin America, the Caribbean, Asia, Africa in the 1950s and 1960s. But as we know, dominant nationalism has always been heterosexist and misogynist; women have always been viewed as the cultural transmitters. So, I am discomforted by the nation and I am perennially suspect of it. Whether it is Queer Nation, lesbian nation, white American imperial nation, or black middle-class nation. It poses a big problem" (Frilot 1996). Alexander's suspicion is not ignorant of the various uses to which nationalisms have historically been put, but this recognition does not prevent her from keeping a critical distance even from postcolonial nationalisms (and *especially* from them in most of her scholarly work). Imbedded in Alexander's refusal of nationalisms is an important reminder that nationalism extends beyond the purview of the nation-state; she aggressively questions its literal and figurative deployment, its imperial and anticolonial uses, its organizing and exclusionary strategies. Alexander's critical discomfort is instructive in that it encourages us to challenge one of the lingering presumptions about anthropology—which the discipline has by now perhaps put to rest—but which may still haunt black queer anthropology if not addressed directly.

If anthropology no longer requires the ethnographer to leave "home"— and this home was most often conceived not only in nationalist terms but also according to certain hierarchies of civilization—in order to do fieldwork, then it is possible for the anthropologist to apply the methods of the discipline right here at home. And although anthropology no longer requires a transcontinental, transnational, or even a transcultural journey (in an earlier period in the discipline this trip may also have been considered transtemporal as well, presuming to leave modernity for its antecedent), it still requires attention to space, to context, to location in much the same imperfect but revelatory way that it always has. This most cursory sketch of the relationship between anthropology and space is intended to preempt any presumptions that the "proper subject" of black queer diaspora studies must reside outside of US America (at least for the US American anthropologist). This is certainly not the case, and to maintain this extranational stipulation for US American anthropologists not only retards the discipline at an earlier period of its evolution but also effaces the sociocultural complexity of the United States.

Nevertheless, black queer studies in the United States cannot simply turn away from the rest of the black queer diaspora. I propose instead that it be called upon to look outward and inward at once, while recognizing that the dividing boundary itself—like blackness and queerness—is socially constructed (though materially buttressed) and thus far from any kind of incontrovertible essence. Nevertheless, I recognize that there are black queer scholars using anthropological methods (perhaps among others) to study black queer peoples. And in recognizing this possibility, I recognize myself: queer scholar of Afro-Trinidadian and African American descent, born, raised, and educated in the United States, using anthropological methods (among others) to study black queer people (among others) in the Republic of Trinidad and Tobago. I do not presume to be the "rightful owner" or "appropriate surveyor" of black queer diasporas; however, it is unavoidable that the type of black queer diaspora-conscious work I do will carry the unmistakable imprint of my own subjectivity and the various sociocultural milieux from which that consciousness emerges. My engagement is no better or worse inherently than any other, but rather a distinctly marked contribution to the scholarly elaboration of a dynamic black queerness.

Within the body of this book, the four interludes that together comprise an interstitial chapter—From Far Afield: A Queer Travelogue, parts I–IV— provide one means by which to mark the experiential specificity of my engagement with this black queerness. In others words, these interludes are intended to function not as parenthetical breaks from my analysis of queer artistry and activism in T&T but rather as windows into the range of experiences that have made my analysis conceivable. In fact, keen attention in these entries to the complicated interaction between subjects—whether corporeal or ideological—reveals in the quotidian a naked infrastructure for the articulation of our theoretical expansion of the erotic and the present insistence on a particular approach to black queer diaspora research methods. One of the principal contributions of these interludes to the conversations they introduce and conclude comes to light if we expand the "dialogue model" of Friends For Life's Chatroom into a structuring frame for this entire project.

My volunteer work with FFL and regular participation in the Chatroom since the very beginning of my research have not only allowed but actually encouraged me to craft this analysis out of various actual and figurative conversations facilitated by FFL. Many of these influenced the writing of my chapters only after having first been marked in the field of experiences that produced these interludes. Although they are differently voiced texts, the chapters and interludes share the crucial conversations that inform my theoretical propositions while themselves participating in an intertextual dialogue that structures the book. The centrality of this dialogue demands that the interludes not be made peripheral to the body of this project. In fact, I challenge the reader to imagine an alternative perspective that positions the queer travelogue as the central focus, jointed by interstitial chapters. This potential centering of the interludes intentionally exposes my position as a conspicuous interlocutor in the conversations I represent and redeploy throughout this analysis.

By providing a means by which to position myself as a queer Afro-Trinidadian subject *in* the study, the interludes also strategically position me as one of the subjects *of* the study without foreshortening either the analytical or experiential narratives whose juxtaposition is intended to balance the work. However, my exposure as a subject of analysis is intended not simply to contest the privileged absence of the researcher-author that haunts nonreflexive scholarship but also to ease my own discomfort with an uncritical ethnographic voyeurism. My figurative and quite literal laying bare might seem a counterintuitive approach to averting fetishistic curiosity; however, the sobering recognition that textual titillation proves exceedingly difficult to anticipate or prevent prompts a strategy that reaches beyond a crippling refusal to include my experience of queer lifeways in T&T. Instead, the interludes exploit this stimulation (perhaps heightened by my inclusion of the sexually provocative) (1) as a bridge to a broader consideration of sensory intimacy, (2) as an unavoidable path to an interlinked consideration of power hierarchies and sacred metaphysics in quotidian experience, and (3) as an incentive to encourage the reader's attention through the text. Thus, instead of summarily refusing fetishistic voyeurism, this project puts that desirous gaze to work in the service of a broader vision.

Again, the FFL Chatroom provides an instructive model for making effective use of this complicated calculus of desire. If the exciting potential of coming upon a sex partner or perhaps upon a conversation about sex (enhanced by the frisson of taboo) has in large part sustained an over-two-decade-old interest in the Chatroom, then FFL has long used this sexual longing to fulfill a perhaps understated collective desire for nonsexual corporeal proximity, to undergird a community-building politic, and to address spiritual ambivalence all among gay/bisexual men and in the service of combating the HIV/AIDS pandemic. Encouraged by this practical usage of desire, the interludes that precede this chapter put the author's desires *and* the reader's desires to work on behalf of the entire book and its articulation of a new erotic that relies on a situated black queer voiced presence to which my own voice contributes.

If the project of black queer diaspora studies must be at least in part about listening for voices that can propose perspectival shifts from the impermanent places black queer people inhabit and the procreative impermanence that inhabits black queerness, then this endeavor cannot be satisfied with discursive treatments of black queer subjects or the juridical, moral, and theoretical contexts in which black queers find themselves. Nor can this analysis presume to divorce an interest in sexuality from a consideration of those black queer subjects. Black queer studies requires the appearance of black queers not simply as representational abstractions but as situated speaking subjects, whose sexuality necessarily forms part of the conversation: "In-depth, grounded research is frequently sorely missing in transnational studies of sexuality, because these settle too readily for a focus on the surfaces and commonalities of same-sex sexual globalization without adequately understanding the particular historical and social contexts in which these sexualities are embedded" (Wekker 2006, 223). Feminist anthropologist Gloria Wekker calls implicitly for rooted, context-conscious analyses of sexuality that do not trample blossoming specificities in the haste to cultivate a haphazard global same-sexuality. And this call is at once part of a delicate symbiosis between a critique of transnational sexuality studies and a desire to elaborate very specifically situated sexual communities. Wekker describes what seems like a rather intuitive research practice, yet this methodology has proven still rare and exotic in assessments of black queer life. Wekker plants a methodological seed that I have attempted to cultivate in the present study by centering situated black queer speaking subjects in my approach to a black queer diaspora studies project.

Erotic Mobility: An Opening

This methodological emphasis inspires the various listening strategies that have made my theoretical interventions possible. A praxis of voiced presence has been fundamental for the elaboration of our new erotic. As I introduce it, this new eros is an epistemic concept reliant on the articulations of same-sex-desiring artists and activists. Calypso Rose, Peter Minshall, and Friends For Life provide various means by which to heed a hermeneutic and creative challenge extending from Audre Lorde's proposition that we think the political, the sensual, and the spiritual together. And while this expanded erotic will perhaps always bear the imprint of Lorde upon Lewis upon Minshall upon FFL as a result of the particular juxtapositions in the present study, this theoretical proposition certainly has the capacity to travel beyond the conceptual locus of its origin. It is this itinerant potential that makes of a Lordean erotic both the interpretive infrastructure of this book *and* an epistemological intervention with uses perhaps even far beyond those I have imagined. In truth, this new elaboration of the erotic is as much a proposition as it is an offering.

If this present engagement with black queer diaspora studies could not possibly presume to map the entire landscape of possibilities the field contains, so too must this study not endeavor to predetermine the possible sites and subjects of our newly expansive eros. And yet I propose that the constitutive topography of the erotic will henceforth retain—as identificatory landmarks—the variously defined, interrelated conceptualizations of the political, the sensual, and the spiritual. At once mobile and malleable but still able to maintain its coherence, the erotic provides shape to my analysis while at the same time offering an invitation to explore the various forms the concept itself might include depending on the specificities of context, content, and contact in the articulation of the political-sensual-spiritual. With this study, I have drawn a new map to eros—across the overlapping terrain of queer artistry and activism in the Republic of Trinidad and Tobago—but there are myriad alternative routes and entirely distinct cartographies that this journey can only gesture toward and many more that it could never have anticipated at all. And yet the erotic—that archipelagic antiparadise of bridged epistemologies—provides a single destination, a flickering crossroads right at the fleshy intersection between the self and everything else.

NOTES

PORT OF ENTRY

1. Dionne Brand's writing—in epigraphs such as this one—at one time served as a thematic barometer throughout this text. I had hoped to use the poetry and precision of her words not only to introduce the major concepts in each of the following chapters but also to entice those readers unfamiliar with her toward her compelling oeuvre. However, due to permissions complications, this excerpt from *A Map to the Door of No Return* (Brand 2001, 192–94) is one of few morsels of Brand that survive. Still, *Erotic Islands* echoes with her resonance. For all of the original epigraphs, please see my dissertation, *Transfiguring Trinidad and Tobago* (Gill 2010).

2. "Paradise," *OED* Online (Oxford: Oxford University Press, 2017). http://www.oed .com.ezproxy.lib.utexas.edu/view/Entry/137340?rskey=RSWiZx&result=1 (accessed August 23, 2017).

3. Angelique Nixon's *Resisting Paradise: Tourism, Diaspora, and Sexuality in Caribbean Culture* offers a dynamic engagement with the historical legacies, contemporary investments, and emergent contestations of this paradise fantasy, especially as currency within the Caribbean tourism industry (Nixon 2015).

4. T&T became an independent nation in 1962 and a full-fledged republic in 1976. Taken together, several important texts comprehensively recount Trinidad's colonial history, but definitive among them is Bridget Brereton's *A History of Modern Trinidad, 1783–1962*, which certainly has stood the test of time (De Suze 1966; D. Wood 1968; La Guerre and Bissessar [1974] 2005; Brereton 1981). The colonial history of

Tobago—which the British administratively linked with Trinidad in 1889—is not as extensively documented, but what this history lacks in quantity, it makes up for in quality (E. E. Williams [1942] 1993; Laurence 1995; Craig-James 2008).

5. The literary theorist Sarah Dillon's *The Palimpsest: Literature, Criticism, Theory* offers a rigorously comprehensive treatment of the palimpsest as ancient practice and metaphorical reading strategy that lays bare the concept and inspires its expansive symbolic usage (Dillon 2007).

6. Briefly, the fetish is intriguing for this analysis because of its anthropological origins as a spiritual stand-in adopted by psychoanalysis to describe a sexual displacement that often implicitly references power dynamics. Yet again we find ourselves in bed with the spiritual, sensual, and political as linked tropes.

7. The soucouyant figure is by no means limited to T&T folklore. Throughout the Caribbean region, similar figures appear carrying various names: *lazaroons* (Dominican Republic), "old hag" (Guyana/Jamaica/Bahamas), *gage* or *duppy* women (Saint Lucia), *volant* (Haiti/Guadeloupe), and *azeman* (Surinam) (Anatol 2000, 45).

8. A "jumbie" is a (usually unwelcomed or malevolent) spirit in anglophone Caribbean parlance. Used throughout the region, the word "jumbie" (or *jumby* or *jumbi*) is believed to have been derived from the Kikongo word *zumbi*—from whence comes the New World word "zombie"—used to describe an inanimate (soulless) human body commanded by sorcery. However, a jumbie by contrast is most often a disembodied spirit, not a spiritless body ("jumby," OED Online [Oxford: Oxford University Press, 2017]. http://www.oed.com.ezproxy.lib.utexas.edu/view/Entry /102022?redirectedFrom=jumbie [accessed August 23, 2017]).

9. This brief soucouyant tale feeds upon various sources; see Anatol 2000; F. Smith 2006; Parsons 1943; and "Trinidad & Tobago's Folklore and Legends," Triniview .com, http://www.triniview.com/TnT/Soucouyant.htm, and the *Oxford English Dictionary* ("soucouyant," OED Online [Oxford: Oxford University Press, 2017]. http://www.oed.com.ezproxy.lib.utexas.edu/view/Entry/242297?redirectedFrom =soucouyant [accessed August 23, 2017]).

10. The Fula are a people primarily found in present-day Guinea but present throughout Western African. And the Soninke are a Mandé people who are thought to have founded the ancient empire of Ghana, which comprises neighboring regions of present-day Mauritania, Mali, and Senegal.

11. The literary theorist Omise'eke Tinsley proposes another flight path for the soucouyant, aligning her with the black femme (lesbian) whose fantastic presence outside certain frames of recognition is so closely watched in film theorist Kara Keeling's *The Witch's Flight* (Keeling 2007). Tinsley queries the black feminist methodological and theoretical innovations this flying femme might introduce (Tinsley 2015). Inspired in part by thinking through the soucouyant, the work that follows insists on experientially grounded theorizing and plays with writerly registers as the beginning of an answer to Tinsley's soaring question.

1. It is often incorrectly presumed that homosexuality is officially illegal in the Republic of Trinidad and Tobago. In fact, T&T's Sexual Offences Act actually makes no mention of homosexuality per se but instead criminalizes "buggery" (defined as anal intercourse between two men or a man and a woman) and any kind of sex that does not involve sexual intercourse (thus nonpenetrative sex between women, but also oral sex, for instance) unless the partners involved are a married, consenting couple over the age of sixteen (T&T [1986] 2000, 7). For more on the legal and ideological implications of this act, see the work of M. Jacqui Alexander and Yasmin Tambiah (Alexander 1991, 1997; Tambiah 2009). T&T's Immigration Act is the only state-produced document that explicitly mentions "homosexuals." It prohibits entry into the country of persons—other than citizens or residents—who are homosexuals themselves, living on the earnings of homosexuals, or attempting to smuggle in homosexuals (T&T [1969] 1995, 11, 12). Thus, this prohibition in fact applies primarily to homosexual tourists, business people, and the occasional researcher. Nevertheless, these official restrictions have to date never been used to bring a criminal case against any same-sex-desiring person in Trinidad or Tobago. In 2012 however, gay Jamaican lawyer Maurice Tomlinson—on behalf of the advocacy NGO AIDS-Free World—did call significant attention to and begin the legal process of challenging the immigration prohibition with the granted permission of the Caribbean Court of Justice (T&T Guardian 2012; Neaves 2013; JA Observer 2014).

2. This embedded Caribbean queerness reaches beyond a mere assimilationist LGBT inclusion in civic life. In fact, it includes a *longue durée* resistance to various Euro-American activist models and norms around same-sex desire, gender nonconformity and queer community mobilization. And there is a growing body of scholarly work that finally brings careful attention to these remarkably Caribbean queer worlds (Wekker 2006; Tinsley 2010; Allen 2011; King 2014; Nixon 2015; Ellis 2015; Walcott 2016).

3. A composite secondary source history of the study of gender and sexuality in the anglophone Caribbean is best told through the work of Caribbean feminist scholars Christine Barrow (1996); Rhoda Reddock (2004); and Kamala Kempadoo (2004). For primary source materials on Caribbean kinship structures and sexual behavior patterns, see the classic work of Caribbean-born anthropologists Fernando Henriques ([1953] 1968a, [1959] 1960, [1962] 1965, 1968b, 1974); Edith Clarke (1957); and Michael G. Smith (1962a, 1962b, 1965). And on Caribbean masculinity and manhood in particular, see the canonical work of Caribbean anthropologists Peter J. Wilson (1969, 1973) and Barry Chevannes (2001).

4. This does not ignore the fact that some significant scholarly engagement with same-sex-desiring Trinbagonian communities does exist even if these select texts are unpublished, not focused on T&T exclusively, or not book-length, region-based treatments. Nevertheless, the work of M. Jacqui Alexander, Jasbir Puar, and Wesley

Crichlow has certainly cleared a path for the current analysis (Alexander 1991, 2000, 2005; Puar 1999, 2001a, 2001b, 2002, 2009; Crichlow 2003, [2004] 2008).

5. Canadian anthropologist David Murray's *Flaming Souls: Homosexuality, Homophobia, and Social Change in Barbados*—the first book-length ethnographic study of same-sex-desiring communities in the anglophone Caribbean—at once instantiates and resists this exclusion-centered model (Murray 2012). And yet Murray unequivocally warns against the implicit judgment of a presumably hyperhomophobic Caribbean, especially in scholarship and in popular representations so widely circulated in Euro-America (Murray 2012, 5, 87).

6. For a look at one of the beacons of this newest generation of scholars, see Alexis Pauline Gumbs. Her dissertation, "We Can Learn to Mother Ourselves: The Queer Survival of Black Feminism, 1968–1996," and her extensive community-building work beyond the academy (see www.summerofourlorde.wordpress.com) are powerful and passionate indications of where a scholarly and personal commitment to the principles and poetics of Audre Lorde—alongside other queer black feminist visionaries such as June Jordan, Barbara Smith, and Alexis De Veaux—might take us (Gumbs 2010).

7. Before being published in *Sister Outsider* in 1984, "Uses of the Erotic" was first published in pamphlet form by Out and Out Books, a feminist press based in Brooklyn, New York, in October 1978 (De Veaux 2004, 401).

8. Among these texts, Mimi Sheller's magnum opus, *Citizenship from Below: Erotic Agency and Caribbean Freedom*, comes the closest to recognizing the sketches of a larger ideological architecture in Lorde's essay (Sheller 2012). Sheller points toward the distinct reorienting path that I propose we walk in order to understand the deepest implications of a Lordean erotic.

9. In the singular and meticulous biography *Warrior Poet: A Biography of Audre Lorde*, Alexis De Veaux notes the importance of the essay for Lorde herself: "In retrospect, she [Lorde] felt that the passion and energy to return to work [the work of the poet, after Lorde's mastectomy as part of her struggle against cancer] came from having written 'The Uses of the Erotic.' [De Veaux cites an interview Lorde did with poet and friend Adrienne Rich:] 'The existence of that paper enabled me to pick up and go to Houston and California, it enabled me to start working again. I don't know when I'd have been able to write again, if I hadn't had those words'" (De Veaux 2004, 227).

10. This particular Berkshire Conference commemorated the approaching thirtieth anniversary of famed French existential philosopher Simone de Beauvoir's bible of feminist theory *Le deuxième sexe* (*The Second Sex*; 1949).

11. Carson's essay was published two years after Lorde's *Sister Outsider* collection and nearly a decade after the original "Uses of the Erotic" speech at Mt. Holyoke.

12. Attentive readers will note that there is one dichotomy missing in Lorde's description: the political vs. the erotic (which Lorde later specifies as "the sensual").

Again, her audience may provide a clue to explain this omission. Perhaps for a group of female scholars not unfamiliar or altogether hostile to many of the theoretical interventions of feminism, recognizing the link between sensuality (the private) and politics (the public) was by the late 1970s a given. Certainly we still feel the force of the enlightened feminist mantra "the personal is political" as evidently as we feel the ideological and legislative forces pushing back against it with a bullheaded ferocity.

13. While resisting his universalist claims about the necessarily "discontinuous self" in his provocative text *L'érotisme* (*Eroticism*; 1957), it is still possible to agree with famed French philosopher Georges Bataille's insistence that erotic desire is principally a desire to reach beyond the self toward a kind of divine continuity that metaphorically kills the self—or, more precisely, releases the individualist ego (Bataille [1957] 1987, 13, 15, 17, 19, 24). For more on desire, divinity, and collective selfhood, see anthropologist Gloria Wekker's path-breaking monograph *The Politics of Passion: Women's Sexual Culture in the Afro-Surinamese Diaspora*—especially her chapter "Winti, an Afro-Surinamese Religion and the Multiplicitous Self" (Wekker 2006, 83–116).

14. Lewis Gordon identifies philosophical anthropology (and existential anthropology more specifically) as one of the busiest thought crossroads concerned with interrogating this phenomenon of human connection, a kind of interexistence (L. Gordon 2008, 13). Although Lorde's connectivity thesis predates the subdiscipline, her proposition echoes in the work of its founder, anthropologist Michael Jackson. In his *Minima Ethnographica: Intersubjectivity and the Anthropological Project*, Jackson arrives—through Claude Lévi-Strauss, Martin Heidegger, and Maurice Merleau-Ponty—at a conception of being as interconnected existence that reaches from the physical to the metaphysical (M. Jackson 1998, 9).

15. Jackson very soberly warns that an underappreciation—or textual suppression, I might add—of these substantive relationships forged in the field can lead to potential problems of epistemological and political import that ought to be taken seriously as analytical terrain for the discipline of anthropology (J. L. Jackson 2013, 240, 241).

16. My insistence on adding "art" to the classic definition of the aesthetic as the "science of sensory perception" finds powerful affinity with John Jackson's instructive reframing of anthropology itself as an "artscience," borrowing the term from biomedical engineer David Edwards (J. L. Jackson 2013, 28). If the discipline creatively and necessarily confounds the distinction between art and science, then perhaps aesthetics as an art/science of perception provides its steady conceptual and methodological match.

17. Across anthropology, African diaspora studies and queer studies, there already exists a small library of texts in common, and many of these graciously manage to defy aggressive border patrolling among these fields (Murray 2002; Crichlow

2004; Ferguson 2004; Alexander 2005; Johnson and Henderson 2005; Stockton 2006; Wekker 2006; Holcomb 2007; Keeling 2007; Padilla 2007; Braziel 2008; Gaudio 2009; Vogel 2009; Weir-Soley 2009; Scott 2010; Tinsley 2010; Allen 2011; Decena 2011; F. Smith 2011; Holland 2012; Murray 2012; Richardson 2012; Sheller 2012; Bailey 2013; King 2014; McCune 2014; Snorton 2014; Woodard 2014; Nixon 2015).

INTERLUDE I. FROM FAR AFIELD

1. All the names in these interludes have been anonymized using the common names of Trinbagonian medicinal plants. Any similarities between the uses of the plant and the personality of the person to which it corresponds—though humorous—are purely coincidental. For the scientific names of the plants and their uses, see C. E. Seaforth et al., *A Guide to the Medicinal Plants of Trinidad and Tobago* (1983).

CHAPTER 1. INHERITING THE MASK

1. While Trinidad's Carnival is the focus of this chapter, there is a lesser-known Carnival celebrated annually in Tobago as well that some sources suggest began as late as 1946. See Trinidadian dramatist Anthony Hall and bandleader George Leacock's 1998 interview, which includes an excerpt from Tobago Museum curator Eddie Hernandez's unpublished 1996 paper "Carnival and Community in Tobago," for more focused though brief attention to Tobago's Carnival (Hall 1998).

2. A colloquial contraction of the word "masquerade," the word "mas" has come to mean much more in the common Trinbagonian parlance than its origin implies. Peter Minshall has long insisted upon the use of this word to refer collectively to the various performative elements—costume, kinetics, and scale, among others— of the Trinidadian Carnival. Minshall officially and lovingly embraces the title "mas man" as a way to legitimate what he believes is an indigenous Caribbean art form, whose recognition as art is his ultimate cri de coeur (Schechner and Riggio [1998] 2004: 121; Minshall 2015).

3. For Minshall, the mas (his art) is paramount. He is adamant about the fact that his whiteness and gayness must not get in the way of recognizing the integrity of his work. Inspired by his father, he trusts that history will recognize his integrity as a man and an artist so that posterity might get on with the business of attending to his lifetime of work (Minshall 2015).

4. "Carnival," *OED* Online (Oxford: Oxford University Press, 2017). http://www.oed .com.ezproxy.lib.utexas.edu/view/Entry/28104?redirectedFrom=carnival (accessed August 23, 2017).

5. I do not pretend to offer a comprehensive history of Trinidad's Carnival in what follows. Even if such a daunting endeavor were necessary for the present analysis, John Cowley has already attempted it with meticulous detail in his *Carnival, Canboulay, and Calypso: Traditions in the Making* (Cowley 1996).

6. Although Britain passed the Emancipation Act in 1834, this de facto abolition was undermined by a mandated apprenticeship period, which would delay full emancipation and the de jure abolition of slavery in Trinidad and Tobago until August 1, 1838 (Batson and Riggio 2004, 31). Emancipation celebrations in Trinidad and Tobago commemorate this latter date.

7. Among Trinidad whites of this era, antagonisms between the older French Creole plantocracy and the British estate owners and colonial government had existed at least as far back as the British capture of the island in 1797. Carnival proved one of the principal areas of cultural contention. The British colonial government frowned upon it, but the French Creole elite's sometimes-reluctant commitment to the festival explains its resilience in an officially Protestant colony (D. Hill 1993, 212).

8. A gendered noun whose feminine form, *jamette*, is a rather commonplace contemporary descriptor for a presumably "aggressively loose" woman or any woman with a formidable sexual appetite, its masculine form, *jamet*, has quite tellingly faded from use (Campbell 1988, 24). And yet it is not uncommon for women *and* men in T&T and its diaspora to jokingly refer to themselves or disparagingly refer to others as *jamettes*; in these instances, the same uniquely derogatory term both celebrates and polices shameless sexual independence (King 2014, 123–60).

9. The Trinidad-born Dartmouth College drama professor Errol Gaston Hill postulated that contemporary *jouvay* (creolized from the French *jour ouvert*, meaning "daybreak") processions, which mark the official predawn beginning of T&T-influenced Carnivals throughout the diaspora, rose from the ashes of Canboulay after the 1884 ban (E. Hill 1972, 86). *Jouvay* (also *j'ouvert*) not only carries forward many of the performative elements of the Canboulay, but it also preserves its rebellious spirit with trenchant sociopolitical critique offered through humorous mime and satirical dress.

10. An oil-producing island with a nationalized oil industry, Trinidad benefitted tremendously from the 1974 rise in the price of oil following the Arab oil embargo. However, by 1981 oil prices would decline dramatically and Trinidad would suffer the challenges of an oil bust (Green and Scher 2007, 13, 5–6).

11. By the late 1980s, Trinidad's Carnival would take on the character that has come to define it in the global marketplace today; this character is increasingly in direct opposition to the elaborate presentations of the festival's earlier era. The appearance of the band *Savage (Saga)* in 1988 presented an infectious new model for the Carnival experience based on a streamlined economic efficiency. Catering to the fancies of the middle class, the band pared Carnival down to little more than a moving fête in which as many people as possible could be accommodated in costumes of very little notable distinction (usually some minimal assemblage of plastic beads, faux jewels, and synthetic feathers in the colors of the season) while enjoying the

most elaborate sound systems and the VIP company for which they paid a premium (Green and Scher 2007, 6).

12. Grenada-born calypso emperor Slinger "Mighty Sparrow" Francisco is among the most prominent of such famously "foreign" Trinidadians.

13. The phrase "orchid house of an island" is adapted from a 1991 speech that Dr. Minshall delivered upon the conferral of his honorary doctorate of letters from the University of the West Indies (Minshall 1991a, 3).

14. Across the Caribbean diaspora, participation in costumed masquerade is known colloquially as "playing mas." Minshall insists, "The language tells us long before we got here what you're supposed to do: 'play the mas' . . . the very word 'play' is what an actor does with a part. And the very word 'mask' is what every actor knows is the basis of theatre, whether like the ancients you put the mask on or like today you put makeup on and the character is what you wear" (Minshall 2008).

15. Also referred to as *bone-black*, *bone char* or *abaiser* (ivory-black), *animal charcoal* is a black porous pulverized substance consisting near wholly of carbon and obtained as the solid residue from the charring of animal bones. It is a deep rich pigment that can be used to make a luxuriously dark black paint. The seeming oxymoron "ivory-black" highlights the now outmoded convention among artists of using charred ivory ground into oil to create this shadowy pigment ("abaiser," OED Online [Oxford: Oxford University Press, 2017]. http://www.oed.com.ezproxy.lib .utexas.edu/view/Entry/59?redirectedFrom=abaiser [accessed August 23, 2017]).

16. For a seminal treatment of blackface minstrelsy in US American culture, see Eric Lott's *Love and Theft: Blackface Minstrelsy and the American Working Class* (Lott 1993).

17. In Trinidad—as elsewhere in the Caribbean and South America—there is also a tradition of whiteface Carnival masquerade that dates at least as far back as the mid-nineteenth century. Revelers frequently donned oval-shaped wire masks painted white and accentuated with garish "Europeanized" features or may have whitened their own faces into elaborate caricatures of whiteness (Cowley 1996, 111). The legacy of whiteface racial mimicry in Trinidad would be largely inherited by the sailor mas tradition popularized during the American occupation of Trinidad during World War II. For an incisive discussion of that occupation, see Harvey Neptune's *Caliban and the Yankees: Trinidad and the United States Occupation* (Neptune 2007). In fact, Minshall has over the years refined a compelling argument for considering the most elaborate version of this often drunk and disorderly character—the "Fancy Sailor"—as *the* manifestation of an autochthonous Trinidadian surrealism (Minshall 2002, 7, 9; Scher 2003, 59; Schechner and Riggio [1998] 2004, 111).

18. The Jamaican choreographer, social critic, public historian, and vice-chancellor emeritus of the University of the West Indies, Ralston "Rex" Nettleford, christens Minshall the "*bête blanc* [*sic*] of Trinidad Carnival arts" (Minshall 2015; Nettleford 2015, 33). Despite the grammatical error (the feminine noun *bête* requires the femi-

nine adjective *blanche*), his adaptation of the French phrase *bête noire* (literally "black beast")—used to describe an insufferable person, an object of aversion, or a goading pet peeve—is an ingenious neologism that linguistically demonstrates precisely the Carnivalesque racial mimicry and reappropriation under consideration.

19. The Central School of Art and Design is now the Central Saint Martins College of Art and Design, which is widely regarded as one of Britain's preeminent art and design institutions.

20. Quite coincidentally, Minshall would choose for the frontispiece of his thesis the very same portrayal—mas designer Terry Evelyn's *Beauty in Perpetuity*—that introduced Trinidadian theatre scholar Errol Hill's dissertation that the very same year and earned him a doctorate of Fine Arts from Yale University's School of Drama. These two great artist-intellectuals, who had very distinct ideas about Carnival's place among T&T's performative arts, would synchronize again in 1974 when Hill invited Minshall to Dartmouth College to design the costumes and set for his musical drama *Man Better Man* (E. Hill 1972, 26).

21. For the Carnival of 1972, Minshall designed a Josephine Baker costume for Sherry Ann, but did not return to Trinidad to supervise its construction. Instead he sent his mother a meticulously detailed ninety-two-page letter, filled with precise explanatory sketches and assembly instructions. An excerpt from this letter, accompanied by other thumbnail sketches Minshall created over the course of his career, were featured in the exhibition *Looking at the Spirits: Peter Minshall's Carnival Drawings* at the Drawing Center in New York City in 2005 (Camnitzer and Gulick 2005). Perhaps to avoid receiving another tome of instructions via post in 1975, Jean Minshall simply convinced her son to come home.

22. Minshall reviews his nearly three-decade-long rumination on innovative mas design techniques extending from the structure and kinetics of the traditional bat character in his illustrated essay "From the Bat to the Dancing Mobile: Technology in Mas" (Minshall 1991b).

23. When Minshall received Lee Heung's call in 1975, he was designing the small cheekily named band *To Hell With You* for Notting Hill Carnival (Funk 2016, 70). And following fast on the heels of his Trinidad Carnival debut in 1976, the mas man designed *Skytribe*—his fourth consecutive band for London's Carnival.

24. Lost to fading memories and scattered personal photographs for over three decades, Minshall's band, *Paradise Lost*, finally marches into its rightful place in the visual archive of Trinidad Carnival in famed Trinidadian filmmaker and television producer Christopher Laird's 2015 documentary *Paradise Lost* (Funk 2016, 72). The lauded film is inspired and anchored by Minshall's narration of extensive band images from George Tang's photography book *We Kind Ah People* (Tang 2014).

25. For a bit dated but still near comprehensive timeline of Minshall's mas bands and his other works, see the final pages of Richard Schechner and Milla Riggio's

interview "Peter Minshall: a Voice to Add to the Song of the Universe—an Interview" (Schechner and Riggio [1998] 2004, 126–28).

26. The *River Trilogy* is perhaps one of the most narrative-driven of Minshall's mas epics. For the full story of the trilogy, written in endearing T&T Creole English, see Minshall's elaborate tale *Callaloo an de Crab: A Story by Minshall* (Minshall 1984b). For a look at the trilogy itself, see Dalton Narine's documentary *The Minshall Trilogy: A Modern Fable as Street Theatre* (1987), originally produced for Trinidad and Tobago Television but now widely available (Narine [1987] 2011).

27. In 1971—two years before the debut of his first band—Minshall presciently designed the sets and costumes for Trinidadian choreographer and dance legend Beryl McBurnie's production *Cannes Brûlées* in London. A prophetic coincidence, neither McBurnie nor Minshall could have known that this reenactment of Carnival's initiating ritual would foreshadow the rise of a mas man (Minshall 1982).

28. Minshall and his team did not present bands for the Trinidad Carnivals of 1977, 1991, or 1992.

CHAPTER 2. PETER MINSHALL'S SACRED HEART

1. Conceived in the late 1980s, the Callaloo Company was initially an experimental theatre troupe informed by a philosophy of inclusion based on the culinary metaphor of the Trinidadian callaloo—a thick stew of various ingredients often containing dasheen (taro) leaves, coconut milk, and okra—and the improvisational performative repertoire of the Carnival. Located in a World War II–era hangar on the Chaguaramas peninsula of Trinidad's northwestern tip, the company's workshop serves as Minshall's base of operations for the production of mas bands and other large-scale spectacles. This warehouse also houses an extensive archive of Minshall's work. I owe a special debt of gratitude to Todd Gulick, the company's managing director, for providing me with unfettered access to the physical archive at Chaguaramas and to the remarkable archive of his memory (Gulick 2008).

2. Formed in 2004, the Trinidad and Tobago National AIDS Coordinating Committee was a state-run governing body for the various HIV/AIDS interest groups and organizations in T&T. This body oversaw the national response to the epidemic until the government disbanded it in 2011 (T&T 2003; T&T 2005; T&T 2013). However, since late 2015, the government has been preparing to restore it.

3. These headpieces and masks were designed in collaboration with Trinidadian sculptor Anna Serrao, whose elaborate metalwork for the band invoked the legacy of metal craftsmanship in the mas that the legendary mas man Harold Saldenah began in 1955 (E. Hill 1972, 97). Saldenah aside, a pictographic study of Noh masks and costuming that I discovered in the archive among Minshall's sketches for the band indicates that this classical fourteenth-century genre of Japanese musical drama also influenced the design of this metalwork and indeed of the entire band.

4. Dalton Narine's 2009 documentary *Mas Man: Peter Minshall, Trinidad Carnival Artist* provides a visual summary of the band. Narine uses *The Sacred Heart* to frame his extensive treatment of the mas man's oeuvre (Narine 2009).

5. A heart-shaped panel of cloth loosely fastened to the chest and often elaborately embellished with swansdown, sequins and mirrors, the *fol* traditionally adorned fancy stick fighter costumes in Trinidad. These elegant stick fighters claimed victory by knocking off their opponent's fol perhaps as a symbolic gesture of piercing the actual heart (E. Hill 1972, 28). From the French for "mad (meaning "vexed" or "insane") or foolish," *fol* was likely used to describe the defeated stick fighter—understandably frustrated at having been made to look the fool—on this early Francophone island. The mocking Nègre Jardin masquerade is a double-edged caricature of the enslaved field hand. The absurd European Pierrot/Pedrolino masquerade is based on a melancholy dandy character common in French and Italian theatrical comedy. And the fearsome Jab Jab (from the creolized repetition of the French *diable*, or "devil") is a whip-wielding, flamboyant demon masquerade.

6. Minshall's most widely recognized dancing mobiles, *Tan Tan* and *Saga Boy*, are over-ten-foot-high puppets that crouch on the shoulders of the performers (Callaloo Company 2005). They debuted as the Queen and King, respectively, of Minshall's band *Tantana* in 1990 (Ganase 1992).

7. Minshall chooses Fitzwilliam not only to portray this beauty-queen-inspired personage—who holds the sparkling heart of the nation wrapped in a red AIDS ribbon—but also as the model visage for the band's dancing mobile queen Miss Universe: *Tan Tan's Girl Child* (see plate 6), handled by T&T's 2006 Miss Universe delegate Jenna Marie Andre.

8. Minshall also admits the practical expediency of deciding on denim for the design coup of delivering a Carnival band in four weeks without measuring, fitting, or stitching a base garment, relying instead on masqueraders' own skin-tight dungarees (Minshall 2016b). Still, as early as 2005, the mas man had been musing about denim as the hardworking fabric equivalent of the galvanized steel so ubiquitous in T&T and had hoped to one day marry these two proletarian materials in mas (Gulick 2016b).

9. Gulick first met Minshall in 1975 in Hanover, New Hampshire; Errol Hill had invited the mas man up to Dartmouth College to collaborate with him. The two men began their relationship in 1976 when Minshall returned for a one-year professorship in Dartmouth's Drama Department. And after an eight-year long-distance relationship, Gulick moved to Trinidad permanently in 1984 to make mas with Minshall.

10. Written by Shontelle Layne and Sheldon Benjamin, the song "Roll It Gal" was released as a single first in Barbados in 2005 and then in the United Kingdom in 2007.

11. With these surreal "bowl-faced" Dame Lorraines, Minshall foregoes the traditional exaggerated makeup of this brazen mas and characteristically dances the form forward into contemporary performance art (Minshall 2016c).

12. Minshall explicitly resists defining this phallic object as a penis in visual terms in order to maintain a level of abstraction that hopes to preserve a multiplicity of referents for the object. Minshall's phallus is perhaps the penis, but it might also be a warhead or missile, disarmed by the dancing figures in red. In essence, Minshall has created a visual double entendre (at the very least) of the sort one might hear in calypso music (Minshall 2008).

13. For a more extensive treatment than I am able to provide here about the relationship between Trinidad Carnival and the various desires motivating participants and scholars alike, see Karmenlara Seidman's dissertation "'Mas' Is Desire: The Erotic, Grotesque and Visionary in Trinidad Carnival" (Seidman 2008).

14. The *Trinidad Guardian* newspaper also reported protests by members of the Hindu community who were offended by "the resemblance of a sailor costume to their deity Lord Shiva in the posture called Nataraja" (Shears-Neptune 2006). Although Minshall did eventually modify the costume in response to this disquiet, several Hindu leaders nevertheless remained dissatisfied with HALLELUJAH.

15. A masterful storyteller, Minshall delivers the wry "punch line" of this exchange without missing a beat: "She then gave me lots of pencils and paper to draw" (Laughlin et al. 2006).

16. The phrase "find a place, make a stage" is part of the infectious chorus of soca artist Fay-Ann Lyons's hit song "M.A.S. (Make a Stage)" (2007). This tune has secured its place in the cultural memory in large part because it serves as an anthem for the first Trinidad Carnival without the Savannah stage. Masqueraders were quite literally forced to "make a stage" of the streets.

INTERLUDE II

1. The Community Chatroom Experience is an open support group primarily for gay Afro-Trinidadian men that meets weekly in Port-of-Spain for conversation about a range of topics. I was a part of the attempt to launch a Tobago-based version of the group. This will be discussed in more detail in chapter 6.

CHAPTER 3. ECHOES OF AN UTTERANCE

1. Since the early 1970s, soca music's rising popularity has only contributed to the century-old aural legacy of the calypso music genre (D. Hill 1993, 283). Although its etymology is as feverishly contested as its parentage, soca is reputed to have been one of the many children of the calypsonian Garfield "Lord Shorty" Blackman (later known as "Ras Shorty I" after a conversion to Rastafarianism). Marrying the traditional calypso to various pulsing rhythmic patterns from the Indian subcontinent, this Afro-Trinidadian musician (most likely among others) stripped calypso

to its rhythmic Creole soul. The "soul of calypso"—*soca*—danced from her mother's womb (Riggio 2004).

2. Tobago-born University of Pennsylvania–trained folklorist J. D. Elder has written what is perhaps the most thorough ethnographic description of a Trinidadian stick-fight in his 1966 " 'Kalinda': Song of the Battling Troubadours of Trinidad" (Elder 1966).

3. Elder notes this particular all-women's kalinda on Carriacou, the very Grenadian island on which Audre Lorde situates a heritage of Caribbean female same-sex desire (Lorde 1982).

4. A white shop clerk, Norman "Richard Couer de Leon" LeBlanc, would quite unwittingly lampoon governor Sir Hubert Jerninham into a permanent place in calypso infamy (Elder 1967, 113).

5. *Sans humanité* (literally "without humanity" in French, becomes *santimanité* in French Creole and acquires the meaning "without pity or mercy") was a popular calypso refrain—with its accompanying melody and verse structure—that was heard especially during extemporaneous derisive song contests between seasoned calypsonians well into the twentieth century.

6. Following her personal preference, throughout this study I will refer to Dr. Sandy-Lewis—who received her honorary doctorate from the University of the West Indies in 2014—using her unhyphenated married name, Lewis.

7. For a more detailed engagement with Spiritual Baptists—also referred to as "Shouter Baptists," indicating the highly vocal nature of worship—please see George E. Simpson's "The Shouters Church" (Simpson 1980), Eudora Thomas's *A History of the Shouter Baptists in Trinidad and Tobago* (E. Thomas 1987), Hazel Gibbs De Peza's *My Faith: Spiritual Baptist Christian* (Gibbs De Peza 1999), Patricia Stephens's *The Spiritual Baptist Faith: African New World Religious History, Identity and Testimony* (Stephens 1999), Kenneth Lum's *Praising His Name in the Dance: Spirit Possession in the Spiritual Baptist Faith and Orisha Work in Trinidad, West Indies* (Lum 2000), and Frances Henry's *Reclaiming African Religions in Trinidad: the Sociopolitical Legitimation of Orisha and Spiritual Baptist Faiths* (Henry 2003).

8. The Trinidad-born, Oxford-educated Dr. Eric Eustace Williams would serve as the titular head of the colonial government and then as the first leader of a newly independent Republic of Trinidad and Tobago from 1956 until his death in 1981.

9. Thelma "Lady Trinidad" Lewis sang "Advice to Every Woman" as early as 1937, and Edna "Lady Ïère" Thomas-Pierre—who sang in the Original Young Brigade tent alongside her husband—both preceded Calypso Rose by at least a decade (Dikobe 2003, 39–41; Dunn and Horne 2008). It is quite likely that there is still an entire chorus of female calypsonians across time periods still to be discovered by calypso scholarship.

10. The Road March title is a people's choice award given to the artist whose song is played most frequently at certain judging stations all along the Carnival parade route.

11. Despite the fact that Lewis migrated to New York City in 1974—where she still currently resides when not on tour or at home in T&T—she continued to participate quite actively in Trinidad's national calypso competition during the Carnival season. This diasporic participation is not uncommon even today in the calypso competition.

12. Over the course of her career, Lewis has accumulated a flood of other awards in Trinidad and Tobago, in the Caribbean region, and internationally. An honorary citizen of Belize and an official ambassador-at-large for Liberia, Lewis has championed a form of international "musical diplomacy" (sharing Trinbagonian culture as well as introducing other nations, such as Belize or Liberia, or peoples, such as the Garifuna, to her global audiences in song) still largely unknown to Caribbean artists, with the legendary exception of Robert Nesta Marley.

13. Lewis stutters ever so slightly when she speaks, and yet in song her voice is as fluid as it is powerful. She shares this trait with one of her most acclaimed mentors, Aldwyn "Lord Kitchener" Roberts, who was known to stutter significantly in speech but never in song.

14. Dionne Brand *In Another Place, Not Here* (Brand 1996, 16).

15. Dr. Rohlehr, who retired in 2007, was professor of West Indian literature at the University of the West Indies and a meticulous archivist of the calypso music genre.

16. Calypso music also proves correlatively to be quite an elaborate archive of Trinbagonian femininity as represented—for better or worse—by men as well as women.

17. To insist on the sociocultural significance of this sex-gender differentiation ought not to be misinterpreted as an investment in the ontological separation of the two concepts. Feminist theorist Judith Butler has taken pains to deconstruct the "naturalness" of sex, revealing it to be a social construction not simply parallel to gender but primarily reliant upon it for coherence (Butler [1990] 1999). I am indebted to anthropologist Edward Akintola Hubbard for his elegant reminder to continually unmask sex (Hubbard 2014). And yet even socially constructed distinctions—such as race—have very tangible material lives.

18. Although a relatively new field, Caribbean masculinity studies has inherited this sex-gender blindness from its parent field—Caribbean gender studies—in which femininity (and perhaps even feminism) is seemingly always confined to the female body and thus presumed to be the rightful and "natural" domain of women only (Ramírez et al. 2002; Reddock 2004).

19. The widely influential Austrian psychiatrist Sigmund Freud founded the psychoanalytic school of psychology. And the oft-cited French psychoanalyst and psychiatrist Jacques Lacan offered what is perhaps the most sustained treatment of "the phallus" in the modern Euro-American thought tradition.

20. "Palette," OED Online (Oxford: Oxford University Press, 2017). http://www.oed.com.ezproxy.lib.utexas.edu/view/Entry/136302?redirectedFrom=palette (accessed August 23, 2017).

1. Famed Trinidad-born writer and Nobel Laureate V. S. Naipaul has proposed acerbically that "it is only in the calypso that the Trinidadian touches reality" (Naipaul quoted in Regis 1999, xi). And yet that reality can also be cunningly playful, mockingly defying the realness of the "real" with an infinite series of masks each more—or less—believable than the last until an interest in the masque itself finally overcomes a desire to look behind it (D. Hill 1993, 216–17). In this respect, calypso perhaps amplifies a whisper we hear in most artistry about the profound work artifice consistently does on the real.

2. For the most elegantly masterful treatment of Caribbean sweetness as sensual trope across time and geography, but especially when shared between women, please savor Omise'eke Tinsley's *Thiefing Sugar: Eroticism between Women in Caribbean Literature* (Tinsley 2010).

3. Gay Trinidadian master poet, activist and calypso connoisseur Colin Robinson encouraged my attention to the naughty triple entendre that here rests upon "business"—also potentially referring to the genitals (male or female)—and "bust," which may refer to either a literal damaging of the genitals or to the figurative Trinbagonian colloquial verb "to break" often used to describe (male) ejaculation (Robinson 2009). Therefore, the thinly veiled reference here may also be to sex-induced injury and orgasm at once.

4. The chorus of "Palet" harkens back to the earliest bilingual calypsos of 1898, sung primarily in English, but with French Creole choruses. This retention demonstrates the persistence of French Creole words and phrases in Trinbagonian common parlance certainly up through the 1950s and into the contemporary period.

5. Maude Dikobe's dissertation *Doing She Own Thing: Gender, Performance, and Subversion in Trinidad Calypso* contains perhaps the most balanced scholarly engagement—though confined to only two sentences in her over-two-hundred-page work—with the question of Lewis's sexuality (Dikobe 2003). Although Dikobe cites Davies's indirect refusal of Lewis's same-sex desire, she insists that Lewis—like the noted blues singer Gertrude "Ma" Rainey—"has refused to say whether she is lesbian or not" (Dikobe 2003, 112). Perhaps the comparison of Lewis to Rainey is an apt one considering that neither woman had necessarily to call herself a "lesbian" in order to revel in her same-sex desire. By most accounts, Rainey was bisexual, though there may be no telling how Rainey herself identified. I will shortly address Lewis's relationship to the word "lesbian"; for now, it is vital to emphasize that refusing "lesbian" does not necessarily preclude same-sex desire.

6. Aubrey Lewis, who was himself no stranger to same-sex desire, passed away on January 12, 1983. During a casual afternoon swim in Tobago, Calypso Rose recounted to me in a gregarious whisper the story of another beach trip she took with Mr. Lewis in Saint Thomas during which she claims to have witnessed him

thrusting away at the behind of a moaning gentleman while hidden belly-deep in the sea (L. M. Lewis 2014).

7. Combining the oral histories and fiction of twenty-seven queer Caribbean women living in the region and in diaspora, Rosamund Elwin's *Tongues on Fire: Caribbean Lesbian Lives and Stories* is a peppery testament to an invisibility made material (Elwin 1997).

8. Lewis underwent invasive surgery for breast cancer in 1996 (Persad 2009). Tragically, the sexual assault of women globally is of such pandemic proportions that it belies the homophobic presumption that rape makes women queer. If that were consistently the case, lesbians, bisexuals, and trans men would be a vast global majority.

9. Although the righteousness of the Spiritual Baptist faith—outlawed from 1917 until the repeal of the "Shouter Ordinance" in 1951—was by no means self-evident before the mid-twentieth century, followers of the faith would likely have disdained calypso and calypsonians on the same moral grounds as the islands' more well-respected Christian denominations.

10. In 1987, while still performing widely, Lewis became an ordained Christian minister (Guilbault 2007, 109).

11. Even as a so-called sex song, "Palet" pushes far beyond the parochial implications of that phrase by earnestly—though no less playfully—calling easy sex-gender presumptions into question. In other words, if it is that sex is always pregnant with a double entendre that refers at once to sexual differentiation (male/female) and sexual intimacy, Lewis's "Palet" as a *sex* song actually takes sex (and gender) much more seriously—by attending to this double entendre—than the categorization would at first imply.

12. From a press release about the study Dr. Parnia and his team began in 2008 at the University of Southhampton.

CHAPTER 5. A GENERATION WITH AIDS

1. Although he has been largely erased from the widely accepted AIDS origin narrative in the United States, Robert Rayford's untimely death in 1969 from what frozen tissue and blood samples indicated nearly two decades later to be AIDS-related complications makes him a controversial first AIDS casualty over a decade before the disease begins to claim the health of mostly white gay men in Los Angeles (Crewdson 1987, Kolata 1987, McMichael 2007, Kerr and Barton 2015). The tragic story of this African American teenager (who took his first and last breath in St. Louis, Missouri) offers an archive of unanswered questions that could potentially reveal so much more about the longer history of HIV/AIDS in African America. And yet, Rayford has suffered a second violent death at the hands of an historical silence that sets a question mark as his tombstone and continues as though he never existed.

2. There had long been considerable controversy over whether the scientists at the Pasteur Institute or the American biomedical researcher Robert Gallo and his team at the National Institutes of Health should be credited with discovering this new retrovirus. Gallo and his colleagues also published several articles in the same issue of *Science* in 1983. However, the Nobel committee summarily decided against Gallo in 2008 by awarding the Nobel Prize in Physiology or Medicine jointly to Françoise Barré-Sinoussi and Luc Montagnier for discovering the virus that causes AIDS (Andersson 2008). For a detailed and nuanced engagement with this contestation and a variety of others over the first decade of the epidemic, see Steven Epstein's *Impure Science: AIDS, Activism, and the Politics of Knowledge* (1996); on the Gallo-Montagnier brouhaha, see especially pages 66–78.

3. Of these twenty-five "national indicators of the implementation of the *Declaration of Commitment on HIV/AIDS*," four (numbers 8, 9, 14, and 23) specifically mention *most-at-risk* populations, while one (number 19) specifically monitors men who have sex with men (UNAIDS 2008b, 17). I will address the categories "most-at-risk" and "men-who-have-sex-with-men" in more detail later in this chapter, but it suffices to identify here a distinction between the two—however subtle or unintended—in the language of the UN indicators precisely because of a troubling tendency to conflate the two in official reporting globally.

4. The benefit of this large body of data makes the 2008 UNAIDS *Report on the Global AIDS Epidemic* one of the most comprehensive evaluations of the epidemic on the global, regional, and national levels (UNAIDS 2008b, 19). I cite this report so extensively because it provides a particularly accurate world map of the pandemic in a specific historical moment.

5. Over thirty years later, Dr. Bartholomew is adamant that the AIDS epidemic in the anglophone Caribbean—what he calls the "British Caribbean"—was discovered first in Trinidad despite the Jamaica claim, which he contends has long been false and unsubstantiated (Bartholomew 2016).

6. The Caribbean Epidemiological Center (CAREC) is a region-wide public health information hub, service provision coordinator, and consulting organization. And the Pan American Health Organization is the World Health Organization's regional office for the Americas.

7. The T&T government's National HIV/AIDS Strategic Plan (NSP) for 2013–18 expects to reduce HIV prevalence to less than 1 percent by its conclusion (T&T 2013, xv).

8. Since 2011, various provisional state-coordinated entities attempted to fill the vacuum left by the disbanded NACC; however, by late 2015, the government began preparing to reinstate it. Tobago has had a slight distance from this tumult thanks to the steady resolve of the Tobago House of Assembly (THA)—a semiautonomous governing body that manages the affairs of the island as a subcommittee of the nation's Parliament. Formed in 2005, the THA's Tobago HIV/AIDS Coordinating

Committee (THACC) directly—and uninterruptedly—oversees the island's response to the epidemic, giving special attention to Tobago's specific needs, risks, and resources (T&T 2003, ii–iii, 40–41, 77–78; T&T 2013, xv).

9. As early as 1983, the CDC identified the first groups thought to be at highest risk for HIV infection and transmission. These four groups—homosexuals, heroin (or other intravenous drug) users, hemophiliacs, and Haitians—came to be known as the "4 H's." Although the CDC has significantly revised its assessment of HIV risk since the early 1980s, the life-threatening stigma suffered by each group of once presumed "disease carriers" remains. And after decades of prejudice-facilitated devastation, hemophiliacs remain the singular exception to the rule of unshakable stigma (Feldman and Bayer 1999; Resnik 1999).

10. Among the seven Caribbean nations that did report on the MSM indicator, it is estimated that Cuba and Trinidad and Tobago reported the lowest condom use rates—at approximately 40 to 59 percent—among the populations of MSM surveyed (amFAR 2008, 23).

11. To be fair, the nation's NSP in 2013–18 identifies what it calls "high risk lifestyle habits" as major impediments to fighting the epidemic; these high-risk behaviors include "multiple partnering, unprotected sex, drug use (including alcohol) and transactional sex" (T&T 2013, 16, 21). Although none of these behaviors is inherently high-risk for HIV infection if one is using safer sex precautions or having unprotected sex with partners of known HIV status, at least this shift has encouraged a national focus on behavior and overall sexual health as vital for HIV/AIDS prevention.

12. In T&T (and likely beyond), this insistence on "MSM" as an identity and not a behavior category summarily ignores one of the most concentrated and yet neglected communities of mostly nongay/bisexual-identified MSM: inmates in the nation's prison system, where a dubiously estimated 15 percent of men may be living with HIV. In this context especially, "the stigma associated with MSM contributes to a deep-seated sense of shame, resulting in their nonreporting of incidents of sexual violence, risk taking and reluctance to seek health and social services including medical treatment" (T&T 2013, 12, 13).

13. There is scant data solely on HIV transmission among "women-who-have-sex-with-women" (WSW)—an infrequently used category in the generally male-biased international HIV/AIDS literature. However, there are significant reports on sexually transmitted infections (including HIV) involving woman-to-woman sex (Brevier et al. 1995; Fethers et al. 2000; Bauer and Welles 2001; Friedman et al. 2003). And similar to the data on MSM, these reports shed little light on the actual sexual practices the term "WSW" occludes—practices that can include oft ignored woman-to-woman penetration (Young and Meyer 2005, 1147). Ignorance of these sexual behavior patterns perpetuates the dangerous fallacy that WSW are not at risk for HIV transmission and thus not a necessary target group for HIV/AIDS

prevention and care services—placing all wsw at an even greater risk of (re) infection. In fact, female same-sex practices, in addition to larger structural factors—including sexual violence—may render wsw much more vulnerable to HIV than is generally presumed (UNAIDS 2009a, 3).

14. Dr. Bartholomew deserves commendation for including attention to actual sexual practices among msm in his study. At such an early stage in the epidemic, he understood the importance of and provided a model for attending to sexual practices even within gay and bisexual male populations. Unfortunately—over three decades later—Dr. Bartholomew's model is still terribly overlooked (Bartholomew et al. 1987, 2605, 2607).

15. A report on a European Union–funded and THA-run qualitative data collecting initiative from 2008 is still the only formal report to my knowledge on Tobago's msm populations (Padmore 2008). Unfortunately, this otherwise detailed assessment of a sample of twenty men provides no statistical data on HIV prevalence among these Tobagonian msm (also recruited largely through HIV/AIDS organizations) and thus no means by which to make a comparison across msm populations on both islands.

16. These were Barbados, Grenada, Saint Lucia, and Trinidad and Tobago during the first phase of the study and Antigua and Barbuda, Dominica, Saint Kitts and Nevis, and Saint Vincent and the Grenadines during the second phase (CAREC 1996, 1; CAREC [1998] 2000, 1).

17. A total of 131 msm participated as interview subjects—either as part of sixteen focus groups or twenty-three individual interviews—over the two phases of the study (CAREC 1996, 3; CAREC [1998] 2000, 6). To my knowledge, this still represents the most ample pool of subjects for a regional study of Caribbean msm.

18. Born in Port-of-Spain, Trinidad, in 1959 and openly gay from as early as 1989, the formidable Godfrey Sealy—a celebrated playwright, electric performer, and tireless activist—was the first openly HIV-positive AIDS awareness advocate in T&T (Sealy 1995; Sylvester 2003). A veritable giant of the T&T theater community, Sealy was best known for his troubling play *One of Our Sons Is Missing* (1988), one of the earliest dramatic treatments of HIV/AIDS in the anglophone Caribbean (Sealy [1988] 2005). Sealy died from AIDS-related pneumonia on April 26, 2006, at the age of forty-six (*T&T Express* 2006; Richards 2006; D. James 2007; Loubon 2009). I had the remarkable privilege of sitting with him for a two-hour interview just seven months before his passing, and I found the charismatic activist and performer to be most resilient despite his worsening health (Sealy 2005).

CHAPTER 6. BETWEEN TONGUE AND TEETH

1. The Chatroom, which had been on hiatus since 2012, resumed for three months before being disbanded again in 2015—with funding from the joint regional project of the Jamaica-based Caribbean Vulnerable Communities Coalition and El Centro de Orientación e Investigación Integral, based in the Dominican Republic

(Jordan 2014, 2015; Sinnette 2016). After a series of violent attacks and at least five reported murders of gay men in the Curepe, Chaguanas and Woodbrook areas of Trinidad from late 2016 into early 2017, Friends For Life attempted unsuccessfully to resume the Chatroom at the prompting of artist and gay community leader Cyrus Sylvester (Padmore 2017). The program is still awaiting further funding.

2. Although it was founded in 1997, Friends For Life did not become an officially registered nongovernmental, not-for-profit organization until January 20, 1999 (Padmore et al. [1999] 2005, 1, 8; D. James 2002, 12; D. James 2003, 5; Jordan and Padmore 2003, 2; NACC/FFL 2008, 18).

3. While the majority of Friends For Life's founders were self-identified gay men, Kendra Bernard-Emmanuel and Portia Guichard—heterosexual cis women—had become close to Padmore while working with him on sexual and reproductive health programs previous to Thomas's tragic death (Padmore et al. [1999] 2005, 1; Jordan 2010).

4. CAREC hosted this HIV/AIDS training session and network-building forum for the Caribbean Forum for Lesbians, All-sexuals and Gays (C-FLAG), a region-wide collective initiated in 1995 by Orguyo—a Curaçao-based association of gay men and lesbians.

5. Delano Ray Richmond-Thompson was a dear friend and a former member of FFL's board of trustees (Padmore et al. [1999] 2005, 11). His spirit transitioned November 24, 2014.

6. Formed in 1974, Jamaica's Gay Freedom Movement (GFM) is thus far the earliest documented LGBT rights advocacy organization in the Caribbean region. The digitized GFM archive is publicly available through the Digital Library of the Caribbean at www.dloc.com/icirngfm.

7. Diagnosed HIV-positive in 1990, Stanforde's spirit transitioned on October 25, 2001. He was only forty-seven years old.

8. The LGBT community in T&T also organized its first AIDS memorial in 1994. And by 1998, this memorial would mark the beginning of a week of activities celebrating Gay Pride in T&T (Jordan 2003, 5; 2010). Nearly two decades later, PRIDE T&T continues to flourish; the festivities and programs now unofficially extend from the last Sunday in June to the last Saturday of July (Jordan 2015).

9. As the only existing gay organization in T&T at the time, Friends For Life would also effectively inherit the entire TnT M4M Project and subsume the surviving membership of the TnT M4M collective.

10. Founded in 1993, the International HIV/AIDS Alliance is a transnational network of organizations that provide technical and financial assistance to thousands of NGOs and community-based organizations globally (www.aidsalliance.org). The organization's programs rely heavily on local leadership and bottom-up community mobilization. The Alliance's regional program in the Caribbean began in 2003 with the principal support of the United States Agency for International Development

(USAID). But by September 2014 the Alliance was no longer commissioned to directly support programs in T&T—under USAID mandate—presumably because of a saturation of donor agencies in the country, and its Caribbean regional office based in Trinidad was shuttered (Jordan 2010, 2015).

11. From June to December 2002 FFL organized a food bank and monthly food-distribution initiative to provide nonperishable goods primarily to HIV-positive clients who were temporarily unemployed. As part of this "I Can–You Can" project—which included a fundraising component to supplement donated provisions—the organization claims to have distributed well over a thousand food hampers (Jordan and Padmore 2003, 4; Jordan 2005, 7).

12. Primarily self-identified gay men in T&T use the derogatory adjectival or adverbial referents "real" and "hen-down" to refer almost exclusively to hyperfeminine gay men or anything associated with a flamboyant male effeminacy. Padmore uses these terms here as a way to mark a presumably undesirable effeminacy with which he quite proudly identifies.

13. Despite the claim in FFL's official literature that it offers services for lesbians and nongay or bisexual identified MSM, the organization has not been successful at executing programs geared specifically toward these populations (Jordan 2003; Jordan and Padmore 2003, 2, 4; Padmore et al. [1999] 2005, 1). Between 2003 and 2005, FFL was able to provide a meeting space as a show of support for an autonomous lesbian Chatroom, and the organization did attempt a short-lived, closed support group for bicurious men. However this work simply pales in comparison to the work FFL continues to do with gay/bisexual-identified MSM populations.

14. The Alliance grant allowed Friends For Life to hire two full-time staff members—a program director and a program assistant—as well as two part-time staff members—an administrative assistant and a reception clerk—for a two-year period (Jordan 2003, 2).

15. My last visit to Trinidad previous to beginning my formal research is especially vivid in my memory because my summer holiday coincided with the ultimately unsuccessful Jamaat al Muslimeen coup d'état attempted on July 27, 1990.

16. The fact that the Alliance's Caribbean region secretariat was itself shut down in August 2014, purportedly for misappropriation of funds, does not excuse FFL's financial mismanagement but perhaps sets it in a larger context (Jordan 2015).

17. Not exclusive to T&T parlance, the colloquial term "bullerman"—often shortened simply to "buller" (pronounced "bullah")—has also been formally documented in Barbados, Grenada, Saint Lucia, and Saint Vincent and the Grenadines (CAREC 1996, 6; CAREC [1998] 2000, 14). In T&T, "bullerman" is often used exclusively as a derogatory referent for homosexual, bisexual, or tellingly effeminate men. This slur is also occasionally used within gay communities to disparage someone or something deemed distasteful, or much less frequently by gay men as a reclaimed neutral self-referent. Although often equated with the term "faggot," that comparison

gives some sense of the force of the word by sacrificing attention to the particular meaning of the term in context. At the core of "bullerman" is the vulgar verb "to bull," which is roughly identical to the verb "to fuck" (also frequently used in T&T). Although the use of the verb "to bull" (like "to fuck") is not restricted to male same-sex acts, the noun "bullerman" is used primarily to indict the presumably gay man for "bulling" a man (instead of a woman). The word "bullerman"—or "bull-a-man" as it is sometimes spelled b-u-l-l-a-m-a-n—draws attention to a social fixation on the act of one man *penetrating* another. The principal irony of the term, though, is that the man most likely to be disparaged as a "bullerman" is the man ignorantly presumed to be the penetrated partner because of his apparent effeminacy. "Faggot" follows an entirely different psychosocial and etymological logic.

18. In 2007, I had the opportunity to experience the challenges of initiating a Chatroom firsthand when I assisted in convening the first series of FFL Chatroom meetings in Tobago. Over a three-month period—from May 28 to July 23—I witnessed a total of eight Chatroom sessions facilitated by Eswick Padmore (who resided in Tobago from October 2006 to March 2010). The Tobago Chatroom began meeting only intermittently after July 23 and has since disbanded.

19. Calypso music may seem to offer a melodious, centuries-old counter-example to this claim in large part because of the persistence of sex and sexuality—of various kinds—as fertile tropes for the song tradition. However, the genre's sly reliance upon double entendre sings a chorus to the point Sinnette makes about the propensity of Trinbagonians—even at their most bawdy—to rely upon the strategic art of indirection.

20. Friends For Life also anticipates and respects the presence of nonbelievers in its fold. In fact, the common ground of love and respect for personal convictions that sustains the organization's leadership also provides an exemplary model for the fellowship of the Chatroom, which—unlike most religious or spiritual orders—accepts even atheists into its communion (Jordan 2016).

21. Of course, this is not to say that there have not been and will not continue to be Chatroom sessions devoted explicitly to discussions of religion, spirituality, and sexuality. In fact, on July 22, 2009—as part of a series of activities commemorating the fifteenth anniversary of Gay Pride celebrations in T&T—FFL convened a special Chatroom session devoted specifically to a discussion of religion and homosexuality tellingly titled "Homosexuality and Religion: a Theology of Inclusion."

22. This notorious delay of official government funding for FFL's Chatroom is especially baffling considering that T&T's 2003 *Five-Year National HIV/AIDS Strategic Plan* (NSP)—the document that effectively brings the NACC into existence—explicitly mentions not only Friends For Life but also the Chatroom in particular as key for HIV prevention among MSM populations (T&T 2003, 23, 47). A draft NSP from 2010 and the NSP from 2013 make no explicit mention of FFL or the Chatroom and continue to suffer from an appalling lack of current, comprehensive,

or consistent statistical data on the nation's MSM populations (T&T 2010, 2013). The Interim HIV/AIDS Secretariat—the NACC's replacement since 2008—has over nearly a decade provided FFL with only small grants (for a combined total of about five thousand US dollars from a budget of millions of US dollars annually) to do World AIDS Day programming (Jordan 2015).

23. Jacquelyn Fields is without a doubt the most prominent lesbian presence in Friends For Life. A longtime member of the organization's board of trustees and an outspoken HIV/AIDS activist and community builder in Trinidadian lesbian circles, Ms. Fields will be—in part—the subject of my concluding chapter.

24. For a poetically precise treatment of the relationship between contagion and contact, see Priscilla Wald's *Contagious* (Wald 2008).

CONCLUSION

1. In her classic essay "Man Royals and Sodomites: Some Thoughts on the Invisibility of Afro-Caribbean Lesbians," Jamaican-Canadian author and editor Makeda Silvera marks this disappeared presence (Silvera 1996). Nearly a decade later, African Caribbean-American scholar and performance artist Rosamond King penned a poetic addendum, "More Notes on the Invisibility of Caribbean Lesbians," that she meticulously extends in her book *Island Bodies: Transgressive Sexualities in the Caribbean Imagination* (King [2005] 2008; King 2014, 93–122). With artful irony, these two lesbian-identified Afro-Caribbean women affirm their absented presence through the presentation of their seeming absence.

2. Jacquelyn Fields has intermittently served on Friends For Life's board of trustees since July 2003.

3. The marriage of these homonyms is part of the ideological legacy of the late godfather of (black British) cultural studies, Stuart Hall.

4. I was able to orchestrate a lengthy—and quite challenging—conversation about the formation and seeming dissolution of this Lesbian Chatroom with seven same-sex-desiring women who attended a day trip to Trinidad's Las Cuevas beach in June 2008. This extended group interview—the only one I was able to conduct with same-sex-desiring women—would not have been possible without the invaluable networks and assistance of Jacquelyn Fields.

5. Or perhaps it might be more appropriate to suggest that the Lesbian Chatroom has become an apparition—coming to view and slipping away just as startlingly, depending on whom you ask. Perhaps this collective ephemeral presence has a different kind of power: the power of the unseen. In any instance, even if some bodies know exactly where to find that vanishing Chatroom, my male body stands perpetually outside of that circle. And this is as it should be.

6. In her remarks in 2004 and the subsequent interview I conducted with her, Fields not only unapologetically describes herself as a "lesbian" but is rather aggressive about policing the borders of "true" lesbianism, explicitly excluding bisexual

women and women who may be questioning their sexual orientation (Fields 2004b). However, during our follow-up conversation in 2008—although she continues to refer to herself as a "lesbian" and still believes that same-sex-desiring women are *really* lesbians at heart—Fields had acquiesced to the prevailing semantic politics of the moment that positioned "lesbian" as a foreign term and required the continuing search for newer terminology (Fields 2008).

7. I do not intend to imply here that same-sex-desiring women do not also participate in penetrative intercourse; however, foregrounding coitus between women—sans penetration—encourages a conceptualization of sensuality that has the potential to shift the focus away from one particular kind of sex and perhaps ultimately away from sex altogether.

8. I remind the reader that Spiritual Baptism is an Afro-Caribbean syncretic faith. For more on the tradition in the Caribbean, see the extant literature documenting its emergence and spread (Herskovits and Herskovits 1947; Simpson 1980; Glazier 1983; E. Thomas 1987; Gibbs De Peza 1999; Lum 2000; Henry 2003).

9. This particular biblical tale, so prominent in homophobic popular discourse across the Caribbean region, informs the remarkably ambiguous legal term "sodomy" (the intimate inheritance of British colonial law) popularly believed to refer to anal intercourse between men. More precisely, though, the term refers to any and all of the "sinful behavior" believed to have been practiced in the city of Sodom. The uncertainty about these practices—and doubts about whether it was sexual indecency alone that caused the city's destruction—is precisely what lends the term "sodomite" an elusive ambiguity.

10. Unfortunately, neither Tobago nor Tobagonians appear in this work.

11. Puar originally began her research in Trinidad on chutney music—a syncretic Indo-Caribbean music genre—but subsequently changed her research focus while in the field (Puar 1999, 124–26; 2009, 1–2). And she decided, based on ethical considerations, not to pursue the publication of her dissertation as a book.

12. For the extensive earlier formulation of the concept of "queer(/ed) ethnography" on which this later reiteration is based, please see the third chapter of Puar's doctoral dissertation, "Queer/ed Ethnographies and the Multisited/sighted Informants" (Puar 1999, especially 110–23).

13. For one of the most rigorous and determined efforts at carrying outward the project of queer studies beyond the boundary of sexual object-choice in the emergent field of queer Caribbean studies, see Nadia Ellis's *Territories of the Soul: Queered Belonging in the Black Diaspora* (Ellis 2015). Also a steady engagement with the conceptualization and affective investments of black diaspora, Ellis's text is certainly no less compelling for being in direct contrast to the ideological and emotional cartography of the African diaspora that guides the present study.

14. Jafari Allen provides an elegantly comprehensive assessment of a diaspora-conscious black queer studies project in "Black/Queer/Diaspora at the Current

Conjuncture," the introduction to his guest-edited special double issue of the lesbian and gay studies journal GLQ (Allen 2012, 211–48).

15. Importantly, E. Patrick Johnson has edited a highly anticipated sequel to the 2005 text. *No Tea, No Shade: New Writings in Black Queer Studies* features the voices of younger scholars influenced by the first volume as well as more work from beyond the bounds of the United States (Johnson 2016).

16. Holland's foreword, " 'Home' is a Four-letter Word," attends—though briefly—to the very situated reflection on black queer life (in this instance, her own) that I argue is so vital for black queer studies. In returning to North Carolina for the conference, Holland must negotiate an uneasy return to the home state of her maternal kin—from whom she has been uncomfortably estranged—in the service of an academic field for which she has been one of the most patient midwives (Holland 2005, ix–xiii).

17. If Shari Frilot's documentary film about the conference is an accurate representation, *Black Nations/Queer Nations?* was a decidedly international/translocal gathering; one easily notes participants from South Africa, Kenya, Sierra Leone, Ghana, Trinidad, India, Britain, and various regions of the United States (Frilot 1996).

Aching, Gerard. 2002. *Masking and Power: Carnival and Popular Culture in the Carib-bean*. Minneapolis: University of Minnesota.

Adisa, Opal Palmer, and Donna Aza Weir-Soley. 2010. *Caribbean Erotic: Poetry, Prose and Essays*. Leeds: Peepal Tree Press.

Alexander, M. Jacqui. 1991. "Redrafting Morality: The Postcolonial State and the Sexual Offences Bill of Trinidad and Tobago." In *Third World Women and the Politics of Feminism*, edited by Chandra Mohanty et al., 133–52. Bloomington: Indiana University Press.

———. 1997. "Erotic Autonomy as a Politics of Decolonization: Anatomy of Feminist and State Practice in the Bahamas Tourist Economy." In *Feminist Genealogies, Colonial Legacies, Democratic Futures*, edited by M. Jacqui Alexander and Chandra T. Mohanty, 63–100. New York: Routledge.

———. 2000. "Not Just (Any)*Body* Can Be a Citizen: The Politics of Law, Sexuality, and Postcoloniality in Trinidad and Tobago and Bahamas." In *Cultures of Empire: Colonizers in Britain and the Empire in the Nineteenth and Twentieth Centuries*, edited by Catherine Hall, 359–76. New York: Routledge.

———. 2005. *Pedagogies of Crossing: Meditations on Feminism, Sexual Politics, Memory, and the Sacred*. Durham, NC: Duke University Press.

Allen, Jafari. 2011. *¡Venceremos? The Erotics of Black Self-Making in Cuba*. Durham, NC: Duke University Press.

———. 2012. "Introduction: Black/Queer/Diaspora at the Current Conjuncture." GLQ: *A Journal of Lesbian and Gay Studies* 18, nos. 2–3:211–48.

Allen, Jafari, and Omise'eke Tinsley. 2012. "A Conversation Overflowing with Memory: On Omise'eke Natasha Tinsley's 'Water, Shoulders, into the Black Pacific.'" *GLQ: A Journal of Lesbian and Gay Studies* 18, nos. 2–3:249–62.

Allsopp, Richard, ed. 1996. *Dictionary of Caribbean English Usage.* London: Oxford University Press.

Altman, Dennis. 2001. *Global Sex.* Chicago: University of Chicago Press.

Alturi, Tara L. 2001. *When the Closet Is a Region: Homophobia, Heterosexism, and Nationalism in the Commonwealth Caribbean.* Working Paper Series. Cave Hill, Barbados: University of the West Indies—Centre for Gender and Development Studies.

Anatol, Giselle. 2000. "Transforming the Skin-Shedding Soucouyant: Using Folklore to Reclaim Female Agency in Caribbean Literature." *Small Axe* 7 (March): 44–59.

Anderson, Benedict. 1983. *Imagined Communities: Reflections on the Origin and Spread of Nationalism.* London: Verso.

Andersson, Jan. 2008. *Presentation Speech, Nobel Prize in Physiology or Medicine 2008.* Stockholm: Karolinska Institute.

Andrews, George Reid. 2004. *Afro-Latin America, 1800–2000.* Oxford: Oxford University Press.

Appiah, Anthony. 1997. "Is the 'Post-' in 'Postcolonial' the 'Post-' in 'Postmodern'?" In *Dangerous Liaisons: Gender, Nation, and Postcolonial Perspectives,* edited by Anne McClintock et al., 420–44. Minneapolis: University of Minnesota Press.

Bagoo, Andre. 2013. "Owners Hope to Get $25M for Property." *Trinidad and Tobago Newsday* (Port-of-Spain), March 21.

Bailey, Marlon. 2013. *Butch Queens Up in Pumps: Gender, Performance, and Ballroom Culture in Detroit.* Ann Arbor: University of Michigan Press.

Baldwin, James. 1985. *The Evidence of Things Not Seen.* New York: Holt, Rinehart and Winston.

Baral, Stefan, et al. 2007. "Elevated Risk for HIV Infection among Men Who Have Sex with Men in Low- and Middle-Income Countries, 2000–2006: A Systematic Review." *PLoS Medicine* 4(12): e339. https://doi.org/10.1371/journal.pmed.0040339.

Bargery, George P., comp. 1934. *A Hausa-English Dictionary and English-Hausa Vocabulary.* London: Oxford University Press.

Barré-Sinoussi, Françoise, et al. 1982. "Isolation of a T-Lymphotropic Retrovirus from a Patient at Risk for Acquired Immune Deficiency Syndrome (AIDS)." *Science* 220 (4599): 868–71.

Barrow, Christine. 1996. *Family in the Caribbean: Themes and Perspectives.* Edited by Christine Barrow. Kingston, Jamaica: Ian Randle.

———. 1998. *Caribbean Portraits: Essays on Gender Ideologies and Identities.* Edited by Christine Barrow. Kingston, Jamaica: Ian Randle.

Bartholomew, Courtenay. 2016. Personal communication with author, April 13.

Bartholomew, Courtenay, et al. 1983. "The Acquired Immune Deficiency Syndrome in Trinidad: A Report on Two Cases." *West Indian Medical Journal* 32:177–80.

———. 1984. "AIDS on Trinidad." *The Lancet* 323, issue 8368: 103.

———. 1985. "Racial and Other Characteristics of Human T Cell Leukaemia/Lymphona (HTLV-I) and AIDS (HTLV-III) in Trinidad." *British Medical Journal* 290:1243–46.

———. 1987. "Transmission of HTLV-I and HIV among Homosexual Men in Trinidad." *Journal of the American Medical Association* 257 (19): 2604–8.

Bataille, Georges. [1957] 1987. *Eroticism.* Translated by Mary Dalwood. London: Marion Boyars.

Batson, Dawn, and Milla Cozart Riggio. 2004. "Trinidad Carnival Timeline." In *Carnival: Culture in Action: The Trinidad Experience*, edited by Milla C. Riggio, 31–38. New York: Routledge.

Bauer, G. R., and S. L. Welles. 2001. "Beyond Assumptions of Negligible Risk: Sexually Transmitted Diseases and Women Who Have Sex with Women." *American Journal of Public Health* 91:1282–86.

Benítez Rojo, Antonio. [1992] 2001. *Isla que se repite* [The repeating island: The Caribbean and the postmodern perspective]. Translated by James Maraniss. Durham, NC: Duke University Press.

Bethell, Leslie. 1998. *A Cultural History of Latin America: Literature, Music, and the Visual Arts in the 19th and 20th Centuries.* Edited by Leslie Bethell. Cambridge: Cambridge University Press.

Bettelhiem, Judith, et al. 1988. *Caribbean Festival Arts: Each and Every Bit of Difference.* Seattle: University of Washington Press.

Birth, Kevin. 1999. *Any Time Is Trinidad Time: Social Meanings and Temporal Consciousness.* Gainesville: University Press of Florida.

———. 2008. *Bacchanalian Sentiments: Musical Experiences and Political Counterpoints in Trinidad.* Durham, NC: Duke University Press.

Boellstorff, Tom. 2005. *The Gay Archipelago: Sexuality and Nation in Indonesia.* Princeton, NJ: Princeton University Press.

Bond, George, et al., eds. 1997. "The Anthropology of AIDS in Africa and the Caribbean." In *AIDS in Africa and the Caribbean.* Boulder, CO: Westview Press.

Bowman, Wayne. 2006. "Minshall Is Back: Call to Arms for the Faithful." *Trinidad and Tobago Express* (Port-of-Spain), February 2.

Brand, Dionne. 1990. *No Language Is Neutral.* Toronto: Coach House Press.

———. 1996. *In Another Place, Not Here.* New York: Grove Press.

———. 1999. *At the Full and Change of the Moon: A Novel.* New York: Grove Press.

———. 2001. *A Map to the Door of No Return: Notes to Belonging.* Toronto: Doubleday.

Brathwaite, Kamau. 1974. *Contradictory Omens: Cultural Diversity and Integration in the Caribbean.* Mona, Jamaica: Savacou Publications.

Braziel, Jana Evans. 2008. *Artists, Performers, and Black Masculinity in the Haitian Diaspora*. Bloomington: Indiana University Press.

Brennan, Denise. 2004. *What's Love Got to Do with It? Transnational Desires and Sex Tourism in the Dominican Republic*. Durham, NC: Duke University Press.

Brereton, Bridget. 1979. *Race Relations in Colonial Trinidad, 1870–1900*. Cambridge: Cambridge University Press.

———. 1981. *A History of Modern Trinidad, 1783–1962*. Kingston, Jamaica: Heinemann.

———. [1975] 2004. "The Trinidad Carnival in the Late Nineteenth Century." In *Carnival: Culture in Action: The Trinidad Experience*, edited by Milla Riggio, 53–63. New York: Routledge.

Brevier, P. J., et al. 1995. "Women at a Sexually Transmitted Disease Clinic Who Reported Same-Sex Contact: Their HIV Seroprevalence and Risk Behaviors." *American Journal of Public Health* 85:1366–71.

Burg, Barry R. 1995. *Sodomy and the Pirate Tradition: English Sea Rovers in the Seventeenth-Century Caribbean*. New York: New York University Press.

Burgess, Muriel. 1999. *Shirley: An Appreciation of the Life of Shirley Bassey*. London: Arrow.

Butler, Judith. 1993. "The Lesbian Phallus and the Morphological Imaginary." In *Bodies That Matter: On the Discursive Limits of "Sex."* New York: Routledge.

———. [1990] 1999. *Gender Trouble: Feminism and the Subversion of Identity*. New York: Routledge.

Byrd, Rudolph, et al. 2009. *I Am Your Sister: Collected and Unpublished Writings of Audre Lorde*. Edited by Rudolph Byrd et al. Oxford: Oxford University Press.

Cáceres, C. et al. 2006. "Estimating the Number of Men Who Have Sex with Men in Low and Middle Income Countries." *Sexually Transmitted Infections* 82, Suppl. 3 (2006): iii3–iii9. PMC. August 24, 2017.

Callaloo Company. 2005. *Biography of Peter Minshall*. www.callaloo.co.tt/minshall (site under construction as of August 23, 2017).

Camara, Bilali. 2000. "An Overview of the AIDS/HIV/STD Situation in the Caribbean." In *The Caribbean AIDS Epidemic*, edited by Glenford Howe and Alan Cobley: 1–21. Kingston, Jamaica: University of the West Indies.

Camnitzer, Luis. 2005. "The Keeper of the Lens." In *Looking at the Spirits: Peter Minshall's Carnival Drawings*. The Drawing Center's Drawing Papers #56. New York: Edward Hallam Tuck Publication Program.

Camnitzer, Luis, and Todd Gulick. 2005. *Looking at the Spirits: Peter Minshall's Carnival Drawings*. Catalogue. The Drawing Center's Drawing Papers #56. New York: Edward Hallam Tuck Publication Program.

Campbell, Susan. 1988. "Carnival, Calypso, and Class Struggle in Nineteenth-Century Trinidad." *History Workshop Journal* 1988 26 (1): 1–27. Oxford: Oxford University Press.

Caribbean Epidemiology Center (CAREC). 1996. "Gay Research Initiative on AIDS Prevention in the Caribbean [Phase 1]." Unpublished report. Brader Brathwaite and Godfrey Sealy (authors). [Provided courtesy of Dr. Brader Brathwaite at the University of the West Indies.]

———. [1998] 2000. "Gay Research Initiative on AIDS Prevention in the Caribbean [Phase 2]." Brader Brathwaite and Godfrey Sealy (authors). Port-of Spain: CAREC.

Carson, Anne. 1986. *Eros: The Bittersweet*. Princeton, NJ: Princeton University Press.

Chauncey, George, and Elizabeth A. Povinelli. 1999. "Thinking Sexuality Transnationally." *GLQ: Journal of Gay and Lesbian Studies* 5 (4): 439–50.

Chevannes, Barry. 2001. *Learning to Be a Man: Culture, Socialization, and Gender Identity in Five Caribbean Communities*. Cave Hill, Barbados: University of the West Indies Press.

Chin, Timothy. 1997. "'Bullers' and 'Battymen': Contesting Homophobia in Black Popular Culture and Contemporary Caribbean Literature." *Callaloo* 20, no. 1 (1997): 127–41.

Clarke, Edith. 1957. *My Mother Who Fathered Me: A Study of the Family in Three Selected Communities in Jamaica*. London: University Press of the West Indies.

Cobley, Alan. 2000. Introduction to *The Caribbean AIDS Epidemic*, edited by Glenford Howe and Alan Cobley: xvi–xxii. Kingston, Jamaica: University of the West Indies.

Coffin, John, et al. 1986. "What to Call the AIDS Virus?" *Nature* 32, May 1. London: Nature Publishing Group.

Cohen, Cathy J. 1997. "Punks, Bulldaggers, and Welfare Queens: The Radical Potential of Queer Politics?" *GLQ: A Journal of Lesbian and Gay Studies* 3 (4): 437–65.

Columbus, Christopher. 1969. *The Four Voyages of Christopher Columbus; Being His Own Log-Book, Letters and Dispatches with Connecting Narrative Drawn from the Life of the Admiral by His Son Hernando Colon and Other Contemporary Historians*. Edited and translated by J. M. Cohen. New York: Penguin.

Constanine-Simms, Delroy, ed. 2001. *The Greatest Taboo: Homosexuality in Black Communities*. Los Angeles: Alyson Books.

Cowley, John. 1996. *Carnival, Canboulay, and Calypso: Traditions in the Making*. Cambridge: Cambridge University Press.

Cozier, Christopher. 2008. Interview by author, January 8, St. Ann's, Trinidad.

Craig-James, Susan E. 2008. *The Changing Society of Tobago, 1838–1938: A Fractured Whole. Volume I: 1838–1900*. Arima, Trinidad and Tobago: Cornerstone Press.

———. 2008. *The Changing Society of Tobago, 1838–1938: A Fractured Whole. Volume II: 1900–1938*. Arima, Trinidad and Tobago: Cornerstone Press.

Crewdson, John. 1987. "Case Shakes Theories of AIDS Origin." *The Chicago Tribune* (Chicago), October 25.

Crichlow, Wesley Eddison Aylesworth. 2003. *Buller Men and Batty Bwoys: Hidden Men in Toronto and Halifax Black Communities*. Toronto: University of Toronto.

———. [2004] 2008. "History, (Re)memory, Testimony, and Biomythography: Charting a Buller Man's Trinidadian Past." In *Our Caribbean: A Gathering of Lesbian and*

Gay Writing from the Antilles, edited by Thomas Glave, 101–31. Durham, NC: Duke University Press.

Crowley, Daniel. 1959a. "Toward a Definition of Calypso (Part I)." *Ethnomusicology* 3 (2): 57–66. Champaign: University of Illinois Press.

———. 1959b. "Toward a Definition of Calypso (Part II)." *Ethnomusicology* 3 (3): 117–24. Champaign: University of Illinois Press.

———. 1966. "Folk Etymology and Earliest Documented Usage of 'Calypso.'" *Ethnomusicology* 10 (1): 81–82. Champaign: University of Illinois Press.

Cruz-Malavé, Arnaldo, and Martin F. Manalansan IV, eds. 2002. *Queer Globalizations: Citizenship and the Afterlife of Colonialism*. New York: New York University Press.

Dann, Graham. 1987. *The Barbadian Male: Sexual Attitudes and Practice*. London: Macmillan Caribbean.

Dass, Shelly. 2008. Interview with Peter Minshall, January 30, *The Big Story*, Cable News Channel 3 (CNC3).

Davies, Carole Boyce. 1990. "'Woman Is a Nation . . .': Women in Caribbean Oral Literature." In *Out of the Kumbla: Caribbean Women and Literature*, edited by C. Davies and Elaine Fido: 165–93. Trenton, NJ: Africa World Press.

Decena, Carlos Ulises. 2011. *Tacit Subjects: Belonging and Same-Sex Desire among Dominican Immigrant Men*. Durham, NC: Duke University Press.

De Mille, Agnes. 1991. *The Life and Work of Martha Graham*. New York: Random House.

De Suze, Joseph A. 1966. *The New Trinidad and Tobago: A Descriptive Account of the Geography and History of Trinidad and Tobago*. London: Collins.

De Veaux, Alexis. 2004. *Warrior Poet: A Biography of Audre Lorde*. New York: Norton.

Dikobe, Maude. 2003. *Doing She Own Thing: Gender, Performance, and Subversion in Trinidad Calypso*. Unpublished PhD diss., Department of African American Studies, University of California, Berkeley.

Dillon, Sarah. 2007. *The Palimpsest: Literature, Criticism, Theory*. London: Continuum.

Donnell, Alison. 2005. "Sexing the Subject: Writing and the Politics of Caribbean Sexual Identity." In *Twentieth-Century Caribbean Literature: Critical Moments in Anglophone Literary History*: 181–250. London: Routledge.

Donovan, Stephen, and Trevor A. Jackson, eds. 1994. *Caribbean Geology: An Introduction*. Jamaica: University of the West Indies Press.

Douglas, Debbie, et al. 1997. *Ma-Ka Diasporic Juks: Contemporary Writing by Queers of African Descent*. Edited by Debbie Douglas et al. Toronto: Sister Vision Press.

Douglas, Mary. [1966] 2002. *Purity and Danger: An Analysis of Concepts of Pollution and Taboo*. London: Routledge.

Dunn, Geoffrey, and Michael Horne. 2008. *Calypso Dreams*. Documentary film. Port-of-Spain: In for a Penny, In for a Pound Productions.

Dutta, Kavery. 1988. *One Hand Don't Clap*. Documentary film. New York: Rhapsody Films.

Dzidzienyo, Anani, and Suzanne Oboler. 2004. *Neither Enemies nor Friends: Latinos, Blacks, Afro-Latinos*. New York: Palgrave Macmillan.

Elder, Jacob Delworth. 1964. "Color, Music and Conflict: A Study of Aggression in Trinidad with Reference to the Role of Traditional Music." *Ethnomusicology*. Vol. 8, No. 2 (May): 128–36. Champaign, IL: University of Illinois Press.

———. 1966. "'Kalinda': Song of the Battling Troubadours of Trinidad." *Journal of the Folklore Institute* 3 (2): 192–203.

———. 1967. "Evolution of the Traditional Calypso of Trinidad and Tobago: A Socio-Historical Analysis of Song-Change." Unpublished PhD diss., Department of Folklore, University of Pennsylvania.

———. 1998. Cannes Brûlées. *TDR: The Drama Review* (Trinidad Carnival Special Issue), 42 (3): 38–43.

Ellis, Nadia. 2015. *Territories of the Soul: Queered Belonging in the Black Diaspora*. Durham, NC: Duke University Press.

Elwin, Rosamund. 1997. *Tongues on Fire: Caribbean Lesbian Lives and Stories*. Edited by Rosamund Elwin. Toronto: Women's Press.

Epstein, Steven. 1996. *Impure Science: AIDS, Activism, and the Politics of Knowledge*. Berkeley: University of California Press.

Fanon, Frantz. [1961] 1963. *Damnés de la terre* [The wretched of the earth]. Translated by Constance Farrington. New York: Grove Press.

———. [1952] 1967. *Peau noire, masques blancs* [Black skin, white masks]. Translated by Charles Lam Markmann. New York: Grove Press.

Feldman, Eric, and Ronald Bayer, eds. 1999. *Blood Feuds: AIDS, Blood, and the Politics of Medical Disaster*. New York: Oxford University Press.

Ferguson, Roderick A. 2004. *Aberrations in Black: Toward a Queer of Color Critique*. Minneapolis: University of Minnesota Press.

Fethers, K., et al. 2000. "Sexually Transmitted Infections and Risk Behaviors in Women Who Have Sex with Women." *Sexually Transmitted Infections* 76:345–49. London: British Medical Association.

Fields, Jacquelyn. 2004a. "Remarks Delivered at the Inaugural Lesbian Night of Trinidad and Tobago's Tenth Annual Pride Week Celebration." July 8, Woodbrook, Trinidad.

———. 2004b. Interview by the author, July 8, Woodbrook, Trinidad.

———. 2008. Follow-up interview by the author, June 2, Woodbrook, Trinidad.

The Foundation for AIDS Research (amFAR). 2008. *MSM, HIV, and the Road to Universal Access—How Far Have We Come?* New York: amFAR.

Franco, P. R. 2007. "The Invention of Traditional Mas and Politics of Genders." In *Trinidad Carnival: The Cultural Politics of a Transnational Festival*, edited by G. Green and P. Scher: 25–47. Bloomington: Indiana University Press.

Frazier, Edward Franklin. 1932. *The Negro Family in Chicago*. Chicago: University of Chicago Press.

———. 1939. *The Negro Family in the United States*. Chicago: University of Chicago Press.

Friedman, S. R., et al. 2003. "HIV Prevalence, Social Marginalization, Risk Behaviors, and High-Risk Sexual and Injection Networks among Young Women Injectors Who Have Sex with Women." *American Journal of Public Health* 93:902–6. Washington, DC: American Public Health Association.

Frilot, Shari. 1996. *Black Nations/Queer Nations? Lesbian and Gay Sexualities in the African Diaspora*. Directed by Shari Frilot. New York: Third World Newsreel.

Funk, Ray. 2016. "The History of Paradise: On Peter Minshall's Paradise Lost." *Caribbean Beat* 137:68–72.

Ganase, Patricia. 1992. "Lord of the Dance: 'Masman' Peter Minshall Took the Revolutionary Techniques of His Carnival Bands to the Opening of the Olympics." *Caribbean Beat* 3: http://caribbean-beat.com/issue-3/lord-dance-peter -minshall#axzz4qtnWSHuJ. Accessed August 26, 2017.

Gaudio, Rudi. 2009. *Allah Made Us: Sexual Outlaws in an Islamic African City*. Sussex, UK: Wiley-Blackwell.

Gibbs De Peza, Hazel Ann. 1999. *My Faith: Spiritual Baptist Christian*. St. Augustine, Trinidad and Tobago: University of the West Indies.

Gill, Lyndon K. 2010. "Transfiguring Trinidad and Tobago: Queer Cultural Production, Erotic Subjectivity and the Praxis of Black Queer Anthropology." Unpublished dissertation, Department of African and African American Studies and the Department of Anthropology, Harvard University.

Glave, Thomas. 2008. *Our Caribbean: A Gathering of Lesbian and Gay Writing from the Antilles*. Edited by Thomas Glave. Durham, NC: Duke University Press.

———. 2010. Personal communication with author, February 20.

Glazier, Stephen D. 1983. *Marchin' the Pilgrims Home: Leadership and Decision Making in an Afro-Caribbean Faith*. Westport, CT: Greenwood Press.

Glick, Michael, et al. 1994. "Necrotizing Ulcerative Periodontitis: A Marker for Immune Deterioration and a Predictor for the Diagnosis of AIDS." *Journal of Periodontology* 65:393–97.

Gopinath, Gayatri. 2005. *Impossible Desires: Queer Diasporas and South Asian Public Cultures*. Durham, NC: Duke University Press.

Gordon, John. 1970. *Jim Dine*. New York: Praeger/Whitney Museum of American Art.

Gordon, Lewis. 2000. *Existentia Africana: Understanding Africana Existential Thought*. New York: Routledge.

———. 2008. *An Introduction to Africana Philosophy*. Cambridge. Cambridge University Press.

Gottlieb, Michael, et al. 1981. "Pneumocystis Pneumonia—Los Angeles." *Morbidity and Mortality Weekly Report* 30 (21): 1–3.

The Government of the Republic of Trinidad and Tobago (T&T). [1969] 1995. *Immigration Act, 1995*. Port-of-Spain: The Republic of Trinidad and Tobago.

———. [1986] 2000. *Sexual Offences Act, 2000*. Port-of-Spain: Republic of Trinidad and Tobago.

———. 2003. *Five-Year National HIV/AIDS Strategic Plan: January 2004–December 2008*. Port-of-Spain: Republic of Trinidad and Tobago. Also available online at www.hiv .health.gov.tt.

———. 2005. The National AIDS Coordinating Committee, Office of the Prime Minister, www.opm.gov.tt. Accessed May 1, 2010.

———. 2010. *Draft Five-Year National HIV and AIDS Strategic Plan*. Port-of-Spain: The Republic of Trinidad and Tobago.

———. 2013. *The National HIV and AIDS Strategic Plan 2013–2018*. Port-of-Spain: The Republic of Trinidad and Tobago.

Green, Garth L., and Philip Scher. 2007. *Trinidad Carnival: The Cultural Politics of a Transnational Festival*. Edited by Garth L. Green and Philip Scher. Bloomington: Indiana University Press.

Green, James, N. 1999. *Beyond Carnival: Male Homosexuality in Twentieth-Century Brazil*. Chicago: University of Chicago Press.

Guilbault, Jocelyne. 2007. *Governing Sound: The Cultural Politics of Trinidad's Carnival Musics*. Chicago: University of Chicago Press.

Gulick, Todd. 2008. Interview by author, April 14, Callaloo Company in Chaguaramas, Trinidad.

———. 2016a. Personal correspondence with author, April 26.

———. 2016b. Personal correspondence with author, April 28.

———. 2016c. Personal correspondence with author, May 3.

———. 2016d. Personal correspondence with author, May 4.

———. 2016e. Personal correspondence with author, May 5.

———. 2016f. Personal correspondence with author, May 9.

Gumbs, Alexis Pauline. 2010. "We Can Learn to Mother Ourselves: The Queer Survival of Black Feminism, 1968–1996." PhD dissertation, submitted to the Department of English, Duke University.

Guy James, Ronald. 2008. Interview by author, April 13, St. James, Trinidad.

Gwaltney, John Langston, ed. 1980. *Drylongso: A Self-Portrait of Black America*. New York: Random House.

Halberstam, J. Jack. 1998. *Female Masculinity*. Durham, NC: Duke University Press.

Hall, Anthony. 1998. "They Want to See George Band: Tobago Mas According to George Leacock." *Drama Review* 42 (3): 44–53.

Hanchard, Michael. 1994. *Orpheus and Power: The Movimento Negro of Rio de Janeiro and São Paulo, Brazil, 1945–1988*. Princeton, NJ: Princeton University Press.

———. 1998. "Black Cinderella? Race and the Black Public Sphere in Brazil." In *Racial Politics in Contemporary Brazil*, edited by Michael Hanchard: 59–81. Durham, NC: Duke University Press.

Henriques, Fernando. [1959] 1960. *Love in Action: The Sociology of Sex*. New York: Dutton.

————. [1962] 1965. *Prostitution and Society: A Survey*. New York: Citadel Press.

————. [1953] 1968a. *Family and Color in Jamaica*. London: Eyre and Spottiswoode.

————. 1968b. *Modern Sexuality*. London: MacGibbon and Kee.

————. 1974. *Children of Caliban: Miscegenation*. London: Secker and Warburg.

Henry, Frances. 2003. *Reclaiming African Religions in Trinidad: The Socio-Political Legitimation of the Orisha and Spiritual Baptist Faiths*. Kingston, Jamaica: University of the West Indies Press.

Herdt, Gilbert. [1981] 1994. *Guardians of the Flutes: Idioms of Masculinity*. Chicago: University of Chicago Press.

Herskovits, Melville J., and Frances S. Herskovits. 1934. *Rebel Destiny: Among the Bush Negroes of Dutch Guiana*. New York: McGraw-Hill.

————. 1936. *Suriname Folk-Lore*. New York: Columbia University Press.

————. 1937. *Life in a Haitian Valley*. New York: A. A. Knopf.

————. 1947. *Trinidad Village*. New York: A. A. Knopf.

Hill, Donald. 1993. *Calypso Callaloo: Early Carnival Music in Trinidad*. Gainesville: University Press of Florida.

Hill, Errol. 1967. On the Origin of the Term Calypso. *Ethnomusicology* 11 (3): 359–67.

————. 1972. *The Trinidad Carnival: Mandate for a National Theatre*. Austin: University of Texas Press.

Hogan, Peter. 2008. *Shirley Bassey: Diamond Diva*. London: André Deutsch.

Holcomb, Gary Edward. 2007. *Claude McKay, Code Name Sasha: Queer Black Marxism and the Harlem Renaissance*. Gainesville: University Press of Florida.

Holland, Sharon. 2000. *Raising the Dead: Readings of Death and (Black) Subjectivity*. Durham, NC: Duke University Press.

————. 2005. "Foreword: 'Home' is a Four-Letter Word." In *Black Queer Studies: A Critical Anthology*, edited by E. Patrick Johnson and Mae G. Henderson: ix–xiii. Durham, NC: Duke University Press.

————. 2012. *The Erotic Life of Racism*. Durham, NC: Duke University Press.

Hubbard, Edward Akintola. 2014. Personal communication with author, October 10.

Jackson, John L. 2013. *Thin Description: Ethnography and the African Hebrew Israelites of Jerusalem*. Cambridge, MA: Harvard University Press.

Jackson, Michael. 1998. *Minima Ethnographica: Intersubjectivity and the Anthropological Project*. Chicago: University of Chicago Press.

Jackson, Trevor A., ed. 2004. *Caribbean Geology into the Third Millennium: Transactions of the Fifteenth Caribbean Geological Conference*. Wanstead, Barbados: University of the West Indies Press.

Jamaica Observer (*JA Observer*). 2014. "CCJ Grants Jamaican Homosexual Leave to Challenge Legislation in T&T and Belize." May 8.

James, David. 2007. "We Must Never Forget Godfrey's Struggle." *Trinidad Guardian* (Port of Spain), December 1.

James, Dennis. 2002. "MSM: No Political Agenda—Trinidad and Tobago." [Subsequent to this inaugural issue, the name of the newsletter would be changed to *Free Forum*]. PRIDE 1 (1). Port of Spain: MSM: No Political Agenda. From the author's personal archive. Austin, Texas.

———. 2003. "T&T: MSM—History and Development of HIV/AIDS Education." Unpublished document. From the late Dennis James's personal archive. St. Clair, Trinidad.

Johnson, E. Patrick. 2003. *Appropriating Blackness: Performance and the Politics of Authenticity*. Durham, NC: Duke University Press.

———. 2008. *Sweet Tea: Black Gay Men of the South*. Chapel Hill: University of North Carolina Press.

———. 2016. *No Tea, No Shade: New Writing in Black Queer Studies*. Durham, NC: Duke University Press.

Johnson, E. Patrick, and Mae G. Henderson. 2005. "Introduction: Queering Black Studies/ "Quaring" Queer Studies." In *Black Queer Studies: A Critical Anthology*, edited by E. Patrick Johnson and Mae G. Henderson: 1–20. Durham, NC: Duke University Press.

Joint United Nations Programme on HIV/AIDS (UNAIDS). 2008a. *Caribbean AIDS Epidemic Update: Regional Summary*. Geneva: UNAIDS.

———. 2008b. *Report on the Global AIDS Epidemic*. Geneva: UNAIDS.

———. 2009a. *UNAIDS Action Framework: Universal Access for Men Who Have Sex with Men and Transgender People*. Geneva: UNAIDS.

———. 2009b. *AIDS Epidemic Update*. Geneva: UNAIDS.

———. 2012. *Report on the Global AIDS Epidemic*. Geneva: UNAIDS.

Jordan, Kerwyn. 2003. Interview by author, August 7, Port of Spain, Trinidad.

———. 2005. Profile on Friends For Life. Friends For Life Archive. Port of Spain, Trinidad.

———. 2006. Biography of Friends For Life. Friends For Life Archive. Port of Spain, Trinidad.

———. 2008a. The Community Chatroom Experience 2007–2008. Friends For Life Archive. Port of Spain, Trinidad.

———. 2008b. "Chatroom Evolution." Presentation delivered at the Community Chatroom Experience Facilitator and Behaviour Change Counseling Educator Training Workshop, July 18–20, St. Augustine, Trinidad.

———. 2010. Personal correspondence with author, February 15, 22, and 25.

———. 2014. Personal communication with author, December 16.

———. 2015. Personal correspondence with author, January 8 and 27, and March 15.

———. 2016. Personal correspondence with author, April 17.

Jordan, Kerwyn, and Eswick Padmore. 2003. "Prejudice and Discrimination: A Nationwide Response." Project funding proposal submitted to the International HIV/AIDS Alliance. Friends For Life Archive. Port-of-Spain, Trinidad.

Joubert, Caroline. 2007. *L'odyssée de Jim Dine: A Survey of Printed Works from 1985–2006.* 1st ed. Caroline Joubert, commissariat. Göttingen, Germany: Steidl.

Julien, Isaac. 1994. *The Darker Side of Black.* Film. London: Arts Council of Great Britain.

Keeling, Kara. 2007. *The Witch's Flight: The Cinematic, the Black Femme, and the Image of Common Sense.* Durham, NC: Duke University Press.

Kelly, John Dunham. 1991. *A Politics of Virtue: Hinduism, Sexuality, and Countercolonial Discourse in Fiji.* Chicago: University of Chicago Press.

Kempadoo, Kamala. 2004. *Sexing the Caribbean: Gender, Race, and Sexual Labor.* New York: Routledge.

———. [2004] 2009. "Dying for Sex: HIV/AIDS and Other Dangers." In *Sex, Power, and Taboo: Gender and HIV in the Caribbean and Beyond*, edited by Dorothy Roberts et al.: 3–32. Kingston, Jamaica: Ian Randle.

Kerr, Theodore and Joss Barton. 2015. "There is a Huge Impact That Not Telling Robert's Story Has on the Past, Present and Future of AIDS." Visual AIDS BLOG. https://www.visualaids.org/blog/detail/ted-kerr-st-louis. Accessed August 23, 2017.

King, Rosamond. [2005] 2008. "More Notes on the Invisibility of Caribbean Lesbians." In *Our Caribbean: A Gathering of Lesbian and Gay Writing from the Antilles*, edited by Thomas Glave: 191–96. Durham, NC: Duke University Press.

———. 2014. *Island Bodies: Transgressive Sexualities in the Caribbean Imagination.* Gainesville: University Press of Florida.

Knight, Franklin W. [1978] 1990. *The Caribbean: The Genesis of a Fragmented Nationalism.* New York: Oxford University Press.

Knight, Franklin W., and Colin A. Palmer, eds. 1989. *The Modern Caribbean.* Chapel Hill: University of North Carolina Press.

Koestenbaum, Wayne. 1991. "The Queen's Throat: (Homo)sexuality and the Art of Singing." In *Inside/Out: Lesbian Theories/Gay Theories*, edited by Diana Fuss: 205–34. London: Routledge.

Kolata, Gina. 1987. "Boy's 1969 Death Suggests AIDS Invaded U.S. Several Times." *The New York Times* (New York), October 28.

Kuklick, Henrika. 1991. *The Savage Within: The Social History of British Anthropology, 1885–1945.* Cambridge: Cambridge University Press.

Kulick, Don. 1998. *Travesti: Sex, Gender, and Culture among Brazilian Transgendered Prostitutes.* Chicago: University of Chicago Press.

Lacan, Jacques. 1977. "The Signification of the Phallus." In *Écrits: A Selection.* Translated by Alan Sheridan. New York: W. W. Norton.

La Guerre, John G., and Ann Marie Bissessar. [1974] 2005. *Calcutta to Caroni and the Indian Diaspora.* Edited by John La Guerre and Ann Marie Bissessar. St. Augustine, Trinidad and Tobago: University of the West Indies Press.

Laird, Christopher. 2015. *Paradise Lost*. Documentary film. Produced by Christopher Laird and Ray Funk. Port of Spain, Trinidad.

Laird, Judith. 1989. *Women in Calypso*. Television documentary. Port-of-Spain: Trinidad and Tobago Television.

Laughlin, Nicholas, et al. 2006. "Masman." *Caribbean Beat*, no. 79. http://caribbean-beat .com/issue-79/masman-peter-minshall#axzz4qtnWSHuJ. Accessed August 26, 2017.

Laurence, K. O. 1995. *Tobago in Wartime, 1793–1815*. Wanstead, Barbados: University of the West Indies Press.

Layne, Shontelle, and Sheldon Benjamin. [2005] 2007. "Roll It Gal." *Soca Queen*. Compact disc. Composed by Shontelle Layne and Sheldon Benjamin. Performed by Alison Hinds. Bridgetown, Barbados: 1720 Entertainment.

Lee, R. K., et al. 2005. "Many Partnered Men: A Behavioural and HIV Seroprevalence Study of Men Who Have Sex with Men in Trinidad." Unpublished report. Port-of-Spain: Caribbean Epidemiology Center.

———. 2006. "Risk Behaviours for HIV among Men Who Have Sex with Men in Trinidad and Tobago." Abstract. Toronto, Canada: AIDS 2006—XVI International AIDS Conference 13–18 August.

Lévi-Strauss, Claude. 1966. *Pensée sauvage* [The savage mind]. Chicago: University of Chicago Press.

Lewis, Linden, ed. 2003. *The Culture of Gender and Sexuality in the Caribbean*. Gainesville: University Press of Florida.

Lewis, Maureen Warner. 1991. *Guinea's Other Suns: The African Dynamic in Trinidad Culture*. Fitchburg, MA: Majority Press.

Lewis, Linda McCartha [Sandy-Lewis]. [1968] 2005. "Palet." *The Best of Calypso Rose: Calypso Queen of the World*. Compact disc set. Port-of-Spain: Caribbean Music Group Limited.

———. 2007. Interview by author, January 18, 2007, New York City.

———. 2009. Personal communication with author, August 14.

———. 2010. Personal communication with author, March 26.

———. 2014. Personal communication with author, December 6.

Lewis, Samella. 1995. *Caribbean Visions: Contemporary Painting and Sculpture*. Alexandria, VA: Art Services International.

Livingstone, Marco. 1998. *Jim Dine: The Alchemy of Images*. New York: Monacelli Press, 1998.

Lomax, Derek W. 1978. *The Reconquest of Spain*. London: Longman.

Lorde, Audre. 1982. *Zami: A New Spelling of My Name*. Watertown, MA: Persephone Press.

———. [1978] 1984. "Uses of the Erotic: The Erotic as Power." In *Sister Outsider: Essays and Speeches*: 53–59. Trumansburg, NY: Crossing Press.

Lott, Eric. 1993. *Love and Theft: Blackface Minstrelsy and the American Working Class*. New York: Oxford University Press.

Loubon, Michelle. 2009. "Sealy's Life Hailed on World AIDS Day." *Trinidad Guardian* (Port-of-Spain), December 4.

Love, Heather. 2012. Public conversation with author, March 19, University of Pennsylvania.

Lum, Kenneth Anthony. 2000. *Praising His Name in the Dance: Spirit Possession in the Spiritual Baptist Faith and Orisha Work in Trinidad, West Indies.* Amsterdam: Harwood Academic Publishers.

Mahabir, Cynthia. 2001. "The Rise of Calypso Feminism: Gender and Musical Politics in the Calypso." *Popular Music* 20 (3): 409–30.

Maison-Bishop, Carole. 1994. "Women in Calypso: Hearing the Voices." Unpublished PhD diss. submitted to the Department of Educational Foundations at the University of Alberta.

Malinowski, Bronislaw. 1927. *Sex and Repression in Savage Society.* London: K. Paul, Trench, Trubner.

———. 1929. *The Sexual Life of Savages in North-Western Melanesia: An Ethnographic Account of Courtship, Marriage, and Family Life among the Natives of the Trobriand Islands, British New Guinea.* London: Routledge.

Manalansan, Martin F., IV. 2003. *Global Divas: Filipino Gay Men in the Diaspora.* Durham, NC: Duke University Press.

Martin, Cedrianne. 2009. "One in Five MSM May Be HIV Positive." *Trinidad Express* (Port of Spain), May 31.

Massiah, Joycelin. 1986. *Women in the Caribbean: A Selection of Papers Based Primarily on the Women in the Caribbean Research Project.* Edited by Joycelin Massiah. Mona, Jamaica: Institute of Social and Economic Research, University of the West Indies.

McClintock, Anne. 1995. *Imperial Leather: Race, Gender, and Sexuality in the Colonial Contest.* New York: Routledge.

McCommie, Dennis. 2008. Interview with Peter Minshall, *Cock-a-Doodle-Doo*, Gayelle Television, February 2.

McCune, Jeffrey Q. 2014. *Sexual Discretion: Black Masculinity and the Politics of Passing.* Chicago: University of Chicago Press.

McMichael, W. Pate. 2007. "The Pre-Pandemic Puzzle." *St. Louis Magazine* (St. Louis), August 31.

Mead, Margaret. 1935. *Sex and Temperament in Three Primitive Societies.* London: Routledge.

Mendes, John. [1986] 2003. *Cote ci Cote La Trinidad and Tobago Dictionary.* Arima, Trinidad and Tobago: Zenith Services Limited.

Mercer, Kobena. 1994. *Welcome to the Jungle: New Positions in Black Cultural Studies.* New York: Routledge.

———. 1996. "Decolonisation and Disappointment: Reading Fanon's Sexual Politics." In *The Fact of Blackness: Frantz Fanon and Visual Representation*, edited by Alan Read: 114–31. London: Institute of Contemporary Arts.

Merriam, Alan P. 1964. *The Anthropology of Music.* Evanston, WY: Northwestern University Press.

Meyer, Ilan, and Rebecca Young. 2005. "The Trouble with 'MSM' and 'WSW': Erasure of the Sexual: Minority Person in Public Health Discourse." *American Journal of Public Health* 95 (7): 1144–49.

Middleton, Richard. 2006. "Appropriating the Phallus? Female Voices and the Law-of-the-Father." In *Voicing the Popular: On the Subjects of Popular Music.* New York: Routledge.

Miller, Daniel. 1994. *Modernity, an Ethnographic Approach: Dualism and Mass Consumption in Trinidad.* New York: Berg.

———. 1997. *Capitalism: An Ethnographic Approach.* New York: Berg Publishers.

Miller, Errol. 1986. *Marginalization of the Black Male: Insights from the Development of the Teaching Profession.* Mona, Jamaica: Institute for Social and Economic Research, University of the West Indies Press.

———. 1991. *Men at Risk.* Kingston: Jamaica Publishing House.

Minshall, Peter. 1982. Guggenheim Fellowship application. Callaloo Company Archive. Chaguaramas, Trinidad.

———. 1984a. Guggenheim Fellowship project summary report. Callaloo Company Archive. Chaguaramas, Trinidad.

———. 1984b. *Callaloo an de Crab: A Story by Minshall.* Callaloo Company Archives. Chaguaramas, Trinidad.

———. 1985. "The Use of Traditional Figures in Carnival Art." Speech given at the First National Conference on the Performing Arts, June 25, Trinidad. Callaloo Company Archive. Chaguaramas, Trinidad.

———. 1991a. "Address by Recipient: Peter Minshall." Speech given at the ceremony to confer the Honorary Degree of Doctor of Letters, University of the West Indies. November 2. Callaloo Company Archive. Chaguaramas, Trinidad.

———. 1991b. "From the Bat to the Dancing Mobile: Technology in the Mas." An illustrated essay. Callaloo Company Archive. Chaguaramas, Trinidad.

———. 1993. "The Power of the Mask." Address delivered at the opening of *The Power of the Mask* exhibition at the National Museum of Scotland, August 11. Callaloo Company Archive. Chaguaramas, Trinidad.

———. 1995. "Carnival and Its Place in Caribbean Culture and Art." In *Caribbean Visions: Contemporary Painting and Sculpture*, 49–57. Alexandria, Virginia: Art Services International.

———. 1998. Keynote adddress delivered at the Caribbean Consultation on HIV/AIDS, June 3–5, Port-of-Spain, Trinidad. Callaloo Company Archive. Chaguaramas, Trinidad.

———. 2002. "Minshall at CCA7." Illustrated presentation to accompany the exhibition *1981*, curated by Chris Cozier. October 23. Callaloo Company Archive. Chaguaramas, Trinidad.

———. 2005. "Play Yourself! The Production That Peter Minshall Has Been Running for 64 Years." Interview by B. C. Pires. *Trinidad Express*, September 25.

———. 2006. "The Sacred Heart." Rough video footage of the band's stage presentation. February 28. Port of Spain, Trinidad. Callaloo Company Archive. Chaguaramas, Trinidad.

———. 2008. Personal communication with author, July 9.

———. 2013a. "Masman/Artist." In *Carnival: Theory and Practice*, edited by Christopher Innes, Annabel Rutherford, and Brigitte Bogar, 315–38. Trenton, NJ: Africa World Press.

———. 2013b. "Nignorance and Enwhitenment." In *Carnival: Theory and Practice*, edited by Christopher Innes, Annabel Rutherford, and Brigitte Bogar, 3–24. Trenton, NJ: Africa World Press.

———. 2015. Personal communication and correspondence with author, October 4.

———. 2016a. Personal correspondence with author, March 27.

———. 2016b. Personal communication and correspondence with author, April 2.

———. 2016c. Personal communication with author, April 21.

Mintz, Sidney Wilfred, and Richard Price. 1992. *The Birth of African-American Culture: An Anthropological Perspective*. Boston: Beacon Press.

Mohammed, Patricia, ed. 2004. *Gendered Realities: Essays in Caribbean Feminist Thought*. Wanstead, Barbados: University of the West Indies.

Moore, Brian. 1998. "The Colonial Elites of 19th-Century Guyana." In *The White Minority in the Caribbean*, edited by Howard Johnson and Karl Watson, 109–15. Princeton, NJ: Weiner.

Moore, Gillian. 2006. "Minshall Calls His Faithful: Masman Comes 'Heartical' for C2K6." *Trinidad Guardian* (Port of Spain), February 4.

Munasinghe, Viranjini. 2001. *Callaloo or Tossed Salad? East Indians and the Cultural Politics of Identity in Trinidad*. Ithaca, NY: Cornell University Press.

Muñoz, José Esteban. 1999. *Disidentifications: Queers of Color and the Performance of Politics*. Minneapolis: University of Minnesota Press.

Murray, David A. B. 2002. *Opacity: Gender, Sexuality, Race, and the "Problem" of Identity in Martinique*. New York: Peter Lang.

———. 2012. *Flaming Souls: Homosexuality, Homophobia, and Social Change in Barbados*. Toronto: University of Toronto Press.

Mysliwec, Karol. 1998. *Eros on the Nile*. Ithaca, NY: Cornell University Press.

Naipaul, V. S. [Vidiadhar Surajprasad]. 1962. *The Middle Passage; Impressions of Five Societies, British, French, and Dutch, in the West Indies and South America*. London: A. Deutsch.

Narain, Jai, et al. 1989. "Epidemiology of AIDS and HIV Infection in the Caribbean." *Pan American Health Organization Bulletin* 23 (1–2): 42–49.

Narine, Dalton. [1987] 2011. *The Minshall Trilogy: A Modern Fable as Street Theatre*. Documentary film. Port of Spain: Create Space Studios.

———. 2009. *Mas Man: Peter Minshall, Trinidad Carnival Artist.* Documentary film. Port-of-Spain: King Carnival Productions.

National AIDS Coordinating Committee of Trinidad and Tobago (NACC). 2006. *United Nations General Assembly Special Session on HIV/AIDS Country Report: Republic of Trinidad and Tobago.* Port-of-Spain: Republic of Trinidad and Tobago.

———. 2008. *United Nations General Assembly Special Session on HIV/AIDS Country Progress Report: Republic of Trinidad and Tobago.* Port-of-Spain: Republic of Trinidad and Tobago.

National AIDS Coordinating Committee of T&T and Friends For Life (NACC and FFL). 2008. *Funding Agreement Packet.* Friends For Life Archive. Port-of-Spain, Trinidad. [N.B.: the page numbers for this document represent the order in which the materials appear in the packet.]

Neaves, Julien. 2013. "Gay Lawyer Fights TT, Belize Laws." *Trinidad and Tobago's Newsday* (Port of Spain), November 13.

Neptune, Harvey. 2007. *Caliban and the Yankees: Trinidad and the United States Occupation.* Chapel Hill: University of North Carolina Press.

Nettleford, Rex. 2015. "Carifesta: In Search of Regional Unity." *National Dance Theatre Company Journal* 6:28–33.

Newman, Paul. 2007. *A Hausa-English Dictionary.* New Haven, CT: Yale University Press.

Newton, Esther. [1972] 1979. *Mother Camp: Female Impersonators in America.* Chicago: University of Chicago Press.

———. 1993. *Cherry Grove, Fire Island: Sixty Years in America's First Gay and Lesbian Town.* Boston: Beacon Press.

Nixon, Angelique. 2015. *Resisting Paradise: Tourism, Diaspora, and Sexuality in Caribbean Culture.* Jackson: University of Mississippi Press.

Noel, Nikolai. 2008. Interview by author, June 6, St. Augustine, Trinidad.

Nunley, John. 1993. "Peter Minshall: The Good, the Bad, and the Old in Trinidad Carnival." In *Imagery and Creativity: Ethnoaesthetics and Art Worlds in the Americas,* edited by Dorthea S. Whitten and Norman E. Whitten, Jr., 288–307. Tucson: University of Arizona Press.

Obolo, Pascale. 2005. *Calypso at Dirty Jim's.* Documentary film. Paris: Maturity Music Limited and Dynamo Productions.

———. 2011. *Calypso Rose: Lioness of the Jungle.* Documentary film. Paris: Maturity Music Limited and Dynamo Productions.

O'Callaghan, Joseph F. 2003. *Reconquest and Crusade in Medieval Spain.* Philadelphia: University of Pennsylvania Press.

Ottley, Rudolph. 1992. "Calypso Rose." In *Women in Calypso,* Part I. Arima, Trinidad and Tobago.

Owens, Emily A. 2009. "Are You Sisters? The Impossibility of Black Lesbian Subjectivity." Honor's thesis, Harvard University, Cambridge, MA.

Padilla, Mark. 2007. *Caribbean Pleasure Industry: Tourism, Sexuality, and* AIDS *in the Dominican Republic*. Chicago: University of Chicago Press.

Padmore, Eswick, et al. 1999. *Friends For Life: Constitution*. Friends For Life Archive. Port-of-Spain, Trinidad.

———. 2003. Interview with author. July 5.

———. 2008. "Tobago Vulnerable Populations: HIV/AIDS Counseling and Support to Men Who Have Sex with Men (MSM), MSM Transactional Sex Workers (MSM-SWS), and MSM Subpopulations (MSM-SP) for the Tobago HIV/AIDS Coordinating Committee Secretariat (THACCS)—A Technical Report." Unpublished report. Eswick J. S. Padmore, consultant. Friends For Life Archive. Port-of-Spain, Trinidad.

———. 2017. Personal communication with the author. August 24.

Parnia, Sam, et al. 2014. "AWARE—Awareness During Resuscitation—A Perspective Study." *Resuscitation Journal* 85: 1799–805. London: Elsevier.

Parsons, Elsie W. C., ed. 1943. *Folk-Lore of the Antilles, French, and English*. Edited by Cindy Patton and Benigno Sánchez-Eppler. New York: American Folklore Society.

———. 2000. *Queer Diasporas*. Durham, NC: Duke University Press.

Pearse, Andrew. 1956. "Mitto Simpson on Calypso Legends of the Nineteenth Century." *Caribbean Quarterly* 4 (3–4): 250–62.

———. [1956] 1988. "Carnival in Nineteenth-Century Trinidad." Trinidad Carnival issue of *Caribbean Quarterly* 4 (3–4): 4–42.

Persad, Seeta. 2009. Documentary on Calypso Rose to be released. *Trinidad and Tobago's Newsday* (Port-of-Spain), July 22.

Phillips, William D., and Carla R. Phillips. 1992. *The Worlds of Christopher Columbus*. Cambridge: Cambridge University Press.

Pines, Jim, ed. 1992. *Black and White in Color: Black People in British Television since 1936*. London: British Film Institute.

Pires, B. C. 2006a. "The Heart of a Mas." Interview with Peter Minshall. *Trinidad and Tobago Express* (Port-of-Spain), December 31.

———. 2006b. "No Fear of Falling: The Sacred Heart Is Peter Minshall's First Band in Three Years." Interview with Peter Minshall. *Trinidad Express* (Port of Spain), February 19.

Plato. [385–370 BC] 2008. *The Symposium*. Cambridge: Cambridge University Press.

Prieur, Annie. 1998. *Mema's House, Mexico City: On Transvestites, Queens, and Machos*. Chicago: University of Chicago Press.

Puar, Jasbir K. 1999. "Transnational Sexualities and Trinidad: Modern Bodies, National Queers." Unpublished PhD diss., Department of Ethnic Studies, University of California, Berkeley.

———. 2001a. "Global Circuits: Transnational Sexualities and Trinidad." *Signs* 26 (4): 1039–65.

————. 2001b. "Transnational Configurations of Desire: The Nation and Its White Closets." In *The Making and Unmaking of Whiteness*, edited by Birgit B. Rasmussen et al: 167–83. Durham, NC: Duke University Press.

————. 2002. "Circuits of Queer Mobility: Tourism, Travel and Globalization." *GLQ: A Journal of Lesbian and Gay Studies* 8 (1–2): 101–37.

————. 2007. *Terrorist Assemblages: Homonationalism in Queer Times.* Durham, NC: Duke University Press.

————. 2009. "Chutney to Queer and Back: Trinidad, 1995–1998." *Caribbean Review of Gender Studies* 3 (November). http://sta.uwi.edu/crgs/november2009/journals /JasbirKPuar.pdf. Accessed August 26, 2017.

Quevedo, Raymond. 1983. *Atilla's Kaiso: A Short History of Trinidad Calypso.* St. Augustine, Trinidad and Tobago: University of the West Indies.

Ramírez, Rafael L. et al., eds. 2002. *Caribbean Masculinities: Working Papers.* San Juan, PR: HIV/AIDS Research and Education Center, University of Puerto Rico.

Randel, Don. 1986. *The New Harvard Dictionary of Music.* Entries for "Voice" and "Singing," 749–50, 926–27. Edited by Don Randel. Cambridge, MA: Harvard University Press.

Reddock, Rhoda. 1994. *Women, Labour, and Politics in Trinidad and Tobago: A History.* Atlantic Highlands, NJ: Zed Books.

————. 2004. *Interrogating Caribbean Masculinities: Theoretical and Empirical Analyses.* Edited by Rhoda Reddock. Mona, Jamaica: University of the West Indies.

Reddock, Rhoda, and Dorothy Roberts. 2009. Introduction to *Sex, Power and Taboo: Gender and HIV in the Caribbean and Beyond.* Kingston, Jamaica: Ian Randle.

Regis, Louis. 1999. *The Political Calypso: True Opposition in Trinidad and Tobago, 1962–1987.* Kingston, Jamaica: University of the West Indies.

Resnik, Susan. 1999. *Blood Saga: Hemophilia, AIDS, and the Survival of a Community.* Berkeley: University of California Press.

Rich, Adrienne Cecile. [1980] 1986. "Compulsory Heterosexuality and Lesbian Existence." In *Blood, Bread, and Poetry: Selected Prose, 1979–1985.* New York: Norton.

Richards, Peter. 2006. *Caribbean: Gay, HIV-Positive, and Totally Fearless.* May 2. Inter Press Service News Agency. http://www.ipsnews.net/2006/05/caribbean-gay-hiv -positive-and-totally-fearless. Accessed August 26, 2017.

Richardson, Matt. 2012. *The Queer Limit of Black Memory: Black Lesbian Literature and Irresolution.* Columbus: Ohio State University Press.

Riggio, Milla, ed. 1998. "Introduction: Resistance and Identity." TDR: The Drama Review (Trinidad Carnival special issue): 7–23.

————. 2004. *Carnival: Culture in Action: The Trinidad Experience.* New York: Routledge.

Riverside Studios. 1986. *Callaloo by Minshall.* Exhibition catalogue. London: Riverside Studios.

Roberts, Dorothy, et al. 2009. *Sex, Power and Taboo: Gender and HIV in the Caribbean and Beyond*. Edited by Dorothy Roberts et al. Kingston, Jamaica: Ian Randle.

Robinson, Colin. 2009. Personal communication with author. March 24.

Rohlehr, Gordon. 1990. "Calypso and Society in Pre-Independence Trinidad." Port of Spain: G. Rohlehr.

———. 2004. "I Lawa: The Construction of Masculinity in Trinidad and Tobago Calypso." In *Interrogating Caribbean Masculinities: Theoretical and Empirical Analyses*, edited by Rhoda Reddock: 326–403. Kingston, Jamaica: University of the West Indies Press.

Rouse, Irving. 1992. *The Tainos: Rise and Decline of the People Who Greeted Columbus*. New Haven, CT: Yale University Press.

Rubin, Gayle S. 1984. "Thinking Sex: Notes for a Radical Theory of the Politics of Sexuality." In *Pleasure and Danger: Exploring Female Sexuality*, edited by Carole S. Vance. 267–319. Boston: Routledge and K. Paul.

Schechner, Richard, and Milla Riggio. [1998] 2004. "Peter Minshall: A Voice to Add to the Song of the Universe—An Interview by Richard Schechner and Milla Cozart Riggio [conducted February 14, 1997, in Port-of-Spain, Trinidad]." In *Carnival: Culture in Action—the Trinidad Experience*, edited by Milla Cozart Riggio: 170–93. New York: Routledge.

Scher, Phillip. 2003. *Carnival and the Formation of a Caribbean Transnation*. Gainesville: University Press of Florida.

Scott, Darieck. 2010. *Extravagant Abjection: Blackness, Power, and Sexuality in the African American Literary Imagination*. New York: NYU Press.

Seaforth, C. E., et al. 1983. *A Guide to the Medicinal Plants of Trinidad and Tobago*. London: Commonwealth Secretariat.

Sealy, Godfrey. 1995. "We Are Our Own Worst Enemies." In *HIV and AIDS: The Global Inter-connection*, edited by Elizabeth Reid, 40–55. Hartford: Kumarian Press and the United Nations Development Program.

———. [1988] 2005. "One of Our Sons Is Missing." In *You Can Lead a Horse to Water, and Other Plays*, edited by Judy Stone, 107–61. Oxford: Macmillan Caribbean.

———. 2005. Interview by author, September 3, Woodbrook, Trinidad. Copy courtesy of Kerwyn Jordan.

Seidman, Karmenlara. 2008. "'Mas' Is Desire: The Erotic, Grotesque and Visionary in Trinidad Carnival." Unpublished PhD diss., Department of Performance Studies, New York University.

Senior, Olive. 1991. *Working Miracles: Women's Lives in the English-Speaking Caribbean*. Bloomington: Indiana University Press.

Shakespeare, William. [1611] 2008. *The Tempest*. Edited by Stephen Orgel. Oxford: Oxford University Press.

Shears-Neptune, Valdeen. 2006. "Minshall Mas Under Fire Again: Blasphemy—RC Group." *Trinidad Guardian* (Port of Spain), February 20.

Sheller, Mimi. 2003. *Consuming the Caribbean: From Arawaks to Zombies.* London: Routledge.

———. 2012. *Citizenship from Below: Erotic Agency and Caribbean Freedom.* Durham, NC: Duke University Press.

Silvera, Makeda. 1996. "Man Royals and Sodomites: Some Thoughts on the Invisibility of Afro-Caribbean Lesbians." In *Lesbian Subjects: A Feminist Studies Reader*, edited by Martha Vicinus. 167–77. Bloomington: Indiana University Press.

Silverman, Kaja. 1992. "The Lacanian Phallus." *Differences: A Journal of Feminist Cultural Studies* 4 (1): 84–115.

Simpson, George Eaton. 1980. "The Shouters Church." In *Religious Cults of the Caribbean: Trinidad, Jamaica, and Haiti.* Rio Piedras: University of Puerto Rico—Institute of Caribbean Studies.

Sinnette, Luke. 2007. Interview by author, July 9, Petit Bourg, Trinidad.

———. 2008. "NACC/FFL Chatroom Pilot Project: Apr. 1–Oct. 31, 2008." Invitation letter to the Chatroom facilitators training workshop, July 1. Friends For Life Archive. Port of Spain, Trinidad.

———. 2016. Personal correspondence with author, April 14.

Smith, Faith. 2006. "Soucouyant." In *Encyclopedia of African-American Culture and History: The Black Experience in the Americas*, edited by Colin Palmer et al.: 822. New York: Macmillan Reference.

———. 2008. Conversation with author, November 4.

———. 2011. *Sex and the Citizen: Interrogating the Caribbean.* Charlottesville: University of Virginia Press.

Smith, Hope Munro. 2004. "Performing Gender in the Trinidad Calypso." *Latin American Music Review* 25 (1): 32–56.

Smith, Michael G. 1962a. *Kinship and Community in Carriacou.* New Haven, CT: Yale University Press.

———. 1962b. *West Indian Family Structure.* Seattle: University of Washington Press.

———. 1965. *The Plural Society in the British West Indies.* Berkeley: University of California Press.

Smith, Raymond Thomas. 1962. *British Guiana.* London: Oxford University Press.

———. 1988. *Kinship and Class in the West Indies: A Genealogical Study of Jamaica and Guyana.* Cambridge: Cambridge University Press.

———. 1996. *The Matrifocal Family: Power, Pluralism, and Politics.* New York: Routledge.

Snorton, C. Riley. 2014. *Nobody Is Supposed to Know: Black Sexuality on the Down Low.* Minneapolis: University of Minnesota Press.

Stephens, Patricia. 1999. *The Spiritual Baptist Faith: African New World Religious History, Identity, and Testimony.* London: Karnak House.

Stocking, George W. 1987. *Victorian Anthropology.* London: Collier Macmillan.

Stockton, Kathryn Bond. 2006. *Beautiful Bottom, Beautiful Shame: Where "Black" Meets "Queer."* Durham, NC: Duke University Press.

Stoler, Ann Laura. 1995. *Race and the Education of Desire: Foucault's History of Sexuality and the Colonial Order of Things.* Durham, NC: Duke University Press.

———. 2002. *Carnal Knowledge and Imperial Power: Race and the Intimate in Colonial Rule.* Berkeley: University of California Press.

Sylvester, Cyrus. 2003. Interview by author, July 23, Woodbrook, Trinidad.

Tambiah, Yasmin. 2009. "Creating (Im)moral Citizens: Gender, Sexuality and Lawmaking in Trinidad and Tobago, 1986." *Caribbean Review of Gender Studies*, no. 3. https://sta.uwi.edu/crgs/november2009/journals/Tambiah.pdf. Accessed August 26, 2017.

Tang, George. 2014. *We Kind Ah People: The Trinidad Carnival Bands of Stephen Lee Heung.* San Francisco: Blurb.

Thomas, Deborah. 2011. *Exceptional Violence: Embodied Citizenship in Transnational Jamaica.* Durham, NC: Duke University Press.

———. 2012. Public conversation with author and Heather Love, March 19, University of Pennsylvania.

Thomas, Eudora. 1987. *A History of the Shouter Baptists in Trinidad and Tobago.* Tacarigua, Trinidad: Callaloux Publications.

Thompson, Delano Ray. 2007. Interview by author, November 7, Lowlands, Tobago.

Tinsley, Omise'eke Natasha. 2008. "Black Atlantic, Queer Atlantic: Queer Imaginings of the Middle Passage." GLQ: *A Journal of Lesbian and Gay Studies* 14, nos. 2–3: 191–215.

———. 2010. *Thiefing Sugar: Eroticism between Women in Caribbean Literature.* Durham, NC: Duke University Press.

———. 2015. Personal conversation with the author on March 9.

Trexler, Richard C. 1995. *Sex and Conquest: Gendered Violence, Political Order, and the European Conquest of the Americas.* Ithaca, NY: Cornell University Press.

Trinidad Express (Express). 1986. "Individual of the Year—Courtenay Bartholomew." January 1.

———. 2006. "Godfrey Sealy Laid to Rest." May 2.

Trinidad Guardian (Guardian). 2001. "Geoffrey Stanforde Dies after Illness." October 27.

———. 2012. "Gay Activist Takes Govt to Court." November 29.

TnT M4M. 1999. *Caribbean M4M 2000: Draft Project Proposal.* September 7. Port-of-Spain: Trinidad and Tobago M4M in collaboration with the Joint United Nations Programme on HIV/AIDS (UNAIDS).

Trouillot, Michel-Rolph. 1992. "The Caribbean Region: An Open Frontier in Anthropological Theory." *Annual Review of Anthropology* 21:19–42.

———. 2003. *Global Transformations: Anthropology and the Modern World.* New York: Palgrave Macmillan.

Turley, Hans. 1999. *Rum, Sodomy, and the Lash: Piracy, Sexuality, and Masculine Identity.* New York: New York University Press.

Turner, Victor Witter. [1969] 1977. *The Ritual Process: Structure and Anti-structure.* Ithaca, NY: Cornell University Press.

————. 1987. *The Anthropology of Performance*. New York: PAJ Publications.

————. [1982] 1992. *From Ritual to Theatre: The Human Seriousness of Play*. New York: PAJ Publications.

Visweswaran, Kamela. 1994. *Fictions of Feminist Ethnography*. Minneapolis: University of Minnesota Press.

Vogel, Shane. 2009. *The Scene of Harlem Cabaret: Race, Sexuality, Performance*. Chicago: University of Chicago Press.

Wade, Peter. 1992. "The Racial Order and National Identity, The Study of Indians and Blacks in the Racial Order, and Unguia: History and Economy." In *Blackness and Race Mixture: The Dynamics of Racial Identity in Colombia*. Baltimore: Johns Hopkins University Press.

————. 1993. *Blackness and Race Mixture: The Dynamics of Racial Identity in Colombia*. Baltimore: Johns Hopkins University Press.

Walcott, Derek. 1984. *Midsummer*. New York: Farrar, Straus, Giroux, 1984.

Walcott, Rinaldo. 1997. *Black Like Who? Writing, Black, Canada*. Toronto: Insomniac Press.

————. 2000. *Rude: Contemporary Black Canadian Cultural Criticism*. Edited by Rinaldo Walcott. Toronto: Insomniac Press.

————. 2005. "Outside in Black Studies: Reading from a Queer Place in the Diaspora." In *Black Queer Studies: A Critical Anthology*, edited by E. Patrick Johnson and Mae G. Henderson: 90–105. Durham, NC: Duke University Press.

————. 2007. "Somewhere Out There: The New Black Queer Theory." In *Blackness and Sexualities*, edited by Michelle Wright and Antje Schuhmann: 29–40. Berlin: Verlag.

————. [2005] 2008. "Fragments of Toronto's Black Queer Community: From a Life Still Being Lived." In *Our Caribbean: A Gathering of Lesbian and Gay Writing from the Antilles*, edited by Thomas Glave: 360–67. Durham, NC: Duke University Press.

————. 2016. *Queer Returns: Essays on Multiculturalism, Diaspora, and Black Studies*. London, Ont., Canada: Insomniac Press.

Wald, Priscilla. 2008. *Contagious: Cultures, Carriers, and the Outbreak Narrative*. Durham, NC: Duke University Press.

Ward, Irving, et. al. 2006. Photo caption. *Trinidad Guardian* (Port-of-Spain), January 30.

Warner, Michael. 1993. *Fear of a Queer Planet: Queer Politics and Social Theory*. Minneapolis: University of Minnesota Press.

————. [1999] 2000. *The Trouble with Normal: Sex Politics and the Ethics of Queer Life*. Cambridge, MA: Harvard University Press.

Warner-Lewis, Maureen. 1991. *Guinea's Other Suns: The African Dynamic in Trinidad Culture*. Dover, MA: Majority Press.

Watt, William Montgomery, and Pierre Cachia. 1965. *A History of Islamic Spain*. Edinburgh, Scot.: Edinburgh University Press.

Weinbaum, Batya. 1999. *Islands of Women and Amazons: Representations and Realities*. Austin: University of Texas Press.

Weir-Soley, Donna Aza. 2009. *Eroticism, Spirituality, and Resistance in Black Women's Writing*. Gainesville: University Press of Florida.

Wekker, Gloria. 1997. "One Finger Does Not Drink Okra Soup: Afro-Surinamese Women and Critical Agency." In *Feminist Genealogies, Colonial Legacies, Democratic Futures*, edited by M. Jacqui Alexander and Chandra Talpade Mohanty, 330–52. New York: Routledge.

———. 2006. *The Politics of Passion: Women's Sexual Culture in the Afro-Surinamese Diaspora*. New York: Columbia University Press.

Weston, Kath. 1991. *Families We Choose: Lesbians, Gays, Kinship*. New York: Columbia University Press.

———. 1996. *Render Me, Gender Me: Lesbians Talk Sex, Class, Color, Nation, Studmuffins*. New York: Columbia University Press.

———. 1998. *Long Slow Burn: Sexuality and Social Science*. New York: Routledge.

———. 2002. *Gender in Real Time: Power and Transience in a Visual Age*. New York: Routledge.

Williams, Dave. 2008. Interview by author, February 6, Belmont, Trinidad.

Williams, Eric Eustac. 1944. *Capitalism and Slavery*. Chapel Hill: University of North Carolina Press.

———. 1970. *From Columbus to Castro: The History of the Caribbean, 1492–1969*. London: Deutsch, 1970.

———. [1942] 1993. *History of the People of Trinidad and Tobago*. London: A. Deutsch.

Williams, Jason. 2008. "Synergy Nights on Synergy Television." Interview with Peter Minshall, March 12. Callaloo Company Archive.

Wilson, Peter J. 1969. "Reputation and Respectability: A Suggestion for Caribbean Ethnography." *Man* 4 (2).

———. 1973. *Crab Antics: The Social Anthropology of English-Speaking Negro Societies of the Caribbean*. New Haven, CT: Yale University Press.

Wilson, Samuel M. 1997. *The Indigenous People of the Caribbean*. Edited by Samuel M. Wilson. Gainesville: University Press of Florida.

Wood, Donald. 1968. *Trinidad in Transition: The Years after Slavery*. London: Oxford University Press.

Wolf, Eric R. 1982. *Europe and the People without History*. Berkeley: University of California Press.

Wood, Elizabeth. 1994. "Sapphonics." In *Queering the Pitch: The New Gay and Lesbian Musicology*, edited by Phillip Brett et al.: 27–66. New York: Routledge.

Woodard, Vincent. 2014. *The Delectable Negro: Human Consumption and Homoeroticism within U.S. Slave Culture*. Edited by Justin A. Joyce and Dwight A. McBride. New York: New York University Press.

World Bank. 2001. *HIV/AIDS in the Caribbean: Issues and Opinions.* Prepared by Patricio Marquez et al. Washington, DC: International Bank for Reconstruction and Development/World Bank.

World Health Organization (WHO). 2009. *Prevention and Treatment of HIV and Other Sexually Transmitted Infections among Men Who Have Sex with Men and Transgender Populations.* Prepared by Sarah Hawkes. Geneva: WHO.

Yelvington, Kevin. 1995. *Producing Power: Ethnicity, Gender, and Class in a Caribbean Workplace.* Philadelphia, PA: Temple University Press.

Young, Rebecca, and Ilan Meyer. 2005. "The Trouble with 'MSM' and 'WSW': Erasure of the Sexual-Minority Person in Public Health Discourse." *American Journal of Public Health* 95 (7): 1144–49.

condom usage: men-who-have-sex-with-men and, 150, 157, 234n10; *The Sacred Heart* and, 58, 67–70

Cozier, Christopher, 55, 64

cross-dressing, 36, 68. *See also* Dame Lorraine character

Cuba, 144, 234n10

Curaçao, 236n4

Dame Lorraine character, 67–70, 228n11, *P10–14*

Davies, Carol Boyce, 112–14, 231n5

desire: use of term, xxii; art-making as, xxii, xxiii; community building and, xx, 10–11, 212–15; eros and, 8–9, 10, 220n11; fetishization and, xxii–xxiii, xxvi, xxvii, 117, 207, 214, 218n6; Friends for Life and, 175–78, 238n21; grassroots activism and, 1–2, 175–78, 200–201, 238n21; historical consciousness and, xxx; as paradoxical desire, 10; political-sensual-spiritual framework and, 10–11. *See also* erotic, the; same-sex desire

De Veaux, Alexis, 220n6, 220n9

Dikobe, Maude, 231n5

Dillon, Sarah, 218n5

Dominica, 235n16

Dominican Republic, 144, 218n7, 235n1

Doris, Loren, *100*

double entendre, 16, 104–6, 231n3, 232n11, 238n19

Eastman, Mark, *P15*

Edwards, David, 221n16

El Centro de Orientación e Investigación Integral (Dominican Republic), 235n1

Elder, Jacob Delworth, 89, 229nn2–3

Ellis, Nadia, 240n13

Elwin, Rosamund, 115, 232n2, 232n7

emancipation, 32–34, 32–35, 38–39, 89, 223n6

erotic, the: blackness and, 215–16; black queer diaspora studies and, 198–99; Carnival and, 31–32, 205; collective selfhood and, 221n13; as community building, 10–11, 159, 205; eros and, 8–9, 10, 220n11;

erotic knowledge, 9–11, 221n13; femininity and, 7–8; fieldwork reflection methodology, 11–12; grassroots activism and, 15; historical consciousness and, xxviii; as methodology, 205; mortality theme and, 10–11, 203–4; as organizing hermeneutic, 2; "Palet" and, 205; as paradoxical desire, 10; political-sensual-spiritual and, 182–85, 199, 215–16, 220n8, 220n12, 221n14; the political *vs.*, 220n12; *Sacred Heart* and, 205; same-sex desire and, 203–4, 205, 215–16; sensoryscape of the erotic, 15; sex-gender conflation and, 7–8; sight and visual erotic aesthetics, 15–16, 36–37, 46–49, 52–62, 62–63, 67–70, 202; sound and vibration erotic aesthetics, 16, 110–12, 120–25; touch and sensation aesthetic experiences, 11, 16–17, 175–78, 182–85, 201–2. *See also From Far Afield: A Queer Travelogue*

ethnography: as methodology, 11–15; narrative voice and, 12–13; queer ethnography, 206–8, 208–15, 240n12; of same-sex desire, 2–4, 13–15; situated subjectivity and, 13, 198, 209–10, 213–14

Family Planning Association of Trinidad and Tobago (FPATT), 162, 163

femininity: calypso and, 111, 112–13, 230n16, 230n18; calypso musicianship and, 111, 112–13, 230n16, 230n18; Caribbean region and, 230n16, 230n18; Carnival and, 224n18; effeminacy, 237n17; the erotic and, 7–8; female masculinity, 104, 106, 112–13; heterosexual matrix, 113; masculinity and, 230n18, 237n11; same-sex desire and, 111

fetish/fetishization and, xxii–xxiii, xxvi–xxvii, 31–32, 117, 207, 214, 218n6;

Fields, Jacquelyn, 197–205, 239n2, 239n4, 239n6, 239n23

Fitzwilliam, Wendy, 61, 227n7, *P9*

Five-Year National HIV/AIDS Strategic Plan (2003), 147, 233n7, 238n22

Francisco, Slinger "The Mighty Sparrow," 98, 112, 224n12

Freud, Sigmund, 101, 102–3, 105, 230n19

Friends for Life (FFL): bisexual intimacy and, 167, 175–78, 214–15, 237n13; challenges and vulnerabilities, 171–73; community building and, 165–72, 175–78, 205, 212–15, 214–15; Community Chatroom Experience, 159, 228n1; desire and, 175–78, 238n21; dialogue model, 213–15; the erotic and, 205; food distribution initiative, 237n11; founding of, 159–65, 235nn2–3; funding of, 16, 166–70, 236n10, 238n22; HIV/AIDS awareness and, 164–65, 167; International HIV/AIDS Alliance and, 166, 168–70, 172–73, 182, 236n10, 237n14, 237n16; lesbianism and, 198–99, 237n13, 239n23; membership, 235n3, 239nn2–3; men-who-have-sex-with-men and, 237n13; mortality theme and, 159–63, 178–81, 184–85, 204; NACC funding, 182–83, 238n22; Eswick Padmore and, 161–70; political-sensual-spiritual framework and, 182–85; sensuality and, 175–78, 238n21; socioeconomic class and, 16, 167–68, 170; spirituality and, 75–76, 178–81, 238nn20–21; staffing, 237n14; TnT M4M Project, 165, 236n8; touch and sensation aesthetic experiences and, 11, 16–17, 175–78, 182–85, 201–2; women and, 235n3, 239n23

Frilot, Shari, 241n17

From Far Afield: A Queer Travelogue, 12–13, 15, 19–29, 77–86, 127–39, 187–95, 213, 222n1

Gay Freedom Movement (Jamaica), 236n6

gay men: use of terms, 3, 175, 237n12, 237n17; effeminacy and, 3, 237n12, 237n17; stigma and, 152–53. *See also* men-who-have-sex-with-men (MSM); same-sex desire; sexual behavior

Gay Pride (T&T), 199–201, 236n8

Gay Research Initiative, 156–58

gender: black femmes and, 218n11; calypso music and, 16, 99–100, 230n16; Caribbean region and, xxvii–xxix, 2–4, 219n3, 230n18; chantuels/chantuelles, 88–89, 88–91, 90, 98; the erotic and, 7–8; female masculinity, 104, 106, 112–13; femininity

and, 230n16, 230n18; gender nonconformity, 207, 208, 219n2; heterosexual matrix, 113; Jamette Carnival, 35–36, 90–91, 223n8; kinship structures and, 2–4, 219n3; masculinity and, 99–100, 104, 106, 112–13; queerness and, 207, 208, 219n2; sex-gender conflation, xxviii–xxx, 7–8, 99–100, 112–14, 113, 218n11

gender play: Canboulay and, 88–89; chantuels, 88–89, 90, 98; female masculinity, 104, 106, 112–13; parody, 15–16; picong, 105, 106; stickfighting and, 88–91, 98, 105, 227n5, 229n2

Gervais, Cleveland, 161–62

Globe Cinema, 53–54

Gordon, Lewis, 5–6, 221n14

grassroots activism: aesthetic experiences and, 15–17, 54–62, 75–76, 175–78, 202; art-making as, 1–2, 10–11; calypso musicianship as, 1–2; Caribbean Forum for Lesbians, All-sexuals and Gays (C-FLAG), 236n6; Carnival as, 1–2; community building and, 171–73, 183–85, 200–201; desire and, xxiii, 1–2, 175–78, 200–201, 238n21; the erotic and, 15; Gay Freedom Movement (Jamaica), 236n6; intimacy and, 200–201; masquerade design (mas) as, 1–2; Orguyo (Curaçao), 236n6; political-sensual-spiritual and, xxii, xxiii, 10–11, 183–85; same-sex desire and, 1–2, 175–78, 238n21; sensuality and, 1–2, 175–78, 238n21; touch and sensation aesthetic experiences and, 11, 16–17, 175–78, 182–85, 201–2. *See also* Fields, Jacquelyn; Friends for Life (FFL); HIV/AIDS prevention and care services

Grenada, 89, 229nn2, 235n16, 237n17

Guichard, Portia, 161–62, 235n3

Gulick, Tod, 63, 226n1, 227n9

Gumbs, Alexis Pauline, 220n6

Guy, Sherry Ann, 44–46, 225n21, *P1, P2*

Guyana, 37–39

Haiti, 141, 144, 218n7, 234n9

Halberstam, J. Jack, 104

Hall, Stuart, 239n3
HALLELUJAH (1995), 47, 55, 70–71, 72,
228n14
Henderson, Mae G., 210
Herskovits, Frances and Melville, 2–4
Hill, Errol Gaston, 92, 223n9, 225n20,
227n9
Hinds, Alison, 67, 69
HIV/ AIDS: overview, 141–43, 233n2; Caribbean region and, 144–46, 145–46, 154–57,
166, 170, 233n5, 233n6, 235n16, 236n10,
237n14, 237n16; condom usage, 150, 157,
168, 175, 177–78, 234n10; critique of HIV/
AIDS discourse, 16; cultural orientation
and, 141–42; geographic orientation and,
141–42; Jamaica and, 144–46, 233n5; limitations of global data, 146–48; men-who-
have-sex-with-men and, 149–50, 154–57;
mortality theme and, 74–76, 142–48; risk
and, 148, 150–54, 233n3, 234n9, 234n11;
stigma and, 56, 58–60, 65, 70, 141–42,
148, 151, 152, 234n9, 234n12; Trinidad and
Tobago and, 146–48, 159, 233n5, 233n8,
235n15; women-who-have sex-with-
women HIV transmission, 234n13. See also
HIV/AIDS prevention and care services;
National AIDS Coordinating Committee
(NACC)
HIV/AIDS prevention and care services:
community building and, 201–2, 205;
condom usage, 58, 67–70, 150, 157, 168,
175, 177–78, 234n10; as grassroots activism, 1–2; International HIV/AIDS Alliance
and, 166, 168–70, 172–73, 182, 236n10,
237n14, 237n16; mortality theme and,
159–63, 178–81, 184–85, 204; most-at-risk
populations (MARP), 148, 150–54, 233n3,
234n9; MSM as identity vs. behavior
category, 234n12; pleasure and, 75–76;
same-sex-desiring women and, 199–202;
sensuality and, 15; stigma/destigmatiza-
tion, 56, 58–60, 65, 141–42, 148, 151, 152,
234n9, 234n12; Tobago and, 233n8; touch
and sensation aesthetic experiences and,
11, 16–17, 175–78, 182–85, 201–2. See also

Community Chatroom Experience (the
Chatroom); Friends for Life (FFL); HIV/
AIDS; Sacred Heart, The (2006)
Holland, Sharon, 211, 241n15
Hubbard, Edward Akintola, 230n17

International HIV/AIDS Alliance (UK), 166,
168–70, 172–73, 182, 236n10, 237n14,
237n16
intimacy: community building and, 200–201;
grassroots activism and, 175–76; queer
intimacy, xxix; spiritual intimacy, 178–79,
181; spirituality and, 202–3, 203–5.
See also bisexual intimacy

Jackson, John L., 13, 14–15, 221n1n15–16
Jackson, Michael, 221n14
Jamaica, 144–46, 218n7, 233n5, 235n1,
236n6
James, Ronald Guy, 59–60
jamette: use of term, 35–36, 223n8; Canbou-
lay Riots and, 90–91; Jamette Carnival,
35–36, 90–91, 223n8
Jamette Carnival, 35–36, 90–91, 223n8
Johnson, E. Patrick, 210, 241n15
Jordan, Kerwyn L., 160–62, 161, 168, 183
jumbies, xxviii, xxix, 24, 218n8, frontis

kaiso, 89–90, 92–93
kalinda tradition/stickfighting, 36, 88–91, 98,
105, 227n5, 229n2
Kant, Immanuel, 15
Keeling, Kara, 218n11
Kempadoo, Kamala, 4
King, Rosamond S., 239n1
kinship structures, 2–4, 219n3

Lacan, Jacques, 101–3, 105, 230n19
Lee Heung, Stephen and Elsie, 46, 225n23
Lesbian Chatroom, 200, 237n13, 239nn4–5
lesbian/gay activism. See Fields, Jacquelyn;
grassroots activism; HIV/AIDS prevention
and care services
lesbianism: use of term, 152–53, 239n6;
bisexual intimacy and, 231n5, 239n6;

Naipaul, V. S., 231n1

National AIDS Coordinating Committee (NACC): *Five-Year National HIV/AIDS Strategic Plan* (2003), 147, 233n7, 238n22; Friends for Life funding, 182–83, 238n22; National AIDS Programme, 146–47, 163; UN country progress report and, 143, 146–48, 155–56

National AIDS Coordinating Committee (NACC): overview of, 146–47, 233n8, 238n22; Minshall Carnival band support, 51, 58

Nettleford, Ralston "Rex," 224n18

Nieves, Timothy, 162

Nixon, Angelique, 217n3

NSP. *See Five-Year National HIV/AIDS Strategic Plan* (2003)

Orguyo (Curaçao), 236n4

Original Young Brigade tent, 97–98, 229n9

Padmore, Eswick: Chatroom facilitators training, 183–84; on effeminacy, 167, 237n12; Friends for Life and, 160–70, 161–70; images of, 161, 162; sexual intimacy within organizations and, 175–76; spiritual intimacy within organizations and, 178–79, 181; Tobago Chatroom and, 238n18

"Palet" (1968): use of term palet, 104–5; double entendre and, 16, 104–6, 231n3, 232n11, 238n19; the erotic and, 109, 205; gender and, 16; lesbian phallus and, 16, 102–4; lyrics, 107–9; masculinity and, 99–100; phallic symbolism, 16, 99–100, 101–6, 117; political-sensual-spiritual and, 16, 120–25; *The Sacred Heart and,* 202–3; same-sex desire and, 16, 110–12; sensual symbolism and, 110–12; as sex song, 120–21, 232n11; song structure, 111, 231n4

palimpsest, the, xxiv, 44, 218n5

Pantin, Brian, 59–60, 60–61

paradise, xxii–xxiii, xxv–xxvii, 46, 217n3

Paradise Lost (1976), 46, 66, 225n24

Parnia, Sam, 123–25, 232n12

Paul, Kerwin, 59, 60–61, *P9*

phallus 16, 102–4, 104–5, 228n12

Philip, Theophilus, "The Mighty Spoiler," 97

political, the: the erotic *vs.,* 220n12; HIV/AIDS awareness and, 75–76; lesbians and, 200; mas and, 57–58; political alliances, 200–201; sensoryscape of the erotic and, 15. *See also* political-sensual-spiritual framework (tropic trinity)

political-sensual-spiritual framework (tropic trinity): as anti-oppression strategy, 11; art-making and, xxii, xxiii, 11; community building and, 10–11, 183–85; desire and, 10–11; the erotic and, 9–11, 182–85, 199, 215–16, 220n8, 220n12, 221n14; female sexual agency, xxvii–xxx; Friends for Life and, 182–85; grassroots activism and, xxii, xxiii, 10–11, 183–85; lesbian phallus and, 16, 102–4; Audre Lorde and, 199, 216, 220n8, 220n12, 221n14; mas and, 76; in "Palet" (1968), 120–25; *The Sacred Heart* and, 75–76; sensoryscape of the erotic and, 15; the soucouyant and, xxix–xxx; temporality as, xxiv–xxv; as tropic trinity, xxx. *See also* black queer diaspora framework

Providence, Antonio, 161–62

Puar, Jasbir K., 206–8, 219n4, 240nn11–12

queerness: bisexual intimacy and, xxix, 207; community-building work and, 220n6; gender nonconformity, 207, 208, 219n2; queer ethnography, 206–8, 208–15, 240n12; queer studies, 240n13. *See also* black queer diaspora framework

race: American blackface minstrelsy and, 43; blackface minstrelsy, 42–43, 224nn15–16; race play, 15–16, 34–37, 224n17; whiteness and, 37–40, 82, 222n3, 224n17

race play, 15–16, 34–37, 224n17

Rayford, Robert, 232n1

Reggio, Milla Cozart, 40–41, 225n25

Republic of Trinidad and Tobago (T&T): overview of, xxiii–xxiv, 217n4; abolition of slavery, 223n6; AIDS memorial (1994), 236n8; blackness and, 38–40; as cultural

Republic of Trinidad and Tobago (T&T) (cont.) contact zone, xxiii–xxv; *Five-Year National HIV/AIDS Strategic Plan* (2003), 147, 233n7, 238n22; HIV/AIDS and, 150–54, 155–56, 159, 233n5; homosexuality laws and, 219n1; oil industry and, xxi, 36–37, 223n10; temporal quilting and, xxii–xxiii; Tobago House of Assembly and, 233n8, 235n15; Trinbagonian term, 96; whiteness and, 38–40. *See also* Tobago

Rich, Adrienne, 114, 220n9

Richmond-Thompson, Delano Ray, *164*, 236n5

River Trilogy (1983–1985), 47, 55, 65, 226n26

Roberts, Aldwyn "Lord Kitchener," 98, 230n13

Robinson, Colin, 231n3

Robinson, Edith, 97

Rohlehr, Gordon, 99–100, 102–6

"Roll It Gal" (2005), 67, 227n10

Sacred Heart, The (2006): condom usage, 58, 67–70; Dames Lorraine characters, *P10–P14*; Mark Eastman in, *P15*; the erotic and, 15–16, 36–37, 46–49, 53–62, 62–63, 67–70, 202; HIV/AIDS awareness campaign and, 58–59, 69–70, 74, 75–76; humor and, 67–70; images and sketches of, 53, 54, 56, 57, 61, *P3–6*, *P8*, *P9*; "Miss Universe—Tan Tan's Girl Child" (2006), 227n7, *P6*; mortality theme and, 74–76; "Palet" and, 202–3; political-sensual-spiritual and, 75–76; reconciliatory unity theme, 55–62; samurai-cowboy heroism theme, 52–53, 58–59, 62; sensuality and, 62–67; sight and visual erotic aesthetics of, 15–16, 36–37, 46–49, 52–62, 62–63, 67–70, 202; Son of Sagaboy, 58–60, 227n6, *P8*; spiritual/religious influences on, 70–75; use of heart metaphor, 54–55, 56–57

Saga Boy mobiles, 58–60, 227n6, *P8*

Saint Kitts and Nevis, 235n16

Saint Lucia, 235n16, 237n17

Saint Vincent and the Grenadines, 89, 235n16, 237n17

Saldenah, Harold, 37, 226n3

same-sex desire: artistic expression and, 1–2, 64; Calypso Rose and, 112–16, 231n5; Caribbean region and, 2–4, 3–4, 111–12, 115–16, 141–42, 206–8, 219n1, 219n4, 220n5; Carnival and, 31–32; colloquial terms for, 175, 237n17; community building and, 1–2, 200–202, 219n3; criminalization of, 219n1; the erotic and, 203–4, 205, 215–16; ethnography of, 2–4, 13–15; femininity and, 111; grassroots activism and, 1–2, 175–78, 238n21; HIV/AIDS prevention and care services and, 199–202; Peter Minshall and, 63–66, 222n3; "Palet" (1968) and, 16, 110–12; same-sex desiring women, 198–202, 239n3, 239n6, 240n7; spirituality and, 203–4. *See also* lesbianism; women-who-have-sex-with-women (WSW)

Samuel, Peter, 60

Sandy, Altino, 94, 97

Sandy, Dorchea (née Ford), 94

Sandy-Lewis, Linda McCartha Monica. *See* Calypso Rose: musicianship; Lewis, Linda McCartha Monica Sandy (Calypso Rose)

Sappho, 8

Savage (Saga) (1988), 223n11

Schechner, Richard, 40–41, 225n25

Sealy, Godfrey, 156, 157, 235n18

sensuality: aesthetics and, 15, 62–67, 67–70, 202; calypso masculinity and, 99–100; community building and, 183–85; the erotic and, 15, 220n12; Friends for Life and, 175–78, 238n21; grassroots activism and, 1–2, 175–78, 238n21; HIV/AIDS awareness and, 75–76; the political and, 220n12; sensoryscape of the erotic and, 15; Victorian morality and, 35–36, 91. *See also* political-sensual-spiritual framework (tropic trinity)

Serrao, Anna, 226n3

sex-gender conflation, xxviii–xxx, 7–8, 99–100, 112–14, 113, 218n11

sexual behavior: anal intercourse, 151–52, 153, 219n1, 240n9; bisexual intimacy and, xxviii–xxx, 239n6; female homosexuality, 3–4; female sexual agency, xxvii–xxx; HIV/